crafts
Illustrated designs and techniques

by

Clois E. Kicklighter
Dean, School of Technology
Indiana State University
Terre Haute, Indiana

Ronald J. Baird
Professor, Industrial Technology
Eastern Michigan University
Ypsilanti, Michigan

South Holland, Illinois
THE GOODHEART-WILLCOX COMPANY, INC.
Publishers

Library of Congress Catalog Card Number 86-7606
International Standard Book Number 0-87006-592-0

2345-86-098

Library of Congress Cataloging in Publication Data

Kicklighter, Clois E.
  Crafts, illustrated designs and techniques.

  Includes index.
    1. Handicraft.   I.   Baird, Ronald J., joint author
II. Title.
TT157.K43   745   86-7606
  ISBN 0-87006-592-0

INTRODUCTION

CRAFTS, Illustrated Designs and Techniques provides basic instruction in 39 different crafts. This book covers exciting traditional craft areas as well as many contemporary ones. Anyone interested in learning new crafts or exploring advanced level activities will find CRAFTS enlightening and rewarding. The chapters are arranged in alphabetical order for your easy reference.

Several full color photos of craft projects, ranging from simple to complex, are presented at each chapter's beginning. This gives you an opportunity to select from a vast source of over 400 project ideas. Each chapter has a description of the craft and suggested projects to enable you to quickly gain an insight into the craft. After the brief description, comes discussion and illustrations of the materials and tools generally required. Next, a well illustrated, step-by-step procedure shows you how to complete the craft project.

The thrill of creating a valuable project is a long-lasting joy to the craft person. As you gain skills and appreciation for projects construction from CRAFTS, Illustrated Designs and Techniques, may you receive the same thrilling experience!

CONTENTS

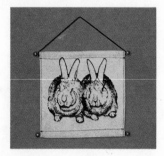

Every successful craft project combines creativity with good design. The most successful are those where the craftsperson has understood well the principles and elements of design and skillfully put them to work.

Chapter 1
DESIGNING CRAFT PROJECTS

Few human experiences are as interesting or rewarding as designing and making something uniquely your own. This is particularly true in a highly technical society where mass production provides an unending supply of identical products. There is genuine pleasure in creating something that is "one of a kind."

Craft projects are usually the work of one person. In design, function and use of materials, craft projects impose no limits. Ordinarily, projects are developed out of a need or desire for a certain object. At other times, the project is created simply for the pure joy of working with tools and materials. In this last sense, it becomes a hobby. But in every instance the craft project serves one or both of two purposes:
1. Beauty.
2. Function.
These terms will be discussed in greater detail later. For now, they are the basis for designing and solving craft problems.

A successful project begins with a design. This is a plan of what the project will look like and how it will be made. The design will usually be accompanied by sketches and dimensions. The latter are important, particularly when the item being crafted is complicated. Planning as you go in such situations is a wasteful approach to craftwork.

BASICS OF DESIGN

If your designs are to produce pleasing results, it is important that you develop a feel for good design. Design involves elements and principles that must be understood before they can be used effectively.

Elements are the visible parts of a project. They give it substance. The elements are: line, form, mass, texture and color. Color includes hue, value and chroma.

Principles are simply guides that apply to all design work. They are not rules, which we must fear to break,

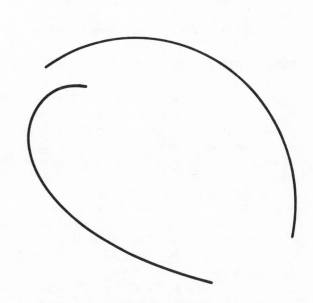

Fig. 1-1. Lines are one of the important elements in design. They may be straight, curved, sloped or curved free form.

but observations about the nature of the visible world. Principles help us decide what looks good and what does not. Good design, then, depends on the principles of proportion, balance, contrast, rhythm and unity or harmony.

Lines are the most basic of the design elements. Fortunately there are only three kinds, Fig. 1-1:
1. Straight. They may be horizontal, vertical, or slanted.
2. Arcs of a circle where rate of curve is unvarying.
3. Free-form curves which may vary in direction.

But designing with lines may still be difficult even with only three kinds used on a flat surface. Lines must be joined to form shapes. How can they be used to form pleasing shapes? How do we join them to change direction? There are simple guidelines we can follow to answer such questions.

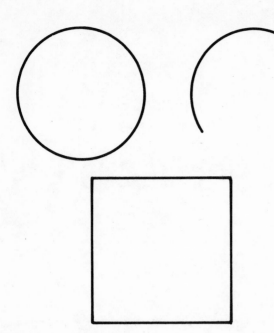

Fig. 1-2. Overuse of circles, squares or arcs of a circle can become monotonous since they are static shapes (lack motion).

STRAIGHT LINES AND ARCS OF CIRCLES

Our use of lines varies little from their appearance in nature. The straight line appears frequently in shapes such as snowflakes and crystal formations. Circles and their arcs are familiar in the shapes of planets or water droplets. Still, the designer uses such lines more for their function than their appeal.

The circle and square are monotonous shapes. The eye tends to follow these lines right back to their starting point. The circle is an enclosing line possessing unity but lacking observable motion and direction. Arcs of circles also lack motion. Their continuous use becomes monotonous, Fig. 1-2.

However, functional design demands the use of these lines. We live in a fairly flat, constructed world which requires straight lines for table tops, books, building materials and the like.

Arcs and circles follow a similar course. The wheel on an automobile, a ball bearing or a baseball make use of the circle as a function of design.

Even so, straight lines, arcs or circles play an important role in aesthetic (artistic) design. We will show this later as we study the enclosing of design shapes and forms.

FREE-FORM CURVED LINES

One of the designers most valuable lines is the free-form curve. It comes from the volute or spiral figure, Fig. 1-3.

The spiraled line of the volute unwinds at an even rate. If extended inward or outward, it will never touch or cross itself. Any section of the volute is a smoothly

Fig. 1-3. A flowing free-form curved line is obtained from a volute.

curved line which is not an arc of a circle. Its free-form curves are appealing since they show motion and are "lively." A wave in the ocean or a leaning blade of grass are good examples of the free-form curve. These curved lines are found in most aspects of nature. Picture the graceful lines of an animal, stones or shells at the oceanside or a rose bud. These are all free-form, flowing, curved lines, Fig. 1-4.

Fig. 1-4. These curved lines are used in good design work.

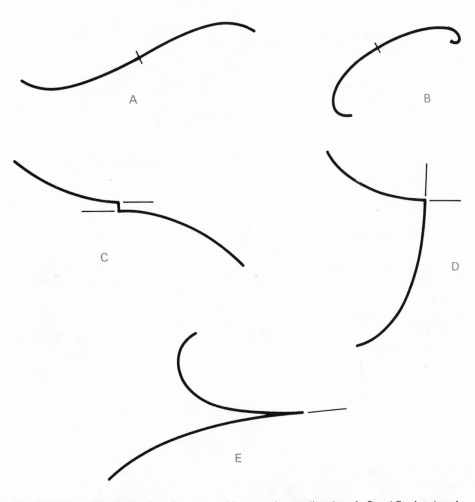

Fig. 1-5. Methods of joining free-form curved lines to change direction. A, B and E—A point of tangency. C—Abrupt change by using a bead. D—A shoulder break, perpendicular to a point of tangency

COMBINING CURVED LINES

Free-form, curved lines may be combined in a number of ways to provide pleasing results. But some general rules must be followed since random use of these lines is generally unsatisfactory. Study the following methods of combining free-form lines (elements) and observe the quality of their form. These methods are only guidelines. They are not unbreakable rules. Yet, they are valuable in developing a feeling for good design.

When two or more curved lines are used in sequence, it is necessary to make some type of break or abrupt change in direction. See Fig. 1-5. The change in direction may be made by using:

1. A shoulder which is an area next to a higher or bigger area.
2. A bead which is a rim, a band or a molding.
3. A point of tangency. This is the spot where lines moving in different directions touch.

At a point of tangency, the ends of the curved lines should either be parallel or perpendicular to each other. Fig. 1-6 shows interesting applications of curved lines.

BEAUTY

Handicrafters who can design objects of beauty and function have become highly sensitive to form and shape. They direct their attention to emotional appeal in a finished product as they design. Therefore, they are directly concerned with BALANCE, UNITY, PROPORTION, COLOR, and TEXTURE. Good design attempts to clarify these qualities, in combinations or separately. A good designer knows how and when they should be used. The blending of these principles and elements is the high point in sensitivity to design.

FORM OR SHAPE

Some simple shapes using the concepts already discussed, illustrate good characteristics of project design. The following guidelines should help.

1. Try to be consistent in the use of lines to enclose a shape. When using straight lines, try staying with that style. Straight lines generally look best when they move toward or away from each other. Straight parallel lines are normally used more for function

9

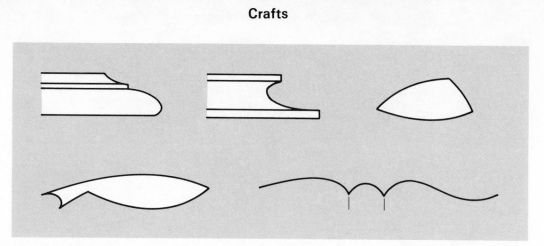

Fig. 1-6. Pleasing use is made of curved lines to enclose shapes and form design styles.

and decoration. (Lines running side by side which never get closer together are called parallel.) Straight lines which are not parallel provide for many interesting design possibilities, Fig. 1-7.

2. Free-form curved lines are often used to enclose a form or shape for craft projects. For practice, make some sketches of a project using curved and straight lines. Follow the guidelines for making a break in the curved line or for changing direction.

BALANCE

Balance is involved in every project. It is not so much a physical matter as it is a "visual" quality. An object properly balanced gives the visual appearance that it will stand up alone. Symmetry (equal on both sides) is the most commonly known form of balance. This is often called FORMAL balance, Fig. 1-8. All the elements at either side of a center line are equal. Most of the commercially produced items we use daily are formally balanced.

To add interest to your craft projects you may use IN-FORMAL balance. This is achieved by opposing unequal design elements on either side of a center line. Though elements are not the same weight, there is an overall feeling of balance, Fig. 1-9.

The attention-getting quality of an element is what lends "weight" to its part of the design balance. Used in equal proportions, red is "heavier" than yellow because of its brilliance and darker value. If used against a smooth background, a coarse texture is "heavier" than a smooth one. A larger area is naturally heavier than a small one.

UNITY

Another principle used in developing a pleasing design is unity (or harmony). Elements of the design —its lines, colors, textures, and shape — must be compatible. (Everything must seem to belong in the design.)

Fig. 1-7. Tapered straight lines provide attractive shape for this chair.

Fig. 1-8. This necklace represents the use of formal balance. Design elements are the same on each side of the project.

Fig. 1-9. The design elements appear to be equally balanced on each side of this piece of pottery.

10

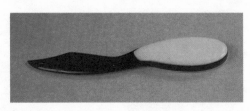

Fig. 1-10. Careful use for shape, color, and texture provide unity for this letter opener.

Fig. 1-11. Simplicity in line and color makes this aluminum ladle an attractive design.

Overuse of materials is an obvious example of poor design. Having four or five different materials, colors, textures or shapes causes design difficulty. One or two would provide a more pleasing effect, Fig. 1-10.

Unity requires honest use of materials. Plan your projects so that the material supports the design idea. Metal picture frames do not have the warmth of wood. Needlepoint has little charm when stitches are made with plastic thread. A serving tray made from rusted wire is not attractive.

Unity also requires restraint on the part of the designer in decoration or color. Beauty lies in simplicity, Fig. 1-11.

Remember, an object has unity when it contains no opposing lines, no colors or textures in conflict. It has unity when all its elements are properly arranged to serve its primary function or use.

Fig. 1-12. Proportion is represented here by the use of color, texture and unity.

PROPORTION

In craft designing, think of proportion as the relationship in size and shape between design elements. Proportion is established primarily through division of surfaces. It is, therefore, directly dependent upon balance, unity, color and texture. Each of these qualities adds something to the pleasing proportions of a project, Fig. 1-12. In other words, proportion is basically a combination of balance and unity to give a project visual interest and beauty.

Fig. 1-13. There is often great beauty in the natural color of the materials.

COLOR

Color plays a major role in craft project design. When appropriate to function, liberal use of strong color provides excitement to many projects. Some craft projects, especially those made from natural materials, take a great deal of their beauty from the color of the material, Fig. 1-13. Paint would spoil the color of a silver bracelet, a walnut serving tray or a stone sculpture. Their natural color is pleasing.

The color or colors to be applied to a craft project are often determined by function. Enameled earrings, for example, lend themselves to brilliant color. On the other hand, a knitted hammock should have subdued, restful colors, Fig. 1-14. Those who have mastered design select colors that bring out the effect they want.

Fig. 1-14. The importance of color selection is shown in this functional hammock. (Joan Kicklighter)

11

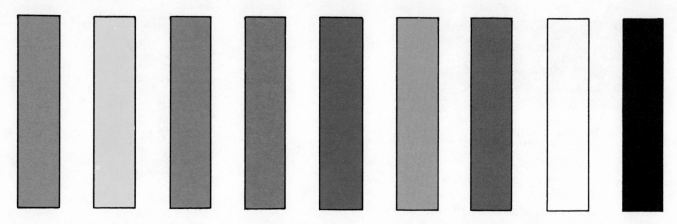

Fig. 1-15. A great deal of emotion can be obtained through the use of vivid colors.

The following observations about color may serve as a guide in selecting suitable project materials and finishes, Fig. 1-15. Reading left to right:

1. Red is the most popular color and has the greatest power to attract. It is positive and exciting.
2. Yellow is bright and cheerful. Gay and lively, it symbolizes the sun.
3. Blue is cool and serene, giving a feeling of peace.
4. Green appears to be more passive than active. It tends to be neutral in its emotional effect. It is generally considered the most restful of colors.
5. Purple gives an air of nobility and courage. It provides an impressive effect, rich and stately.
6. Violet is similar to blue but is more solemn and subdued. It is cool and retiring.
7. Brown is found in nature in varying shades. Thus, it gives the impression of natural materials. It often produces a rich effect.
8. White is stimulating, light and delicate. It is generally used with other colors to give a luminous feeling.
9. Black gives a sense of smart formality. It is somber and profound.

TEXTURE

Another design tool at your disposal is texture. Every craft material, from the rough side of a piece of bark to the smooth surface of glass, has some degree of texture. Deep or heavy textures are more stimulating and attention-getting. To achieve some balance in designing projects, different surfaces used together should show varying, modest degrees of texture, Fig. 1-16. Very coarse and highly polished surfaces generally do not compliment each other. Often, craft materials provide their own textured surfaces and should be used as such. Examples are leather, wood, metal, yarn and sea shells. Each has its own degree of texture. Textured surfaces may also be artificially produced by etching, sanding, chipping, weaving, machining or finishing. You should be aware of texturing possibilities when designing.

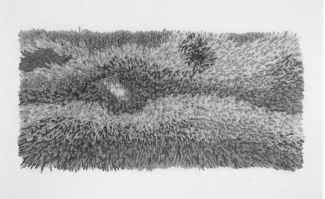

Fig. 1-16. Interesting use of texture in a woven rug.

Fig. 1-17. This functional juice glass is made from a cut bottle.

FUNCTION

Often an object is said to be functional if it does the job it was intended to do. This may well be true, but there is more to be said for function when you are designing a craft project. Mechanical function involves the properties of the material, Fig. 1-17. You must also frequently consider the following five factors:

1. The strength of the material you are using.
2. The forces or pressures required of it.
3. Its ability to withstand heat, cold or moisture.
4. Resistance to rust or tarnish.

Study the materials you are planning to use for any project. See if they are well suited for what you want them to do.

There are other functions that many projects must serve. The primary function may be to give pleasure through its form, color, line or texture as in Fig. 1-18. Other functions of a project may be to:

1. Show ownership.
2. Convey a message.
3. Simply provide the pleasure of using skill and expressing feelings through craftwork.

THE DESIGNING PROCESS

The final venture in the study of design is to make something and see how it works. As you can probably see by now, some craft projects require little or no designing. A little designing is necessary to make a rug or frame a picture. You need to plan what you will do about certain qualities the project will have:

1. The shape and size.
2. What colors you want to use and where.
3. The texture of materials.

More formal designing is usually necessary when you plan a project that requires considerable forming or shaping. A leather handbag, a gold ring, a woven basket or a carved wood candy dish are typical examples. The following procedure should serve as a guide:

1. Since "form follows function," your first step is to decide on the exact purpose of the project. Will it meet the needs you have in mind (for example, to

Fig. 1-18. Pleasing shape and line are the function of this wall hanging.

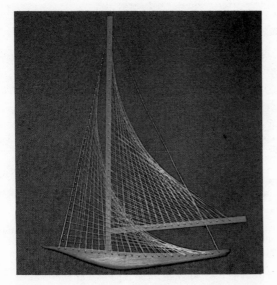

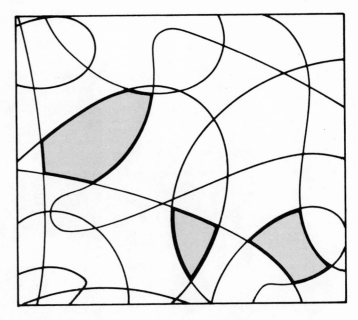

Fig. 1-19. How to develop design shapes by using the scribble method.

give viewing pleasure, show ownership, make a statement, provide recreation)?

2. Look for ideas that may help you come up with a pleasing design. Look through books, magazines or visit stores. You may find something you like. Take notes or make a quick sketch so you will remember such things as shape, size, color or texture.

3. Sketch alternative designs until you have a shape or form that is the most pleasing and satisfying.

4. If your project is a free-form design, the scribble method, Fig. 1-19, may be used to get good shape ideas.

5. When you have decided on the design, you will probably want to make a pattern, final sketch or drawing of the project. For most craft projects, your design should be made full size so that you can trace it onto the materials you have chosen.

6. Gather the necessary materials. Some materials such as sea shells, bottles or stones are free. Others run from fairly inexpensive to quite costly, like silver, foreign woods and stained glass. Choose your materials wisely. The quality of your project and the satisfaction you get from it will depend on their properties.

7. Whatever finishing or fastening materials are required—paints, sealers, varnishes, waxes, glues, screws and nails—should be at hand.

Now you are ready to use the tools and follow the procedures found in any of the following craft chapters.

Project suggestions for basketry. A—Straw basket and interesting swirl weave pattern. B—Hanging planter made with large reed and flat bindings. C—Wood base basket with dowel stakes. D—Small reed basket. E—Woven base basket with slightly flared sides. F—Picnic plate holder and matching napkin ring made from reed. G—Fancy woven reed shovel. H—Plastic woven base basket. I—Watering can with arrangement of plastic flowers. J—Coiled hot pad of raffia. K—Woven tray with handles. L—Raffia basket with wood base and willow frame. M—Lady's purse with decorative design. N—Flower basket with wrapped handle. O—Reed trivet with lacy edges. P—Coiled rope basket with cord binding.

14

Chapter 2
BASKETRY

Basketry is the art or craft of weaving useful and decorative containers from natural or synthetic materials. The possibilities for variety in shape, size and pattern are unending. Basket weaving is easy to do and suitable materials abound. The beautiful basket in Fig. 2-1 is just one example of this creative craft.

MATERIALS

Fig. 2-2 shows an assortment of basketry materials. Since you may not be familiar with them, each is described.

Reed, the easiest obtained and simplest to use, comes from the core of the rattan or cone palm. This is a tropical climbing plant which grows to a length of over 500 ft. (about 150 m). Special machines cut the core into round or flat shapes of various sizes. Round reed is produced in sizes from 0 to 10. Fig. 2-3 shows the approximate sizes. Sizes 2 and 3 are most often used for weaving. Size No. 4 is most used for the spokes or stakes. No. 8 is used for handles.

Three widths of flat oval reed (flat on one side and oval on the other) are generally used in basketry: 1/4, 3/8 and 1/2 in. (Corresponding metric widths would be about 6 mm, 10 mm and 13 mm.)

While willow is a traditional material for basket construction, it is more difficult to work. Master the strokes or stitches using reed before attempting to weave with willow.

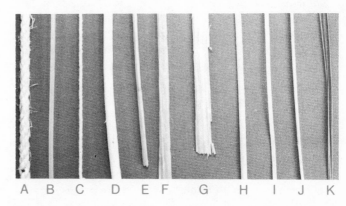

Fig. 2-2. Basketry materials. A—Hemp rope. B—Plastic strand. C—Cord. D—Willow. E—Wheat straw. F—Raffia. G—Wide flat reed. H—Oval reed. I—Flat reed. J—No. 6 round reed. K—Pine straw.

Fig. 2-1. Wood-base basket.

DIMENSIONS		
Size No.	Millimetres	Inches
0	1.2	3/64
1	1.5	1/16
2	2.0	5/64
3	2.4	3/32
4	2.75	7/64
5	3.2	1/8
6	4.2	11/64
7	5.0	13/64
8	6.0	15/64
9	7.0	9/32
10	8.0	5/16

Fig. 2-3. Sizes of round reed.

Hong Kong grass is coarse and may be twisted to form a continuous length. It is available in a natural shade and in colors.

Raffia, used in coiled basketry, is available in a variety of colors as well as natural. It comes from the dried leaves of a palm frond found mainly in Madagascar. This material can be split easily from end to end.

Straw, suitable for weaving, comes from several sources. Grain straws, such as wheat or rye, are best because the joints are long. Pine straw, from the longleaf pine or southern pine, reaches a length of 18 in. (45 cm). Pine needles should be dry when used. Early fall is the best time for gathering them.

Synthetic materials, mainly plastics, have become available in recent years. Plastic strands can be woven in much the same way as natural materials. Many colors and sizes are produced for a wide variety of textures and effects.

TOOLS

Few tools are required for basketry, Fig. 2-4. A very sharp knife will do for cutting the weaving materials. A pair of roundnose pliers is another essential tool needed for bending and squeezing the reed. Squeezing is necessary to prevent breaking of fibers. An awl opens up spaces in the weaving when you wish to put in new stakes or a handle. A reed cutter or a diagonal cutter are useful tools and make the work easier. A blunt tapestry needle will be required for coiled basketry and raffia work. Be sure that the needle has a large eye.

TERMS

Basketry has a number of unfamiliar terms which must become a part of your vocabulary:

BASE — bottom of the basket. Some are woven; others are made from a flat piece of wood or other material with holes around the edge to receive the stakes. Baskets are usually woven from the base upward.

FOOTING — row of weaving worked under the base when a solid base is used.

PAIRING — using two reeds at the same time, working one stroke with each reed alternately. Two reeds may also be used side by side as if they were one.

PIECING WEAVERS — technique of working a new weaver into the basket when the previous weaver is used up.

SIMPLE or PLAIN WEAVING — passing a single weaver over one stake and under the next in an alternating pattern. An odd number of stakes must be used.

STAKES or SPOKES — upright reeds forming the foundation upon which the basket is woven.

STROKE — name given to one complete movement of the weaving reed. For example, a stroke in a plain

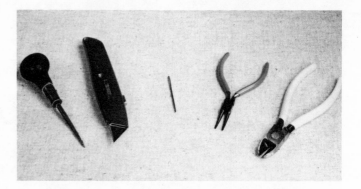

Fig. 2-4. Tools needed for basketry work include (left to right) an awl, sharp knife, tapestry needle, roundnose pliers and side cutting pliers.

Fig. 2-5. Basket base is made from 1/4 in. (6 mm) plywood.

weave is completed when the weaver is passed in front of one stake and behind the next stake.

UPSETTING — fixing the stakes firmly in place using a three-ply coil weave.

WALING — strip of braided weavers (two or more) used to accent and strengthen basket work.

WEAVERS — reed, cane straw or other basketry materials used to weave the sides and sometimes the base of a basket.

PLAIN WEAVING WOOD-BASE BASKETS

The following procedure may be used for nearly any basket, tray or article formed on a wood base.

1. Purchase a precut base or cut one out of 1/4 in. (6 mm) plywood or other material suitable for your project. Smooth the edges and sand the surface if plywood is used, Fig. 2-5.

2. Lay out and drill an odd number of holes about 5/8 in. (16 mm) apart and 1/4 in. in from the edge around the outside of the base. The holes should be large enough to accept the reed selected for the project, Fig. 2-6. Put a finish on the base which will be functional and attractive.

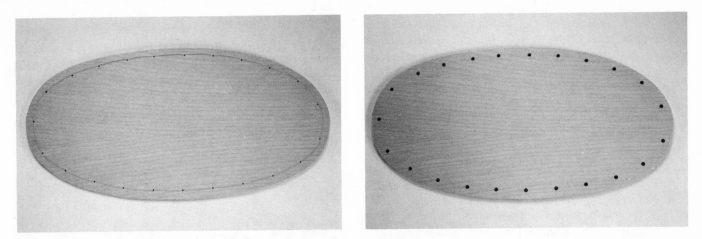

Fig. 2-6. Preparing base to receive the stakes. Left. Mark the location holes. Right. Drill holes in proper location. Note that an odd number of holes has been drilled.

3. Count the holes and cut the same number of stakes from No. 4 reed. Make them long enough for the project selected. Be sure to allow for about 3 1/2 in. (9 cm) extra length. This will project through the base of the basket. Next, soak the reeds in water for a few minutes before pushing them through the holes in the base, Fig. 2-7.

4. With the bottom of the base facing up, begin weaving the base border by taking one stake and bending it down in front of the first stake to the right and behind the next stake as in Fig. 2-8. Continue this pattern until you reach the starting point. The last stakes are tucked into the first ones woven. See Fig. 2-9.

5. Soak the weavers in water for a few minutes before beginning to weave, Fig. 2-10. Set the

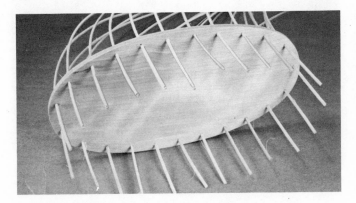

Fig. 2-7. Reed stakes are in place with about 3 1/4 in. (9 cm) of reed projecting through the base.

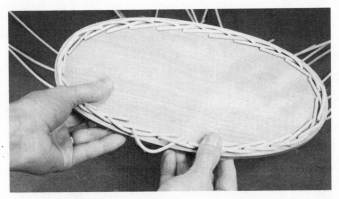

Fig. 2-9. End base border back where it started. Last stake is tucked under to hold it in place.

Fig. 2-8. Beginning to weave base border. Ends of stakes bend more easily if dampened first.

Fig. 2-10. Soaking weavers in a bucket of water for several minutes before using them, makes them more pliable.

project upright on the workbench and select a weaver about 4 ft. (1 m long). Longer weavers are hard to handle. Place the weaver between two stakes with one end extending about an inch (2 or 3 cm) inside the stake, Fig. 2-11. Now, move the weaver in front of the first stake on your right and then behind the next one. Continue this pattern until you use up the first reed. The weaving should not be too tight and the stakes must remain vertical for a straight-sided basket.

6. When the first weaver is used up, pick up a new piece, letting the new reed cross in front of the old one behind a stake. Leave the remaining ends resting against a stake, Fig. 2-12. The ends may be trimmed when the project is completed.

7. Continue weaving until the proper height is reached.

8. Trim the stakes to the proper length, Fig. 2-13. Leave enough to finish off the top.

9. There are several possible borders for finishing the project. The simplest is the scallop. Begin by forcing open the space beside a stake with an awl. Insert the end of the stake to the immediate left. Push it down into the weave as shown in Fig. 2-14. If the stakes are too long, trim them to the right length.

10. Trim ends where weavers were joined, Fig. 2-15, and examine your work for shape and tightness. Let the wood dry completely; then singe off curled and hanging fibers with a match or cigarette lighter. Be careful not to set the project on fire.

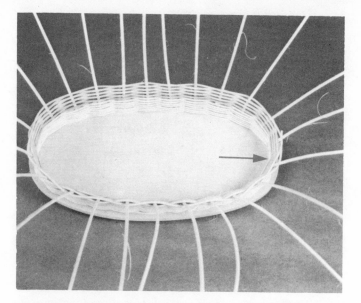

Fig. 2-12. Second weaver has been used up and the end rests behind a stake (arrow).

Fig. 2-13. When basket has reached the desired size, stakes should be trimmed, leaving several inches of reed with which to finish the border.

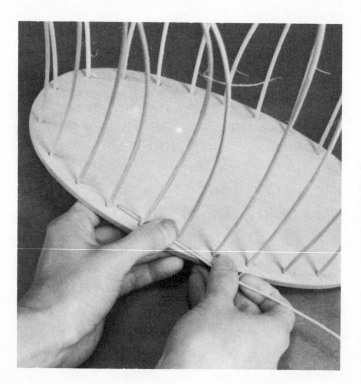

Fig. 2-11. Begin first weaver on top side of base.

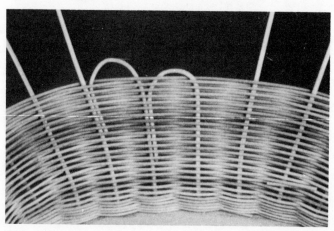

Fig. 2-14. Beginning scallop weave to finish basket. End of each stake is forced down beside stake to its left.

PLAIN WOVEN-BASE BASKETS

A woven-base basket, Fig. 2-16, is harder to construct than wood-base designs. The simplest woven-base baskets use one weaver while more complex designs use two or more. Use the following procedure for woven-base baskets with one weaver:

1. Select materals. Use No. 4 reed for stakes and No. 2 or smaller for the weavers. The amount of material needed will depend on the size of your project.

2. Lay out all the stakes. Each will consist of two reeds for added strength. Keep the four double stakes going in one direction fairly close together. Then, at a right angle, weave two double stakes which will help secure the previous stakes. Proceed by weaving in one double stake at a time until all are woven in. Be sure to alternate the crossings of each pair of weavers. Clamp the corners with clothespins or hold the proper shape with wire brads nailed into a work board, Fig. 2-17. Adjust the stakes so that all are the same length.

3. Select a long weaver and, starting at a corner, weave a circle around the stakes, Fig. 2-18. This

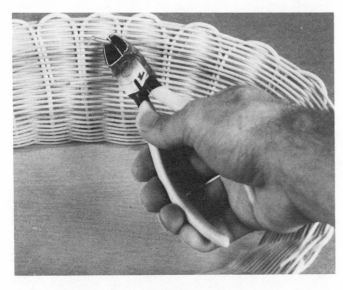

Fig. 2-15. Trim ends of all weavers with side cutting pliers.

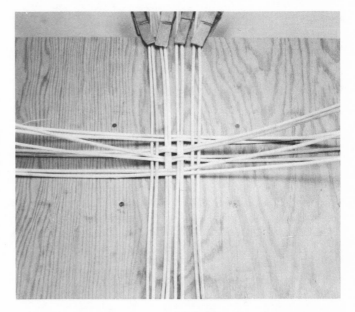

Fig. 2-17. Beginning a woven-base basket. Use double reeds for added strength and a better looking basket.

Fig. 2-16. Woven-base basket.

Fig. 2-18. First weaver is in place. Notice that one double short stake has been added to form an odd number. Try to keep stakes evenly spaced as you work.

will form the circular base of the basket, so be sure that it is as round as possible. When you have completed the first row, insert a short double stake at that corner. This gives the uneven number of stakes needed for plain weaving.

4. Continue to weave, alternating each new row with the preceding one, over and under the stakes, Fig. 2-19. Using the pliers as in Fig. 2-20, bend the stakes up as you weave to form the desired shape. Fig. 2-21 shows an early development of the basket sides. When the basket is the proper height, finish it off with a border, Fig. 2-22. Use the procedure described for wood-base baskets.

5. Trim the ends of weaves and examine your work.

ATTACHING HANDLES

Whatever the design, the basket handle must be strong enough to support the weight of the contents. In addition to being functional, it should complement the overall basket design. The handle described is made from No. 7 to No. 10 reed or willow, depending on the size of the basket and materials available. This piece is called the bow. Follow the steps described:

1. Cut the reed to length, Fig. 2-23. Be sure to allow for the ends which must be pushed down into the sides of the basket. Soak the reed until it is pliable.

2. Point each end of the reed for 2 or more inches (about 5 cm). See Fig. 2-24. Use an awl to spread the weavers apart, Fig. 2-25. Push one end into

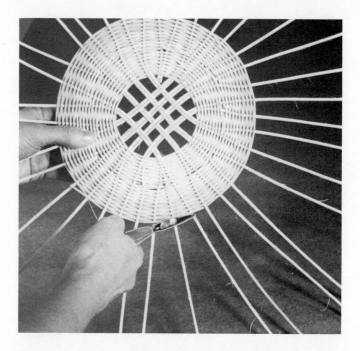

Fig. 2-20. Bend stakes upward with roundnose pliers to begin sides of basket. Soak base in water before bending stakes. It prevents breaking of stakes.

Fig. 2-21. After stakes are bent, weavers keep them vertical.

Fig. 2-19. Woven base is taking shape after third weaver is in place. Double stakes have been spread apart and are now used as single stakes. This produces a finer weave and a tighter basket.

Fig. 2-22. Weaving scalloped edge on top of basket. If stakes are dry, soak them again before this operation.

each side of the basket midway along the side. If the handle is to be wrapped, the end of the wrapping or winding reed is pointed and threaded down along the handle into the basket to secure it. The material is then spiral wrapped around the handle and secured on the other side. Make the wrapping long enough so that it will not need to be pieced. Fig. 2-16 shows a completed basket with a wrapped handle.

COILED BASKETRY

Coiled basketry is usually worked with some form of raffia. Raffia is easy to use, economical and available in colors. It is stitched around a foundation of heavier material. Stitches must be neatly done for a nice appearance.

Reed is one of the most frequently used foundation materials. Sizes from No. 4 to No. 7 are popular. Rope foundations may be used, but usually do not provide as much firmness.

Sew the coils with a blunt tapestry needle. Never use a sharp needle; it tends to split the raffia stitches. Stitches must cover the foundation completely and are always sewn from front to back and away from you. Stitches are generally sewn from right to left; however, you may sew from left to right if it is easier.

The method for making a coiled basketry article follows:

1. Point the end of the reed and dampen it well. If rope is used, remove several strands to form a long, tapered end, Fig. 2-26. Coil the sharpened end on itself as closely as possible.

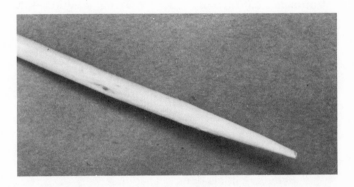

Fig. 2-24. Sharpen ends of handle so they can be forced down into weavers.

Fig. 2-25. Using an awl, spread the weavers apart to receive handle.

Fig. 2-23. Willow bow is being fitted to this basket. Measurement is taken by bending it to fit basket. Soak it in water for 30 minutes before bending.

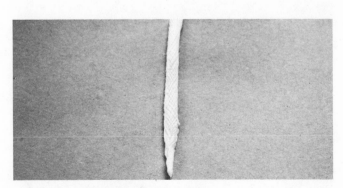

Fig. 2-26. Foundation material for coiled basket should be shaped to a point to begin coil.

2. Lay the end of the raffia over the center of the foundation material and work over it until the end is covered, Fig. 2-27. Sew round and round into the center opening until the coil is covered completely.

When you reach the starting point, you may begin a specific stitch. One of the easiest and most popular for coiled basketry is the Lazy Squaw or long and short stitch, Fig. 2-28. This stitch consists of one long loop going into the previous row or coil and one short stitch going around the foundation (outside coil) only. As each new coil is added, the long stitches go into the space under short stitches of the previous row.

3. When a new piece of raffia is needed, lay the old end and the new one together, Fig. 2-29, along the top of the foundation. Work over both of them until they are covered.

4. Add a new piece of reed or rope by removing some material from the end of each piece for an inch or more. Lay them together to be covered as though they were one. The joint should not show in the finished work if it is done properly.

5. As work progresses, it will be necessary to put two stitches in one space from time to time, because the article is getting larger and more stitches are required to cover the foundation. When sewing a flat

Fig. 2-29. Adding new piece of raffia to coils. Hold ends down and cover them as stitching continues.

Fig. 2-30. Flat coil illustrates how stitches radiate from center.

Fig. 2-27. Begin the coil by sewing around the tightly coiled end until the beginning point is reached. Cover foundation rope completely.

Fig. 2-28. Lazy Squaw stitch is used here to form the design. This stitch is made with one long and one short stitch. Long stitches go into the center of coil. Short stitches wrap around foundation only.

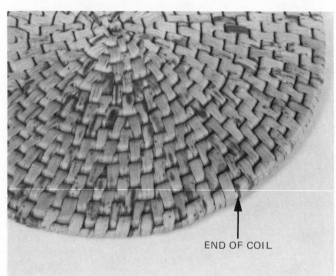

END OF COIL

Fig. 2-31. End coil by shaving off the reed or other foundation material until a point is reached. Weave to the point (see arrow) to complete project.

coil, such as the base of a basket, the lines radiate from the center, Fig. 2-30.

6. The transition from the base of the basket to the sides may be made by sewing the reed or rope foundation on top of the preceding coil. This may be an abrupt shift or gradual change depending on the shape desired. The same diameter must be maintained if the sides of the article are to be vertical.

The lines on the sides of a coiled basket will form a spiral effect which is attractive.

7. When the work has reached the final stage, finishing off is very important. Shave off the foundation reed very gradually and continue working until it is covered, Fig. 2-31. Fasten off the raffia neatly by working it under and over alternate rows of coils and cutting it off on the inside.

A wooden base with dowel stakes tipped with small wooden balls provide the basic framework for this attractive plain-woven reed basket. Use of cream with brown accents, suggest natural materials.

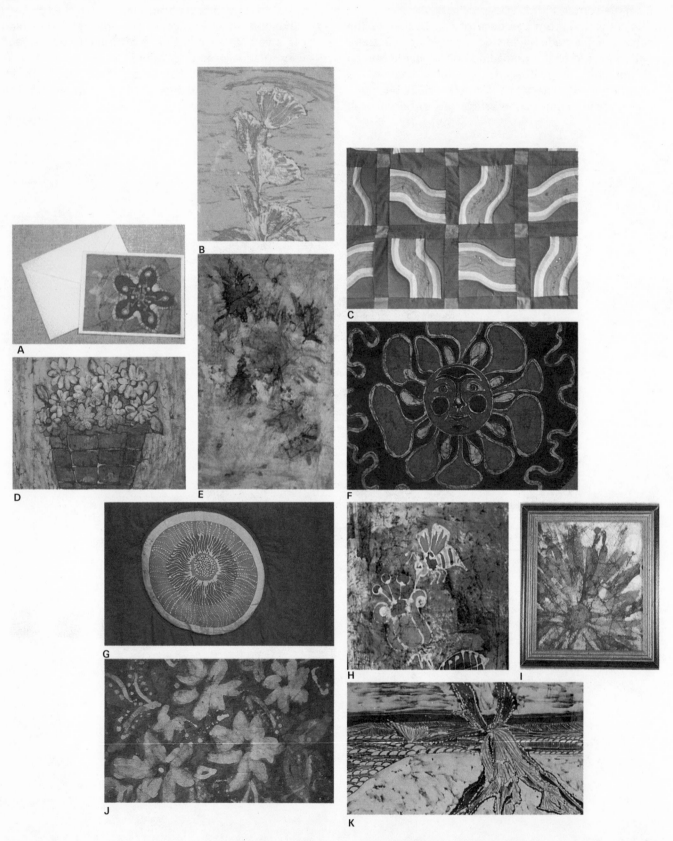

Batik project suggestions. A—Handmade card with batik applied to fabric face of card. B—Fine detail is key element of this batik picture. C—Patchwork quilt made from batik squares and pieces. D—Batik picture made with brush and tjanting tool. E—Fabric decorated with batik flower design. F—Stylized face design of tjanting batik. G—Wall hanging. H—Picture using brush and tjanting techniques. I—Floral design in gold and earth tones. J—Floral pattern in brush batik. K—Batik piece in which primary design is developed with tjanting tool.

Chapter 3
BATIK

Batik is a method of printing on cloth using a wax deposit to control dyeing in design areas. One or more colors may be used, making possible many exotic designs and color combinations. Batik may be used to decorate clothing, wall hangings or anything made from cloth. It is truly a unique and creative craft. See Fig. 3-1.

MATERIALS AND TOOLS

Relatively few materials and tools are required to produce batik articles. The basics include fabric, wax, dye, applicators — such as brushes or tjanting (pronounced ''chantin'') tools — and containers for dye and wax, Fig. 3-2.

FABRIC

The choice of fabric for batik is important. The material should be firm and smoothly woven, not coarse or with a pile. A thin cotton fabric, such as a bed sheet, works very well. Silk, linen and wool are also good materials. White cloth produces the most vivid colors, but a light pastel sometimes gives pleasing results. New material should be washed and ironed to remove the sizing which is in all new cloth.

WAX

Wax is as important as the cloth for a batik project. Usually, a mixture of half paraffin and half beeswax produces a good consistency. Paraffin alone is too brittle while beeswax is expensive and tends to clog some batik tools. If you prefer not to mix your own, you can purchase specially prepared batik wax in hobby and craft shops. Wax should be carefully heated to between 300 and 350 °F (149 and 176 °C) in a double

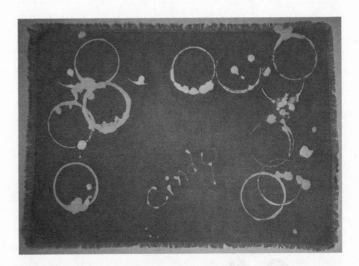

Fig. 3-1. Place mat is decorated with stamp batik. (Cindy Kicklighter)

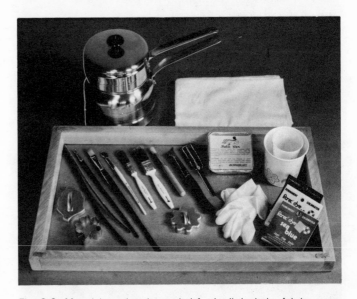

Fig. 3-2. Materials and tools needed for batik include: fabric, wax, dye, applicators, frame, double boiler, rubber gloves and containers for dye.

boiler or on an electric hot plate. CAUTION: Wax is highly flammable. Be very careful. Keep a box of baking soda nearby to extinguish an accidental fire.

DYE

Dye is another critical material. Several different types are available, but many are difficult to mix or have other disadvantages. A multipurpose or liquid instant dye is recommended for the beginner.

These dyes are produced in a broad range of colors, may be used cold and will work on most fabrics. They do have one disadvantage — they have limited color fastness.

Another good dye for batik work is a cold-water ''reactive'' dye. Being color fast, it will withstand repeated washing, is simple to use and is available in many colors. However, it can be used only with natural fiber materials (cotton, linen, jute and satin).

BRUSHES AND TJANTING TOOLS

The wax design may be applied using a brush, stamp or tjanting tool. Brushes of all sizes are useful depending on the specific design, Fig. 3-3. Finer detail requires a smaller brush. Stiffer bristles help to work the wax into the fabric. Batik stamps may be made from many items found around the home, Fig. 3-4. Collect articles with interesting shapes that could be used for future projects.

The tjanting tool has a handle, reservoir and a small spout, Fig. 3-5. A thin stream of wax can be poured from the tool to make fine lines and other delicate details. You may purchase a tjanting tool or make one from cardboard or tin. Since the wax is hot, the tool must have a handle.

Brushed and tjanting batik is usually performed with the material tightly stretched in a frame. Most any type of frame will do the job. An old picture frame or a canvas stretcher will be fine. Stamp batik is done on a flat surface over wax paper without a frame.

Fig. 3-4. Pipe stem cleaners, paper cups and cookie cutters make good batik stamps.

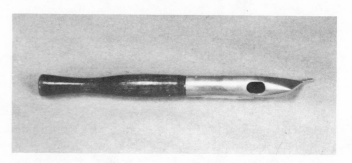
Fig. 3-5. Typical tjanting tool is made of brass with a wooden handle.

Fig. 3-6. Work is ready to begin on a stamp batik project. Cloth has been cut to size for a place mat.

Fig. 3-7. Stamp made from pipe stem cleaner is dipped into hot wax and immediately pressed against cloth. Note wax paper under cloth.

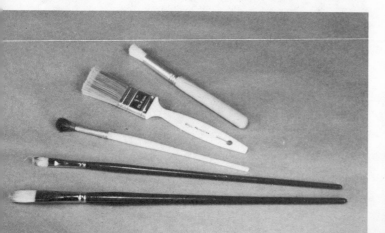
Fig. 3-3. Brushes of all sizes are useful for batik.

CONTAINERS

Two containers are required for this process. A plastic bucket is ideal for dyeing the article.

Dye should not be mixed in a metal container. Use a glass or enameled pan. A double boiler is recommended for melting the wax. (This is a pot placed inside another deeper pot which contains water.) The water is heated and, in turn, heats the wax in the inner container. A regular pan may be used if watched carefully.

STAMP BATIK

A good beginning batik project is one which uses a stamp to create the design. Articles which lend themselves to this process are table mats, napkins, T-shirts and pennants. The following steps will help you through your first project.

1. Select the article you wish to decorate. Prepare cold-water dye in one or more colors. Heat the wax, select a suitable stamp and spread out a large piece of waxed freezer paper. Protect the work area with newspapers. Fig. 3-6 shows the work ready to begin.
2. Place the wax paper on the newspapers and lay the article on the wax paper. Heat the wax to between 300 and 350 °F (149 to 176 °C). Make the pattern by dipping the stamp into the hot wax and stamping the fabric with it as in Fig. 3-7. Dip the stamp each time you use it. These waxed areas will be untouched by the first dyeing application.
3. When the wax is dry, carefully peel off the wax paper, Fig. 3-8. Avoid cracking the wax as you remove the paper.
4. Mix the dye and let it cool. If used too warm, it will melt the wax and ruin your design. The lightest colored dye is generally used first in batik. Dye the fabric in a large shallow pan for about 30 min. Try not to break the wax, Fig. 3-9. Remember that the colors will appear darker when wet. Rinse in cold water and hang up to dry.
5. If you plan to have more than one color, place the fabric on wax paper again and stamp more designs, Fig. 3-10. The first designs will be white and the second designs will be the color of your first dye. The background will be the color of the two dyes mixed together.
6. Peel off the wax paper when the wax is dry and dye with the second color. Rinse in cold water and dry.
7. When the article is dry, remove the wax by ironing the fabric between paper towels. Work over a thick padding of newspaper. Continue ironing until no wax is left in the cloth, Fig. 3-11.
8. Remove toweling and view finished product. Evaluate the process and make mental notes for the next time.

Fig. 3-8. Peel off wax paper after design has been completed.

Fig. 3-9. Dye first color in cold-water dye.

Fig. 3-10. More designs are stamped on the cloth for the second color.

Fig. 3-11. Iron out wax using newspapers, paper towels and hot iron.

BRUSH BATIK

When large areas are to be waxed, brush batik is generally used. See the hanging in Fig. 3-12. Choose a brush size appropriate for the work, Fig. 3-13. Small brushes can also be used for intricate designs. The fabric is stretched over a frame during brushing. (See Materials and Tools.)

The following steps are recommended for brush batik:

1. Select the materials for the project and plan the general theme of your design. Attach the fabric to the frame with tacks or staples. If your project is very large, you should wax one section at a time.
2. Heat wax to the proper temperature (300 to 350 °F or 149 to 176 °C) and begin to apply the wax design you have chosen. Fig. 3-14 shows a swirl pattern being applied with a large brush. These areas will remain white after the first dye bath.
3. When the wax is dry, remove the fabric from the frame and dye the first color. A very interesting effect can be achieved by wadding the cloth to create small cracks in the wax, Fig. 3-15. Rinse in cold water and hang up to dry.
4. When the fabric is dry, tack it on the frame again. Apply wax for the second series of designs, Fig. 3-16. Use the same procedure as before. Areas waxed this time will be the color of the first dye.
5. When the wax is dry, dye the second color. Rinse in cold water and hang up to dry. If you wish to add other colors, continue using the same procedure.
6. Remove the wax by ironing between paper towels on newspaper. Wash in cold water or dry clean the article. Press out the wrinkles.

TJANTING BATIK

When fine detail is desired in a batik design, a tjanting tool may be used. Modern versions of this ancient tool may be purchased at craft and hobby shops which carry batik supplies.

To use the tjanting tool:

1. Fill the reservoir with hot wax by immersing it in the wax, Fig. 3-17. This will melt any hardened wax in the tool and help it maintain the heat longer. Wipe the tool clean with a rag and hold the rag under the spout to avoid accidentally dripping wax on your fabric, Fig. 3-18.
2. Practice making a line with the tjanting tool, Fig. 3-19. Learn to flow the wax onto the material at a constant rate of speed; then, quickly put the rag under the spout when a line is completed. About one or two drops per second is the proper rate of flow.

Two factors will affect the rate of flow:
1. Temperature of the wax.

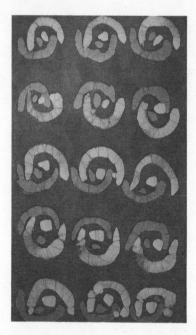

Fig. 3-12. Brush batik wall hanging.

Fig. 3-13. Any of these brushes may be used for a batik project. Size and type will depend on size and design of the project. Cloth has been attached to wood frame with stapling gun.

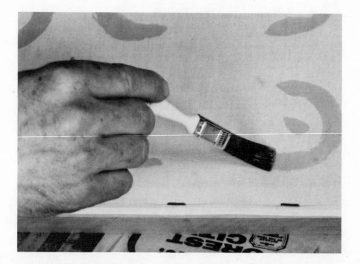

Fig. 3-14. Swirl pattern is being applied with large brush. Wax must be hot to penetrate cloth properly.

2. The size of the opening in the spout.

Both can be controlled. If the opening is too small, open it with a very fine needle. Squeeze it together if it is too large.

The waxing and dyeing procedure for tjanting batik is exactly the same as for brush batik. In fact, the two methods may be used together if desired. After you have mastered the use of the tools, you can make many interesting and beautiful articles.

Fig. 3-17. Step 1. Fill tjanting tool by immersing it in hot wax. Allow tool to heat up to the temperature of the wax before removing it.

Fig. 3-15. Dye the lightest color first.

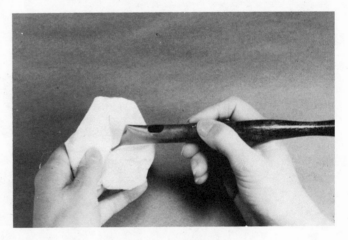

Fig. 3-18. Hold a cloth under the tjanting spout to prevent wax from dripping on cloth.

Fig. 3-16. Apply second color design with brush and hot wax.

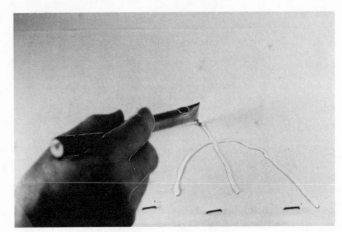

Fig. 3-19. Waxing a line with the tjanting tool. Finer detail is possible because of the small spout.

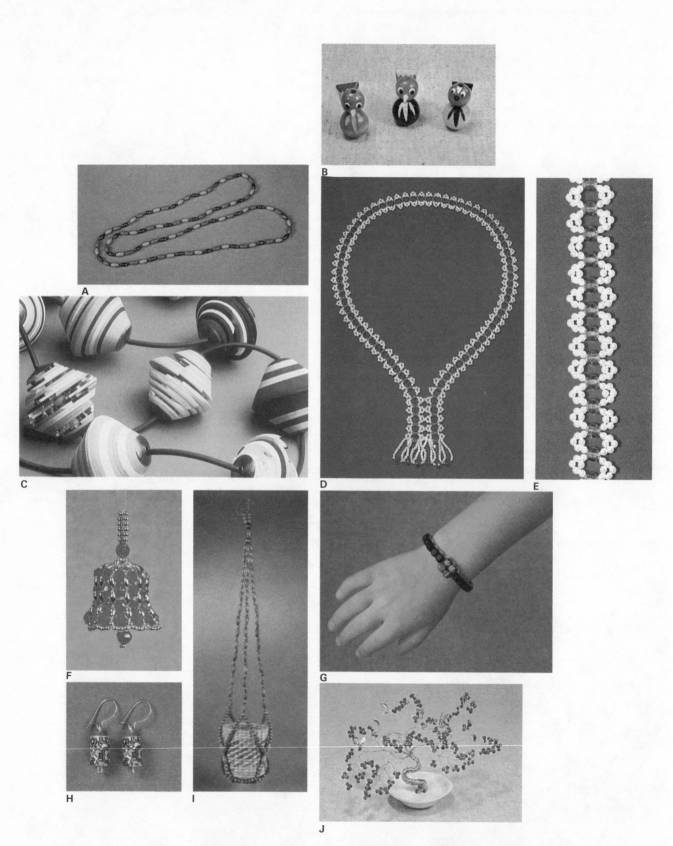

Project suggestions for beadwork. A—Necklace using three colors of beads. B—Trio of petite birds fashioned from large wood beads. C—Decorative bead necklace made from plastic laminates. (Formica Corp.) D—Complex bead necklace. E—Closeup of beadwork used in D. F—Bell of red and silver beads. G—Bracelet of square wood beads laid side by side using two-needle method. H—Earrings fashioned from ceramic beads and silver findings. I—Beaded hanging planter strung with 50 lb. monofilament fishing line. J—Bead tree made of wire and beads.

Chapter 4
BEADWORK

Beadwork is almost as old as civilization itself. Beads have been associated with religion, superstition, relaxing, communication, games, barter and personal adornment. American Indians are known for their exquisite bead craft.

Beading is a craft with impressive possibilities. Articles of jewelry, clothing, wall hangings, room dividers, trivets and place mats are but a few of the products that incorporate beads. They are also used with other crafts such as weaving, knitting, crocheting and macrame. The simplicity or complexity of a beadcraft project, Fig. 4-1, depends on the skill and interest of the individual.

MATERIALS AND TOOLS

Materials used in beadwork include beads of many sizes and colors, needles, thread and jewelry parts. Several hand tools are also required and looms must be used for certain projects.

BEADS

Much of the fun of beadwork is in selecting the beads. Anything that can be strung on a string may be used. Beads are available in a multitude of materials, shapes and sizes, Fig. 4-2. Some beads are so small that they are only a few millimetres in diameter; others measure several inches or centimetres.

Beads may be made of wood, metal, clay, shell, bone, cork, jade, porcelain, pearl, opal, plastics, glass and many other materials. You can also make them from paper, seeds, leather, pasta, buttons or other items found around the home. There is no end of sources for beads.

SEED BEADS are the smallest available. They are round, hollow, and generally made from plastic, metal or glass.

ROCAILLES (pronounced ''row-ki-reh'') are similar to seed beads except that they have square holes. They may be substituted for seed beads.

BUGLE BEADS are about the same diameter as seed beads but are longer.

E BEADS are about three times bigger than seed beads.

Fig. 4-1. Beadcraft is simple to do and the results are craft items of great beauty.

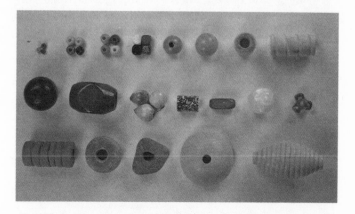

Fig. 4-2. This assortment of common beads includes tiny seed beads, glass, plastic, ceramic, stone and large wooden beads.

When the neckace is long enough, remove the needle from the thread.

7. Slip off the anchor bead on the other end of the thread. Tie in a square knot with the desired amount of tension on the string. (You will have four ends rather than two if the thread was doubled.) Place a dab of cement on the knot. This is called a knotted closing. See Fig. 4-12.

8. Thread a needle onto one of the ends and go through two beads and knot it around the main thread. Go through two more beads and knot it around the main thread again. Cement the knot and cut this thread.

9. Repeat Step 8 with the other end. Note: If you are using monofilament thread, make a square knot and put a drop of cement on the knot. Then make another knot on top of the first one. Cut the monofilament near the knot.

If you wish to use jewelers' findings to close your necklace, choose a bead cup, jump ring, hook or necklace end, Fig. 4-13. Tie these findings securely and cement the knots.

TWO-NEEDLE CROSS THREADING NECKLACES

Once you have tried beading with a single needle, you might wish to try two-needle beading or dual-strand stringing.

1. First, thread a needle on each end of a length of button twist yarn or other thread. Center an oval bead on one needle and run the other needle through the bead from the opposite direction, Fig. 4-14, view A.
2. Center the oval bead on the thread.
3. String a round bead on each needle as shown in Fig. 4-14, view B.
4. String an oval bead on one needle and run the other needle through from the opposite direction as in Fig. 4-14, view C.
5. Continue this procedure until the desired length is reached, Fig. 4-14, view D.
6. Close by knotting or add jewelry findings.

TWO-NEEDLE PARALLEL THREADING NECKLACE

1. Thread a needle on both ends of a thread.
2. Center two round beads on the thread, Fig. 4-15, view A.
3. Run both needles, one at a time, through a large bead from the same direction, Fig. 4-15, view B.
4. Run one needle through one small bead, and the other needle through another small bead.
5. Run both needles through another large bead.
6. Continue this pattern until the desired length is reached, Fig. 4-15, view C.
7. Secure the ends of your beadwork.

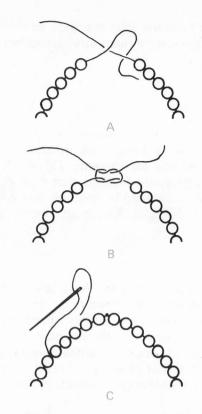

Fig. 4-12. Simple knotted closing. A—Start of knot. B—Square knot completed. C—Use needle to thread end back through several beads.

Fig. 4-13. Necklace has hook and chain so length can be adjusted.

SEED BEAD DAISY DESIGN

1. Thread the needle and double the thread. String one bead and go through it again to secure it as an anchor bead, Fig. 4-16, view A. Leave about 6 in. (152 mm) of thread at the end.
2. String 10 white beads and then eight red beads.
3. Go back through the first red bead. String one white bead for the center of the daisy, then go on through the fifth red bead to form the daisy, Fig. 4-16, view C. Pull the daisy tight against the white beads.
4. String 10 more white beads and eight red or yellow beads.
5. Repeat the previous procedure until the desired length is reached, Fig. 4-17.
6. Secure the ends in an accepted manner.

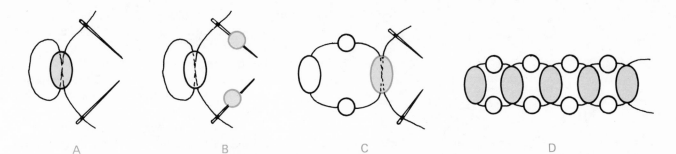

Fig. 4-14. Two-needle cross threading bead project. A—Center an oval bead on one needle and run other needle through bead from opposite direction. (The thread has a needle on each end.) B—String a round bead on each needle. C—Repeat first step by stringing an oval bead on one needle and running other needle through from opposite direction. D—Completed strand using the two-needle cross threading approach.

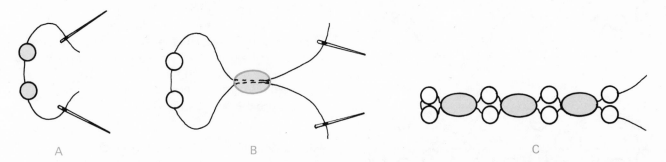

Fig. 4-15. Two-needle parallel threading. A—Begin by threading two round beads on the thread. B—Thread both needles through a large bead from the same direction. C—Series of beads have been strung using the two-needle parallel threading technique.

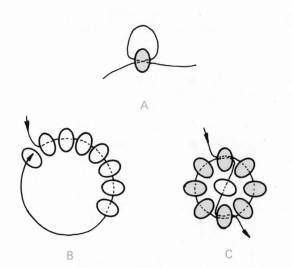

Fig. 4-16. Producing a seed bead daisy design. A—Anchor one bead. B—Partially completed design. C—Completed daisy.

Fig. 4-17. Seed bead daisy design produces attractive necklace.

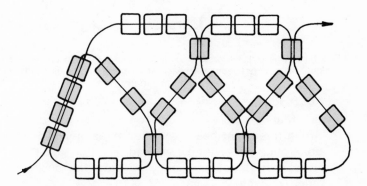

Fig. 4-18. Chevron chain is formed by stringing seven dark beads and then three light beads. Run the needle back through the first four dark beads. String three more light beads and then three dark. Pass the needle back through the seventh dark bead. Repeat the procedure as many times as necessary to produce the length desired.

CHEVRON CHAIN DESIGN

The chevron chain design is frequently made with dark beads along the edges and light beads inside. But the sample design described here has four dark beads in the V of the chevron and three light beads along the sides. Chain may also be made with other combinations of beads in the same proportions of five and four, six and five, etc., depending on the width you desire.

1. String seven dark beads on a thread leaving about 5 in. at the end. Follow the procedure in Fig. 4-18.
2. String three light beads and go back through the

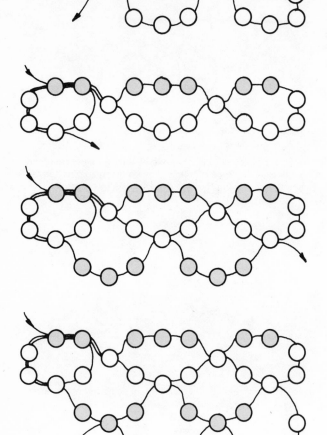

Fig. 4-19. This series illustrates the procedure for the Mexican lace design. This type of beadwork looks best when light and dark beads are used to form pattern.

first four dark beads.
3. String three light beads and then three dark. Then, go through the seventh dark bead.
4. Repeat the procedure until you have the desired length of chevron chain.
5. Secure the ends.

MEXICAN LACE DESIGN

The Mexican lace design is an open beadwork technique used to create an intricate pattern. It has many applications and is rather easy to learn. The procedure is illustrated in Fig. 4-19.
1. Select two colors of beads for your design.
2. Thread a two dark, one light, three dark, one light sequence until seven beads are strung (left to right). Then string two more dark beads. This will finish the first row.
3. Start the second row (right to left) by stringing four light beads. Then go back through the third bead from the end of the first row. This is a light bead. Pull the string tight.

4. String three more light beads, and, still moving to the left, go through the next light bead in the first row. Pull tight.
5. Continue the pattern until you reach the last light bead in the first row. (This was the first light bead that you strung.) Go through this bead and the two dark beads next to it.
6. String four more light beads and go through the two dark beads at the left end of the first row, from right to left. Come back down through three of the four beads just added.
7. String three dark beads. Moving from left to right, go through the bottom center bead of the nearest loop in the previous row.
8. Repeat Step 7 until you have gone through the last center bead at the right side of the row.
9. String four light beads and go back through the center bead of the first loop of the previous row. You are now moving from right to left.
10. Continue until the article is the desired size.
11. Secure the ends by knotting.

BEAD WEAVING WITHOUT A LOOM

Weaving beads without a loom produces a pattern of diagonal rows. There are two methods. The one-thread method is used for items with an even number of rows while two threads are used for articles with an odd number of rows.

Even row (one-needle) method. This method is called TWILL BEADING or PEYOTE BEADING. It produces a solid texture and can be formed around a core of rope to develop a spiral pattern. All beads must be of uniform size with a hole large enough for the thread to pass through twice.

Fig. 4-20. Bead weaving using even row (one-needle) method. This technique produces a solid texture and may be used to form a spiral pattern around a cylindrical surface.

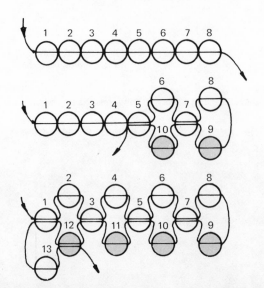

Beadwork

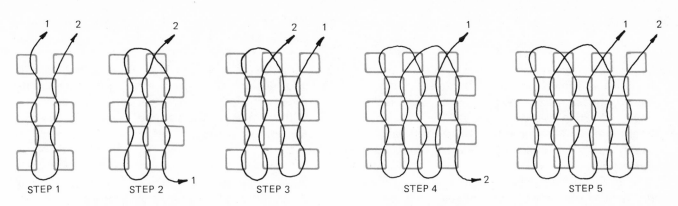

Fig. 4-21. Step-by-step procedure for bead weaving using the odd row (two-needle) method.

1. Select two colors of seed beads or round beads (light and dark).
2. Thread the needle with the appropriate thread and tie a knot about 2 in. (5 cm) from the end.
3. String eight light beads and slide them down to the knot as in Fig. 4-20.
4. String one dark bead and go back through the third bead from the needle (the seventh bead strung). Pull the thread tight.
5. String another dark bead and go back through the fifth bead of the first row. Pull the thread tight.
6. Continue the pattern until the end of the second row is reached.
7. String a light bead and move from the left to the right. Go through the first dark bead in the previous row. Pull the thread tight.
8. Add another light bead and go through the next dark bead in the previous row. Continue this procedure until you reach the desired length.
9. Secure the threads by weaving back and forth through one row for three beads. Knot around a connecting thread, and work back through three more beads and knot again. Cut the thread.

Odd row (two-needle) method. Refer to Fig. 4-21 as you read the following steps. Refer also to the sample shown in Fig. 4-22.

1. Put a needle on each end of the thread and string two beads on one needle. Move them halfway down the length of the thread. Pass both needles, in the same direction, through a third bead. String

another bead on each needle and then pass both needles through a sixth bead. String another bead on each needle forming a band five beads wide.

2. Bring the left-hand thread (marked "1" in the illustration) down through the top, right-hand bead. Pass the No. 1 thread down through a new bead, then through the right-hand bead just below. Continue in this manner until the No. 1 thread is passed through the right-hand bead in the bottom row.
3. Pass thread No. 1 through a new bead, then up through the right-hand bead directly above. Continue in this manner until thread No. 1 emerges from the top.
4. Note that the threads are again side by side at the top of the work. But thread No. 2 is on the left side of thread No. 1. Pass thread No. 2 down through the bead just added. Continue threading downward as you did with thread No. 1, until thread No. 2 emerges from the bottom of the work.
5. Start back up the work with thread No. 2 as you did with thread No. 1. Continue upward until thread No. 2 comes out the top. Thread No. 2 is now on the right side of thread No. 1.
6. Weave the pattern until you reach the size you want. Finish off as you did in the even row method.

Fig. 4-22. This sample of bead weaving is done with the odd row method.

Fig. 4-23. First, draw a design of what is to be developed on the bead loom. Use a pencil so you can easily erase as the design evolves.

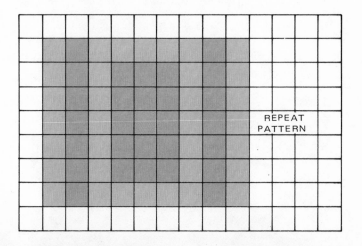

REPEAT PATTERN

LOOMED BEADWORK

Bead weaving on a loom allows several strands of beading to be woven at once. However, the length and width of the loom limits the size of the project.

1. Plan your design on graph paper or special beading paper indicating colors as in Fig. 4-23.
2. Begin threading the loom with beading thread. Tie the thread to the single nail at one end of the loom. Pass the thread over both bolts, Fig. 4-24, and loop it around the nail at the other end of the loom. It is best to start at one side and space the threads accurately as you proceed. These are known as the WARP threads. Double the two outside warp threads to provide added strength. When you have enough threads on the loom, tie the end to the nail. The procedure is essentially the same if a box loom is used. However, the threads are wrapped around the frame on the bottom and top, Fig. 4-25.
3. Thread your needle and wax a comfortable length of beading thread. Tie the weaving thread around the warp thread on the side away from you, about 6 in. or 15 cm from the end.
4. String one row of beads onto the needle according to your design. Push the beads down on the weaving thread.
5. Hold the threaded beads under the warp threads. With your finger, arrange the beads so each one is between two warp threads. The hole in each bead should be slightly above the warp threads.

6. Push the needle through the row of beads again making sure that it is above the warp threads. See Fig. 4-26 and Fig. 4-27.
7. Continue in this manner until you have finished your design. When your weaving thread becomes too short, tie it around a double warp thread and, with the needle still attached, push it back through the next to last row of beads. Knot it around itself in the middle of the row. Pull it through the rest of the row and cut it off. Begin a new thread by pulling it through the last row worked. Knot it around the double warp threads. Fig. 4-28 shows the completed design.
8. End off your loomed beadwork in one of several ways. Cut your work from the loom leaving the warp thread long enough so that each one can be woven and knotted back into the work. This procedure sometimes distorts the ends. Another method is to make a selvage (a narrow tape effect) by running weft (weaving threads) over and under the warp threads for 1/2 in. (13 mm) while the work is still on the loom, Fig. 4-29. Cover this selvage with cement. When it is dry, cut it from the loom.

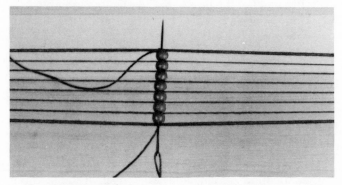

Fig. 4-26. Step 6 in attaching the first row of beads onto the beading loom. Needle is being passed through the beads over top of warp threads. Pull thread through beads to complete first row.

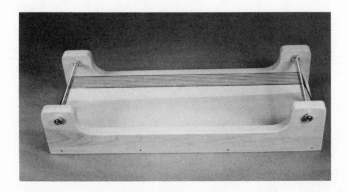

Fig. 4-24. This bead loom has been strung and is ready for work to begin. Warp threads are evenly spaced the width of a bead. Be sure to double the outside threads for added strength.

Fig. 4-25. Beading is underway on box loom. Note that warp threads are wrapped around frame on this type of loom.

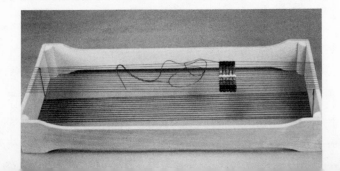

Fig. 4-27. Pressing the beads up between the warp threads with the finger and running the needle back through the beads above the warp threads.

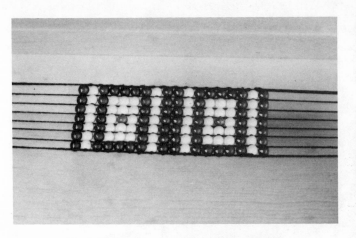

Fig. 4-28. Design with pattern repeated twice.

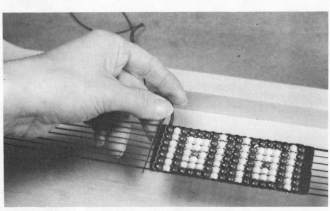

Fig. 4-29. Making selvage edge by weaving beading thread back and forth across warp threads. The right-hand side is complete.

Block printing project suggestions. A—Leaf print made by rolling technique. B—Large peacock printed on rice paper from woodcut. C—Print made on colored paper to give two-color effect. D—Woodcut, itself, suitable for display E—Symmetrical animal design. (Bobbe Bergsma Krebs) F—Three-color print has ship motif. (Paul Wolner) G—Three-color print from linoleum block. H—Vegetable print stationery. I—Piece of fabric printed with repeat pattern using linoleum blocks. J—Colorful woodcut print suitable for framing. K—Advanced woodcut work. L—Single color block print with modernistic design. M—Block printing on foil. N—Matted linoleum block print outlining main features of design. O—Flowered composition for block print.

Chapter 5
BLOCK PRINTING

Block printing, Fig. 5-1, is a simple method of reproducing several copies of a design or symbol. The rubber stamp, familiar to everyone, is one example. The design can be carved onto any one of several common household items. Successful block printing has been done with potatoes, carrots, gum erasers, wood or linoleum.

In block printing you simply cut away the material around the design and then cover the design with ink. When the raised surface comes in contact with the paper, the inked design is left on the paper. Printing from any kind of raised surface is called RELIEF PRINTING. Other types of hand reproduction will also be covered in this chapter.

MATERIALS AND TOOLS

Most block printing requires paper. Regular writing paper, newsprint, parchment, rice paper or poster board may be used. Generally, very porous paper will produce a blurred image. Shiny, coated paper will smear if used with water base ink. Experiment with different papers before selecting one for your project. Fig. 5-2 shows some of the common materials and tools used in block printing.

INKS

Choice of ink is an important decision in block printing. You can use either water base or oil base materials. Many people prefer an oil base. Such inks spread easily and produce bright, dense colors. Disadvantages include longer drying time and greater difficulty in cleanup. Solvents such as kerosene, benzene or painters' naphtha, needed for cleaning tools and spills, have a disagreeable odor. Moreover, the task of cleaning up is messy in itself and dirty rags must be carefully

Fig. 5-1. Block print design in several colors.

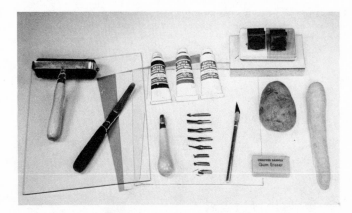

Fig. 5-2. Block printing tools and materials include brayer, piece of glass, paper, inks, carving instruments, stamp pad, stamps, palette knife and block materials such as wood, linoleum and vegetables.

41

disposed of to avoid fire hazard. CAUTION: Follow the directions on the solvent container. These chemicals are dangerous!

Water base paints produce a flat, dense color and dry very quickly. They are also cheaper. Cleanup is easy since it can be done with water. Soiled cleanup rags can be cleaned and reused. On the other hand, water base paints do not spread as easily as oil base paints.

Generally, inks are thinly spread on a piece of glass with a BRAYER, Fig. 5-3. The brayer is simply a roller with a handle. The roller should be 5 or 6 in. (127 or 152 mm) wide. This is large enough for most projects.

BLOCK MATERIALS

You will need a piece of block material for carving your design. Use a potato, or an eraser for small projects. Linoleum or wood are better for larger, more complex designs. Experiment with various materials. Select the one that seems most appropriate for your project.

Carve your design with a sharp knife or carving tool similar to those shown in Fig. 5-4. Some of the carving blades are U-shaped and some are V-shaped for making various cuts. When possible, cut away from yourself to prevent injury should the tool slip. Fig. 5-5 shows a design being cut in a piece of linoleum.

MAKING A VEGETABLE BLOCK PRINT

To make a vegetable block print, assemble the following materials: a large, firm potato or carrot, an X-acto knife or carving tools, a stamp pad or water base ink and a sheet of paper. A piece of glass and a brayer may be substituted for the stamp pad.

PROCEDURE

1. Wash the vegetable and cut it in half. Draw a design on the freshly cut surface. Carve away the unwanted portion to form the design, Fig. 5-6.

Fig. 5-3. The brayer should have a thin, even coating of ink.

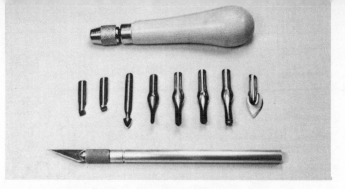

Fig. 5-4. An X-acto knife and linoleum carving tool with an assortment of blades are excellent for carving designs.

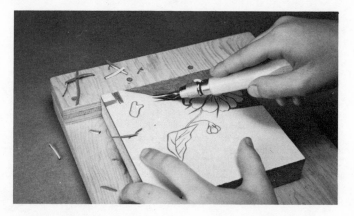

Fig. 5-5. Carving out the background around a design on linoleum block. Always cut away from the body to prevent injury.

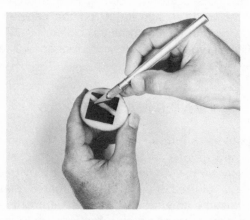

Fig. 5-6. Carving out a design on a potato. Ink has been added to the potato surface so that it is easier to see the design.

Fig. 5-7. Printing an image with the potato stamp. Stamp pad was used for inking.

2. Ink the carved image surface. Press the potato or carrot against the stamp pad or ink the surface with the brayer. Test it on a piece of scrap paper, Fig. 5-7. Note the amount of pressure needed to make a good print. Also, notice that the print is the reverse of your design, Fig. 5-8. This is important to remember. *The image is always reversed.*

3. Print your design on writing paper, napkins or place mats, Fig. 5-9. You now know how to make vegetable block prints and can design projects involving this process.

MAKING ERASER BLOCK PRINTS

Gum erasers are recommended for making eraser printing blocks. They are easily carved and the eraser surface picks up water base ink very well. The tools and materials required include an eraser, carving tools, carbon paper, stamp pad, water base ink and papers.

PROCEDURE

1. Draw the design on a piece of paper, indicating which areas will be raised for printing, Fig. 5-10. The lined area represents the image.

2. Using a piece of carbon paper and your pattern, trace the design on the eraser, Fig. 5-11. Carve away the material around your design.

3. Ink the block and test it on a piece of scrap paper. The area which has been carved away could be printed another color if you make a negative block for the second color. This can be done by stamping the design on a sheet of paper and tracing the design on a second eraser. Carve away the image made by the first block. Fig. 5-12 shows the positive and negative blocks and the design that each makes.

4. Carefully make several designs using one eraser block. Then fill in the second color using the other

Fig. 5-9. Series of designs made with vegetable stamps.

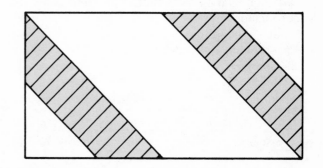

Fig. 5-10. Eraser block print design drawn on paper The lined area represents the desired image.

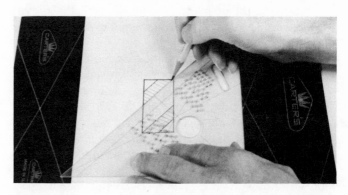

Fig. 5-11. Trace design on eraser using carbon paper under drawing. Eraser was carefully positioned under the drawing.

Fig. 5-8. The stamp (potato) makes a reverse image from the design cut into it.

Fig. 5-12. Positive and negative prints made with two eraser blocks. The second block was made by carving away the image of the first.

block, Fig. 5-13. This technique could be used for making wrapping paper, for producing a border design on a poster or for many other project designs.

MAKING LINOLEUM BLOCK PRINTS

Most experienced craft workers use linoleum for making block prints. It carves easily and produces prints with very fine detail. Available in large sizes it may be purchased mounted on a wood backing.

MATERIALS AND TOOLS

In addition to the linoleum block, materials and tools needed include:
1. A piece of glass for spreading the ink.
2. Brayer for inking the design.
3. Oil base ink.
4. Carving tools.
5. Paper

PROCEDURE

1. Draw the design on the block, and carve out the background area, Fig. 5-14.
2. When the design is carved, as in Fig. 5-15, spread a small amount of ink on the glass. Roll the brayer back and forth in several directions to coat it evenly with ink.
3. Roll the brayer across the linoleum block, Fig. 5-16, until raised portions are covered with ink.
4. Try printing the block on a piece of scrap paper, Fig. 5-17. Remember, a large block will require more pressure than a small one. Print your design on napkins, place mats, T-shirts, or other projects.

Now that you know the art of making block prints, you can make more elaborate designs in several colors. Fig. 5-1 shows the design in three colors. Each color is carved on a separate block. Blocks must be carefully aligned during printing.

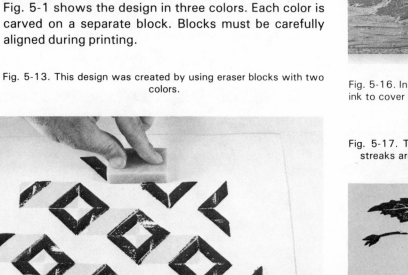

Fig. 5-13. This design was created by using eraser blocks with two colors.

Fig. 5-14. Carving out a daisy design on a block of linoleum. Be sure to cut away from you. Carve the details first and then remove the background. Cut about 1/16 in. (1-2 mm) of the material away.

Fig. 5-15. Properly carved linoleum block. White portions are higher, will receive ink.

Fig. 5-16. Ink linoleum block design with the brayer. Use just enough ink to cover the design. Do not fill in small details such as veins and leaves.

Fig. 5-17. Trial printing of block to check design. Dark spots and streaks are high spots which must be removed from the block.

OTHER HAND PRINTING TECHNIQUES

Several other methods of hand printing produce results similar to block printing. They use the same basic materials: ink, paper and some instrument for applying pressure. These hand printing methods are rubbing, rolling, offsetting and masking.

RUBBING

Making a rubbing is a creative and direct way to print a pattern or design. All you need for this technique is a textured surface, brayer, wooden spoon and paper. Articles such as textured wallpaper, embossed designs, woven pieces and naturally textured materials may be used for rubbings.

PROCEDURE

1. Ink your brayer with oil base or water base ink and apply the ink to the textured surface, Fig. 5-18.
2. Place a piece of paper over the inked surface and apply pressure to the paper with the back of a flat wooden spoon. Start rubbing in the center and work toward the edges.
3. Remove the paper when the entire surface has been rubbed and check for details, Fig. 5-19. Experiment with various textured surfaces, Fig. 5-20 and different papers and ink.

ROLLING

Objects such as a feather, leaf, fern frond (leaf) or twig make ideal items for rolling. This technique picks up the very finest details and produces an accurate image of the object. You will need a rolling pin in addition to paper, ink, brayer and the object itself.

PROCEDURE

1. Apply ink to the object using a brayer. Do this on newspapers or scrap paper.
2. Carefully place the inked object on the printing paper, Fig. 5-21, and cover it with another piece of

Fig. 5-19. Place sheet of paper over textured surface which has been inked. Rub paper with back of wooden spoon. Image will be formed on back of paper.

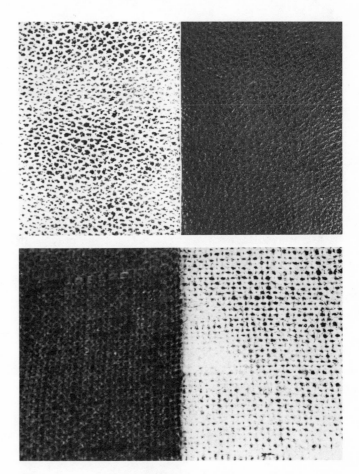

Fig. 5-20. Two examples of rubbings indicate the variety of textures which may be created. Top. Leather. Bottom. Coarse sacking material.

Fig. 5-21. Inked fern leaf is placed on print paper and is ready to form image.

Fig. 5-18. Applying ink with the brayer to a textured surface to make a rubbing print.

paper. If you ink both sides of the object, you can make two similar prints at once.

3. Use the rolling pin to apply pressure to the paper, Fig. 5-22. Be careful not to move the paper as you roll. Taping it down helps to hold it in place.

4. When the impression has been made, remove the top piece of paper and the object. Inspect the results, Fig. 5-23. Try several other objects and see what interesting prints you can develop. Fig. 5-24 shows another leaf print.

OFFSETTING

In offsetting, an inked image is formed on a surface such as an uninked brayer. The image, so formed, is then transferred or offset, to the desired surface. Textured or embossed articles work well for this printing technique. Since the image is formed on the cylindrical roller, the pattern can be repeated several times to cover large surfaces.

PROCEDURE

1. Ink the surface of your object with a brayer. If underlying paper picked up ink, transfer the inked object to a clean sheet. Now, either clean the brayer or use a second clean one to offset the image on the roller. Be careful to get a clear, sharp image.

2. Roll the image onto a clean sheet of paper, Fig. 5-25. You may repeat the pattern several times before cleaning and starting the process all over again.

Prints with several colors may be made, but each color must dry before applying the next. Again, use your imagination and experiment to produce various effects. Fig. 5-26 shows a four leaf clover design and its offset image for comparison.

MASKING

MASKING is a technique for creating designs or patterns using thin pieces of paper or other materials placed over an inked area to prevent the ink from reaching the paper underneath. A brayer is used to spread the ink over a smooth piece of wood, linoleum or other work surface.

PROCEDURE

1. Ink a work surface as large as the print you plan to make.

2. Cut out interesting shapes from paper or place other objects such as leaves, feathers or string on the work surface in the desired location, Fig. 5-27.

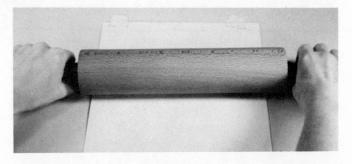

Fig. 5-22. Cover leaf with another sheet of paper and apply pressure with rolling pin. Press hard to get good image. Several layers of newspaper under printing area may help to improve results.

Fig. 5-23. Fern leaf image after rolling has been completed.

Fig. 5-24. A leaf print produces very fine detail using the rolling method.

3. Place a piece of paper over the surface and apply pressure by rubbing or rolling with a clean brayer. Carefully remove the printing paper and inspect your results, Fig. 5-28. Overprinting with other colors may be done in the same manner after previous colors are dry.

Fig. 5-25. This print was produced by offsetting the image on a clean brayer and rolling it on the print paper.

Fig. 5-27. An inked surface with paper masking strips in place to make print. Place print paper over inked surface and masking strips. Roll with clean brayer to form print.

Fig. 5-26. Four leaf clover print made by offsetting. Right. Inked object. Left. Image transferred to paper.

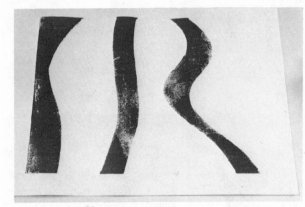

Fig. 5-28. Print made by masking method.

Bottle cutting project ideas. A—Set of four juice glasses made from throw-away bottles. B—Glass mug with cherry handle. C—Clear, cut glass leaded and stained. Simulated paste leading does not contain lead. D—Colorful hanging planter. E—Cut bottle fashioned into cheese cover. F—Vase. G—Attractive candle holder is sand-filled. H—Paper clip holder. I—Tall container for breadsticks. J—Parfait glass from parts of two bottles. K—Flower vase from short, curved bottle. L—Flower vase from tall clear bottle. M—From colored bottle to colorful sugar bowl. N—Brown bottle candy container. O—Kitchen canister. P—Soft drink glass. Q—Walnuts served in clear, cut bottle.

Chapter 6
BOTTLE CUTTING

Careful cutting transforms useless or discarded bottles into functional and fascinating glassware. Your imagination is the only limit to the variety of bottle cutting projects you can make. How about soda, sundae and beverage glasses? Interesting vases and candle holders? Or terrariums, bowls and dip dishes? You might even want to make a charming kitchen canister or a hanging glass planter. The latter combines bottle cutting with macrame'. Recycling of used empty bottles into decorative items, Fig. 6-1, also benefits the ecology in a small way.

MATERIALS AND TOOLS

Naturally, bottles are the main material. Quite a few are needed. Use simple ones for practice. Save beautifully shaped and colored ones for your projects. See Fig. 6-2.

There are many sources for obtaining them. Ask your friends or neighbors to save them for you. Restaurants, pharmacies, drugstores or science laboratories also have a variety of bottles. You may also find just what you need at garage or rummage sales, thrift shops and secondhand stores.

It is usually advisable to avoid bottles having embossed lettering or decoration that cannot be removed. While not always undesirable, such markings generally detract from the beauty of the finished product.

Other materials you will need are:
1. A range of silicon carbide abrasive grits and wet or dry abrasive papers.
2. A lapping plate for smoothing cut glass edges. A thin sheet of steel or an old cookie tin will do.
3. A candle for heating the glass.
4. Cold water for cooling.
5. Decorating materials for finishing projects. A few popular ones are glass coloring stains, a tube of liquid metal, decals, glitter, acrylic paints, assorted

Fig. 6-1. Drinking glass with decal crest added.

Fig. 6-2. Bottles come in many interesting shapes and colors. Round, smooth ones are easiest to cut.

Fig. 6-3. Materials for bottle cutting include turpentine, silicon carbide grit and paper, glass stain, simulated leading and a plain wax candle.

hardware and any paste-ons you may wish to select.

Basic materials are shown in Fig. 6-3. They may be purchased at most hobby and craft stores.

The only tool needed is a bottle cutter. Three basic types are available:

1. Vertical, Fig. 6-4, top.
2. Horizontal, Fig. 6-4, bottom.
3. Hot wire cutter. This type, not shown, requires an electrical source for heating. In other respects, it is like the horizontal cutter.

CUTTING THE BOTTLE

If this is your first attempt at bottle cutting, practice on clear, round containers like soda or catsup bottles. You can throw them away if your cutting operation is not satisfactory. However, your skill develops quickly and you will want to get on to those beautifully shaped, colored bottles.

USING HORIZONTAL CUTTERS

To use a horizontal bottle cutter:

1. Always wear safety glasses or goggles to protect your eyes from chips of flying glass during all operations.
2. Remove labels from the bottle and wash it inside and out.
3. Position the bottle on the cutting machine with the bottom against the back gage support, Fig. 6-5. If the back gage has different levels to support the bottle, use the one that enables you to make the best possible contact between bottle surface and cutter blade. The front of the bottle should make direct contact with both the front support bracket and cutter blade.
4. Make the cut on a straight up and down part of the bottle when first beginning. Making a cut on the curved neck of a bottle is more difficult and will be shown later.
5. Adjust the back gage to hold the bottle at the point

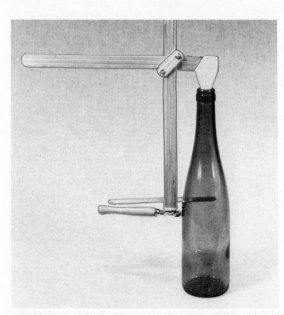

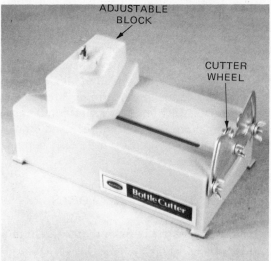

ADJUSTABLE BLOCK

CUTTER WHEEL

Fig. 6-4. Bottle cutters. Top. Vertical bottle cutter is inexpensive and simple to operate. Bottom. Typical horizontal cutter. Cutter wheel can be raised and lowered. Block slides left and right or can be removed entirely.

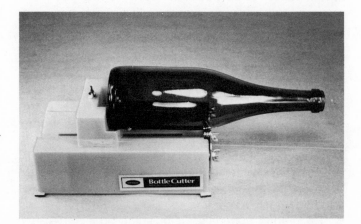

Fig. 6-5. Ready for cutting, bottle rests on back gage support at right angle to cutting wheel.

where you want to make the cut. Position the gage by loosening the thumbscrew. Slide it into position and gently tighten. An extremely large bottle may be cut by removing the back gage and positioning the bottle on the frame as shown in Fig. 6-6.

SCORING

After setting the back gage so that the cutter is in contact with the clean, smooth, parallel side of the bottle, you are ready to score, (scratch) the glass.

1. Hold the bottle against the cutter as shown in Fig. 6-7. Apply a slight downward pressure on the bottle while rotating it toward you. Keep the bottle firmly held against the back gage to insure a straight score.
2. Try to use a steady, even pressure to produce a *light score.* The scored line should look like a fine scratch on a window pane. As you are scoring, you should hear a light scratching sound. If the scoring action has a harsh grating sound, you are pressing too hard and making too deep a cut. Deep cuts dull the cutter and the bottle will not separate with a smooth edge. *This is probably the most important part of bottle cutting.*
3. Try to make a long continuous score, not a series of short, uneven scratches. Make your score just once around the bottle until the ends meet. *Do not cut over a scored line a second time.* It will only produce a deep cut and a ragged edge.
4. If you have not made a clean, straight scored line, do not waste time trying to score over it again. Just discard the bottle.

SEPARATING THE BOTTLE

Under stress, glass will fracture at its weakest point. The scored line has provided the weak point and a temperature shock will separate the bottle.

1. Fill a deep plastic pail with ice cold water and set it next to your work area.
2. Place a low candleholder near the edge of the table. Light the candle and heat the bottle along the scored line, Fig. 6-8. CAUTION: remove the cap or stopper from the bottle because the expanding warm air inside could cause it to explode. Slowly rotate the bottle, keeping the tip of the flame about 1/4 in. (half a centimetre) below the scored line. Continue rotating the bottle for about four or five turns.
3. Since glass is a poor conductor of heat, the ends of the bottle will not get too hot to hold. Rest your arms on the table so you can hold the bottle steady. After rotating it about 30 seconds over the flame, dip the bottle in the pail of cold water as demonstrated in Fig. 6-9.

Fig. 6-6. If a bottle is too long it is placed on frame with back gage support removed.

Fig. 6-7. Scoring is started by rotating the bottle toward you with light pressure against the cutting wheel.

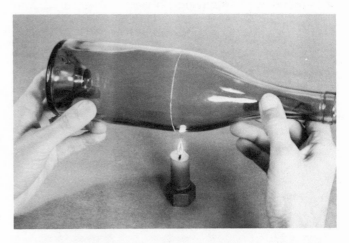

Fig. 6-8. Heat scored line over candle flame with a rotating motion.

Fig. 6-9. Dip bottle into cold water after heating scored line.

51

4. If the bottle has been scored and heated correctly, the bottle will separate in the pail of water, Fig. 6-10. Should it fail to separate, try a slight snapping motion. This will usually separate the bottle as shown in Fig. 6-11. If the bottle still does not separate, do not force it apart. Dry the bottle, heat if over the candle again and repeat the cold water bath. You may have to repeat this procedure two or three times on heavy, thick-walled bottles.

5. Another good method of separating the scored bottle is to rub an ice cube around the scored line after heating. In either cooling method, if the break is not complete, hold it in the light and you can see where the crack has not gone completely through the glass. Reheat that area and cool again.

SMOOTHING THE ROUGH EDGES

The edges of the cut glass may be fairly flat but rough. They will also be very sharp. Do not rub them with your fingers. Smooth the rough edges in the following manner:

1. Pour a small amount of silicon carbide (grit size 120) onto your lapping plate. Add enough water to the glass rim.

2. Rotate the rough edges of the cut glass around and around while applying downward pressure. Continue until the surface is smooth and all rough spots have been removed, Fig. 6-12. Work from a coarse to a very fine grit.

3. Final smoothing is done on a sheet of silicon carbide wet or dry paper placed on a flat surface. Wet

Fig. 6-11. Snapping motion of hands should separate bottle if it did not separate in water.

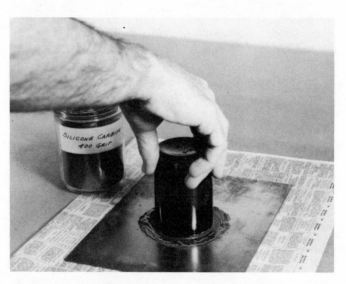

Fig. 6-12. Smooth rough edges of cut bottle on lapping plate with wet silicon carbide grit.

Fig. 6-10. Bottle should separate with a clean break.

Fig. 6-13. Rub cut edge on fine "wet or dry" paper.

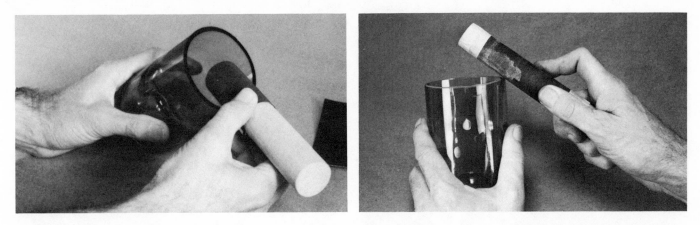

Fig. 6-14. Left. Smooth inside edge with "wet or dry" paper wrapped around dowel rod. Right. Smooth outside edge in similar manner.

4. Since the outside and inside edges will still be sharp, they, too, must be smoothed. Wrap a strip of 200 grit paper around a large dowel rod and polish these edges to a smooth finish, Fig. 6-14.
5. The best possible finish is produced by heating the edges with the candle flame after sanding with abrasive papers. The completed bottle, ready for decorating, is shown in Fig. 6-15.

ADHESIVES

Some bottle projects will require the use of adhesives to join glass parts. Undoubtedly one of the best adhesives for glass is a clear, two-stage epoxy resin. The epoxy makes a strong bond and dries hard. Use just enough adhesive to lightly coat the surface. Excess adhesive will show and is difficult to remove. Clear silicone adhesives, liquid glass and contact cement are also satisfactory, especially with colored glass. Wood and metal handles, knobs and bases may be glued to glass with ease. Always follow the manufacturer's instructions when using any adhesives.

CUTTING CURVED SURFACE

Scoring the curved surface of a bottle may be done with either the horizontal or vertical bottle cutter. One reason for using the vertical type, since it is more difficult to operate, is to cut curved surfaces that cannot be reached with the horizontal cutter, Fig. 6-16.

To score a curved surface with a horizontal cutter, place the bottle on the step of the back gage support that enables you to make the best contact with the cutter wheel and bottle. Adjust the front bottle support so the bottle rests level, Fig. 6-17.

Check the cutter wheel to make certain it is pointing directly toward the bottle surface. If not, loosen the cutter wheel, rotate it to the correct position and tighten. Proceed with cutting and separating in the same manner as used for straight-sided bottles.

Fig. 6-15. Cut and polished bottle is ready for decorating.

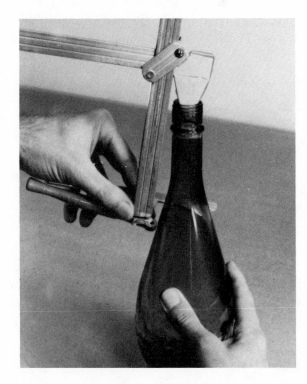

Fig. 6-16. Scoring curved neck of a bottle with the vertical cutter.

Fig. 6-17. Scoring deep curve of bottle neck with bottom on top step of back gage support.

DECORATING CUT BOTTLES

Decorating cut bottles is a matter of individual taste. The possibilities are unlimited. A list of suggestions follow:

1. Decals can be purchased for almost any design or message you wish. Flowers, butterflies, labels for spice jars or cannisters, name tags, initials, fraternity or sorority crests and letters of the alphabet are but a few. Follow directions on the backs of decals for soaking and applying them.

2. Painting designs on bottles is like raised surface painting. Acrylic paints in squeeze tubes and glittering pastes can be applied to your glass creations in raised bands of brilliant color. Just squeeze the tube as you would a cake decorator to make your design. These materials are also good for covering undesirable embossed letters on the glass.

3. Labels that you may want to preserve on old or new bottles can be protected with a few light coats of clear plastic spray. Be careful not to damage the label when cutting and separating.

4. Colorless glass may be made more attractive by staining. The appearance is similar to leaded stained glass windows or lampshades. Simply apply the liquid metal, known as leading, from the tube to the glass surface. Form whatever design you desire. This material dries quickly to a pewterlike finish. Though often called ''liquid solder'' it is nonmetallic. Next brush colored glass stain on the clear glass areas between the leading. Two or three coats of stain may be applied to obtain rich deep colors. Allow each coat to dry thoroughly. Since most glass stains are not waterproof they are generally used for decorative purposes only.

BOTTLE CUTTING PROBLEMS

A few suggestions may help to eliminate bottle cutting problems:

1. Make sure the small cutting blade is rotating freely. If not, loosen the screw that holds the cutter assembly until the blade turns easily.

2. The surface area of the bottle being cut should be absolutely clean. Even finger prints can cause the cutter to slip, producing an irregular scored line. Wipe the glass surface clean with a cloth dampened in turpentine. You will be surprised how much better your results will be.

3. Put a drop of light machine oil on the cutting wheel after every five or six bottles cut. This will help insure proper cutting action and prevent the glass from slivering.

4. Use a small brush to keep the cutting blade clean and free of dirt or paper labels.

Bottle Cutting

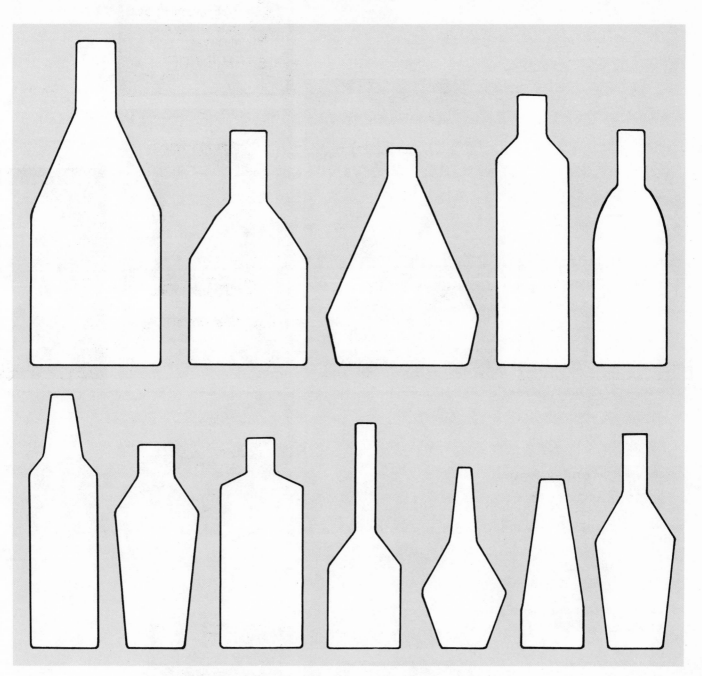

Of bottles there is no end of variety! Part of the fun of bottle cutting is to collect them and dream up unusual ways of using each bottle's unique shape. What would you do with any one of the shapes above?

Sample projects in calligraphy. A—Free flowing script style is appropriate to message on this plaque. B—Combining lettering and photography. C—Illumination of a favorite quote. D—Calligraphic print set off by matting and framing. E—Beautiful lettering executed in brown ink on parchmentlike paper. F—Formal announcement lettered in Old English Text. G—Hand lettering on background of subtly shaded screen print. H—Delicate lettering against finely shaded artwork. I—Art and lettering rendered in pencil and ink. J—Commercial calligraphic print demonstrates wide range of application of this craft.

Chapter 7
CALLIGRAPHY

Calligraphy—the art of beautiful handwriting—is more than simple lettering or penmanship. It is a form of personal expression. It enables the writer to create a more interesting visual impact with words. In the past, calligraphy was used to transcribe sacred texts. These beautiful works were executed with great care adding overtones and illuminations to enhance and glorify the writings, Fig. 7-1.

Today, calligraphers are not restricted to repeating the classic styles. New alphabets have been designed and endless applications have grown from them. Academic diplomas, mottos, old proverbs, invitations and place cards are just a few of the modern uses of calligraphy. A hand-lettered document with decorative flourishes and motifs takes on added importance. It has enduring value to the recipient. With practice and patience, you can learn the skills necessary to transcribe your writings or those of others into objects of lasting beauty.

TOOLS AND MATERIALS

The basic tools of calligraphy include: lettering pens, waterproof ink, pencils, scale, dividers, compass, straightedge and some fine sable brushes, Fig. 7-2.

PENS

Lettering pens (holder and nibs) are available at most art supply stores. Select several styles and sizes for different lettering applications. Fig. 7-3 shows four basic nib shapes. Some have ink reservoirs attached to the underside to reduce the time spent refilling the pen. A fine-line mechanical pen is also useful for making straight lines or some elaborate designs, Fig. 7-4.

Fig. 7-1. This beautiful example of calligraphy demonstrates the exquisite design and detail possible in this art.

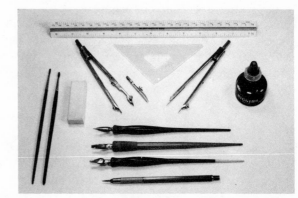

Fig. 7-2. Basic tools needed for calligraphy include lettering pens, waterproof ink, pencils, dividers, compass, straightedge, eraser, scale and fine sable brushes.

INKS

A high-quality waterproof black ink should be used for lettering. Several brands are available and work equally well. Select a container having a dropper for easier filling of pens, Fig. 7-5. Tempera paint, designers' gouache (opaque watercolors) or colored inks may be used for illumination. It is best to try the ink on a sample of the paper you plan to use.

PAPER

While many types of paper are suitable, the most popular are the parchment types in various colors and textures. They are readily available and easy to use.

Other fine papers may be purchased for specific applications. Genuine sheepskin and parchment are still manufactured, but are difficult to use and expensive. Leave this material for the expert.

HAND LETTERING STYLES

Some calligraphic styles are very formal. OLD ENGLISH TEXT is considered a classic of formal lettering. It is probably the most popular of all lettering styles. For that reason alone it should be learned by anyone interested in calligraphy.

Less formal is the lettering style called CHANCERY CURSIVE. It has an entirely different "look" than Old English Text and is used for entirely different purposes.

OLD ENGLISH TEXT

Though not highly readable, Old English Text is unmatched in elegance. The entire alphabet is a combination of 24 elements, Fig. 7-6. These must be mastered before you can letter the alphabet. Fig. 7-7 shows the upper and lower case letters as they are commonly drawn. A square nib pen held at a 45 deg. angle, Fig. 7-8, is used to produce the letters.

The basic lettering technique follows:

1. Place a square nib in the penholder. Using the dropper, place a small amount of ink on the top side of the nib, under the brass fitting or on the underside as in Fig. 7-9. Do not overfill the pen.

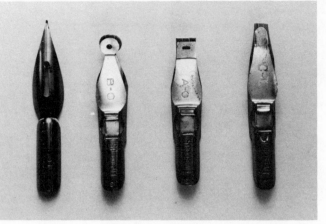

Fig. 7-3. Four common nib shapes used in lettering.

Fig. 7-4. Fine-line mechanical pen has self-contained ink reservoir.

Fig. 7-5. An ink container having a dropper is easy to use.

Fig. 7-6. The 24 elements used in Old English Text letters. These should be mastered before trying to letter the alphabet.

Fig. 7-7. Old English Text alphabet has great dignity.

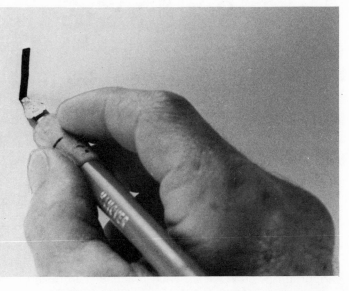

Fig. 7-8. Hold the lettering pen so wide part of tip is at a 45 deg. angle to paper's length when making Old English letters.

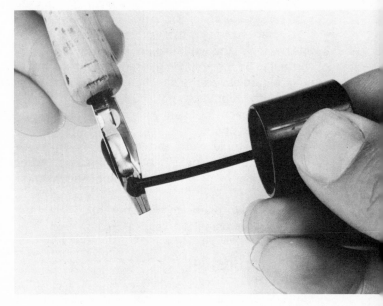

Fig. 7-9. One way to fill a square nib lettering pen with a dropper.

ABCDEFGH
IJKLMNOP
QRSTUV
WXYZ
abcdefghijklmn
opqrstuvwxyz

Fig. 7-10. Chancery Cursive alphabet. This style has simpler strokes and is useful for less formal work.

2. Make a few strokes on scrap paper to start the flow and check that the pen is not overloaded with ink.

3. Hold the pen at a 45 deg. angle, as previously illustrated, and make a vertical stroke. Move from top to bottom. Keep all parts of the pen point in contact with the paper at all times and maintain the 45 deg. angle.

4. Practice each of the strokes shown in Fig. 7-6 until you can make them smoothly. Try to memorize their shapes. Notice that an essential element of this style is the variation in line width. This is controlled by maintaining the same angle at the pen point regardless of the direction the pen is moving.

5. Practice the alphabet until you have a firm mental picture of each letter in your mind. Refer to the alphabet frequently.

6. Choose a simple word and letter it, paying close attention to the spacing between letters. After some practice, you will learn the proper spacing for maximum legibility.

7. You are now ready to try your hand at some creative work using Old English Text.

CHANCERY CURSIVE

Chancery Cursive has a contemporary flair and is ideal for greeting cards, announcements and invita-

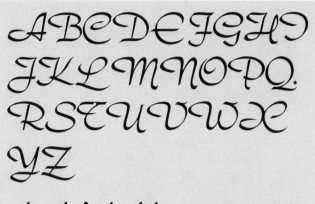

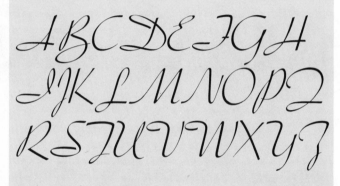

Fig. 7-11. These three lettering styles are useful for a variety of calligraphy projects. The first one is Rondo, the second Trafton Script and the third Bon Aire.

tions. It is well worth learning to use for less formal work.

Fig. 7-10 shows the Chancery Cursive alphabet in upper case and lower case letters. Study the shape and proportion of each letter. Then practice them using a square nib pen. Fig. 7-11 shows three other lettering styles useful for calligraphy projects.

Fig. 7-12. Philosopher's statement is to be lettered in Old English Text and hand illuminated. Sample of the alphabet is close at hand for reference.

HAND ILLUMINATING

Beautiful calligraphy may be combined with hand illumination to add personal expression and artistry to a piece of work. The beginner should choose a brief and simple project with letters 1/2 in. (13 mm) high or larger.

The following steps are basic to the art of hand illumination:

1. Select the copy and a calligraphic style, Fig. 7-12. Pick a simple one for the first try.
2. Select the inks, pens and paper.

Fig. 7-14. Begin to ink lettering. Keep most of project covered with scrap paper to prevent smears or ink spills.

3. Prepare a rough layout and decide if you like the design, Fig. 7-13. Frequently, the first letter of the text is drawn much larger and illuminated.
4. Make the top of the beginning (initial) letter about even with the highest parts of any letters in the first line and the bottom of this letter even with the bottom of the letters in the second line. Fig. 7-14 shows the correct method.

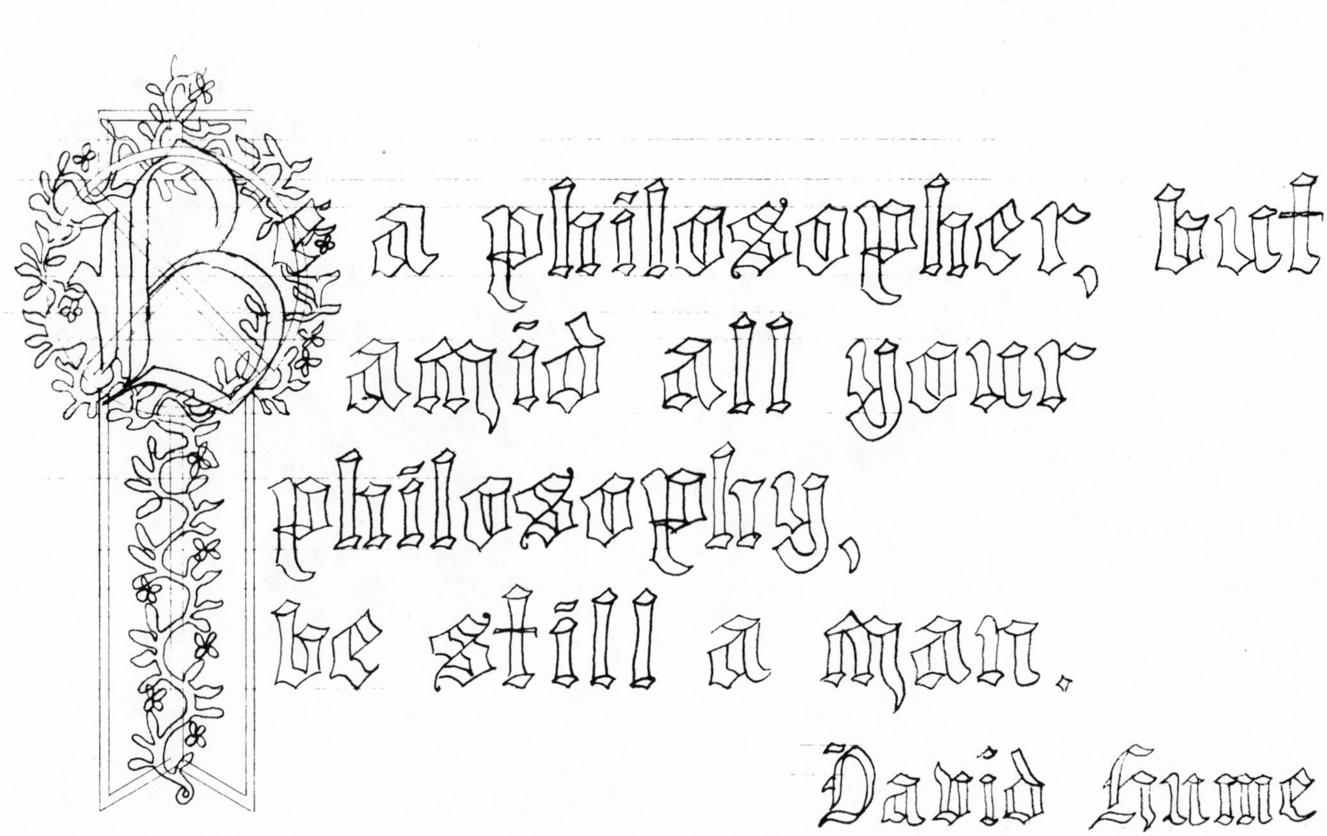

Fig. 7-13. Make rough layout in pencil to check design.

5. Ink the message using the techniques described. Dividers may be used to check the proportions of each letter against examples of the alphabet. Refer to Fig. 7-15.
6. Draw your design lightly first in pencil and then in ink, Fig. 7-16. Outlines of leaves, flowers, spirals or other figures may be made with a mechanical inking pen or one of the standard nibs.
7. Erase pencil lines carefully. Be sure the ink is dry. Guidelines may be left if desired.
8. Fill in empty areas with color using waterproof ink, tempera or designers' gouache. A No. 1 brush may be used for large areas. Use a finer brush for smaller areas. Apply the paint in continuous strokes to achieve flat, solid areas of color, Fig. 7-17. Fig. 7-18 shows the illuminated letter in color as it should appear on the completed project.
9. You may give the finished work an antique look by slightly burning the edge with the flame of a match. Hold the match at the edge of the paper and blow out the flame as soon as the paper catches fire. Practice on scrap first, Fig. 7-19.
10. Display your work.

INKING HINTS

1. Work slowly and try not to make a mistake.
2. Keep equipment clean and in good working order.
3. Do not overfill your pen.
4. Always try out the pen on scrap paper first.
5. Keep a sample of the alphabet style in front of you as you work.
6. Rest your forearm and elbow on the table and let your wrist and fingers perform the movement.
7. Use a soft pencil to draw guidelines and lay out your work. Lines can be erased when the ink is dry. Be sure it is dry!
8. Be consistent in the way you form each letter.
9. Use a sheet of clean paper under your hand to prevent smudges on your work.
10. Ink may be scraped off with some success using an X-acto knife or razor blade held perpendicular to the paper. Scrape very lightly and then erase to smooth the paper.

Fig. 7-16. Ink in the rest of the lettering.

Fig. 7-17. Fill in open areas of the illumination with colored waterproof ink. Apply small amounts to prevent runs.

Fig. 7-15. Check proportions of a letter to be sure it conforms to alphabet sample.

Fig. 7-18. Color illumination executed to check final design and color. It will be used as a guide in completing final project.

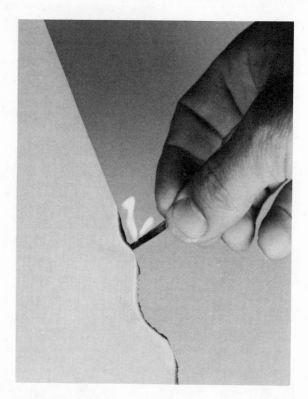

Fig. 7-19. Burning the edge of a piece of parchment will give it an antique appearance. Practice on scrap before trying it on your project.

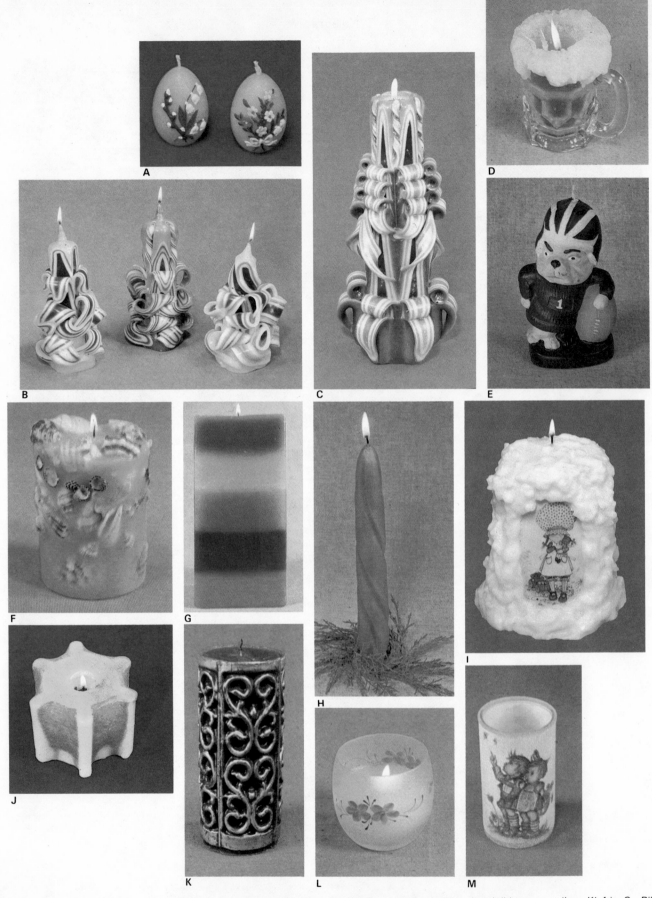

Bakers' dozen of candlemaking ideas. A—Hand decorated egg candles. B—Candles decorated with colored ribbon wax. (Lew Kieft) C—Ribbon wax candle in warm tones. D—Candle cast in mug using wax foam decoration. E—Painted candle made in plastic mold. F—Seashells embedded in hot wax. G—Multicolored milk carton candle. (Linda Baird Kerr) H—Twisted hand dipped candle in two colors. (Lew Kieft) I—Foamed wax decoration around picture. J—Candle decorated with brown sand. K—Filigreed surface decorated in gold. L—Candle cast in cut bottle M—Candle cast in glass.

Chapter 8
CANDLEMAKING

Candles have become very popular as home decor. Their main purpose is to provide a bright and cheerful atmosphere through their beautiful shapes and bright colors.

Making the candles has become an exciting craft medium where you can be as creative as you wish. The process is simple and materials are inexpensive. Yet, the result is your own unique creative effort. Try both simple and complex shapes. Experiment with different designs.

MATERIALS

Candles are made from a good grade of paraffin or candle wax and quality wicking. These may be purchased at most craft and hobby stores. Beeswax is one of the best materials for candles but it is expensive. We suggest a fine quality paraffin. It comes in slab form and can be modified for most candlemaking purposes.

A white, powdery material called stearine is generally added to the paraffin. This makes the candle harder so it will not sag in hot weather. Stearine will also make a candle more opaque, if desired. Carnauba wax and candelilla wax can be substituted for stearine as a hardening agent. Bayberry wax, while expensive, provides a pleasing fragrance.

You will also need:
1. A supply of plain, braided wicking.
2. Special candle dyes for coloring.
3. Caulking.
4. A liquid or spray mold release agent. See Fig. 8-1.

TOOLS AND MOLDS

Few tools and equipment are required for candlemaking. You will need a double boiler and an electric hotplate or range. A candy thermometer can be used to measure the temperature of the hot paraffin. A plastic bucket or wastepaper basket serves well to water cool the mold. Other tools you should have are: an ice pick, knife, scissors, rotary egg beater, pastry brush, measuring spoons, hammer and a pair of pot holders. You should also have a Pyrex measuring cup or kettle with a spout to pour the hot wax. Major tools and equipment are shown in Fig. 8-2.

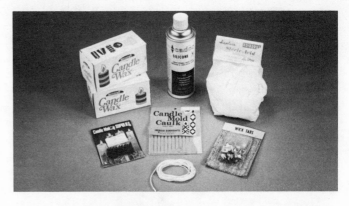

Fig. 8-1. Materials you will need are: candle wax, silicone spray mold release, powdered stearine, coloring dye, caulking, wick tabs and braided wicking.

Fig. 8-2. Equipment needed includes a double boiler, Pyrex measuring cup, egg beater, candy thermometer, knife, wooden spoon, ice pick and pastry brush.

Standard metal and plastic molds are available in a variety of shapes and sizes. But you may already have glass, plastic, cardboard and metal containers that will make ideal molds. See Figs. 8-3 and 8-4.

CASTING A CANDLE

Cover your work area with several layers of newspaper or brown wrapping paper. For safety purposes, melt your wax a good distance from where you will be casting in the molds. Have your tools and materials ready and use the following procedure.

1. Break the wax into small chunks and place it in the double boiler, Fig. 8-5. A 1 qt. (0.95 L) mold will require about 3 lb. (1.5 kg) of wax. When the wax melts, slide the candy thermometer into the boiler so that you will always know the temperature of the wax.
2. Apply an even coat of silicone mold release to the mold, Fig. 8-6.
3. Cut a length of wick a few inches longer than the height of the mold. Insert one end through the hole in the mold bottom, pull it to the top and tie to metal rod, Fig. 8-7.
4. Turn the mold over, draw the wick tight and fasten as shown in Fig. 8-8. Use a sealer to prevent the mold from leaking, Fig. 8-9

   Some commercial molds have a hole at the bottom and a rubber sealing gasket to which the wick is fastened. In such cases, follow the manufacturer's directions for fastening the wick.
5. Fill the water bucket so that all but the last inch of the mold can be submerged for cooling.
6. Check the temperature of the wax, Fig. 8-10. When it reaches 180 to 190°F (82 to 88°C), add about three tablespoons of stearine for each pound of wax, Fig. 8-11. If color is desired, the dye should be added at the same time, Fig. 8-12.

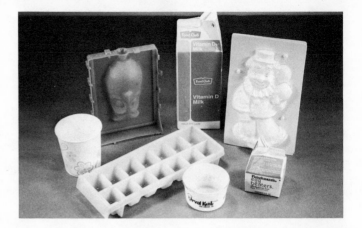

Fig. 8-4. Plastic and cardboard molds for a variety of candle shapes.

Fig. 8-5. Cut small chunks of wax into double boiler.

Fig. 8-3. Assorted metal and glass containers which can be used as molds are to be found around the home.

Fig. 8-6. Applying silicone mold release to commercial metal mold.

Fig. 8-7. Fasten wick to metal bar at top of mold.

Fig. 8-10. Check wax temperature with candy thermometer.

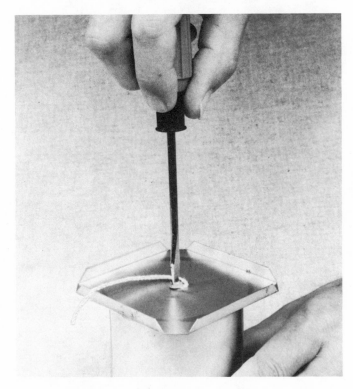

Fig. 8-8. Tighten wick at bottom of mold and hold it in place with metal screw.

Fig. 8-11. Add powdered stearine to melted wax.

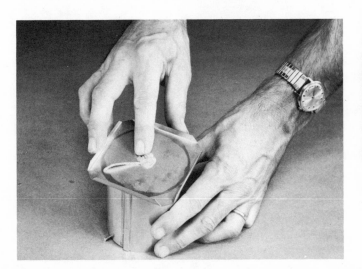

Fig. 8-9. Caulk around screw to seal mold against leakage.

Fig. 8-12. Cut chips from stick dye into melted wax.

Never allow the temperature of the molten wax to go over 200°F (93°C). Stir the mixture carefully with a long wooden spoon until an even color is obtained. Add fragrance just before pouring if desired.

7. Pour enough wax into the Pyrex measuring cup to fill the mold. Then pour into the mold as shown in Fig. 8-13. The pouring cup and mold may be warmed in an oven prior to pouring to keep the wax from cooling too quickly. Use a glove or pot holder when pouring the hot wax. Always check to see that there is water in the bottom of the double boiler. Never allow water to drip into the hot wax.

8. After pouring, place the mold in the water bucket, Fig. 8-14, so that the water level is just below the top of the mold. Do not add more water for cooling since some may get in the mold and spoil the wax surface. When the candle cools for about 30 min., it will shrink. Keep adding wax until the desired level is obtained. Break the cooled wax surface with an ice pick, as necessary, to add more hot wax around the wick. Fill only the low center section. Any wax that goes over the first pouring and seeps down the mold wall may spoil the candle surface. Allow candle to cool completely, at least six hours or overnight.

9. Remove the candle from the mold as shown in Fig. 8-15. If the candle does not slide out of the mold easily, it can be released by pouring hot water on the mold. Check the candle surface. If it is not as smooth as you would like, hold it by the wick and quickly dip it into hot water. Scrape off any mold lines with a knife. Trim the wick, Fig. 8-16. Your candle is now completed.

Fig. 8-14. Place mold in water. Do not allow water to come over top of mold. It will spoil the candle.

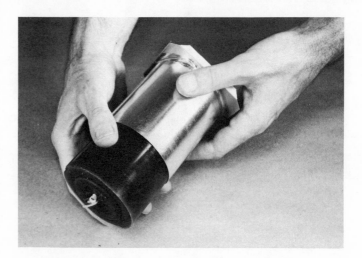

Fig. 8-15. Unfasten wick at mold bottom and gently remove the candle from mold.

Fig. 8-13. Pouring wax into metal mold from Pyrex cup. Pot holder should be used to grip hot cup.

Fig. 8-16. Trim wick about 1/2 in. (13 mm) long with scissors.

10. Many plastic molds are made of two halves that snap together. Attach the wick according to instructions that come with the mold. Place the mold in a shallow pan of cold water to catch any drips. Pour melted wax at about 180°F (82°C) as shown in Fig. 8-17. Allow to cool about six hr. and then add more wax to fill shrinkage at the top. After about four more hours the mold can be unsnapped, opened and twisted carefully to remove the candle, Fig. 8-18. Acrylic paints work well for decorating these candles.
11. Household molds produce nice candles for stacking or as individual pieces, Fig. 8-19. Pour at correct temperatures and use a hot ice pick to make the hole for wicks.

MAKING A HAND DIPPED CANDLE

1. Melt the wax in a double boiler as described for casting. Keep the wax just above its melting point, about 150°F (65°C), so that wax will stick to the candle each time it is dipped. Use a tall boiler for long candles.
2. Cut a length of wicking and tie one end to a small stick or a pencil to make it easy to handle and hang. Dip the loose end in the hot wax and then stretch the wick on a piece of paper and hold until cool, Fig. 8-20. Now rigid, it is ready for further dipping.
3. Quickly dip the wick into the hot wax and withdraw it evenly, Fig. 8-21. Allow the wax to cool in the air until it is fairly hard after each dip. This takes but a few minutes.
4. Continue dipping until the candle is the right

Fig. 8-18. Remove candle from opened plastic mold.

Fig. 8-19. Jello cup mold produces beautiful candle. Wax pieces in ice cube tray are for a stacked candle.

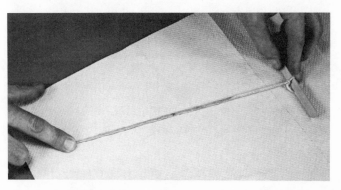

Fig. 8-20. Stretch wax coated wick on paper until cool.

Fig. 8-21. Withdrawing candle from hot wax as thin coating begins to build up.

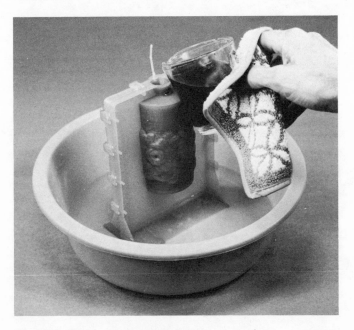

Fig. 8-17. Pour wax into plastic mold which is set in pan of water to catch any drips.

diameter. Hang the candle by the wick, Fig. 8-22, until it has completely cooled and hardened. This will usually take from two to three hours. For a tapered candle, dip the lower half into the wax more frequently.

5. Trim the candle at the bottom as in Fig. 8-23.

HELPFUL HINTS

1. Mold release should be used on most types of molds for easier removal of the candle. Plastic molds generally do not require mold release.
2. Wax-pouring temperatures:
   Metal containers and molds - 180 to 200°F (82 to 93°C).
   Warm glass molds - 170°F (77°C).
   Cardboard molds - 145°F (63°C).
   Plastic molds - 150 to 170°F (65 to 77°C).
3. Decorative, fluffy wax can be made by melting the wax and allowing it to cool until a film forms on the surface. Whip it into a fluffy consistency with a rotary egg beater. Apply foamed wax to the candle with a pastry brush or fork.
4. Glasses or jars can be used as both mold and container. Tie one end of a piece of wicking to a wick tab, Fig. 8-24. Suspend the wick in a container as shown in Fig. 8-25. Pour wax at a low temperature. Allow to cool and trim the wick. Colored wax without stearine will glow through a clear container while burning.

BALL CANDLES

To make a ball candle, fill a half-round mold with wax. Allow wax to harden and remove. Repeat the pro-

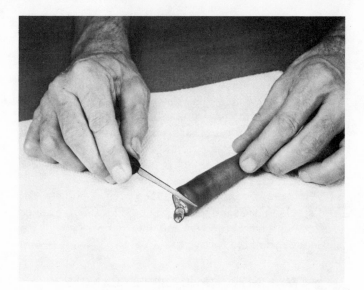

Fig. 8-23. Cut candle to length with sharp knife.

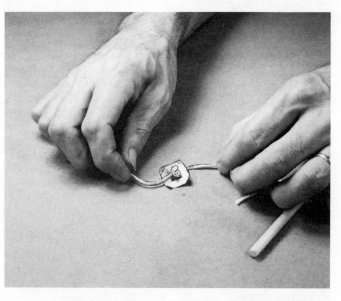

Fig. 8-24. Tie one end of wick to metal wick tab.

Fig. 8-22. Candle is hung up to cool and harden.

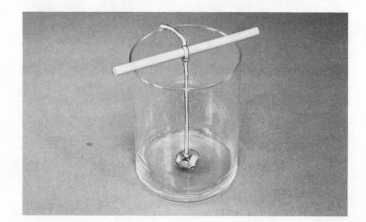

Fig. 8-25. Wick is suspended in glass container with top tied to short piece of dowel rod.

cedure and then center the wick between the two wax halves. Cement the halves together evenly and carefully using melted wax.

STACKED CANDLES

Produce stacked candles by pouring wax into a muffin tin, ice cube tray or cake pan. Circular pieces shaped by the muffin tin can be stacked to any desired height. The flat sheet of wax in a cake pan can be cut into a variety of shapes with a cookie cutter as the wax begins to harden. Stack these pieces to whatever shape you like while cementing each piece to the next with hot wax. Heat an ice pick and press a hole down through the stack of wax pieces. Dip wicking in hot wax, allow it to cool and thread it through the hole.

PAPER-CORE WICKING

Paper-core wicking is available for adding a wick after the candle has been cast. It is considerably stiffer than regular wicking and is easily inserted into a hole made by a hot ice pick.

SAFETY

Wax can catch on fire and burn. Keep a box of baking soda handy to smother a flame in the melting pot. Always use a double boiler to melt wax since it cannot get hot enough to ignite. Keep wax away from an open flame and wear gloves or use pot holders when handling or pouring molten wax. NEVER pour leftover wax into a sink. It hardens quickly and may clog the drain.

Projects suited to plastics casting. A—Cast napkin holder made in a plastic mold. B—Bird in wooded habitat cast in clear resin. C—Plastic candle cast in reusable glass mold. D—Copper design imbedment used as a paper weight. E—Color pigment cast in clear resin. F—Letters cast in carved wood for subdivision or street sign. G—Table setting of cast grapes made in breakable glass molds. H—Cast polyester table figure. I—Kitchen spoon holder. J—Grape decoration using red dye. K—Necklace of surface cast beads. L—Close reproduction of penny greatly enlarged.

Chapter 9
CASTING PLASTICS

The casting of plastic resins into useful and creative craft projects, Fig. 9-1, has an appeal all of its own. Once you have mastered the casting technique, you will, undoubtedly, see the countless possibilities that exist in this unique craft.

Cast projects may be clear, colored or decorated with embedments. A few examples of cast plastics projects are egg timers, desk sets, spoon rests, jewelry, artificial fruit table decorations, lamp bases and valuable objects you may want to preserve by embedment.

MATERIALS

Most cast plastics projects are made with clear liquid polyester resin. A hardener is added to the resin at the time of casting. It causes the resin to solidify in the mold. Casting resins are available in pints and quarts. The hardener is kept in a separate container until it is time to use it. Opaque pigments and transparent dyes may be added to the resin to produce any desired color. These materials are shown in Fig. 9-2. A release agent must be used with many molds to keep the resin from

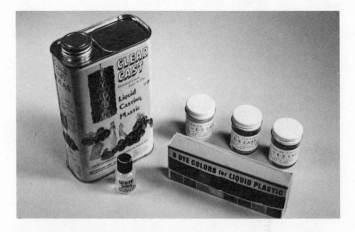

Fig. 9-2. Liquid casting resin and hardener are mixed together as they are used. Opaque and transparent dyes are added to provide a variety of colors in plastic projects.

sticking to the walls of the mold. Molds can be purchased or made from plastic, plaster, wood, glass or metal, Fig. 9-3. You should also have at hand:
1. Paper mixing cups.
2. Stirring sticks.
3. Eye dropper.
4. Metallic glitter.
5. Fasteners or findings.
6. Objects you want to embed, Fig. 9-4.

TOOLS

Few tools are required for casting:
1. Small paintbrush for applying mold release.
2. Tweezers to position articles for embedding.
3. Standard hand and power tools for making wood, metal or plaster molds.
4. File and sandpaper for removing rough edges from cast project.
5. Hand or power drill for making holes in cast plastic.

Fig. 9-1. Coin embedments can be designed as pendants, as wall decorations, mounted as above, or used in a number of imaginative, decorative ways.

73

Fig. 9-3. Top. Commercial plastic molds. Center. Household metal molds. Bottom. Glass molds for casting.

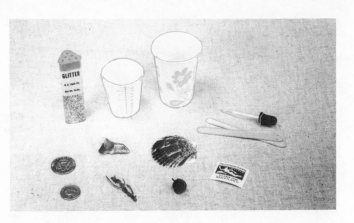

Fig. 9-4. Metallic glitter, mixing and measuring cups, eye dropper and stirring sticks will be needed to mix casting resins. Suitable embedments in the foreground include buttons, medals, leaves, teeth, artificial flowers and pictures or photographs.

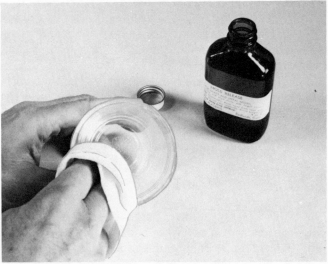

Fig. 9-5. Applying liquid mold release to a glass mold.

CASTING PLASTICS PROJECT

Secure the materials for the project you have planned. Work in a well ventilated area and cover the bench with several layers of paper to catch spills. Use the following procedure for casting:

1. Place the mold on the work table. Apply a thin coating of mold release if necessary, Fig. 9-5. Plastic molds do not require a release agent.
2. Pour the required amount of casting resin into a paper measuring cup, Fig. 9-6. Add the correct amount of hardener specified by the manufacturer, Fig. 9-7. Mix the resin thoroughly with a wooden stirring stick and add dye color if desired.

Fig. 9-6. Pouring correct amount of casting resin into measuring cup.

Fig. 9-7. Add hardener to resin by counting correct number of drops.

3. Pour a surface layer of resin to about one-third the depth of your mold as shown in Fig. 9-8. This is called the three-layer pouring method for casting embedded articles, Fig. 9-9.

4. As soon as the surface layer has begun to gel (thicken), test the surface with a stirring stick, Fig. 9-10. It should be just thick enough to support the weight of the article to be embedded. This usually takes 25 to 30 min.

5. Prepare another mixture of resin and hardener for the positioning layer and pour a small amount into the mold. Gently place the article to be embedded on the resin, Fig. 9-11. Then pour the rest of the positioning layer, Fig. 9-12.

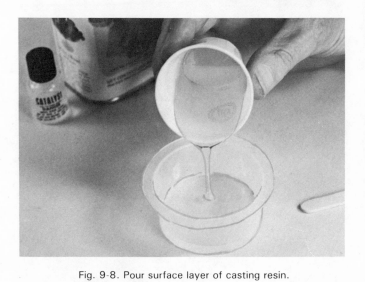

Fig. 9-8. Pour surface layer of casting resin.

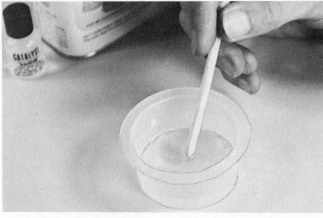

Fig. 9-10. Test surface of first pour with stirring stick.

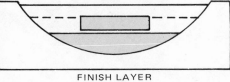

SURFACE LAYER

POSITIONING LAYER

FINISH LAYER

Fig. 9-9. Three-layer pouring method. Surface layer is allowed to thicken until it will support weight of object being embedded.

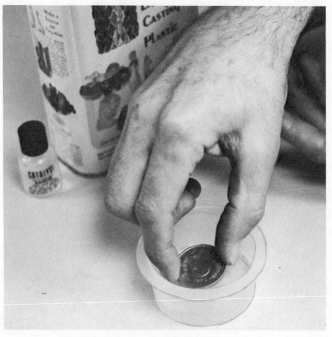

Fig. 9-11. Place article to be embedded into a partial pour of the second or positioning layer. This does away with air pockets and voids when the article is positioned.

6. Mix enough resin and hardener for the finishing layer. Mix dye, opaque coloring or metallic glitter with the resin at this time, if you wish. Pour the resin mix slowly over the embedment at one edge of the mold and fill to the top, Fig. 9-13. Cover the mold and allow to cure overnight.

7. Remove the casting from the mold as in Fig. 9-14. When using glass breakaway molds, wear gloves and tap with a small hammer until all glass has been removed.

8. The top or back of the casting is generally rough or wavy. Place a piece of coarse grit sandpaper on a flat surface and rub the casting back and forth until smooth, Fig. 9-15. Switch to moistened "wet or dry" sandpaper of finer grits (No. 220 to 400) and continue sanding until all scratches have been removed.

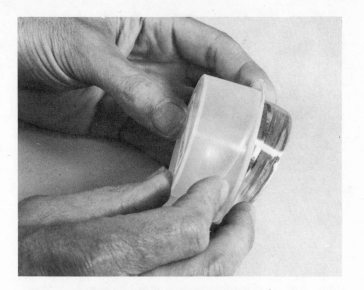

Fig. 9-14. Use pressure on bottom to remove solid casting from plastic mold after material has cured.

Fig. 9-12. Pour positioning layer of resin.

Fig. 9-15. Rub back of casting across strip of coarse sandpaper to produce smooth surface on casting.

Fig. 9-13. Pour finishing layer from one edge to fill mold or cover embedment to desired depth.

Fig. 9-16. Buffing casting with commercial polishing compound. Toothpaste also serves well for polishing.

9. Rub the casting thoroughly with a soft cloth and some polishing compound. Polish vigorously until the casting becomes clear and takes on a bright lustre, Fig. 9-16. Fingerprints and small scratches can be removed from any surface of the casting in the same manner. The completed casting is shown in Fig. 9-17.

HINTS FOR BETTER CASTING

1. Chill glass and ceramic molds and then submerge them in hot water to aid in the release of the casting.
2. Add the exact amount of hardener as specified by the resin manufacturer. During the chemical reaction of curing, the amount of heat given off depends on the amount of hardener used. Too much hardener can create enough heat to crack the casting. Too little hardener may cause the casting to cure very slowly and remain sticky.
3. Be sure your molds and any embedments are dry. Any moisture may turn into steam during curing and create enough pressure to crack the casting.
4. Air bubbles can be brought to the surface of the liquid resin and released with a pin or toothpick.
5. The basic casting procedure is the same for any

Fig. 9-17. Completed casting of embedded coin is mounted on handsome wood base.

type of plastics project. Of most importance is accurate measuring of resin and catalyst (hardener) and complete mixing with catalyst and colors.

6. In the interests of safety, castings made in thin, breakaway glass molds should be wrapped in newspaper and tapped with a hammer to break the glass. Wear gloves and safety glasses for additional protection.

Suggestions for collages and assemblages. A—Assemblage of wood printing type. B—Letter collage. C—Collage based on driftwood theme. D—Dried flower collage. E—Collage of dyed scraps of leather mounted on wood base. F—Freestanding scrap wood assemblage. G—Paper collage of fruit. (Nancy Kermode)

Chapter 10
COLLAGES

Children who make greeting cards by pasting scraps of colored paper and fabric onto note paper are actually making a collage. The name, itself, is the French word for pasting.

A collage is nothing more than an arrangement of "things" fastened to a background. It may be a well-planned arrangement or a random selection and placement of materials. Most any materials can be used but the arrangement usually follows a theme of interest to its designer, Fig. 10-1. For example, a person interested in golf might develop a collage from golf tees and score cards. Someone interested in cooking might combine pictures of food with recipes. Similarly, a forestry enthusiast might combine leaves, twigs and bark into an interesting pattern. Collages are fun to make. You simply let your imagination run free.

Although the technique goes back many centuries, new materials and ideas make the collage an up-to-date craft. Most collages are made for decoration and enjoyment.

In the past, collages were thought of only as flat-work—pasting paper, buttons and felt on a background. Three-dimensional collages, known as assemblages, will be a part of this craft experience. They are made from thick materials such as stones, bottles or parts of a clock. See Fig. 10-2. Many are freestanding, intended to be placed on a table. There is often little difference between a collage and an assemblage.

MATERIALS AND TOOLS

Material for collages and assemblages is unlimited. Many items can be salvaged from scrap. However, there are generally some basic materials needed that must be purchased.

Always select a variety of fairly flat materials from which to create your design. These may include leaves,

Fig. 10-1. This collage is designed around a travel theme. (Marge Baird)

Fig. 10-2. Freestanding assemblage is made from collection of familiar construction scrap.

grasses, magazine clippings, maps, postcards, fabrics or pieces of colored paper.

A large piece of matboard makes a good backing for mounting these materials. Other materials and the tools you will need are shown in Fig. 10-3.

An assemblage usually requires more cutting and fastening of parts. As with a collage, the materials are endless: pieces of metal or wood, old keys, scraps from a lumber yard or disassembled products.

After pieces have been chosen, a number of fastening materials may be required to attach them to each other or to a backboard or mount. See Fig. 10-4. Most assemblages can be put together by doweling, gluing or nailing.

The tools needed depend upon the materials you will be using. However, specialized tools are hardly ever required. Those found in most workshops, such as hammers, drills and saws, will usually meet your needs.

MAKING A COLLAGE

The paper collage is a good beginning project. With virtually no cost, it allows you to select and shape individual pieces of flat material into a design that expresses your interest and mood. For instance, a travel theme might be developed:

1. Look at magazines, travel brochures and postcards. Select pictures dealing with that theme. Gather many more than you will actually use; you may want to refine your ideas as you go along.
2. Select a map to serve as the background. Glue it to a matboard backing, Fig. 10-5. Allow the glue to dry before applying other materials.
3. To start the arrangement, cut out individual pieces and lay them on the map as in Fig. 10-6. Using the overlay technique, cut the pictures to the size and shape you want. Shift the pictures around until you are satisfied, Fig. 10-7.

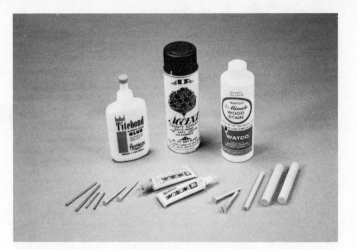

Fig. 10-4. Materials often used to fasten the parts of an assemblage include white glue, spray paint, stain, nails screws, dowels and epoxy cement.

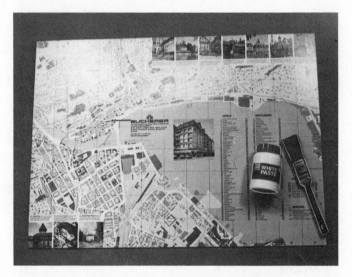

Fig. 10-5. Glue map to matboard with white paste.

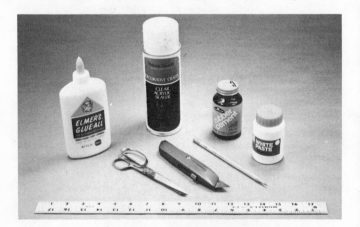

Fig. 10-3. You will generally need white glue, clear plastic spray, rubber cement, white paste, scissors, mat knife, pencil and ruler to make a collage.

Fig. 10-6. Start random picture arrangement on map.

4. The underlay technique is used to show the girl's face in the mountains. Slit the top picture, Fig. 10-8, and slide the face underneath until you have the desired effect, Fig. 10-9.
5. Start gluing pieces to the map with rubber cement, Fig. 10-10, until the collage is complete. Allow rubber cement to dry about one minute before pressing pieces into position.

MAKING AN ASSEMBLAGE

An assemblage is fairly simple to make. Parts, being heavier, are fastened with glue, nails or wood screws. The pieces can be fastened to plywood or other backing material or mounted on a self-supported base.

But more important than the method of attachment is the selection and arrangement of parts. The assemblage is a personal reflection of your feelings and ideas. Try the following procedure to make a freestanding assemblage.

1. Select your theme. The pictured assemblage displays materials used in home construction. Collect as many small products or pieces of building material as possible.
2. Cut a length of 2 x 6 in. lumber to serve as a mounting for the assemblage. Cut the top at an angle. Plane or sand it smooth, Fig. 10-11. Spray coat it with clear sealer.

Fig. 10-9. Slide underlay into desired position.

Fig. 10-10. Apply rubber cement to back of pictures for attachment to the backing.

Fig. 10-7. Rail pass is overlayed on forest picture.

Fig. 10-8. Cut round opening or curved slit to frame portion of picture that will be inserted underneath. This is known as the underlay technique.

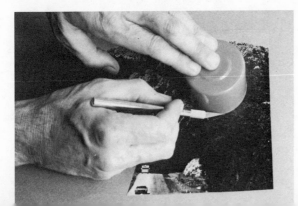

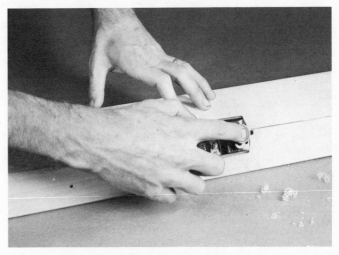

Fig. 10-11. Plane edges of wood mount for smooth finish.

3. Place parts all around the wood mount in an arrangement that satisfies you. Select items for their interesting shapes, colors and texture. Cut parts, as necessary, to fit particular spaces. Drill holes in the mount, Fig. 10-12, and attach parts with dowels, Fig. 10-13.
4. Use white glue, nails and screws to attach other parts. See Fig. 10-14 and Fig. 10-15. Apply stain to wood pieces attached to the mount, Fig. 10-16. Allow stain to dry; brush with a coat of sealer.
5. Cut the base to size from a piece of cedar siding. Spray with one coat of clear sealer and attach with nails, Fig. 10-17. Attach wallpaper strip with white glue to complete the assemblage, Fig. 10-18.

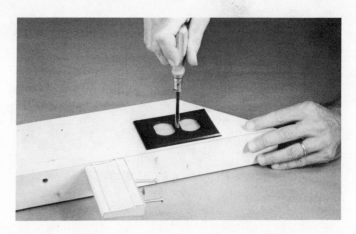

Fig. 10-14. Fasten outlet cover plate to mount with wood screw.

Fig. 10-12. Drill holes in mount for attaching parts with dowels.

Fig. 10-15. Top trim is glued in place with white glue.

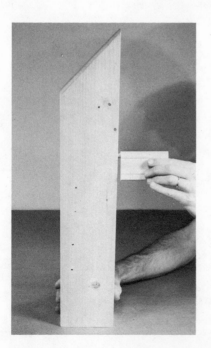

Fig. 10-13. Attach trim piece with dowel and white glue.

Fig. 10-16. Brush stain on side trim piece.

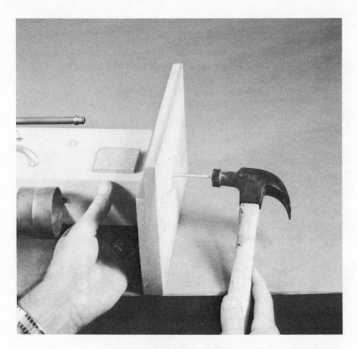

Fig. 10-17. Fasten base to mount with hammer and nails.

Fig. 10-18. Complete assemblage is a conversation piece.

Project suggestions for decoupage. A—Favorite bird decoupaged with matching ribbon. B—Old fashioned dress style decoupaged to matching plaque. C—Lady's purse with carefully arranged decoupage. D—Decoupage plaque mounted and framed. E—Antiqued flower picture decoupaged to oval plaque, mounted and framed. F—Another beribboned winner - a decoupage picture in an oval setting. G—Walnut plaque with card decoupaged to it. H—Rose picture framed in black, red and gold.

Chapter 11
DECOUPAGE

In the 17th century Venetian cabinetmakers cut out paper prints and applied them to their furniture. Today, this craft, DECOUPAGE, is once again very popular. Almost any object can be decorated in this manner. The basic skill is easy to acquire. Simply cut out a scene or picture that you like and glue it to any surface you wish to decorate. Several coats of clear lacquer, varnish or plastic finish are then applied. Boxes, lamps, cans, plaques and furniture are but a few of the objects that can be beautifully decorated. The art is available in old greeting cards, pieces of wallpaper or commercially prepared prints especially designed for decoupage. Fig. 11-1 shows an example of this craft.

Fig. 11-1. A decorative craft once practiced by furniture makers, decoupage survives as a popular handicraft.

TOOLS AND MATERIALS

The few specialized tools and materials needed are stocked by most craft shops, Fig. 11-2.

For most decoupage projects you will need:
1. White glue for attaching prints. Select a type that dries clear.
2. Liquid sealer, acrylic spray or gesso for sealing wood surfaces. Use clear sealer or spray for a natural wood finish. Gesso, a mixture of gypsum and glue, is ideal for painted surfaces and produces a porcelain-like surface.
3. Fine sandpaper, such as No. 400, for smoothing the surface after the sealer is dry.
4. Large scissors for trimming prints and cutting paper to rough size.
5. Manicure scissors for cutting out picture details.
6. X-acto knife or craft knife which may be used instead of a manicure scissors.
7. Varnish, lacquer or water base acrylic. The latter is fast and easy to use. Lacquer is also fast but difficult to use. Do not use it on objects that will be handled a great deal. Clear gloss varnish is best even though it is slow drying.

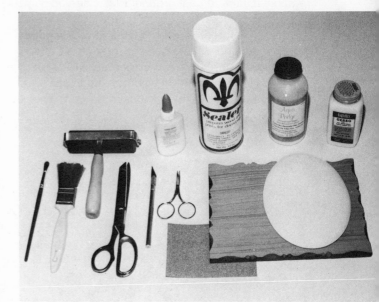

Fig. 11-2. For decoupage you will need: brushes, scissors, brayer, manicure scissors, X-acto knife, sandpaper, white glue, embedding material, gesso, acrylic spray. You will also need a plaque or some other surface to receive the print.

8. Brushes for applying sealers and finishes.
9. Roller or brayer. Either tool is used to press prints onto wood or other mounting surfaces, particularly those that are large and flat.

HOW TO DO DECOUPAGE

The same general steps may be applied to most decoupage projects produced on ceramics, wood, plaster of paris, stone or tin.

1. Assemble tools and materials and plan your project. It is best to work on several projects at once. While one is drying you can be working on another.
2. Prepare the surface. Wood should be sanded as shown in Fig. 11-3. Varnished or waxed furniture should be washed with mineral spirits. Rinse new tinware in a 1:1 solution of water and vinegar. When dry, coat the surface with rust-resistant paint. Do not sand or seal stone; scrub it with soap and water. Ceramic surfaces require no special preparation. Plaster of paris should be smooth sanded.
3. Seal the surface. Use acrylic spray or liquid sealer on wood if it is to have a natural finish, Fig. 11-4. Stain may be applied before the sealer if desired. Wood may be sealed with gesso before painting, Fig. 11-5. Stone may be varnished or lacquered to seal the surface. Sand the surface lightly with fine sandpaper after the sealer has dried. Remove all dust and grit with a cloth. Apply at least two coats of sealer.
4. Paint the surface, Fig. 11-6, if your project requires a painted background. Matte acrylic paint is a good choice for all decoupage projects that are to be painted. It dries fast and looks good. Apply a second coat when the first is dry. Sand lightly with No. 400 sandpaper between coats and wipe clean. Brush on a coat of liquid sealer to protect the surface when the last coat of paint has dried.

Fig. 11-4. Sealer may be sprayed or brushed on plaque.

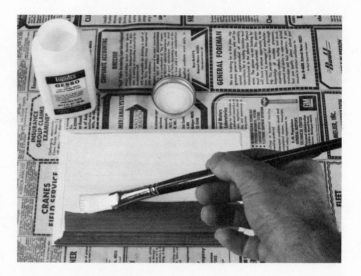

Fig. 11-5. Surface of this plaque is being sealed with gesso. This material produces a porcelain-like surface which is very easy to work on. Always seal the surface before painting.

Fig. 11-6. Painting plaque with matte acrylic paint. Apply two coats and sand lightly with No. 400 sandpaper between coats. Spray surface with liquid sealer after the second coat of paint has dried.

Fig. 11-3. Sand surface of plaque with fine sandpaper.

5. Prepare the prints. First, spray them with several coats of acrylic sealer as shown in Fig. 11-7. This prevents colors from running and makes the paper easier to cut.

   Prints should be made as thin as possible before they are applied to the surface. If a postcard, photograph or other heavy paper is used, it must be thinned. Seal the front with spray. When this is dry, turn the print over and coat the back with white glue. Allow to dry, then peel up a corner on the back side. Place a pencil across it and roll the peeling layer around the pencil. Roll the pencil until the entire layer of paper has been removed. Lightly sand away high spots. The paper should be thin enough now.

   The backing can also be removed after sealing by soaking the print in vinegar and water. This technique requires some practice.

6. Cut out the print, Fig. 11-8. Remove the inside areas first so that you will have something to hold onto while cutting the last part. A craft or X-acto knife works well, Fig. 11-9. Manicure scissors are preferred for cutting irregular edges. Be neat with your cutting and remove all white edges.

7. Apply white glue to the back of the print, Fig. 11-10. Use your finger or a brush to spread the glue.

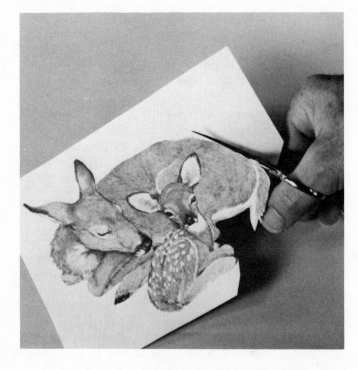

Fig. 11-8. Cut out print with manicure scissors. This print has no inside areas to be removed.

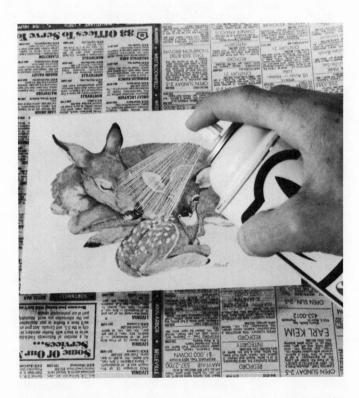

Fig. 11-7. Spraying print with several coats of clear acrylic sealer prevents colors from running. Paper is also made easier to cut.

Fig. 11-9. Using an X-acto knife to cut out an inside area of print. Inside areas are usually cut out first when print is easier to hold.

8. Using your fingers or a pair of tweezers, position the print on the surface to be decorated, Fig. 11-11. Remove air bubbles by rubbing the surface of the print. Work from the center out to the edges, Fig. 11-12. Use a brayer if one is available. Press down (burnish) the edges of the print so a smooth surface is formed. Wipe off excess glue with a damp cloth. Allow the glue to dry.

9. Embed the print, Fig. 11-13. This is a very important operation and it will determine the success or failure of the project. Choose one of the three types of finish: water base (acrylic), lacquer or varnish. Read the directions on the can and apply a number of coats.

   Several coats of the water base may be applied in a single day. Apply only two or three coats of lacquer in a day. Put on only one coat of varnish per day. Steel wool (4/0) or very fine wet or dry sandpaper may be used to remove imperfections between coats. Use as many coats as necessary to build up a glass-like surface. The back side of a wood project ought to be sealed so that it will not absorb moisture and warp.

10. Wax the surface with a fine furniture paste wax, Fig. 11-14. Spray-on wax is not recommended for decoupage projects.

11. Complete final operations such as framing or mounting.

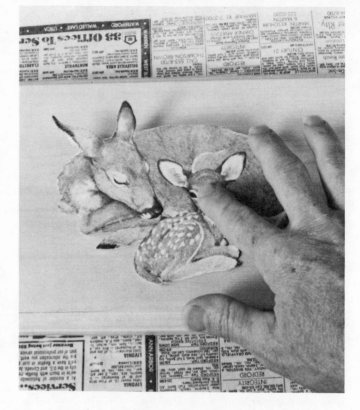

Fig. 11-11. Place print in proper location on plaque and smooth high spots with finger.

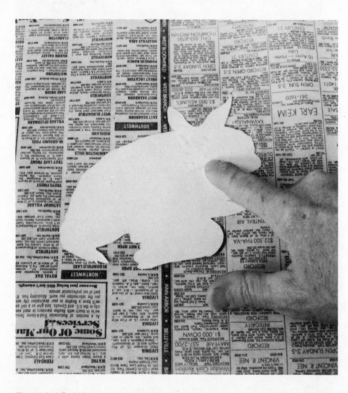

Fig. 11-10. White glue is applied to back of print which is ready to be attached to plaque.

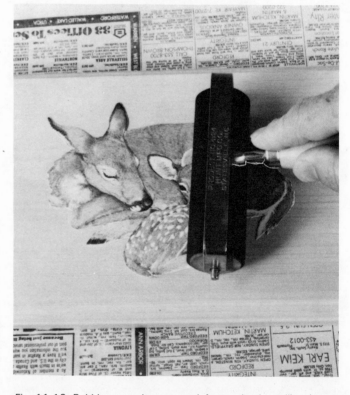

Fig. 11-12. Bubbles may be removed from print by rolling brayer across surface.

Fig. 11-13. Water base acrylic embedding liquid is being used to cover the print and plaque surface. Several coats must be applied to produce the desired results. Steel wool or very fine wet or dry sandpaper may be used to remove imperfections between coats.

Fig. 11-14. Wax plaque with good furniture paste wax. Use soft cloth to polish surface.

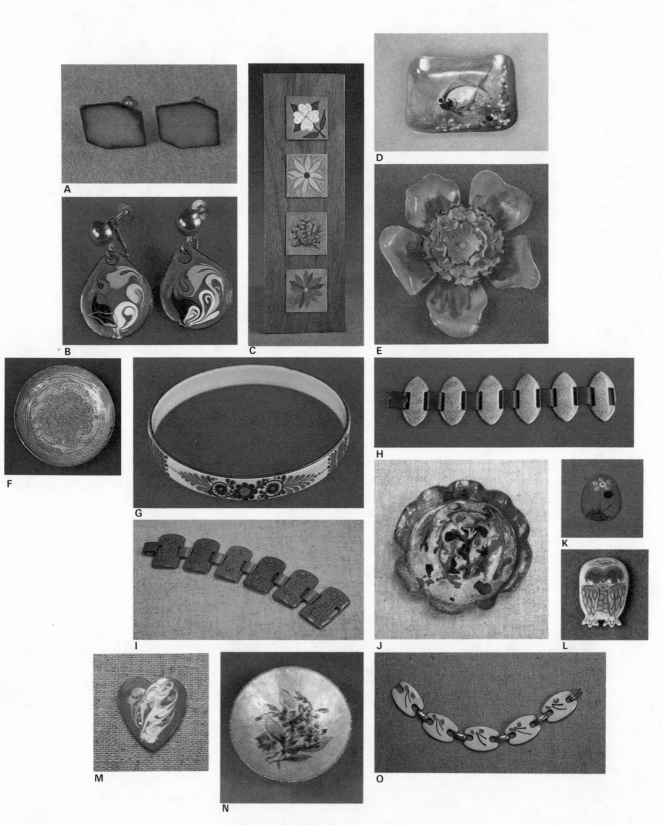

Metal enameling projects. A— Earrings in red with blackened edges. B—Pendant earrings in swirled enamel colors. (Marge Baird)   C—Wall plaque of copper enameled squares mounted on wood. D—Fish design on copper tray. E—Decorative pin is assembled from separate pieces. F—Green enameled tray. G—Enameled bracelet. H—Bracelet with soft pepper finish. I—Copper wire design for bracelet. J—Scalloped tray with swirled design. K—Enameled flower on stickpin. L—Enameled owl design on pin. M—Swirled design on heart shaped pin. N—Pin tray with flower motif on clear enamel base. O—Bracelet with small flower design.

Chapter 12
ENAMELING METAL

Metal enameling is a very old art form based upon a simple process. Specially prepared powdered glass is fused to metal at high temperatures. Since the process can be adapted to so many decorative techniques, the excitment of enameling comes from your own creative expression and the speed with which beautiful craft projects can be made. Enameling of small dishes, fishing lures, wall plaques and inlays make very interesting projects. However, there is no end to the variety of practical jewelry projects you can develop with a little imagination. See Fig. 12-1.

MATERIALS

Enamel is made from finely powdered glass. Metal oxides and chemicals are added for color and elasticity. They are available in:
1. Transparents, through which you can see the metal base.
2. Opaques, which form solid colors and do not permit the passage of light.

Obtain a selection of materials as shown in Fig. 12-2.

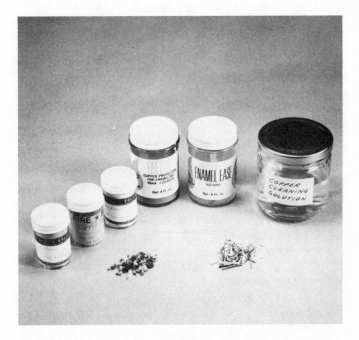

Fig. 12-2. Main materials used in enameling are powdered enamel colors, copper protector, enamel ease (flux) copper cleaning solution, glass chunks and threads.

A   B   C   D

Fig. 12-1. Finished examples of enameling techniques. A—Swirling. B—Glass wire or lumps. C—Stenciling. D—Sgraffito.

Other materials may be needed for special designs.

A number of different metals can be used for enameling; however, copper works extremely well. You can cut and shape your own designs or purchase precut shapes, Fig. 12-3. Jewelry findings are purchased.

EQUIPMENT

Equipment needed for enameling metal includes a good kiln, Fig. 12-4. Fig. 12-5 shows other tools you should have.

You may also want a pair of gloves to protect your hands from the heat of the kiln. If you plan to make some of your own copper pieces, you will also need basic tools for cutting and shaping metal. In that case, include a pair of tin snips, jeweler's saw, an assortment of files, a mallet and a sandbag. Both flat and curved copper pieces for enameling can be made with these tools.

COPPER ENAMELING

These steps are basic to the enameling technique. They will get you started on most projects:

1. Select or cut out the desired shape from a blank of copper. File the metal edges smooth, Fig. 12-6.
2. Clean the copper thoroughly. Enamel will fuse only to a copper surface free of oxides, grease and finger prints. First, clean the surface with steel wool. Then dip the copper piece into a cleaning solution, Fig. 12-7, and rinse in clear water. Use tweezers to hold the piece. Do not touch the surface with your fingers.

   The acid solution, called pickling, is prepared from one part nitric acid and six parts water. This is similar to a commercial copper cleaning solution. NEVER pour water into acid. It may spatter and cause serious burns.

   Copper can also be cleaned by scrubbing it with emery cloth or scouring powder, rinsing in water and drying with a cloth. If the metal is clean enough for enameling, water will cover the surface in a thin film.

3. Brush an even coat of copper protector on the back of the piece to be enameled, Fig. 12-8. Allow to dry thoroughly. This keeps the copper from turning black during firing. The protector will form a scale on the back which flakes off after the piece has cooled.
4. With a brush, apply a coat of enamel ease to the top, Fig. 12-9. Enamel ease acts as a flux causing the enamel to stick to the surface in an even coating.
5. Place the copper on a clean sheet of paper. Sift the desired color of opaque or transparent enamel

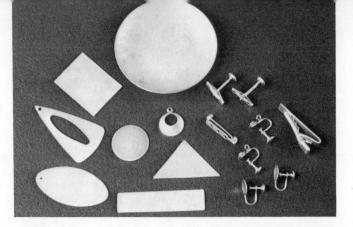

Fig. 12-3. Assortment of copper shapes and jewelry findings are needed for enameling.

Fig. 12-4. Electric copper enameling kiln must produce temperature of 1500 °F (815 °C).

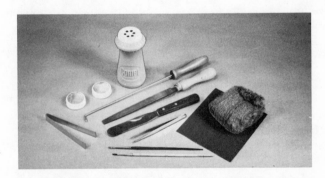

Fig. 12-5. Major tools required for copper enameling work: trivet, tweezers, small paintbrushes, sifters (if enamel jars do not have sifter caps), emery cloth, metal cleaner, steel wool, swirling tools, a flat file, and a spatula.

Fig. 12-6. File copper edges smooth before enameling.

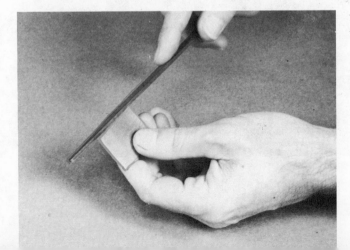

Fig. 12-7. Dip copper into cleaning solution with tweezers.

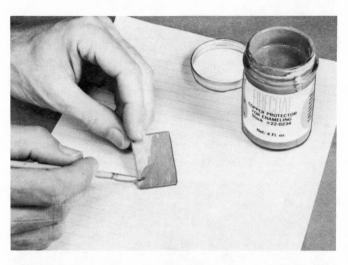

Fig. 12-8. Brush copper protector on underside of copper blank.

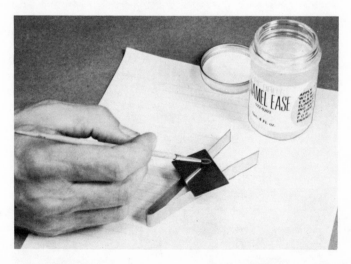

Fig. 12-9. Apply enamel ease to top surface with small brush.

Fig. 12-10. Sift enamel onto wet surface of copper.

Fig. 12-11. Lift copper piece off trivet with spatula.

Fig. 12-12. Cover has been removed and piece to be fired is being placed in the kiln.

over the surface as in Fig. 12-10. Apply the powdered enamel evenly. Cover the whole surface so that no metal shows through.

6. Check the kiln. If it has reached the firing temperature, about 1,500 °F (815 °C), it is hot enough to fuse the powdered glass to the metal surface. Slide a spatula under the copper piece, Fig. 12-11, and carefully place it in the kiln as shown in Fig. 12-12.

7. Collect the enamel spilled by creasing the edge of the paper to form a trough. Pour the enamel back into the container as shown in Fig. 12-13.

8. Carefully watch the firing process. As the enamel begins to melt, the powdered surface will craze, (develop small cracks) become ripply, and then even out to a smooth glossy surface. At this point, remove the piece from the kiln and place it on material, such as asbestos, that will not burn. Allow it to cool. The resulting solid color can be left as is or will serve as a base coat for additional decoration. If the enameling is not thick enough, apply a second coat using the same procedure.

9. When the enameled piece has cooled, file the edges to remove the black scale that forms on the copper during firing. Any fire scale that sticks on the back of the copper piece should also be removed by using abrasive paper and steel wool, Fig. 12-14.

10. Attach findings for jewelry, such as tie clasps, pins, Fig. 12-15, and cuff links, with epoxy cement or soft solder. Brush a coat of clear lacquer on all polished copper surfaces to keep them from tarnishing.

DECORATIVE TECHNIQUES

A number of decorating methods may be used for enameled projects after the base coat has been applied and fired. The most popular decorative techniques are swirling, glass wire or lumps, stenciling, sgraffito and cloisonne. These may be used alone or in combination with each other. A description of each of these decorating techniques follows:

1. SWIRLING. First apply enamel ease. Then dust the base coat with an enamel of another color and place it in the kiln. Lumps of enamel may be used in place of solid color. When the entire surface has melted, use a swirling tool to swirl the molten enamel into a variety of interesting designs, Fig. 12-16.

2. GLASS WIRE or LUMPS. Brush a layer of enamel ease onto the base coat. Locate the threads or lumps on the liquid which will hold them in position to produce your design. Use tweezers to place the threads or lumps making up your design pattern. Place in kiln and fire until they have fused into the base coat, Fig. 12-17.

3. STENCILING. Mask off portions of the base coat and apply contrasting enamel colors to the exposed sections, Fig. 12-18. Fire the piece to fuse the new enamel to the surface. Stencils are generally made by cutting the design out of a stiff material such as a file card.

4. SGRAFFITO. Generally referred to as a drawing process, this technique involves dusting a second

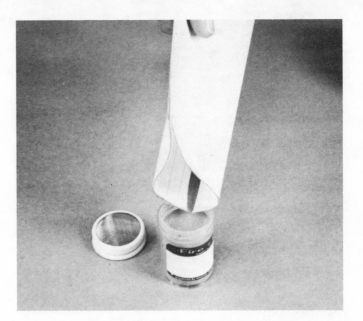

Fig. 12-13. Pour spilled enamel back into container.

Fig. 12-14. Remove fire scale with steel wool.

Fig. 12-15. Solder pin clasp to copper back.

color of enamel over the base coat. Then, using any blunt or sharp tool (even a pencil), scratch the design through the dusted coat, Fig. 12-19. When the design is complete, return the piece to the kiln for final fusing.

5. CLOISONNE. This technique is used to enclose separate design areas or shapes for different colors. Form the design by bending copper wire, cutting and fitting as necessary. Use tweezers to place each wire onto the enameled base. Place in the kiln and fire until the wires fuse into the enamel base. Remove and allow to cool. Fill in the compartments formed by the wire with the different colors of enamel, Fig. 12-20. Return the piece to the kiln for final fusing.

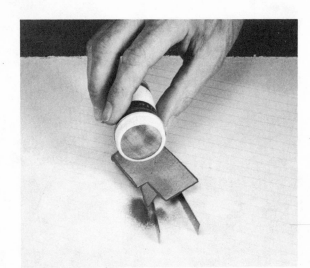

Fig. 12-18. Sift enamel over stencil onto copper.

Fig. 12-16. Swirl design is made on enameled piece with pointed tool. Use care. Tool tip is hot.

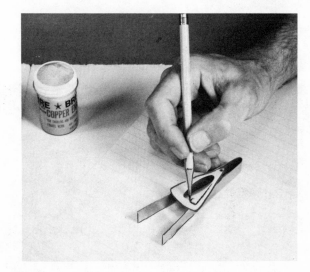

Fig. 12-19. Scratch design through dusted coat of enamel.

Fig. 12-17. Design is produced by fusing lumps into enameled piece.

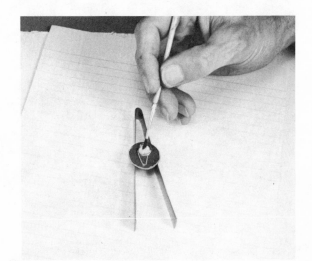

Fig. 12-20. With small paintbrush, fill compartment with enamel level to top of copper wire.

Flowercraft project ideas. A—Burlap flower mounted on decorative plaque. B—Copper foil flowers and butterflies. C—Various natural textures mounted and arranged in an attractive display. D—Feathers and dried flowers arranged in a beautiful bouquet. E—Dried bamboo arrangement in handcrafted pot. F—Burlap and film dip bouquet. G—Large film dip flower. H—Large dried flower arrangement in a dish. I—Fabric flowers with dried flower filler. (Sherry Minton)   J—Bouquet of fabric flowers attached to a single stem. K—Fabric flower with pipe cleaner edges. L—Fabric flowers with dried plants as filler. (Jill Minton)   M—Large feather flower with foam ball center. N—Petite bouquet of dried wild flowers.

96

Chapter 13
FLOWERCRAFT

Flowers, endless in their variety of shapes, colors and textures, represent the best that nature has to offer. Think of the fun and excitement of preserving your favorite blossoms or crafting your own flowers for lasting enjoyment. See Fig. 13-1.

This chapter will show you how to dry natural flowers and make your own from cloth, foil, plastic film and feathers. The possibilities are really unlimited, because beautiful flowers can be made from almost any material. After trying some of these suggested procedures you will more than likely develop many more of your own. So, have fun with this exciting craft!

DRIED FLOWERS

The art of drying flowers reaches back hundreds of years and is more popular today than ever. Few tools and materials are needed and anyone can do it.

TOOLS AND MATERIALS

Tools and materials for drying flowers are shown in Fig. 13-2. The side-cutting pliers will be needed for cutting and bending the florists' wire. Garden clippers are used to trim flower stems. The drying container, 1 or 2 qt. size, should be wide and not too deep. A cover is needed if silica gel is to be used.

Florists' tape (green) may be used to attach the flower stems to the wire. Florists' wire, about 24-gage in 6 in. (152 mm) lengths, is needed to form new flower stems.

Clean, dry masons' sand, beach sand or aquarium sand may be used for sand drying flowers. It should be fine grained and free of foreign material. If beach sand is used, wash it to remove salt. Then sift and oven-dry it. You will need about 3 qts. or 2.5 L for a small batch of flowers.

Fig. 13-1. This beautiful bouquet of freshly cut peonies will last only a few days before the petals begin to fall. Craft flowers, also beautiful, will last an indefinite period—incentive enough to try some of the procedures presented in this chapter!

Fig. 13-2. Tools and materials for drying flowers. Beginning at the lower right and moving clockwise: clippers, side-cutting pliers, small dowel rod, florists' wire, florists' tape, drying container, flowers and container of sand or silica gel.

Silica gel, sold in many garden shops, looks like sand but is lighter weight and highly absorbent. Keep it in a closed container when not in use. Otherwise, moisture from the air will reduce its drying effectiveness. The small diameter dowel will be used to support flower petals when covering them with sand or silica gel.

Probably the most important material is the flowers. The condition of the petals is important. They should be fresh and crisp and their petal tissues filled with water. Flowers purchased from a florist may be freshened by cutting off 1 or 2 in. (25 or 51 mm) from the stems and standing them in water for a few hours. Keep garden flowers fresh by placing them in a bucket of water immediately after cutting, Fig. 13-3. Select only choice specimens for drying.

DRYING FLOWERS IN SAND OR SILICA GEL

Most flowers can be dried in one to three weeks in sand and in less than half that time in silica gel. The thickness of the flower and amount of water it contains will affect the drying time. Usually, only the flower head is dried. Leaves and most of the stem are removed, Fig. 13-4, and replaced with wire, Fig. 13-5. Filler material such as air-dried branches, grain stalks, seed pods and drift wood may be used to fill spaces in an arrangement. See Fig. 13-6.

Drying Positions

Flowers can be dried in three basic positions:
1. Face up.
2. Face down.
3. Diagonal.

Fig. 13-4. Leaves and most of the stem of this trillium are removed before drying.

Fig. 13-5. Florists' wire is inserted in remaining short stem.

Fig. 13-3. These garden flowers were cut and immediately placed in a cup of water to keep them fresh.

Fig. 13-6. These materials are often used to fill spaces in an arrangement of dried flowers.

Large-petal flowers, such as roses or dahlias, are generally dried face up, Fig. 13-7. Stems on these flowers must be cut down to 1 in. long or too much sand will be required for drying.

Longer stems may be retained on flowers dried face down, Fig. 13-8. This position is ideal for small flowers such as single daisies, zinnias and any flower whose petals are on a flat plane.

A diagonal position, Fig. 13-9, works well for drying multipetaled smaller flowers such as marigolds, cornflowers, small roses and wild flowers. Stems may be cut 3 to 5 in. (76 to 127 mm) long when drying face down or diagonally.

Steps for Drying

For drying flowers in sand or silica gel:

1. Pour 1 or 2 in. (25 to 51 mm) of sand or gel into the drying container to support the flowers. See Fig. 13-10.

2. Cut off the stems about 1 in. below the blossoms for flowers being dried face up. A 2 or 3 in. (51 to 76 mm) length of stem may be saved from each flower for reattachment later. Flowers to be dried face down may have stems 3 to 5 in. long. Insert a 6 in. (152 mm) length of florists' wire up the stem and into the base of the flower, Fig. 13-11. Bend the wire so that it will stick up above the drying medium when the flower is drying face up. Flowers dried face down may have straight wires.

Fig. 13-8. Flower is placed in face down position for drying.

Fig. 13-9. Wild flower placed in diagonal position. This flower has a stem about 5 in. (127 mm) long.

Fig. 13-7. Large flower is placed in face up position. It has a short stem and wire is bent upward.

Fig. 13-10. Sand or silica gel in drying container is ready for flower to be dried face up.

3. When drying face up, place the flower on the sand or gel so that the bottom petals are supported, Fig. 13-12. Make an indentation in the drying medium about the same size and shape of the flower to be dried face down. All surfaces should contact the medium. A small ridge of sand or silica gel is formed behind the blossom with the wire projecting upward.

4. Very gently sift the sand or gel around and over the flower. Try to distribute the drying granules evenly over all parts of the flower so the petal shapes and positions are not distorted. Use the wooden dowel to support petals during this operation, Fig. 13-13. Cover the flower with about 1/2 in. sand or gel, Figs. 13-14 and 13-15.

5. If silica gel is used, cover the container so that it is airtight. Sand does not need to be covered. Record contents and date on the container for future reference, Fig. 13-16.

6. Store the flowers for drying. The length of time required is given in the chart, Fig. 13-17.

7. When the flowers are dry, carefully remove them from the sand or gel. Tilt the container so the medium pours out, Fig. 13-18. Grasp the wires as the flowers become visible and gently pull them free. Remove all grains of drying medium clinging to the petals.

8. Straighten the stem wires and add the stem sections you saved, Fig. 13-19.

9. Cover wire and stem with green florists' tape, Fig. 13-20. If petals fall off during these operations, reattach using water-diluted white glue.

Fig. 13-12. Place flower on sand so that bottom petals are supported. Wire must protrude above sand.

Fig. 13-13. Wooden dowel supports flower petals while sand or gel is added gently over flower

Fig. 13-11. Florists' wire is inserted into flower stem. Push wire into stem until it passes through hard part of the flower base. Wire should not be visible on petal side.

Fig. 13-14. Flower is almost covered with silica gel or sand.

Fig. 13-15. Flower is completely covered. Container must then be sealed if silica gel is used.

Fig. 13-16. Container is filled with flowers and silica gel. Masking tape has been placed around lid to insure tight seal. Date has been recorded on cover.

Fig. 13-18. Pour off some of drying medium before removing dried flower. Sand which clings to petals may be removed with a fine artists' brush.

Fig. 13-19. Add stem section which was saved. Slide stem up wire to provide support. Frequently, wire stem is simply wrapped with florists' tape.

FLOWERS	SAND	SILICA GEL
Anemone	3 weeks	3-4 days
Carnation	2-3 weeks	3 days
Clematis	(gel preferred)	12-18 hrs.
Daffodil	2-3 weeks	3-4 days
Delphinium	2-3 weeks	2-4 days
Dogwood	2-3 weeks	(sand preferred)
Feverfew	2-3 weeks	(sand preferred)
Forget-me-not	2 weeks	2 days
Globe thistle	air dry upside down for several weeks	
Hyacinth	3-4 weeks	5-6 days
Hydrangea	2 weeks or air dry	
Iris	(gel preferred)	3-4 days
Larkspur	3 weeks	(sand preferred)
Lilac	2-3 weeks	2-3 days
Lily	(gel preferred)	4-5 days
Lily of the valley	2-3 weeks	2-3 days
Magnolia	(gel preferred)	4-5 days
Marigold	3 weeks	3-4 days
Pansy	(gel preferred)	12-18 hours
Peony	3-4 weeks	5-6 days
Poinsettia	3 weeks	4-5 days
Rhododendron	(gel preferred)	4-5 days
Salvia	air dry upside down for several weeks	
Tulip	(gel preferred)	4-5 days

Note: Keep flowers being dried in sand in a warm, dry place with less than 60 percent humidity.

Fig. 13-17. Table suggests drying times for different flowers.

Fig. 13-20. Wrapping the flower stem with florists' tape. Tape must be stretched to make it stick.

10. Dried flowers may be stored for future use by inserting their stems into blocks of floral foam, Fig. 13-21. Place the foam base in a cardboard box. Put the box in a plastic bag and seal it to keep out dust, light and moisture.
11. Display your real dried flowers.

Some foliage may be preserved successfully with glycerin purchased at a drugstore. Mix one part glycerin to three parts water. Put the stem end of the foliage into a jar filled with this solution. Allow from 3 or 4 days to 3 weeks, depending on the size of the branch. When the upper leaves darken, remove the branches from the jar and hang upside down in a dark, dry place. Some types of foliage which can be preserved using glycerin include: broadleaf evergreens, mountain laurel, Juliana barberry, flowering crab, forsythia, magnolia, needled evergreens (yews), beech, apple, blueberry.

Fig. 13-21. Arrange dried flowers so they will not become deformed during storage. This arrangement works best. Store in dry place.

FOIL FLOWERS

Fashion daisies, mums and other flowers from aluminum, copper and brass foil. These materials may be transformed into dazzling floral arrangements with a few tools and a little creativity.

TOOLS AND MATERIALS

The basic tools required for this craft are tin snips, roundnose pliers, side-cutting pliers, epoxy cement and a pencil or scribe, Fig. 13-22. The snips are needed to cut the petals and leaves to shape. Roundnose pliers are used to shape flower parts. Side-cutting pliers are needed to cut wire to lengths and hold pieces of metal. A pencil or scribe will be needed to outline petals and leaves on the foil.

Flower pieces may be fastened together with epoxy cement or solder. Copper and brass may be either cemented or soldered very easily, but aluminum should be cemented only.

Metal foils may be purchased in hobby or craft shops. Stems may be made from brass, aluminum and copper wire or rod ranging in size from 1/32 to 1/8 in. (0.8 to 3 mm) diameter. Larger flowers will require larger diameter stems. Fig. 13-23 shows a selection of foil and rods.

MAKING FOIL FLOWERS

To make your first foil flower:
1. Draw a pattern for each flower part on a piece of heavy paper or cardboard. Fig. 13-24 shows some sample pattern designs for flowers.
2. Select one of the foils (copper, brass or aluminum) and place the patterns on it for tracing. Trace

Fig. 13-22. Useful tools for making foil flowers.

Fig. 13-23. Foils in thicknesses of .001 and .0005 in. (0.025 and 0.012 mm) are used for flower petals. Rods vary in diameter from about 1/32 to 1/8 in. (0.79 to 3 mm).

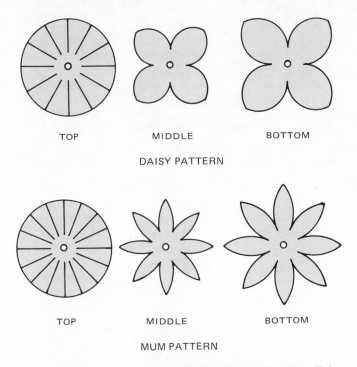

TOP   MIDDLE   BOTTOM

DAISY PATTERN

TOP   MIDDLE   BOTTOM

MUM PATTERN

Fig. 13-24. These patterns form a daisy and mum. The size will depend on how large a flower is desired.

Fig. 13-25. Each flower part has been traced on foil and pieces are ready to be cut out.

around each part, Fig. 13-25.

3. Cut out each part with the tin snips, Fig. 13-26. Be sure to follow the lines closely and make smooth cuts.

4. Cut a stem from wire or rod using the same type of metal that you used for the flower parts, Fig. 13-27. The stem length should be in proportion to the flower size. For example, a 3 in. diameter flower should have a stem about 10 in. long.

5. Shape the flower parts and leaves to look as natural as possible, Fig. 13-28. The roundnose pliers will be useful for this operation.

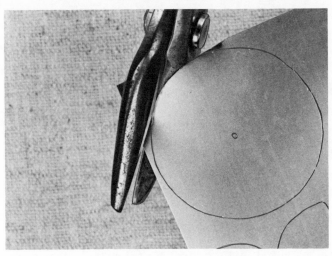

Fig. 13-26. Cutting out each flower part with the snips. Be careful not to cut your finger on sharp foil.

Fig. 13-27. Cutting flower stem to length with side-cutting pliers. Do not use snips for cutting wire.

Fig. 13-28. Shape flower petals with roundnose pliers. Try to make the petals look as natural as possible.

6. Cement or solder the stem to the flower petals, Fig. 13-29. Several layers of petals may be used to form a flower. If more than one layer of petals is used, punch or drill a hole in the center for easier fastening. Attach the top layer first, then the second and so on until all petals are secured to the stem, Fig. 13-30.

7. Cement or solder the leaves to the stem as shown in Fig. 13-31.

8. Apply a clear acrylic spray to the flower, stem and leaves to protect it. When it is dry, display your work. Fig. 13-32 shows two completed foil flowers. A single flower may be mounted on a stone, wood or metal base to achieve a pleasing effect. Groups of flowers may be placed in a container to form a bouquet. A piece of foam in the bottom of a vase will hold the flowers in place.

PLASTIC FILM FLOWERS

Making plastic film flowers is a perfect craft for an individual or a group. It is simple to do, produces beautiful flowers and is truly unique.

TOOLS AND MATERIALS

The only tools required are a pair of side-cutting pliers, scissors and a block of foam. The pliers will be needed to cut wire to length. Scissors are used to cut floral tape and your fingers will shape the wire into petals and leaves, Fig. 13-33.

Materials required for film flowers include a can of liquid plastic film (sold under the trade name, "Fantasy Film"), plain or green florists' wire (about 23 gage), green floral tape and artificial flower centers (stamens). The liquid plastic film is sold in hobby and craft shops in red, yellow, green and blue. The wire, purchased in

Fig. 13-30. Second layer of petals is being attached to stem. A hole has been punched in the second and third petals for easy assembly.

Fig. 13-31. Leaves have been fashioned from foil to match type of flower being constructed. Their stems are wound around the flower stem and then wrapped with foil or florists' tape.

Fig. 13-32. Completed foil flowers add beauty to home decor.

Fig. 13-33. Tools and materials for making plastic film flowers. Photo shows manicure scissors, side-cutting pliers, two sizes of florists' wire, artificial flower centers, florists' tape, a block of styrofoam and a can of plastic film dip liquid.

Fig. 13-29. Cement top layer of petals to stem. If epoxy cement is used, be sure to mix it according to directions on container. Brass, copper and tin flowers may be soldered, if desired.

lengths or rolls, must be easy to bend. Floral tape is used to cover the stem and bind the petals and leaves to the stem. Flower centers add realism to the flowers. Use the block of foam to hold your flower parts while they are drying.

MAKING FILM FLOWERS

To fashion your film flowers:

1. Decide which basic shape of petal and leaf you plan to make. Take a piece of wire and form it into that shape, Fig. 13-34.
2. Dip the wire (petal end down) into the liquid plastic film and remove it. Let excess liquid drip back into the container. The petal area should have a film covering as in Fig. 13-35. If not, dip it again.
3. Press the other end of the wire into a block of foam and allow the film to dry, Fig. 13-36.
4. Make as many petals and leaves as you will need for a complete flower, Fig. 13-37. Cover the can of liquid film as soon as you are finished to prevent evaporation.
5. When the flower parts are dry, select a suitable center for your flower, Fig. 13-38. Using floral tape, attach it to a wire stem.
6. Attach the petals as shown in Fig. 13-39. You should be able to wrap all the petals at once.

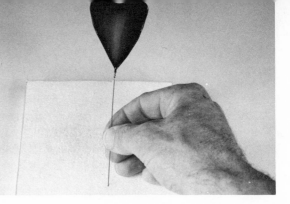

Fig. 13-36. Press petal stem wires into block of styrofoam to support them while drying.

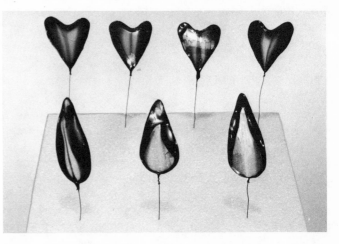

Fig. 13-37. Prepare enough petals and leaves to form a flower.

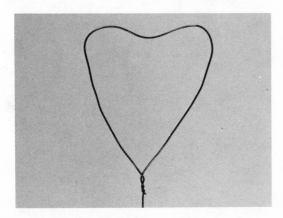

Fig. 13-34. Florists' wire is formed into petal shape.

Fig. 13-35. Petal has proper covering of plastic film.

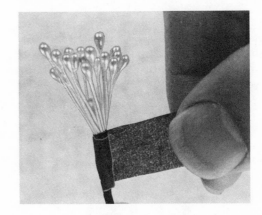

Fig. 13-38. Tape flower center to stem wire using floral tape.

Fig. 13-39. Attaching the flower petals with tape. Petal wires have been trimmed and wound around main stem wire.

7. Continue wrapping the stems together until you reach the location for the first leaf. Add it to the stem and continue wrapping, Fig. 13-40.
8. Add as many leaves as desired and finish wrapping the entire stem, Fig. 13-41.

Now that you know how simple this craft really is, you can make other exotic flower arrangements in vivid colors.

FEATHER FLOWERS

With creativity and imagination you can transform a few colorful feathers into a beautiful flower. Among the possibilities are sunflowers, tulips, hibiscus or other flowers of your own design.

TOOLS AND MATERIALS

You will need a pair of side-cutting pliers to cut wire to length; scissors to shape feathers and cut tape; florists' wire for stems and fastening the feathers together; green floral tape to cover stems; an assortment of colorful feathers and a package of artificial flower centers, Fig. 13-42. Feathers may be purchased from a sporting goods store which handles fly tying supplies or a craft and hobby shop. Kits are also available.

MAKING FEATHER FLOWERS

To make a beautiful feather flower:
1. Plan the type of flower you wish to make. Fix its shape in your mind and select feathers which have a shape similar to the natural flower petals.
2. Wire several artificial flower centers together with florists' wire, Fig. 13-43. This length of wire will also form the stem of the flower.

Fig. 13-41. Completed plastic film flower.

Fig. 13-42. Tools and materials needed to make feather flowers include: scissors, side-cutting pliers, feathers, florists' tape and wire and flower centers.

Fig. 13-40. Attach leaves the same way you attached petals.

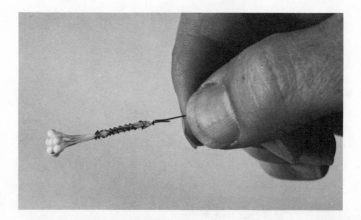

Fig. 13-43. Several flower centers are wired together on the end of a flower stem wire.

Flowercraft

3. Attach a wire to the quill end of each feather to be used in the flower, Fig. 13-44.

4. Select the feathers for the center petals of the flower and attach them to the stem wire around the artificial center, Fig. 13-45. Twist the feather wires around the stem wire and make them a part of it. Wrap these wires with a few turns of floral tape, Fig. 13-46.

5. Add the larger, outer feathers which will form the large flower petals, Fig. 13-47. Wrap all these wires with tape and continue on down the stem until the location of the first leaf is reached.

6. Make a leaf out of a feather or use an artificial leaf and tape it in place along the stem as shown in Fig. 13-48, Continue wrapping the stem until you reach the end.

Fig. 13-46. When flower center has been developed, wrap wire tightly with floral tape.

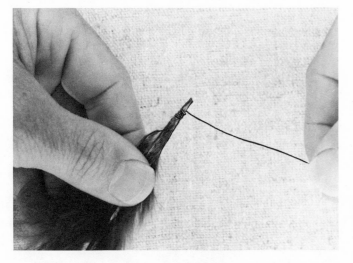

Fig. 13-44. Attach a wire securely to quill end of each feather. Wires will be used to attach feathers to main stem.

Fig. 13-47. Larger feathers are added to build flower shape. Wrap wire around stem.

Fig. 13-45. Place several feathers around flower center and wind wires around stem wire.

Fig. 13-48. Leaf made from a feather is attached in the same manner as the petals.

Crafts

Your feather flower is completed, Fig. 13-49. Make several more and display them as a bouquet.

Figs. 13-50 through 13-54 illustrate another way of making feather flowers. A styrofoam ball forms the center. The feather quills are pressed into the foam to form petals. Another ball is used for the leaves.

Fig. 13-52. Add progressively larger feathers until ball is covered.

Fig. 13-49. Completed feather flower has airy appearance.

Fig. 13-53. Top view of completed flower. Ball is completely hidden.

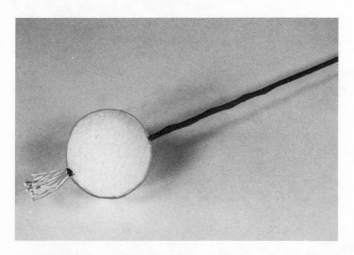

Fig. 13-50. Foam center may be used to form feather flower. Size of ball can be varied according to size of flower you wish. A 1 in. diameter ball will make a flower about 6 in. across.

Fig. 13-51. Press quills of several small feathers into top of ball.

Fig. 13-54. Add another ball to stem and attach long green lacy feathers to form leaves. Bottom foam ball still visible in this photo, is also hidden when flower is completed.

FABRIC FLOWERS

Scraps of cloth left over from a sewing project are ideal for fabric flowers. The flowers are highly decorative and may be made to match furnishings.

TOOLS AND MATERIALS

A pair of side-cutting or diagonal-cutting pliers will be needed to cut wire and pipe stems to length. Chenille pipe cleaners form the frame for each petal and leaf. Florists' wire (23 ga.) is used to attach petals and leaves to the stem wire (16 ga.). Green floral tape is wrapped around the stem. White glue will be needed to attach the fabric to the pipe-cleaner frame. Yarn, pipe cleaners or foam balls may be used to form the flower centers. Fig. 13-55 shows these tools and materials.

MAKING FABRIC FLOWERS

Follow these steps to complete your first fabric flower:

1. Make a cardboard pattern for each petal and leaf, Fig. 13-56. Cardboard works best because the pipe cleaner can be formed around the edge of the pattern.
2. Select a pipe cleaner, your choice of color, and form it around the pattern, Fig. 13-57. Twist the cleaner together two turns at the base of the pattern. Clip off excess leaving only enough to fasten

Fig. 13-56. Cardboard patterns are prepared for petals and leaves.

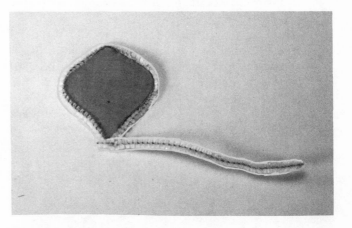

Fig. 13-57. Forming pipe cleaner around pattern. Twist ends together to hold shape.

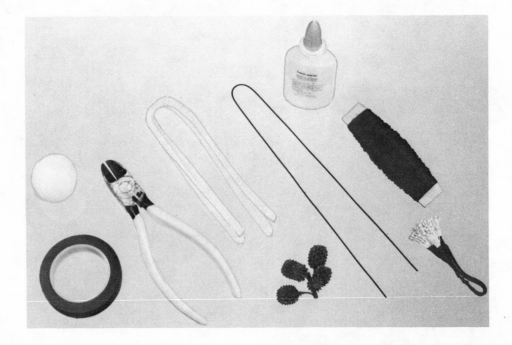

Fig. 13-55. Tools and materials for making fabric flowers, bottom to top, left to right: floral tape, foam ball, side-cutting pliers, pine cones, chenille pipe cleaners, florists' wire, flower centers, yarn and white glue.

the petal to the stem. See Fig. 13-58.

3. Cut a piece of cloth slightly larger than the pipe-cleaner petal frame. Apply a small amount of white glue to one side of the pipe cleaner and place it on the cloth, Fig. 13-59.

4. When the glue is dry, trim the petal, Fig. 13-60.

5. Attach a 23 ga. wire to each petal and leaf, Fig. 13-61, so that they may be fastened to the stem wire.

6. Select the type of center desired and attach it to a stem wire. Use a 16 ga. size wire. Foam centers may be covered with a 2 in. (51 mm) square of cloth and secured with wire on the under side, Fig. 13-62. Trim off the excess cloth.

7. Space the petals evenly around the stem wire and wrap the end of each petal wire around the stem wire. Clip off excess wire.

8. Wrap floral tape around the stem and the petal wires. Continue wrapping until you reach the location of the first leaf. Wire it to the stem and continue wrapping until you reach the location of the next leaf. Wire it to the stem and continue wrapping until finished, Fig. 13-63. Your completed flower should be similar to one shown in Fig. 13-64. For another variety of flower making, see Chapter 34, Shellcraft.

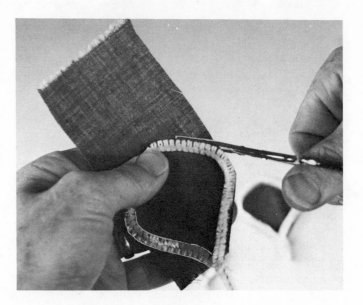

Fig. 13-60. Trim fabric petal to size after it has been glued to frame.

Fig. 13-61. A 23 ga. wire is attached to each petal so that it can be fastened to main stem wire.

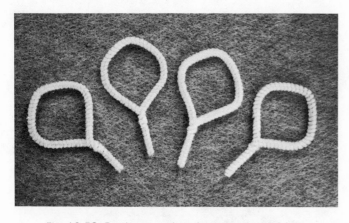

Fig. 13-58. Petals are ready to be covered with fabric.

Fig. 13-59. Fabric is glued to pipe cleaner petal.

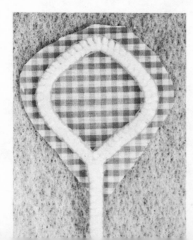

Fig. 13-62. Fabric-covered foam ball makes an excellent flower center. Fabric is fastened with wire.

Fig. 13-63. Wrap flower stem with florists' tape to cover wires.

Fig. 13-64. Completed fabric flower is your own unique creation.

Foam plastic project suggestions. A—Play-a-game foam coasters. B—Cloth covered Christmas tree ornaments. (Fran Nelson)   C—Foam eggs covered with embroidery thread. D—''Big Apple'' kitchen bulletin board. E—Foam desk set. F—Seasonal foam decoration. G—Painted foam sewing caddy. (Marge Baird)   H—Mrs. Santa in foam (Dee Barnhill)   I—Decorated foam snowman. (Dora Johns)

Chapter 14
FOAM FORMS

A fairly new material for useful craft projects is plastic (synthetic) foam. Plastic foams are generally produced by adding air or gas to a plastic resin. The result is a sponge-like material. They may be very flexible like a pillow or quite rigid like a picnic beverage cooler.

For foam craft projects, the rigid type, made from POLYSTYRENE, is used almost exclusively. The most common rigid foam is known as STYROFOAM, its trade name.

The properties of polystyrene foam make it an ideal material for creating both functional and decorative craft projects. Projects might include small serving trays, animal figures, wall hangings, seasonal decorations, kites, puppets, bird feeders, small beverage coolers, toy boats, airplanes, duck decoys and coasters. See. Fig. 14-1.

Fig. 14-1. A Styrofoam ice bucket is but one of the attractive and useful items that can be made with this plastic material.

MATERIALS

Polystyrene foam is available in many forms, Fig. 14-2, and may be purchased at most handicraft shops and art supply stores. It is less expensive to buy large, thick sheets of foam and create your own shapes. Foams come in different degrees of surface smoothness from coarse to very fine. However, some shapes, like a round ball or cone, are quite difficult to carve and might make a trip to a hobby shop worthwhile.

Some of the main advantages of styrene foam are its ease of cutting and shaping, light weight, rigidity, clean white color and good insulation properties. Some foam is available in grey and light blue or green. It also floats like cork, will not absorb water and resists rot or corrosion. Remember these advantages when planning and designing your foam projects.

Although other materials may be combined with foam to develop your project, the basic items are

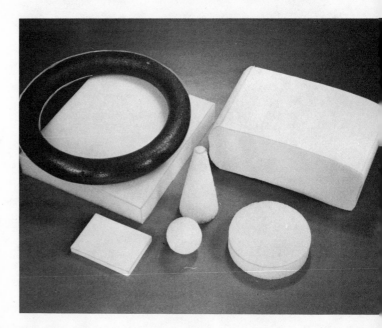

Fig. 14-2. Foam may be purchased in special shapes, sheets or parts of a foam billet.

shown in Fig. 14-3. As you develop skill in working with foam, you will, undoubtedly, want to include other materials. Do not hesitate, give them a try.

TOOLS

Fig. 14-4 indicates the tools necessary to shape or form styrene foam projects. A good steel ruler will serve both for measuring and as a guide for cutting straight lines. Many types of sharp knives and razor blades may be used for cutting and carving. A table model hot-wire cutter is very desirable when cutting thick foam, curves and angular shapes. A hand foam cutter and a wood-burning pencil make it easier to form holes and shape designs. That is all you need. Should you get highly involved in foam craft work, you will find that most power tools work well with foam. A drill press can be used to make holes or parts can be turned on a lathe. However, few projects would require such equipment.

CUTTING AND SHAPING FOAM

There is no end of things that can be made from foam. By using the following procedure you will be able to get the "feel" of each of the tools used in shaping and forming plastic foam.

1. Clamp a strip of wood to the hot-wire cutter table as a guide for making straight cuts. Slowly slide the foam along the guide. Be careful, too much pressure may bend the hot wire, Fig. 14-5.

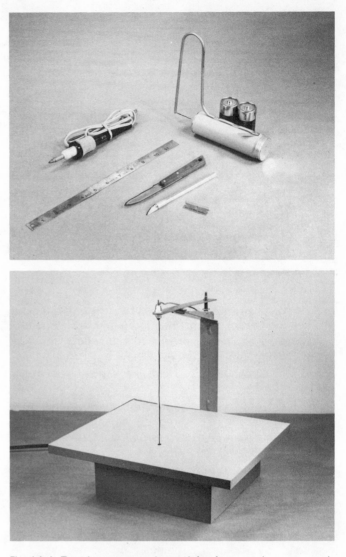

Fig. 14-4. Top. Important tools used for foam work are a wood-burning pencil, hand hot-wire foam cutter, steel rule, knives and a razor blade. Bottom. Electric table model hot-wire cutter. Cutting action is smooth and fast as it melts the foam.

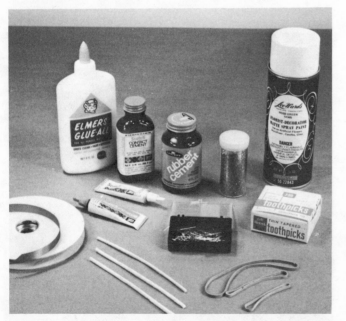

Fig. 14-3. Materials used with foam include white glue, contact cement, rubber cement, glitter, spray paint, ribbon, epoxy glue, pins, toothpicks, pipe cleaners and rubber bands.

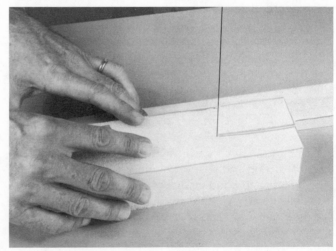

Fig. 14-5. Cutting straight line on hot-wire cutter with strip of wood as a guide. Feed the material slowly.

2. Irregular shapes are easily made on the cutter. Sketch the shape on the foam with a pencil as illustrated in Fig. 14-6.

3. To cut a circle out of a square sheet of foam, locate the center of the square and press a sharp, pointed nail down through it. Place three thicknesses of masking tape on the table surface to hold the nail point. Place the tape about half the diameter of the circle away from the hot wire. Example: to cut an 8 in. circle, place the point of the nail 4 in. from the wire. Press the nail point against the masking tape and rotate the foam as shown in Fig. 14-7. Fig. 14-8 shows the cut completed.

4. Tall cylinders can be made in a similar manner. Cut the head off a small nail and press the blunt end into the bottom of a block of polystyrene foam. Locate the nail (on several layers of masking tape) so the point is the correct distance from the hot wire. Rotate the block against the hot wire to cut the cylinder as shown in Fig. 14-9.

5. The table model hot-wire cutter does the best job. It cuts accurately and leaves a smooth surface due to the melting action of the hot wire on the plastic. However, sharp knives are quite satisfactory if used with care. Use a straightedge and short bladed knife for cutting thin foam sheet, Fig. 14-10. Many projects require irregular designs and deep cuts into the foam surface. Most of these can be made with a knife or razor blade. The technique is similar to carving in wood.

6. Holes are easily formed in foam by using a wood-burning pencil. Use the round tip and enlarge the

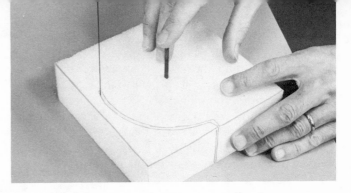

Fig. 14-7. Cutting circle using nail as pivot. Hold a finger on the nail as you rotate the foam with the free hand.

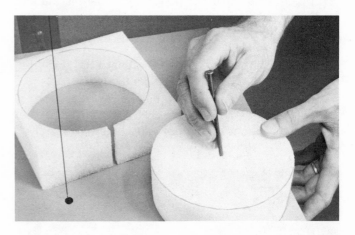

Fig. 14-8. Remove the nail from the center of the completed circle.

Fig. 14-9. Tall cylinder is cut using a nail point (hidden) as a guide.

Fig. 14-10. Cut thin foam sheet with straightedge and sharp knife.

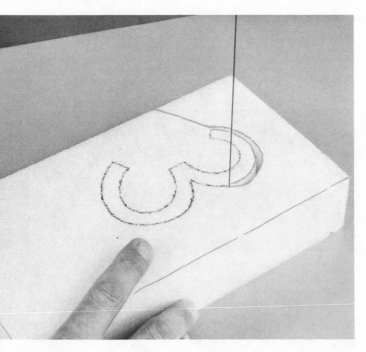

Fig. 14-6. Cutting irregular shapes. Carefully follow sketched lines to cut curves on the hot wire.

hole by rotating the tip as shown in Fig. 14-11. While the plastic is still soft, clean the metal tip with a heavy cloth and gloves.

7. A battery powered hot-wire cutter works extremely well for cutting sheet less than 1 in. thick. Most shapes are easily cut by following a pencil line or design traced from a pattern, Fig. 14-12.

MAKING A FOAM PROJECT

An ice bucket made of polystyrene foam is a good beginning project requiring a number of operations. Use a dense, fine-textured foam. Try the following procedure:

1. Lay out the pattern on thin cardboard and trace the design on 1/2 in. (13 mm) foam as in Fig. 14-13.
2. Use a knife and a straightedge to cut out the tapered sides and bottom, Fig. 14-14. Shape the curved sections on the hot-wire cutter, Fig. 14-15.

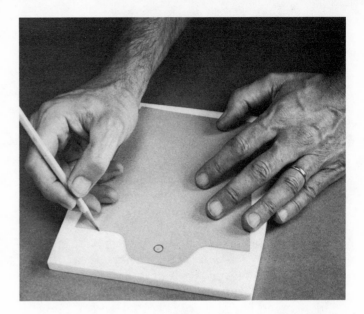

Fig. 14-13. Trace design on foam sheet with soft lead pencil.

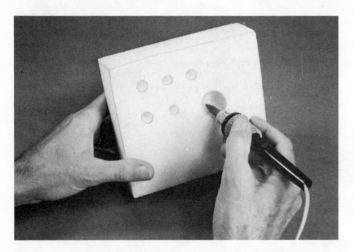

Fig. 14-11. Form (burn) holes with round tip of wood-burning pencil. Use circular motion to enlarge hole.

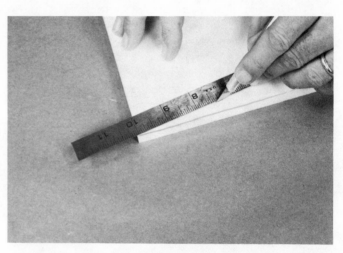

Fig. 14-14. Use knife and straightedge to cut sides and bottom.

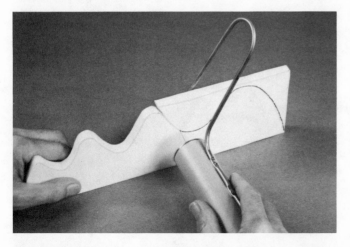

Fig. 14-12. Cutting curves in sheet foam with hand hot-wire cutter. Do not force the cutter. Allow the hot wire to melt the plastic.

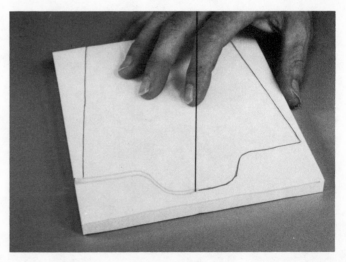

Fig. 14-15. Cut curved handle section with hot-wire cutter.

3. Make 1/4 in. (6 mm) dia. holes for the handle with the wood-burning pencil as shown in Fig. 14-16. With epoxy cement, attach 3/4 in. dia. metal washers over the holes for the handle.

4. Assemble the bucket using epoxy or contact cement. Glue two sides together at a time and hold in place with pins until dry, Fig. 14-17. Fit the bottom inside the walls and glue it in place. Be sure all joints are sealed with glue to prevent leakage.

5. The ice bucket may be decorated or left in its natural color. A good way to finish it is by painting. Use a thin enamel or latex base paint. Since the foamed surface is cellular (has small openings), a thick paint will clog the surface and dry unevenly. Brush on the finish with smooth, even strokes. Designs may be applied using another color of paint, decals, glitter or numerous decorating materials.

SUGGESTIONS

The following suggestions should be helpful when you plan craft projects using polystyrene foam.

1. When using adhesives or paints, try them on scrap pieces of foam to be sure they will not dissolve the surface before using them on your project.

2. Whenever possible, use a hot-wire cutter for final cutting. The heated wire melts the plastic surface as the cut is being made. This leaves a thin film over the cut face adding considerable surface strength. Make your cuts with a slow, even feeding action against the wire. Forcing the foam will bend the wire and produce an uneven cut.

3. Sanding the foam is of little value when preparing to finish surfaces. Faces or edges cut with a very sharp knife or hot-wire cutter will produce the best surfaces.

4. Most polystyrene foam used in craft work will burn. Be very careful when working foam around an open flame. Some fireproof foams are available at craft or hobby stores.

5. When cutting large pieces of foam to usable sizes, a handsaw or hacksaw works nicely.

6. Simple, decorative foam projects like party favors can be joined together with toothpicks, pins or even pipe cleaners.

7. Foam surfaces can easily be decorated or protected by covering them with fabrics, contact paper, printed vinyl film, wallpaper or even veneers.

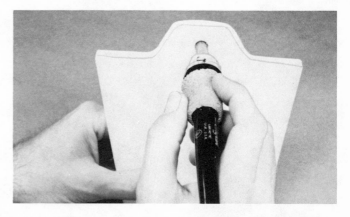

Fig. 14-16. Form hole for handle with wood-burning pencil. Be sure to keep pencil perpendicular to side of bucket.

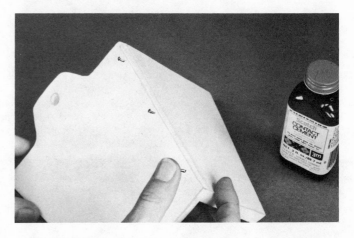

Fig. 14-17. Assembling sides of bucket using pins and glue.

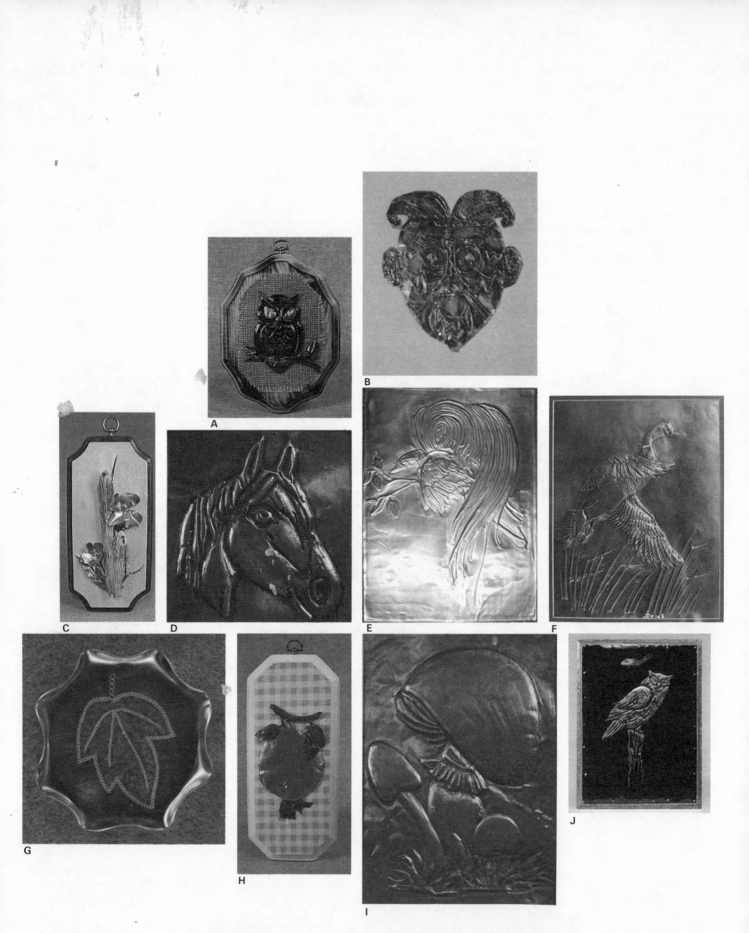

Foil project possibilities. A—Copper foil owl mounted on fabric and framed. B—Foil tooling decorated with glass stain. C—Combining foil tooled flowers with driftwood. D—Copper tooled horse's head with highlighting. E—Aluminum foil peacock. F—Duck in flight. G—Tooling and stippling on aluminum. H—Foil tooling on cast plaster backing. I—Stand of tooled mushrooms. J—Owl on black painted background.

Chapter 15
FOIL TOOLING

Many unique craft projects can be made using foil tooling. The process involves raising and, sometimes, lowering the surface of thin sheet metal with hand tools. Since the metal is quite soft, three-dimensional shapes are easily produced for projects such as crests, desk name plates, wall plaques, book ends, assorted jewelry and pictures. See Fig. 15-1. Many projects will need a frame to complete them. Refer therefore, to the chapter on framing.

As you can see from many of the projects illustrated, foil tooling is a proper craft for those well advanced in creative design. But, happily, it is equally proper for those just beginning to develop design skills.

MATERIALS

Metals generally used for foil tooling are copper, brass and aluminum. Copper, available in both sheets and rolls, is the first choice. It is easiest to tool and decorates nicely through different coloring techniques. See Fig. 15-2. The most commonly used foil is 36 gage—just slightly thinner than a standard file card. Most craft and hobby shops carry it.

Other materials you will need include fine steel wool, masking tape, a rubber pad or layers of felt, epoxy glue, clear finish, thin paper for making design patterns, some plaster of paris, art metal or modeling clay and liver of sulphur. Refer, again, to Fig. 15-2.

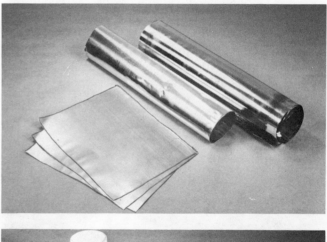

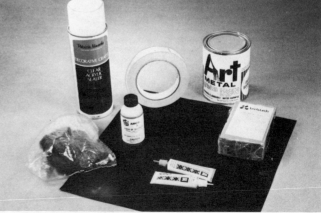

Fig. 15-2. Top. Use sheets and rolls of copper foil for tooling. Bottom. Some additional materials needed are clear acrylic spray, masking tape, art metal, modeling clay, steel wool, liver of sulphur, epoxy glue and a thick rubber pad.

Fig. 15-1. Irish setter worked in copper foil.

TOOLS

Several hand tools are required for the actual tooling process, Fig. 15-3. For most work, a round pointed tool is used to trace the pattern and outline the design. A modeling tool with a smooth spoon end is needed to raise the design. A smoothing tool works well to flatten the background. If these tools are not available, empty ball point pens, smooth ended dowel rods and flat wood sticks can be substituted. Other useful tools are pictured in Fig. 15-4. Special tools and materials for certain mountings or jewelry projects should be acquired as needed.

TOOLING A FOIL PROJECT

The following steps are basic for almost all foil tooling projects:

1. Select or make up your own design and draw it full size on a piece of paper as in Fig. 15-5. Typing paper works very well. Plastic patterns may be used for beginning projects since they require less skill.
2. With a pair of scissors, cut a piece of copper foil to size. (Allow extra material on all sides for mounting or trimming.) Center your design on the foil and fasten it with masking tape, Fig. 15-6.
3. Place the foil, design up, on a rubber pad or layer of felt. A heavy newspaper pad can also be used. Trace the design with the round pointed tool. Use just enough pressure so that trace lines can be

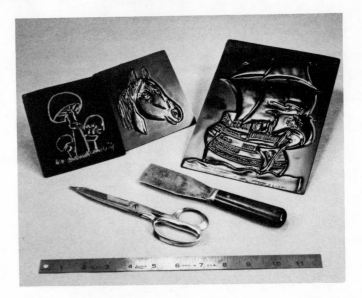

Fig. 15-4. Plastic patterns, putty knife, scissors and straightedge are other useful items for foil tooling.

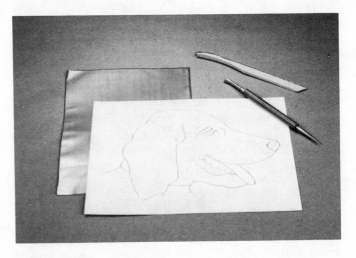

Fig. 15-5. Full size paper pattern of design is ready to be placed over copper foil.

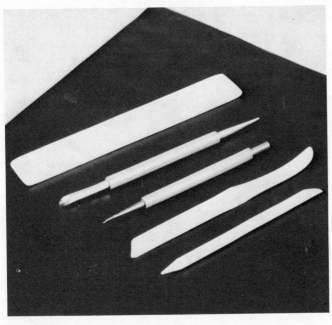

Fig. 15-3. Foil is tooled with (left to right): hardwood spatula, wide metal spoon, metal tracing tool, wood modeling tool and pointed wood tool.

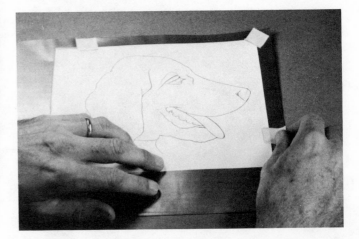

Fig. 15-6. Fastening design to foil. Masking tape holds it in place while you are tracing it.

clearly seen, Fig. 15-7. If a border is planned, trace those lines with the same tool and a straight-edge, Fig. 15-8.

4. Remove the paper from the foil and check all lines. They must be neat and clear. Go over lines that do not show vividly.

5. Turn the foil face down on the padded surface and use the tracing tool to draw another line just inside the traced design, Fig. 15-9. Make this line slightly heavier than the tracing line on the front.

6. With a spoon end modeling tool, gradually depress the foil inside the lines of the design. For larger areas, depress the design with a wide spoon as shown in Fig. 15-10. Try to use soft, sweeping strokes with the modeling tools to maintain a smooth, curved surface. Start with those surfaces that are to be raised the most.

7. Turn the foil over and inspect the raised surfaces. If they are not high enough, continue the raising process. Any detail lines should be depressed with the round pointed tool.

8. Place the foil face up on a hard, smooth surface, such as a piece of glass, marble or hard masonite. Use the hardwood spatula to flatten the metal

Fig. 15-7. Trace design with pointed tracing tool.

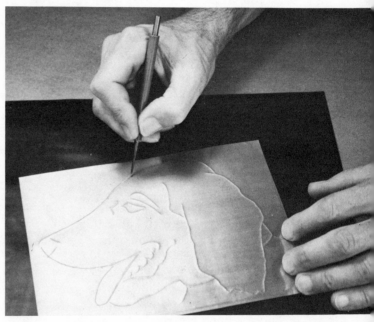

Fig. 15-9. Tool design on backside just inside the traced line.

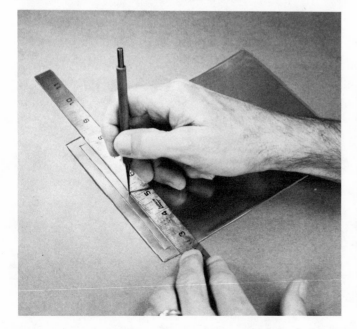

Fig. 15-8. Make border lines with straightedge and pointed tool.

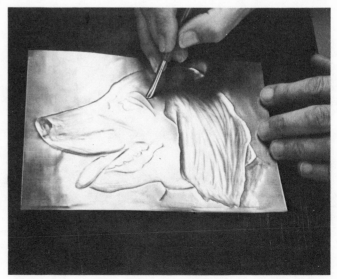

Fig. 15-10. Depress design on backside with wide spoon.

around the outside of the design, Fig. 15-11. Keep the tool flat on the foil and use light smooth strokes as you work along the border of the design. Continue this operation until the background is completely smooth and flat.

You may continue reversing from one side to the other, working the background down and the raised portions up, until you are satisfied with the design shape. You may want to make sharp indentations in some areas of the raised surface such as the dog's nose. Support the raised surface at that point with modeling clay and carefully depress these lines with a pointed tool. The background can be stippled (textured) by using the pointed tool as shown in Fig. 15-12.

9. When tooling is done, fill the remaining cavities on the back to prevent collapse of the design. Plaster of paris, modeling clay or art metal are all satisfactory, Fig. 15-13. Be sure the back is smooth and flat.

10. The face of the foil should be polished with fine steel wool until the surface is a bright copper color and all oxides are removed. If a shiny copper finish is desired, apply two coats of lacquer or plastic spray. This will keep the surface from oxidizing or turning a brownish black.

However, many copper foil projects are made even more attractive by purposely tarnishing the surface. Liver of sulphur, a tarnishing solution, is commercially available for this purpose.

Apply the solution to the copper with a soft cloth or cotton swab until the surface turns to any uniform degree of brown you like. Wash the coloring solution off with water and allow surface to dry. Avoid touching the surface with your hands.

Fig. 15-12. Stipple foil with pointed end of spoon stylus.

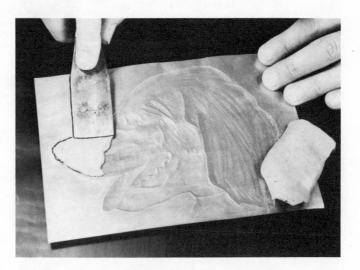

Fig. 15-13. Fill backside depressions with modeling clay.

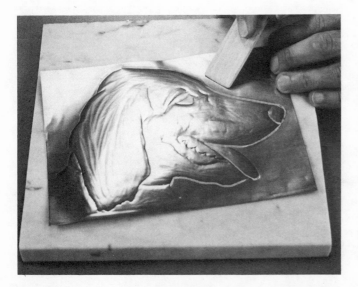

Fig. 15-11. Flatten surface around design with wood spatula.

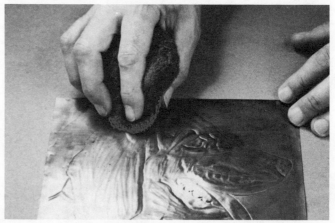

Fig. 15-14. Highlight areas of the design by rubbing with fine steel wool. Work very carefully.

Interesting colors can be obtained by lightly polishing with steel wool to highlight desired areas, Fig. 15-14. Apply a clear finish to protect the surface. The completed foil tooling is shown in Fig. 15-15.

11. Plastic patterns, available in many different designs, make tooling much easier. Simply place the copper foil over the hollow pattern and slowly depress the foil into the design shapes with a spoon modeling tool, Fig. 15-16. It may be necessary to use a pointed tool for fine lines. Complete the project as previously described.

12. Projects such as wall plaques or name plates can be mounted on wood backings with epoxy glue or small copper brads. They may also be attractively matted and framed. Refer to the chapter on framing. Many jewelry projects, made up of two or more foil pieces, can be fastened together by carefully soldering or using epoxy glue.

13. Painting areas of foil projects is another decorating technique. Opaque or transparent acrylic paints work well. Transparent paints allow the copper color to show through and will give many pleasing effects.

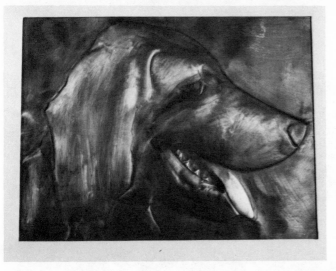

Fig. 15-15. Clear acrylic spray finish protects completed foil tooling.

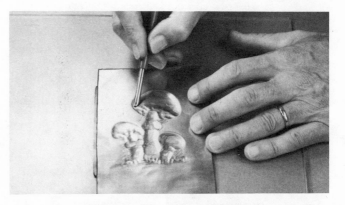

Fig. 15-16. Foil shape may be formed in plastic pattern with the wide spoon tool working from the backside.

Picture framing suggestions. A—Narrow frame with beveled mat for antique picture. B—Circular, one-piece frame used for mounting old family portrait. C—Wide fabric mat and narrow frame lend importance to small print. D—One-piece molded frame with fabric backing makes agreeable setting for medal. E—Dark background and dark, ornate frame complement this 19th century print. F—Contemporary frame of walnut molding enhances velvet backing for key display. (Herb Wilson) G—Background is rich velvet; mat is beveled and in subdued beige. Frame, being similarly subdued in coloring, does not vie with medal for attention. H—Fabric mat and frame trimmed in gold pick up tones of the painting. I—Light oval inside dark, beveled mat emphasizes the small illustration. Frame repeats colors found in the print. J—Oil painting in natural frame has neither mat nor glass covering. K—Dark frame and mat surround and suitably frame the simple detail of line drawing.

Chapter 16
FRAMING

The art of making frames for things you particularly enjoy can be a rewarding craft experience. The main purpose of picture frames is to enhance the beauty of paintings, photographs, and prints. Or they may be employed to attractively display maps, diplomas and a variety of memorabilia. The frame should not detract attention from the artwork it is meant to display. Yet, it should provide a pleasing surrounding for all aspects of the presentation. It is like the blue sky surrounding a puffy white cloud.

Careful attention must be given to frame width, shape, color and texture. Study the artwork before deciding on these features.

Another purpose of the frame is to protect. Dirt and dust, scratches, fading and wrinkles due to humidity can all be significantly reduced by good framing techniques.

Making your own picture frames may be more fun than you think. The possibilities for variety are many.

MATERIALS

Most picture frames can be made with materials and tools that are familiar and not at all difficult to use. Many are described here. Others needed for specialized work are discussed in the framing procedure.

The main material is the stock for the frame itself. Moldings for frames can be purchased in many shapes, Fig. 16-1. You can buy them either finished or unfinished.

Good woods for unfinished frames are poplar, oak and walnut. Poplar is easy to work with and takes well to stain, paint and other finishing methods. Oak is much harder but provides an attractive frame when stained. The beauty of walnut is generally enhanced by a clear finish.

OTHER MOLDINGS

Another source for moldings is your local lumber supplier. There you can obtain many molded shapes used as trim around cabinets and windows in the home. An assortment is shown in Fig. 16-2. A rabbet, the L

Fig. 16-2. Standard lumber yard moldings can be glued together to form interesting frame shapes. Note that a rabbet is formed to hold the picture in each molding.

Fig. 16-1. Stock picture frame moldings. Some are finished and some are unfinished.

shaped section cut from the edge of the moldings, has been prepared to hold the picture in place. Nearly all frames require a rabbet. If equipment is available, you can make your own molding as shown in Fig. 16-3. Other materials required are glass, white glue, mat board, nails, brown paper, masking tape, diamond points, wood filler and finishes, Fig. 16-4.

Fig. 16-4. Materials used for framing are sold in any hardware store.

TOOLS

Some of the basic tools used for framing are shown in Fig. 16-5. A hammer, handsaw, framing square and pliers may also be required. A miter box, Fig. 16-6, or a table saw are necessary for cutting mitered corners. A miter clamp, Fig. 16-7, holds the corners in position during gluing. Use of these tools is explained in the framing procedure.

MAKING A FRAME

Although the cross section of picture frames may vary considerably, construction of a frame follows a fairly standard procedure. Try the following:

1. Select the molding for the frame you plan to make. Determine the length you will need. Add together the following lengths:
   a. The four sides of the picture.
   b. Eight times the width of the molding.
   c. Two inches extra for cutting waste.

   This equals the total length of molding needed to make the frame. For example, a picture 6 by 9 in. using a molding 1 in. wide would require:

   a. $6'' + 6'' + 9'' + 9'' = 30''$
   b. $1'' \times 8 = 8''$
   c. $2''$ cutting waste $= 2''$
   Total needed $= 40''$

Fig. 16-5. Important tools for framing are a bevel mat cutter, steel tape, nail set, glass cutter, mat knife and straightedge.

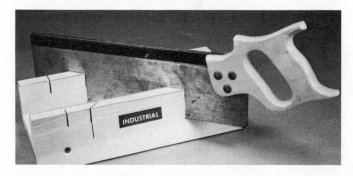

Fig. 16-6. Standard wood miter box with backsaw makes miter cuts or crosscuts.

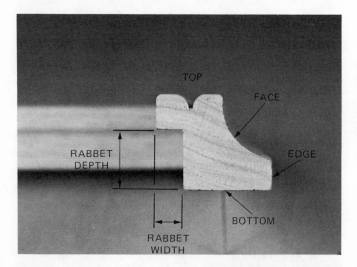

Fig. 16-3. Wood molding made with a router. Terms are those relating to most types of frame moldings.

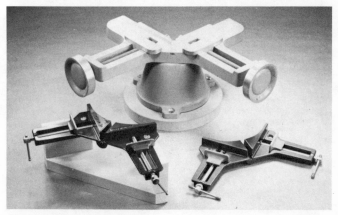

Fig. 16-7. Heavy duty miter clamp and small clamps are useful for holding parts during framing.

2. When framing a picture without a mat, the "rabbet" size is generally used for measuring. This is the opening on the back of the frame into which the 6 by 9 in. (152 x 229 mm) picture is to be fitted. Add about 1/16 in. (1.5 mm) to each strip so the rabbet opening will be slightly larger. This makes it easier to insert the glass and picture. See Fig. 16-8.

3. Cut the long sides first. Set the miter box (or table saw miter gage) at a 45 deg. angle and make your first cut as shown in Fig. 16-9. This will provide a mitered edge for further measurements. Make a pencil mark on the rabbet edge 9 1/16 in. (14 mm) from the first miter cut, Fig. 16-10. Place this strip in the miter box at the opposite 45 deg. angle and cut the molding along the pencil line. Cut the second long side and short sides in the same manner. Accurate miter cutting is necessary so that each corner will be exactly square.

4. When all sides of the frame have been cut, start assembly, Fig. 16-11. Apply white glue to the mitered ends of two molding strips, Fig. 16-12. Place them in the miter clamp, Fig. 16-13, and tighten the clamps.

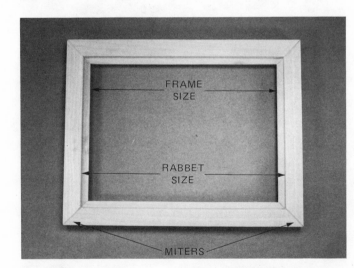

Fig. 16-8. Back of picture frame shows mitered corners and how to measure for rabbet size and frame size.

Fig. 16-9. Making first 45 deg. angle cut on long side of molding. Hold molding tightly against miter box during sawing.

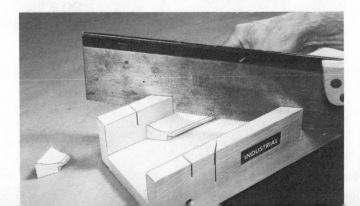

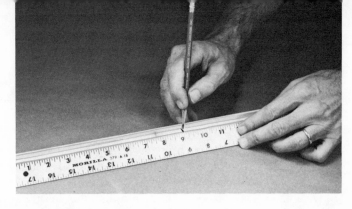

Fig. 16-10. Marking length for second miter cut on rabbet edge of molding. Use sharp pencil.

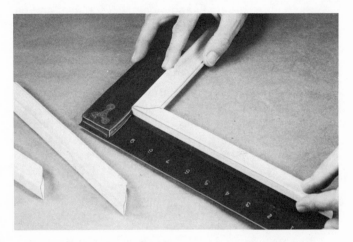

Fig. 16-11. Check miter cuts with try square before assembly.

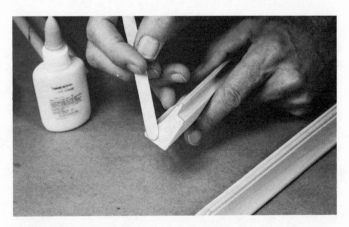

Fig. 16-12. Apply thin coat of glue to mitered ends of molding strips before clamping.

Fig. 16-13. Adjust miters accurately in clamp and tighten.

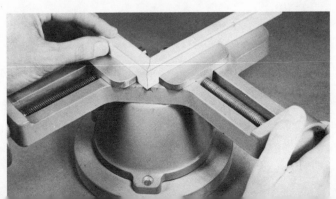

5. Always nail mitered joints while in the miter clamp. Drive a thin finishing nail into the clamped joint as shown in Fig. 16-14. Allow to dry for about a half hour and repeat for the other three corners. Use a nail set to drive the head of the nail below the surface, Fig. 16-15. This hole will be filled later. If the wood is hard, drill a small hole for each nail so the wood will not split, Fig. 16-16.

6. A small, inexpensive miter clamp also works quite well as shown in Fig. 16-17. Fasten the clamp in a vise to make your work more sturdy.

7. Fill the nail holes with wood filler, Fig. 16-18, allow the filler to dry and sand smooth. Stick filler can be used after finish has been applied or on prefinished moldings. Select a matching color and rub into the nail holes. Buff with a soft cloth.

8. Finish your frame by sanding smooth and applying a finish that will go well with the picture. If the wood is to remain its natural color, simply apply two coats of lacquer sealer or a penetrating oil finish. Stains and paints can be used to add a variety of colors, Fig. 16-19. Glazing compounds give the frame an antique appearance, Fig. 16-20.

ASSEMBLING A PICTURE

To secure the glass, picture and backing material into the frame:

1. Cut the glass the same size as the picture. The procedure for glass cutting is illustrated in the chapter on stained glass. Either picture glass or nonglare glass may be used. Window glass is satisfactory but is considerably thicker. Wash the glass thoroughly and dry completely.

2. Measure the backing material. It should be the same size as the rabbet opening in the frame, Fig. 16-21. Cut the backing with a mat knife as shown in Fig. 16-22. Corrugated board or illustration

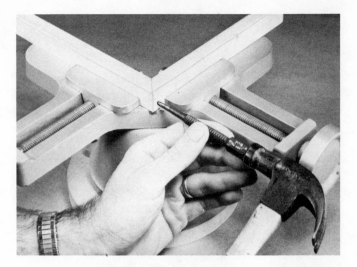
Fig. 16-15. Sink nail head below wood surface with nail set. Heavy duty miter clamp is fastened to workbench.

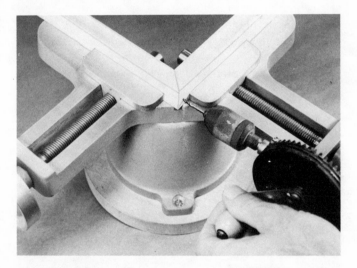
Fig. 16-16. Drill hole for nail with hand drill.

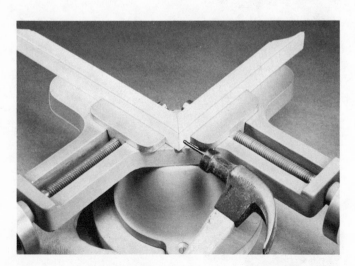
Fig. 16-14. Nail clamped joint with long finishing nail.

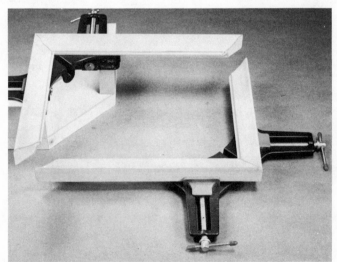
Fig. 16-17. Using small miter clamps for gluing. Four clamps can be used at one time for a complete frame.

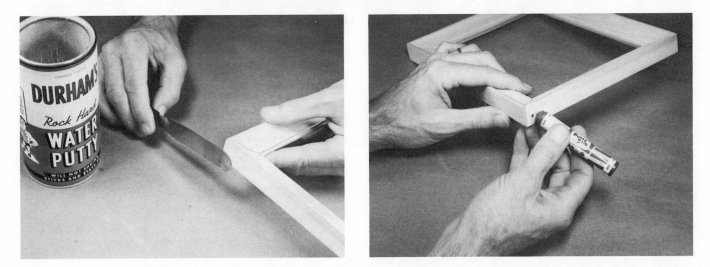

Fig. 16-18. Left. Filling nail holes with wood filler. Right. Putty stick was used to fill nail holes after finishing had been completed. Sticks are sold in choice of colors.

Fig. 16-19. Staining frame for a dark gray finish. Either a rag or a brush is used.

Fig. 16-21. Mark backing material size using frame for pattern. Draw pencil line along rabbet edge. Allow for width of rabbet when cutting.

Fig. 16-20. Apply glazing compound to frame for antique finish.

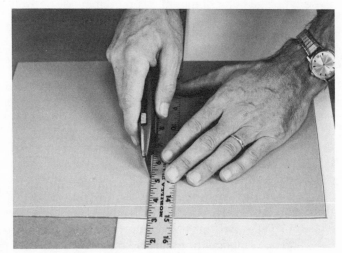

Fig. 16-22. Cut backing material with mat knife and straightedge. Be careful not to damage working surface.

board both work well. However, corrugated board has greater strength for larger pictures. Glass, picture and backing material should be the same size, slightly smaller than the rabbet opening.

3. Place the frame, face down, flat on the covered work area. Assemble the glass, picture and backing, Fig. 16-23, and place them in the rabbet. Use small brads, Fig. 16-24, or diamond points to fasten the assembly as shown in Fig. 16-25. Push fasteners securely into frame.

4. To seal the frame and picture, use heavy brown paper and white glue. Cut the brown paper about 1/8 in. (3 mm) less in width and length than the outside of the frame back. Apply a small amount of white glue along the edges of the back and press the paper firmly in place with your fingers, Fig. 16-26. Be sure the glue forms a continuous seal with the paper to keep out dust.

5. Standard picture hangers work well to hang most picture frames. Small screws or screw eyes attached to either side of the frame back and connected with a fine wire are often used to support heavier frames.

MOUNTING AND MATTING PICTURES

Careful mounting or matting gives emphasis to the color of the picture and may make it appear larger. Mounting simply means that the picture is fastened directly to the face of a larger board and is framed in the usual manner. Matting is similar except that an opening or "window" is cut from mat board. The picture shows through the opening and is separated from the frame on all sides by the width of the mat border. Mat board, ragboard, wallpaper, veneer and a variety of fabrics may be used for mounting or matting. Proceed as follows:

1. When mounting a picture or piece of artwork, select a type and color of mounting board that will go well with the illustration. Determine the amount of margin you want on each side of the picture and cut the mounting board slightly smaller than the rabbet size of the frame.

2. Center the picture on the mounting board by measuring the correct distances from each side. Hold the picture flat and make a light pencil mark on each corner, Fig. 16-27.

3. Place a clean weight on the center of the picture to hold it in place. Lift the top corners, one at a time. Apply a small amount of rubber cement or white paste under each edge, Fig. 16-28. Press down firmly and allow to dry. Assemble the mounting with glass and backing in the standard manner. Fabrics, wallpaper or other thin materials should be glued to a mat board to provide added strength to the mounting board.

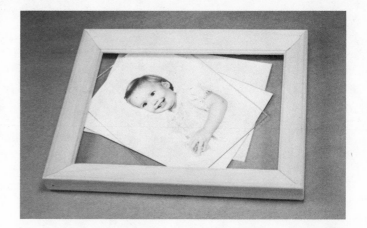

Fig. 16-23. All elements—frame, glass, picture and backing—are now ready for assembly.

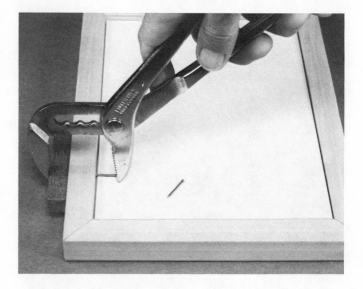

Fig. 16-24. Drive brads with pliers and supporting block. Place about 4 in. apart.

Fig. 16-25. Using diamond points to hold picture in place. Glazier's gun does same job rapidly if one is available.

Fig. 16-26. Brown paper glued to back of frame keeps out dust.

Fig. 16-27. Mark corners of picture with pencil to indicate exactly where picture must be mounted.

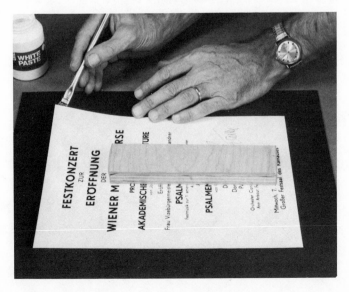

Fig. 16-28. Lift corners and apply white paste.

Fig. 16-29. Lay out opening on back of mat with pencil and rule.

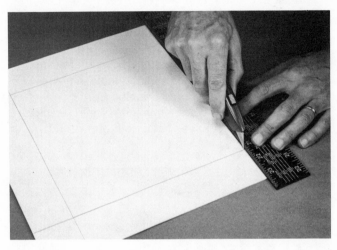

Fig. 16-30. Carefully cut opening with mat knife and straightedge.

MAKING PICTURE MATS

Remember that the color and texture of material used for matting should be carefully chosen to accent the picture.

1. Select the matting material. Determine the width of border you want to show around your picture. This is a matter of personal taste, but as a general rule, the larger the picture the smaller the mat width.

2. When you have determined the mat size, make the frame to fit the mat dimensions. This is the rabbet size of the frame. Cut the mat about 1/8 in. smaller than the rabbet size.

3. Next, place the mat board face down on the work table. Lay out the size of the opening on the back of the mat board using a rule and pencil, Fig. 16-29. Measure accurately from each edge of the mat so the opening will be correctly centered. The opening may overlap the picture as much as desired.

4. Cut out the opening using a sharp mat knife and a straightedge as shown in Fig. 16-30. Make your cuts on top of a scrap piece of mat board so as not to dull the knife or mar the work table. Carefully cut to intersecting lines so the corners are sharp and clean. A slip of the knife can make unsightly scratches.

5. When the opening has been cut out, Fig. 16-31, erase pencil lines and smooth rough edges with fine sandpaper. The making of a bevel cut for the mat opening is shown in Fig. 16-32. A bevel cutting mat knife is more accurate and is worth the cost if you plan to do much picture matting. A bevel cut for the mat opening generally gives a better appearance that a straight cut, Fig. 16-33. The bevel cut can be made by hand with a mat knife and straightedge. However, it is difficult to keep the exact angle for each side of the opening.

6. Apply a small amount of white paste to the inside edges of the mat and center it over the picture, Fig. 16-34. Press down firmly around the edges and allow to dry. Another method is to use paper or linen tape to fasten the picture to the mat. Assemble the glass, picture and backing in your frame. Insert diamond points to hold assembly in place. Seal with brown paper and white glue.

A fabric covering is sometimes desirable for picture matting. Materials such as linen, thin burlap and velvet all work well. Linen is especially easy to apply and provides an interesting texture around artwork. Try the following procedure for preparing a fabric mat:

1. Prepare the mat from regular mat board. Cut it to size for the picture being framed. Make a straight cut for the mat opening rather than a bevel.
2. Cut the fabric about an inch wider and longer than the mat, Fig. 16-35.
3. With the mat face up, spread an even coating of white paste over the entire surface, Fig. 16-36.
4. Center fabric over mat and rub with a soft cloth to make a tight bond, Fig. 16-37.
5. Turn the mat over and use a mat knife to cut an opening in the fabric as shown in Fig. 16-38.
6. Remove the fabric and apply paste to the mat edge the width of the overlapping fabric. Fold fabric over mat edges and rub with a soft cloth until all wrinkles are out, Fig. 16-39.
7. Trim outside edges of fabric flush with the mat and allow to dry. The finished mat is now ready for framing, Fig. 16-40.

Fig. 16-31. Opening has been cut out of mat board.

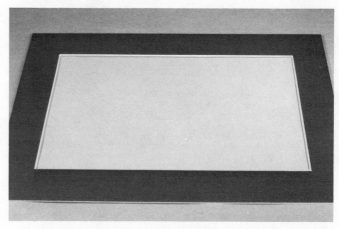

Fig. 16-33. Beveled cut exposes an attractive edge around mat opening. Same bevel angle must be kept on all sides.

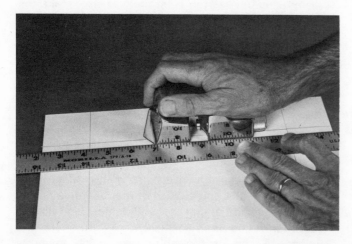

Fig. 16-32. Make beveled cuts with bevel cutter using straightedge as guide.

Fig. 16-34. Picture is centered in mat opening and glued in place.

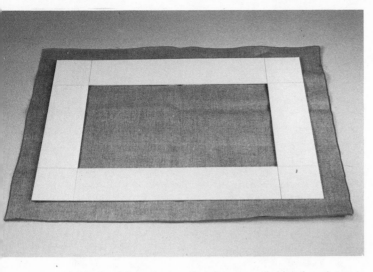

Fig. 16-35. Cut fabric about an inch larger on all sides than the mat.

Fig. 16-38. Make a 1 in. cut at each corner at 45 deg. angle. Then cut out the inside fabric parallel to the mat sides. Allow about 1 1/2 to 2 in. (38 to 51 mm) of fabric to wrap over back of mat.

Fig. 16-36. Spread paste on face of mat. Thin even coat is necessary so that paste will not soak through fabric.

Fig. 16-39. Fold fabric over mat edges and be sure corners of fabric make a tight fit with the mat.

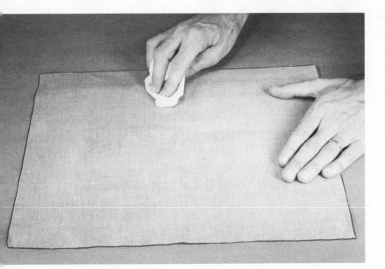

Fig. 16-37. Glue fabric to mat. Work out air bubbles with soft cloth.

Fig. 16-40. Completed fabric mat should look like this.

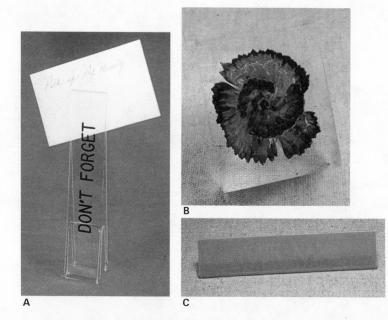

Project ideas for internal carving of plastics. A—Letter carving from the back using burr tool. B—Carved flower in acrylic block with blue and red dye. C—Desk nameplate carved from the back.

Chapter 17
INTERNAL CARVING PLASTICS

Internal carving of solid plastic material is not difficult. It involves the use of clear acrylic plastic, often called Lucite or Plexiglas, into which hollow shapes are carved to produce the design. The design may then be seen through the clear plastic.

A variety of colors may be added to the cavity to enhance the design and provide special effects. Colored dyes are most often used, but the cavity may also be filled with colored sand, powdered plastics or liquids. Left empty it has a frosted appearance.

Typical products of internal carving plastics are desk name plates, bases for penholders, night lights, paper weights (Fig. 17-1), table decorations, letter holders and a variety of jewelry.

MATERIALS

Clear acrylic plastic for carving is sold in standard cube sizes, rods, square bars or in almost any sheet thickness. It is less expensive to cut your project material from bars or thick sheet. But this requires a great deal of sanding and polishing to produce a glasslike smooth surface where cuts have been made.

Other materials include acrylic dyes, patching plaster, an eye dropper or plastic cementing dispenser, felt, sandpaper, buffing compound, toothpaste and fasteners such as jewelry findings. Fig. 17-2 shows plastic stock and some other necessary materials.

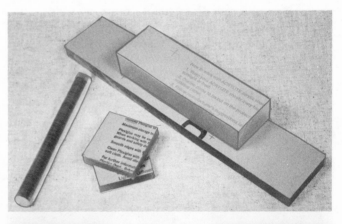

Fig. 17-1. This completed edge carving will make a beautiful desktop decoration or paperweight.

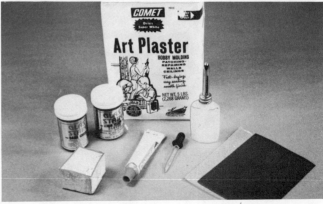

Fig. 17-2. Top. Thick sheets, blocks and rods of acrylic plastic are suitable for internal carving. Bottom. Major materials for internal carving include patching plaster, acrylic dye, buffing compound, toothpaste, eye dropper, dye dispenser, sandpaper and felt.

TOOLS

The most useful tool for internal carving is a motor driven chuck to power the carving drills. A flexible shaft tool works very well since the chuck is lightweight and easily guided for carving. Small, hand-held power drills work almost as well, Fig. 17-3.

An assortment of tapered drills and steel burrs will provide for the variety of cuts you may need to make, Fig. 17-4. You may also need a cloth buffing wheel if it is necessary to polish large surfaces.

MAKING AN INTERNAL CARVING

When you have selected the project you plan to make, secure the acrylic plastic you will need. If pieces must be cemented, refer to the chapter on plastics crafts for directions. Use the following procedure for internal carving.

1. Sand and polish the edges of the acrylic piece to a bright lustre. Use a fine "wet or dry" silicon carbide paper and then buff with buffing compound or toothpaste. Remove the masking paper when you are ready to begin carving.
2. Select a tapered drill of appropriate size and fasten it into the chuck of the hand power tool. Hold the plastic piece in one hand and gently press the tapered drill into the bottom side directly under the center of your design as shown in Fig. 17-5. The depth of the drilled hole can be seen by looking through the side of the plastic, Fig. 17-6. You may want to practice this operation on scrap plastic to get the "feel" of the drilling action.
3. To form the petals of a flower, make cuts by inserting the drill into the plastic at an angle and pivot the drill with a sweeping motion, Fig. 17-7.

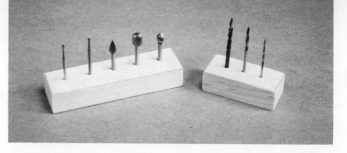

Fig. 17-4. Assortment of tapered drills and steel burrs will speed the task of carving plastic.

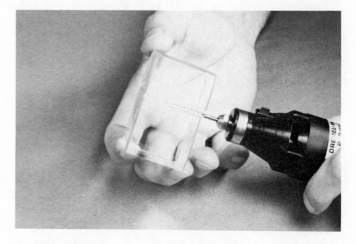

Fig. 17-5. Drill into bottom of acrylic block to begin design.

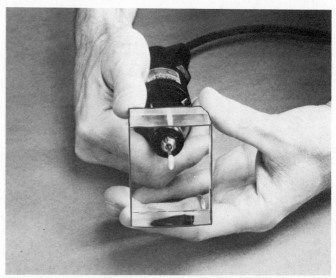

Fig. 17-6. Check on drill depth through side of plastic block.

Fig. 17-7. Slight angling of drill is used to form first petals of flower.

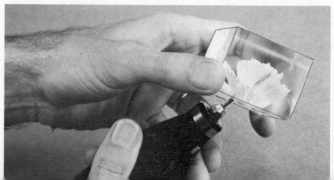

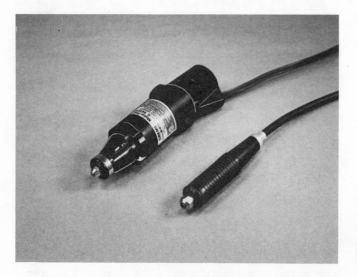

Fig. 17-3. Small power hand tool and flexible shaft tool both work well as power source for carving with the drill.

Try to keep each cut for a petal separated from a previous cut. Continue cutting the petals by tilting the drill to a greater angle as the flower nears completion. Each time the drill is inserted into the original opening to form another petal, try to keep from enlarging the hole more than necessary to complete the job. The sequence for carving a flower is shown in Fig. 17-8.

4. If you plan to add color to the carving, use acrylic dye and an eye dropper or plastic cementing dispenser. The dispenser works very well since the needle opening allows you to place the dye exactly where you want it, Fig. 17-9. Allow one color of dye to dry about 15 min. before adding another.

5. To fill the cavity of the carving, mix some patching plaster with water until it has a putty-like consistency. Press the plaster into the cavity with a putty knife, Fig. 17-10 and smooth the surface. Felt may be glued to the bottom to give the project a finished appearance.

DESIGN HINTS

There are so many design possibilities for internal carving that you may want to consider some of the following:

1. Acrylic sheet, generally 3/8 in. (9.5 mm) thick or less, can be carved from both the back and the edge to produce interesting designs. The cavity may be left frosted or colored with dye and filled with plaster. Use acrylic cement to fasten the bottom edge to a piece of wood or another sheet of plastic.

2. Add interesting color to a carving by filling different sections with colored sand. Use the technique described in the chapter on sand art. Be sure to seal the sand at the opening with a few drops of lacquer or white glue.

3. A variety of surface carvings can be made by using either steel burrs or tapered drills. These carvings are usually made by working from the back side of acrylic sheet. Lay out your design on the back side and carve with the face down on your work table. Name plates, fish, animal figures and symbols work well with this method. Dyes may be used to add color to the project.

4. It is possible to give the design the appearance of a solid color by gathering the carved plastic chips and packing them back in the cavity. Add acrylic dye with an eye dropper and the color will dissolve into the chips and carved surface. The result is a solid opaque color that provides a realistic look.

Safety: Be very careful when using the high speed tapered drills and steel burrs. They are sharp and can cause injury. If forced completely through the plastic or if they slip out of the carving, they could hit your hand.

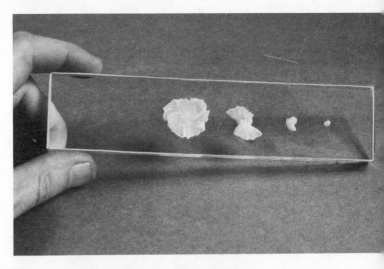

Fig. 17-8. Sequence of forming flower from right to left. First drilled hole, forming flower stigma, first layer of petals and final layer.

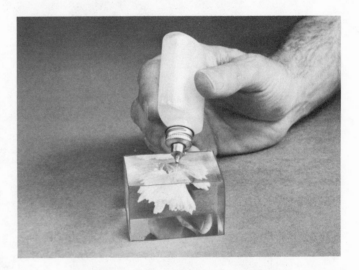

Fig. 17-9. Color flower with plastic dye dispenser.

Fig. 17-10. Fill cavity with patching plaster.

137

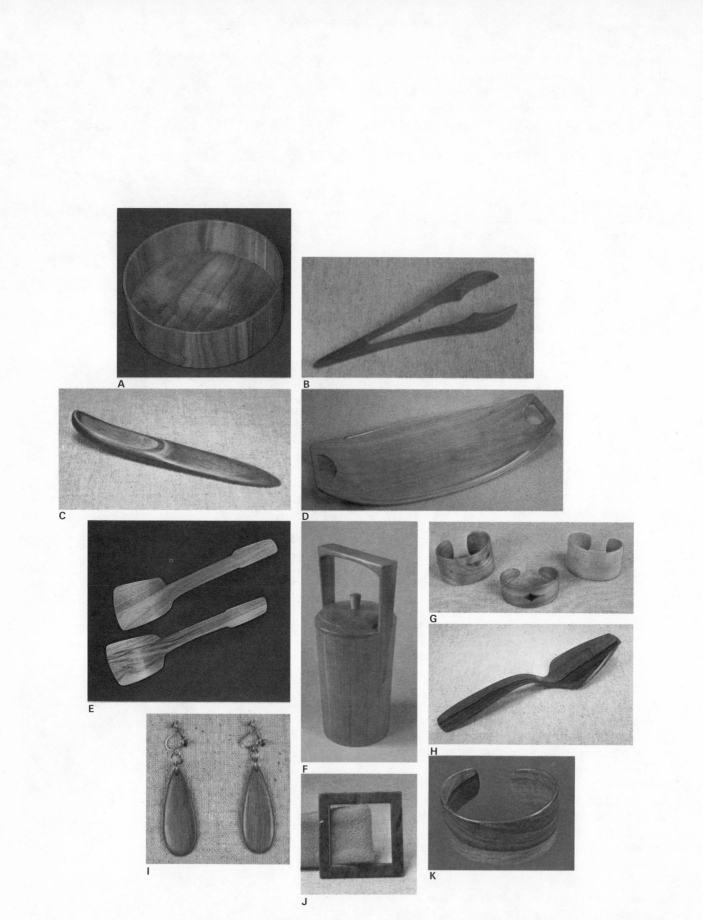

Suggestions for laminating wood products. A—Serving bowl with flat laminated bottom. B—Bun serving tongs. C—Sculptured letter opener. (Mark Lindsay) D—Walnut bread tray. E—Walnut salad servers. F—Ice bucket. G—Walnut and cherry bracelets. H—Rosewood cake server. I—Sculptured earrings. J—Laminated belt buckle. (Mark Lindsay) K—Rosewood bracelet.

Chapter 18
LAMINATING WOOD VENEERS

Gluing together thin sheets of wood veneer to form a solid article is called LAMINATING. Since the veneer is so thin, it can be formed to many desirable shapes. Yet, it retains the strength of much thicker wood. There is very little waste, beautiful grain patterns are easy to find and design possibilities are unlimited.

Serving trays, salad servers, letter holders, cheese spreaders, bowls and a variety of jewelry can be made from wood laminates. Projects of this type are inexpensive and provide a delightful craft experience. Fig. 18-1 shows a veneer butter dish which can be constructed by following a few simple instructions.

MATERIAL

Veneer is available in a wide selection of woods. Make your choice according to desired color and texture. Standard hardwood veneer averages about 1/28 in. (0.9 mm) in thickness. It is available in many widths and lengths. Some of the most beautiful veneers for craft projects are walnut, rosewood, cherry, teak, maple and oak, Fig. 18-2. You will also need some blocks of softwood to make the caul (a form for clamping veneers when gluing), felt, white glue, waxed paper, plastic resin glue, a glue brush, sandpaper and finishing materials.

TOOLS

Tools for laminating should include a bandsaw or jigsaw, hand clamps, wood files, and a coping saw. Some advanced projects may require a wood lathe for turning solid sections. Materials and tools for laminating veneers are shown in Fig. 18-3.

MAKING A LAMINATED PROJECT

Two major processes are required to make a laminated project.
1. The caul must be prepared to shape the veneer sheets.

Fig. 18-1. Veneer butter dish with wooden spreader.

Fig. 18-2. Many beautiful wood veneers are available for laminating.

Crafts

2. The laminated blank of glued veneer sheets must be cut and shaped into the final product.

Try the following procedure for laminating:

1. Design your project and make an accurate sketch of it. Lay out the shape of the caul on thin cardboard and cut out the pattern with scissors.

Make a cardboard pattern for the shape of your laminated project in the same manner. Some patterns are shown in Fig. 18-4.

Fig. 18-5. Trace pattern for caul on softwood block.

Fig. 18-6. Cut the curved shape of the caul on a bandsaw.

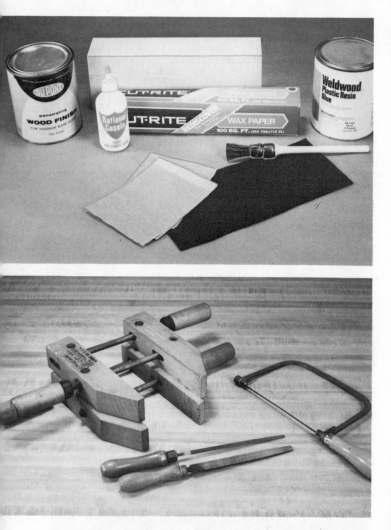

Fig. 18-3. Top. Materials for laminating include a block of softwood, clear finish, white glue, wax paper, plastic resin glue, glue brush, sandpaper and felt. Bottom. Hand tools used for laminating include hand screw clamps, files and a coping saw.

Fig. 18-4. Typical patterns for cauls and laminated projects. They are made of cardboard.

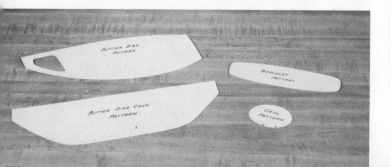

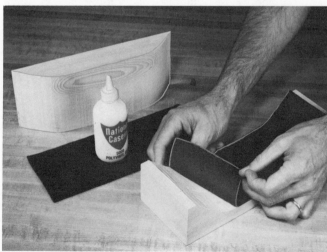

Fig. 18-7. Fasten felt to caul with white glue.

Laminating Wood Veneers

2. Get a block of inexpensive wood at least 1/2 in. larger on all sides than your project pattern. Good clean pieces of construction lumber are fine as caul stock. With a pencil, trace the pattern for the caul as shown in Fig. 18-5.

3. Use a bandsaw to cut the profile (side view) of the caul, Fig. 18-6. Carefully follow the pattern pencil line for a smooth curve. Flat spots or lumps will show up on your laminate.

4. Lightly sand the cut surfaces of the caul. Do not try to remove any irregular surfaces or the two halves will not clamp evenly. Cut out two pieces of felt slightly larger than the caul surface. Apply white glue to each caul surface, press the felt firmly in place, Fig. 18-7, and allow to dry. Trim the excess felt along the edges with a sharp razor blade. Your caul is now ready to make as many laminations as you desire. It can be used over and over again!

5. Select the veneer and cut as many blanks as necessary to get the right thickness. Four or five sheets work well for most projects. Use a paper cutter or a straightedge and sharp knife for cutting. Heavy scissors may also be used. Cut the veneer blanks slightly larger than the caul surface. Also cut two sheets of waxed paper the same size. Make sure all veneer grain runs lengthwise.

6. Lay out the caul and materials for assembly as shown in Fig. 18-8. Mix the plastic resin glue and spread it on all veneer surfaces except those that will form the top and bottom of the project, Fig. 18-9. Apply a very thin coat, enough to wet the surfaces.

7. Place a sheet of waxed paper over the bottom half of the caul. Assemble the layers of veneer and lay them on top of the waxed paper. Cover with another sheet of waxed paper and put the top half of the caul in place, Fig. 18-10. Adjust hand clamps and tighten them firmly on the caul as shown in Fig. 18-11. Allow to dry overnight. The waxed paper will keep glue squeeze-out from getting on the felt or surfaces of your laminate.

Fig. 18-8. Caul, wax paper and veneers are ready for assembly.

Fig. 18-9. Spread plastic resin glue on veneer surfaces.

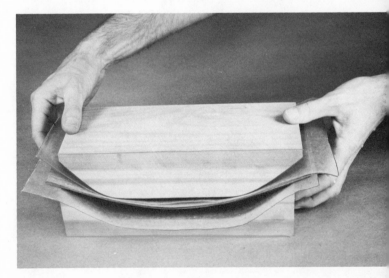

Fig. 18-10. Place top of caul on assembly of veneers covered with waxed paper.

Fig. 18-11. Tighten hand clamps on caul with heavy pressure.

8. When the glue is dry, remove clamps and laminated blank from the caul. Place your design pattern on the laminate and carefully trace it with a pencil, Fig. 18-12. (Never attempt to trace the pattern before laminate is shaped. Veneer strips may slip while gluing.)

9. Carefully cut out the project shape with a coping saw or a bandsaw if the curvature of the laminate is not too great. See Fig. 18-13. Be sure to cut just outside your pencil line.

10. Use files and sandpaper to smooth the edges of the laminate accurately to your pencil lines. Round the edges as desired to give your laminated project a graceful appearance, Fig. 18-14.

11. Apply two coats of a penetrating oil finish or lacquer and rub out smooth with fine steel wool after it has dried. Polish with a coat of paste wax if desired. The completed project with a butter spreader is shown in Fig. 18-15.

CONSTRUCTION HINTS

1. Always use a plastic resin glue for laminating veneers. It is very rigid when dry and will keep your project in the curved shape you planned.

2. Select the most attractively grained veneers for the visible parts of your project. Poorer quality veneers can be used on the inside where they do not show.

3. If your project is small, the caul can be clamped in a woodworking vise. C clamps or a book binding press can also be used if they are available.

4. A high pressure plastic laminate, like Formica, often makes a good top surface for a laminated project. Use it in the same manner as a top layer of veneer.

5. Many round or oval-shaped laminated projects require a one piece caul as shown in Fig. 18-16. Cut the caul to the exact shape of the inside of your project and glue on felt. Wrap waxed paper and the glued veneers around the caul, Fig. 18-17. Hold the lamination in place while tightly wrapping strips of inner tube or rubber bands around it as shown in Fig. 18-18. Allow to dry overnight. Trace pattern on laminate, Fig. 18-19, and cut out with a coping saw. Sand smooth and apply finish. Fig. 18-20 shows the completed project. (Do not attempt to trace pattern on laminate before it is shaped.)

6. Veneers will sometimes break when bent to a small curve. This can be prevented by wetting the veneer strips and preshaping them inside a plastic form , as shown in Fig. 18-21. Allow the pieces to dry before gluing. Refer to Chapter 28 for construction of plastic projects.

7. For special designs, cut openings in handles or other appropriate areas of your project. Drill a hole at the center of the design, insert the coping saw blade and cut to shape. Finish with small files and sandpaper.

8. Flat laminates, such as a cheese spreader or bottom for a bowl, can be made by clamping the veneer pieces between two pieces of thick wood or plywood.

Fig. 18-12. Trace design pattern on curved laminated blank.

Fig. 18-13. Cut out the project with a coping saw.

Fig. 18-14. Sculpture edge of laminated project with sandpaper.

Fig. 18-15. Laminated walnut butter dish. A silver butter spreader has been added.

Fig. 18-16. Oval bracelet caul is also made of wood. Patterns for caul and bracelet are cut from heavy cardboard.

Fig. 18-17. With waxed paper protecting the felt, wrap glued veneers around caul.

Fig. 18-18. Tightly wrap strip of rubber inner tube around veneers to hold them against caul.

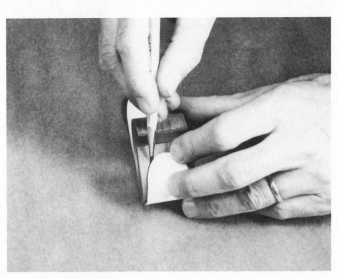

Fig. 18-19. Lay bracelet pattern on shaped piece of wood laminate and trace shape onto laminate.

Fig. 18-20. Completed bracelet has been given a clear finish.

Fig. 18-21. Slide wet veneers into clear plastic form for preshaping.

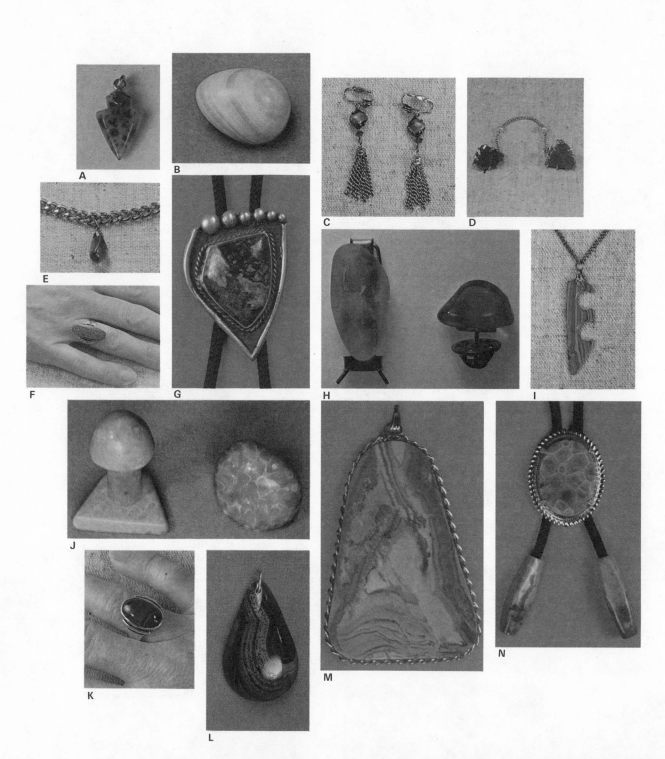

Ideas for stone and gem cutting. A—Moss agate pendant. B—Egg made from polished, stratified stone. C—Polished amethyst gemstones are main feature of these earrings. D—Sweater guard of polished chrysocolla and quartz. E—Tumbled amethyst gem bracelet. F—Goldstone gem set in silver band. G—Western style string tie with turquoise set in bronze. H—Tumbled stones used to make a tie tac and barette. (Chip Kicklighter) I—Jasper pendant in freeform design. J—Paper weights made from Petoskey stone. K—Tiger's eye ring set in silver bezel. L—Malachite pendant in teardrop shape. M—Jasper pendant with silver findings. N—Western style tie featuring a cabochon from Petoskey stone. (The Miner's Den)

Chapter 19
LAPIDARY

LAPIDARY is the art or craft of cutting and polishing stones. Interest in gemstones dates back to antiquity when gem-making or lapidary was a mysterious craft with closely guarded secrets. But modern-day rock collecting and the availability of new equipment and information is causing gem-making to become a favorite hobby across America. It is easy to do and almost anyone can master the skills. Once you learn the basic processes, you can make jewelry, home furnishings, art objects or simply display your handiwork.

MATERIALS

Nature has provided the basic material for this craft in a wealth of beautiful rocks, minerals and gems, Fig. 19-1. You may collect your own or purchase them from a local dealer. There are over 100 kinds of rocks and about 1500 mineral species. Gems are the most prized of all minerals because of their clarity and crystalline qualities.

Traditionally, minerals have been classified as either "precious" or "semiprecious." Diamonds, emeralds,

rubies and sapphires have been considered precious or true gems and other minerals semiprecious. Fig. 19-2 shows a collection of both. The distinction between precious and semiprecious stones is usually ignored today because of the wide variation in quality available. The term "gemstones" is being used to describe any stone worth cutting and polishing.

Fig. 19-2. These gemstones include amethyst, diamond, topas (beige) citrine (yellow), emerald, aquamarine, padparadja (orange), peridot (light green), rose zircon, ruby and smoky quartz.

Fig. 19-1. Rocks, minerals and gems may be found in every state. This assortment includes jasper, selenite, gypsum, quartz, amethyst, copper, agate and petrified wood.

TOOLS

Several pieces of equipment are used in the lapidary craft. They include:

1. A tumbler. This tool provides an easy way to polish gemstones, Figs. 19-3 and 19-4. It can be purchased at a modest cost and will produce highly polished baroque gems (tumbled irregular and unusually shaped stones).

2. Diamond saw. The saw, Fig. 19-5, is needed to cut slabs of stone which may be trimmed and formed into new shapes. Since it represents a sizable investment, you may settle for stones already rough cut. Many craft shops sell pieces of stone already cut to rough shapes.

3. Grinder, sander and polisher. Frequently these three are combined into a single machine, Fig. 19-6. They are necessary to shape the stone and smooth it to the desired luster.

Large flat surfaces of stones may be ground and polished using a vibrating lap, Fig. 19-7. The operation takes several hours, but the result is beautiful especially if slabs are nearly transparent and colorful.

Fig. 19-5. This 6 in. diamond saw has grinder and polisher attached. (Shop-Vac Corp.)

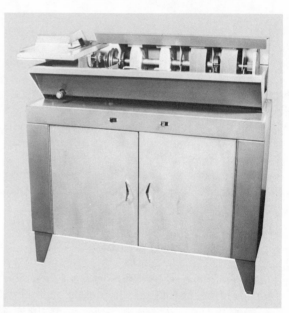

Fig. 19-6. Combination unit includes saw, two grinding wheels, two sanding wheels and polisher. It will perform all operations. (Shop-Vac Corp.)

Fig. 19-3. Tumbler may be used to produce highly polished baroque gems. (Shop-Vac Corp.)

Fig. 19-4. Small sonic tumbler will polish baroque gems very rapidly. (Henry B. Graves Co.)

Fig. 19-7. Vibrating lap may be used to polish large flat stones and slabs. (Shop-Vac Corp.)

GEM MAKING

Gems are most frequently finished in one of three basic forms. The forms are "baroque," "cabochon" and "facet." See. Fig. 19-8. Baroque gems are made by tumbling irregular and unusual shaped stones. Cabochon gems are made by cutting a geometric shape from a slab of stone 3/16 to 1/4 in. (5 to 6 mm) thick. The stone is then ground to a dome shape. Most cabochons are flat on the bottom, but some have a domed surface on the bottom also. Facet gems are generally cut from transparent stones. The facets should be arranged symmetrically and meet at a point.

MAKING BAROQUE GEMS (TUMBLING)

Tumbling is a speedy way of doing what nature has been doing from the beginning of time. Basically, tumbling involves putting a batch of small stones (roughs), Fig. 19-9, of similar hardness into a tumbler barrel, adding coarse abrasive grit and water and tumbling or rotating 24 hours a day for about a week. The process is then repeated with medium grit abrasives and then again with fine grit. The fourth week, polish is used instead of abrasives to attain a high luster. The time required may be slightly shorter or longer depending on the hardness or condition of the stones. Fig. 19-10 shows some tumbled stones.

Tumbled stones may be used for earrings, necklaces, bracelets, cuff links and tie bars. Epoxy adhesive is used to bond the stone and metal together.

Fig. 19-8. The three stones on the left are baroque stones which have been tumbled to produce the smooth, shiny surface. The middle stone is a cabochon which has been cut to shape, ground and polished. It is flat on the back side. The stone on the upper right is a faceted gem which has been ground to a very precise shape.

MAKING CABOCHON GEMS

The cabochon is the oldest and simplest cut and is usually tried first by beginners. An opaque or translucent stone is generally selected to form a variety of geometric outlines. Examples include the oval, square, heart and cross and others. These shapes are shown in Fig. 19-11.

Fig. 19-9. These small stones, similar in hardness, are ready to be polished by tumbling.

Fig. 19-10. These stones were tumbled for many days until they took on a satin luster.

Fig. 19-11. Several typical cabochon shapes which are popular with beginners and those who are experienced.

To make a cabochon:

1. Select a slab of stone 3/16 to 1/4 in. (5 to 6 mm) thick. If you have a diamond slab saw, you can cut the stone yourself; if not, you can purchase the slab already cut from a local dealer, Fig. 19-12. When cutting the slab, use even pressure to produce a straighter and smoother cut.

2. Scribe the desired shape on the slab, Fig. 19-13. A template or pattern is generally used with a pointed aluminum rod or pencil.

3. Cut out the marked area using a diamond blade trim saw. Leave about 1/16 in. (1.5 mm) around the edge for grinding. See Fig. 19-14. Feed the material into the blade slowly to prevent breaking or damage to the blade.

4. Attach the stone to a "dop" stick, Fig. 19-15. A 1/4 in. (6 mm) wooden dowel 4 in. (101 mm) long will work well. The stone will remain attached to the dop stick through grinding, sanding and polishing. A special dop wax secures the stone to the stick. Heat the wax with an alcohol burner and apply some wax to the dowel rod, Fig. 19-16. Quickly, press the waxed dowel to the stone. Hold it steady until it hardens. It may adhere better if the stone is warm.

   Grind the stone freehand to shape using a light pressure, Fig. 19-17. Usually, a 100 grit silicon carbide wheel is used for rough grinding. Finish grinding is done with a 220 grit wheel. Use water as a coolant when grinding, Fig. 19-18. Grinding is generally done from the bottom of the stone toward the top so that chipped edges will be ground off when the top is shaped. Fig. 19-19 shows a cabochon ground to approximate size and shape.

5. Grind the contour on the face of the stone, Fig. 19-20. Work from the bottom edge toward the top.

Fig. 19-13. A template and a pencil or pointed rod are generally used to trace the shape on the slab.

Fig. 19-14. Cabochon has been sawed to rough shape leaving about 1/16 in. around the edge for grinding.

Fig. 19-12. Three slabs cut to 3/16 in. (5 mm) thickness are ready to be made into cabochons.

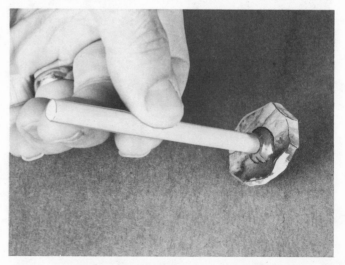

Fig. 19-15. In preparation for grinding, sanding and polishing, shaped stone is attached to wooden dowel.

Lapidary

Fig. 19-16. Apply hot dop wax to the end of a 4 in. (101 mm) long dowel rod. The rod will serve as a handle for grinding, sanding and polishing a cabochon.

Fig. 19-17. Coarse grinding wheel is used to roughly grind the stone to desired shape.

Fig. 19-18. Stone should be cooled in can of water while grinding to prevent softening the wax.

Remove all flat areas to form a perfect dome.

6. Sand the stone to remove grinding marks, Fig. 19-21. Use a 220 grit sanding disc or cloth for coarse sanding and a 320, 400 or 600 grit for finishing. Turn the dop stick slowly and apply gentle pressure. Be careful not to overheat the stone because it could crack from the stress. Continue sanding until there are no flat spots and the surface has a dull shine all over.

Fig. 19-19. Rough shape has been attained after a few minutes of grinding on carbide wheel.

Fig. 19-20. The face of the stone has been contoured working from the bottom edge to the top.

Fig. 19-21. Sand the stone on a coarse wheel.

7. The final step in gem making is polishing, Fig. 19-22. This operation should take only a few minutes if the grinding and sanding have been performed properly. Use a felt, leather or muslin buff with tin oxide, cerium oxide or levigated alumina as a polishing agent. Dampen the buff slightly with water and mix the polishing agent into a thick slurry. Apply the agent to the buff with a brush. Apply light pressure to polish the entire surface of the stone. If the polish sticks to the stone, apply more water. A high luster will develop very quickly, Fig. 19-23.

8. Place the stone in ice water for a few seconds to remove the dop stick. The wax will become brittle and the stone will pop off with light pressure. Scrape off remaining wax with a razor blade and clean the stone with alcohol. Fig. 19-24 shows a wide assortment of finished cabochons ready for mounting.

9. Mount the stone as you desire, using epoxy cement.

FACET GEMS

The art of faceting gems is a highly developed and skilled craft. It demands a knowledge of the optics (refraction and reflection) of gems. In addition, specialized equipment, Fig. 19-25, and a high degree of mechanical skill is required. If you are interested in learning this craft, go to your public library or lapidary dealer for more information.

Fig. 19-23. The completed cabochon has a high luster and is uniform in contour with no flat spots.

Fig. 19-24. Agate and jasper cabochons. Rows 1, 3, 6 and 7 are "polka dot" agate and jasper from Priday Ranch. Photo shows wide variety of colors and patterns found in this deposit. Rows 4 and 5 are Succor Creek Picture Jasper. (Prof's Rock Shop, College Place, Washington).

Fig. 19-22. Polishing the cabochon on a polishing wheel. This wheel of leather and tin oxide is being used as a buffing agent.

Fig. 19-25. This gem faceting machine is appropriate for a beginner. (Henry B. Graves Co.)

Since a diamond saw is expensive, many craftspeople buy pieces of stone, like this one, already cut to rough shape.   (Prof's Rock Shop)

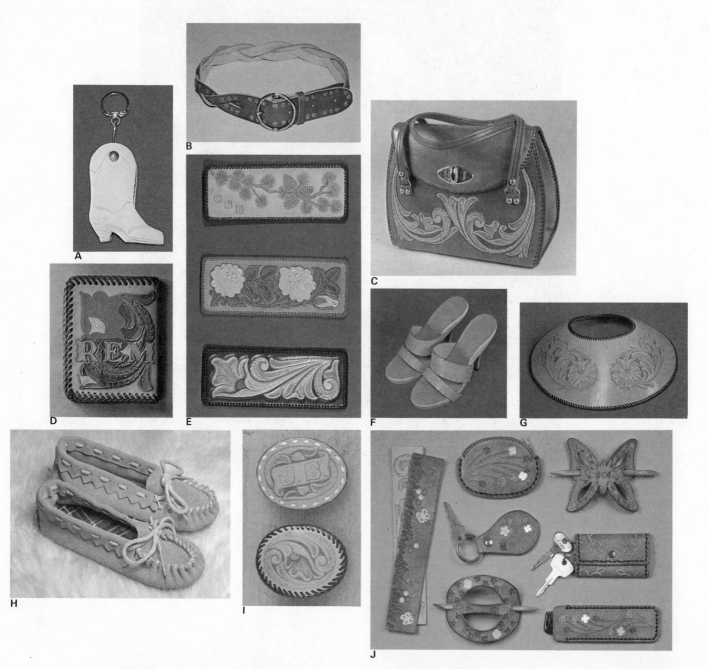

Things to make from leather. A—Key holder. (Chris Kicklighter) B—Braided belt of simple design. C—Lady's purse with carved front. D—Carved and tooled billfold with dyed design. (Robert E. Maguire) E—Three styles of billfold showing variety of tooling possible. F—Handcrafted shoes of leather and maple. G—Unique leather hat. H—Child's moccasins from sueded leather. I—Tooled leather belt buckles. J—Projects for young leathercrafters: barrettes, coin purse, book marks, keyholder, key ring and comb case.

Chapter 20
LEATHERCRAFT

Leather has been used for centuries to provide humans with clothing, shelter, containers and armor. We still use it today for functional as well as decorative items.

Produced in a variety of textures and colors, leather is exceptionally durable and may be carved, tooled or shaped. It can be transformed into articles of clothing, pictures or sculptures. These craft items may be painted, dyed or left natural.

TYPES OF LEATHER

There are many kinds of leather to chose from. Fig. 20-1 shows some of the most common for craft activities.

Cowhide, the most popular, is available in many types and thicknesses. Vegetable tanned cowhide, a natural leather sometimes called tooling leather, is best for carving and stamping. Chrome tanned leather has

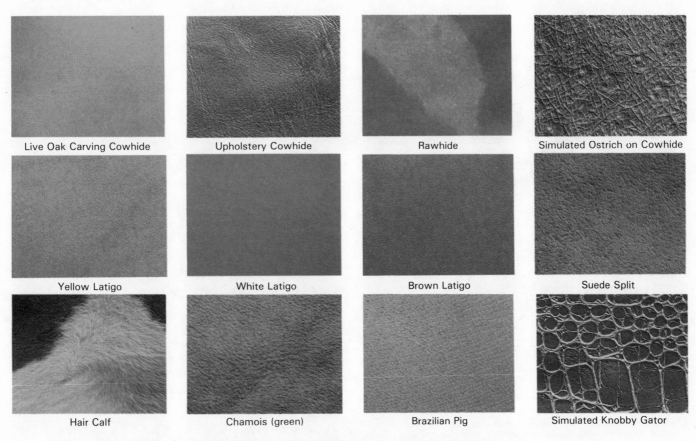

Live Oak Carving Cowhide	Upholstery Cowhide	Rawhide	Simulated Ostrich on Cowhide
Yellow Latigo	White Latigo	Brown Latigo	Suede Split
Hair Calf	Chamois (green)	Brazilian Pig	Simulated Knobby Gator

Fig. 20-1. These types of leather may be used in craft projects.

been treated with chromic salts to produce a tough, firm, water-resistant material. This leather is generally dyed at the tannery and may be recognized by the bluish-green edges produced by the salts. Not generally used for carving and stamping, it is best for shoe uppers, gloves and garments.

Suede is leather whose surface has been buffed or sanded to produce a velvetlike nap. Usually made from lambskin, it is used for garments.

Garment cowhide is thinner and more flexible than leather used for belts, shoes and bags. Most garment leather is dyed and finished before it is sold. The hides are split into layers to produce the right thickness. Splits, the layers taken from the flesh side of the hide, are usually sueded on both sides. Top grain leather is the top layer; only the flesh side has been sueded. The grain side is left smooth.

Leather can be made from any animal skin but most comes from cattle, sheep and goats. Horsehides and pigskins are used to a lesser extent. Hides from domestic animals are also used to produce simulated alligator, sharkskin, ostrich and turtle skins. These are used for luxury items.

LEATHERCRAFT TOOLS

Some basic leathercraft tools are needed to produce carved and stamped leathercraft products. These fall into four categories:
1. Marking and measuring tools, Fig. 20-2.
2. Cutting tools, Fig. 20-3.
3. Other miscellaneous tools, Fig. 20-4.
4. Saddle stamps, Fig. 20-5.

MARKING AND MEASURING TOOLS

These tools prepare the leather for cutting and forming operations. You will need:

Pencil or pen - to prepare patterns and designs and to lay out pieces to be cut. Leather should be marked only where it will not show on the completed product.

Metal square - for measuring lengths and as a straightedge for cutting leather.

Dividers - for transferring distances from patterns to leather, dividing distances into a number of parts and scribing lines.

Tracer modeling tool - for tracing designs and for compressing leather.

Double line marking tool - to mark lines as guides for lacing.

Awl - for marking locations where holes are to be punched.

Spacing wheel - for marking equally distant spaces on the leather before punching holes for sewing.

CUTTING TOOLS

Cutting and shaping of leather requires special knives, shears, gouges and chisels. You will need the following:

Skiving knife - for cutting and thinning the edges of leather. It works equally well on any thickness of leather, but it must be kept sharp.

Shears - for cutting all weights of leather. Lightweight leather may be cut with a pair of household scissors.

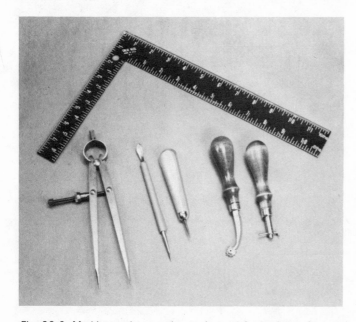

Fig. 20-2. Marking and measuring tools used for leathercraft work include: Top. Metal square. Below, left to right. Dividers, tracer modeling tool, awl, spacing wheel and double line marking tool.

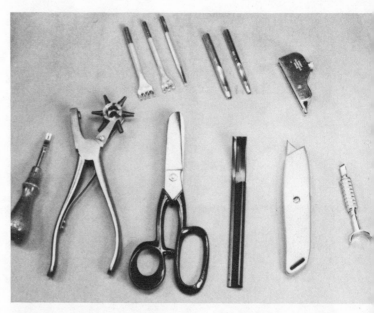

Fig. 20-3. Leathercraft cutting tools needed. Left to right, top row. Thonging chisels (three kinds), punches and edge beveler. Bottom row. Gouge, revolving spring punch, shears, skife, skiving knife and swivel carving knife.

Skife - for skiving or thinning leather edges which are to be joined.

Swivel carving knife - to cut the outline of a pattern into the leather. It is the most important of all leather carving tools.

Gouge - for cutting grooves in the leather or for thinning areas for proper folding.

Thonging chisel - for punching slits or holes through leather for lacing. This tool may have one or more prongs.

Edge beveler - to cut away portions of the edges of leather in preparation for the edge creaser.

Revolving spring punch - for punching holes through leather. It produces six different sizes of holes.

OTHER TOOLS

A number of tools are needed which perform special miscellaneous functions:

Mallet - needed to flatten rubber-cemented leather seams and to tap a thonging chisel or awl through leather when forming holes or slits for sewing. The head of this tool should be made of leather, wood or synthetic materials.

Modeling tools - for compressing small areas of a design on leather.

Edge creaser - for rounding edges of leather which are not going to be laced.

Snap button set - attaches segma and bird-cage snap buttons.

Eyelet setter - for setting eyelets into leather.

Fid - used for opening thong slits.

Lacing needle - used for lacing pieces of leather together.

SADDLE STAMPS

Certain tools produce an imprint that beautifies leather and leaves a design on it. Each has its own special name and purpose:

Background tools - designed to stamp down leather around the design to the depth of the swivel cuts. This activity increases the three-dimensional effect of the design. Many sizes, shapes and textures are available.

Bevelers - used for sloping down one side of the swivel knife cut. This, too, provides a three-dimensional effect. Some have a smooth, burnished surface; other have a textured surface. Available in many sizes.

Camouflage - for decorating stems, leaves, flower petals and fern swirls. It represents veins and folds. Crescent shaped, it is available in several sizes.

Pear shader - produces dished or pear-shaped impressions in flower petals and leaves. Shaped like a tear drop or pear, this tool is available in smooth or textured surfaces and in many sizes.

Veiners - add veins to leaves and produce other decorative effects. Available in several sizes, shapes and curves.

Stops - designed to beautify the end cuts of flowers, stems and leaves. Wedge-shaped, they are made in several sizes with smooth or textured surfaces.

Seeder - makes seeds in flower centers and fern swirls.

Mulefoot - produces a U or V-shaped depression for decorating leaf and flower stems and in front of stop cuts.

Fig. 20-6 shows impressions made with leather stamping tools.

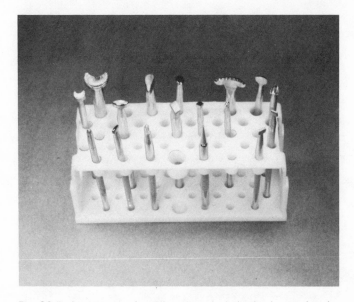

Fig. 20-4. These leathercraft tools are useful. Clockwise beginning at upper right. Lacing needles, eyelet and rivet setters, adjustable creaser, edge creaser, fid, mallet, eyelet setter, dot and grommet setters with anvil, snap button assembly, modeling tools.

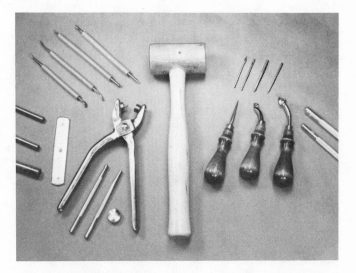

Fig. 20-5. Assortment of saddle stamps includes background tools, bevelers, camouflage tools, pear shaders, veiners, stops, mulefoot tool and seeders.

Fig. 20-6. Variety of impressions can be made using readily available tools.   (Tandy Leather Co.)

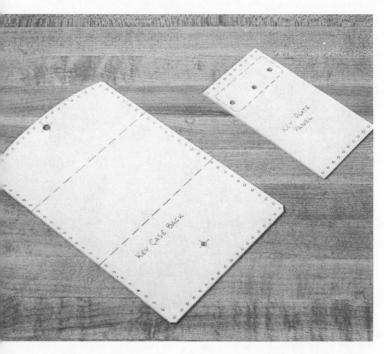

Fig. 20-7. Pattern for a key case is made from cardboard. Fold lines, hole locations and lacing holes are included.

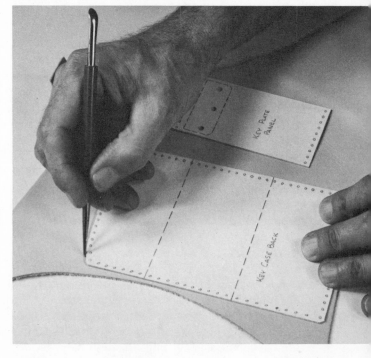

Fig. 20-8. Trace around the pattern with the tracer modeling tool.

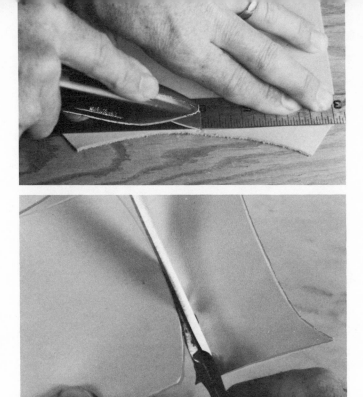

Fig. 20-9. Cut out the project using a straightedge and knife. Top. Use knife and straightedge for straight cuts. Bottom. Use shears for cutting curves.

CARVING AND STAMPING PROCEDURE

Before beginning any leathercraft project, gather the materials and tools for the job. Then follow these steps:

1. Make a template (pattern) from cardboard, nonferrous metal or plastics for each part of your project, Fig. 20-7. Draw the pattern directly on the template material or draw it on a piece of paper and cement the paper to stiffer material. Cut out the template very accurately. Drill holes wherever required and indicate folds. *Do not place your carving design on the template.*

2. Transfer the shape of each template to the proper type of leather, Fig. 20-8. Use a ballpoint stylus or tracing tool to trace the design. *Do not use a pencil or ballpoint pen on the leather. It leaves lines that cannot be removed.*

3. Cut out the leather with knife or shears, Fig. 20-9. Straight edges may be cut more accurately with the knife and a metal straightedge. Curves are easier to cut with shears.

4. Crease edges that will remain exposed before beveling, Fig. 20-10. Bevel those edges with an edge beveler, Fig. 20-11. Push the tool forward away from you.

5. Condition the leather by rubbing a damp (not wet) sponge on the flesh side as evenly as possible, Fig. 20-12. Then, turn the leather over and dampen the grain side (carving surface). The leather will turn a

darker color when wet. When it begins to return to its natural color, it is ready to be carved.

Having the right amount of moisture is important. If too wet, the leather will not hold tool marks. If too dry it will be difficult to tool. Should you be unable to complete the tooling in a single work session, seal the damp leather in a plastic bag to keep it moist. Store in a cool place to prevent molding.

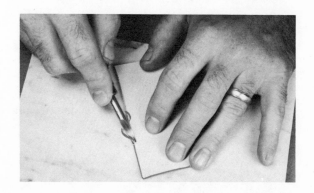

Fig. 20-10. Crease edges before beveling.

Fig. 20-11. Use edge beveler to dress exposed edges.

Fig. 20-12. Condition leather with damp sponge before you transfer design to project. Both sides must be dampened.

6. Transfer your design to the leather, Fig. 20-13. The design should first be drawn on thin tracing paper or clear plastic film (transfer film). Only the outlines of the design which are to be cut with a swivel knife are transferred. Use a ballpoint stylus, pencil or any instrument with a rounded point to retrace all the lines of the design. If transfer film is used, employ a flat tool to imprint the design. A thick piece of glass or marble makes a good backplate. Check the result of the tracing before removing your pattern, Fig. 20-14. Be careful not to mark or scratch the leather; when damp, it is highly sensitive to marks.

7. Practice using the swivel knife on scrap leather of the same kind and thickness as used in your project. Following these instructions should improve your use of the swivel knife:

a. Grasp the barrel with the thumb and middle finger. Place your index finger in the yoke. Place the little finger against the blade, or rest it on the surface of the leather. Fig. 20-15 shows the proper grip.

b. Turn the barrel with the thumb and middle finger to cut curves.

c. Rock the blade slightly forward to form the proper blade angle for cutting. The flat side of the blade must remain straight up at 90 deg. to surface of the leather.

d. The side of the hand or the little finger remains on the work surface to steady the cut.

e. Apply pressure downward with the index finger to embed the blade in the leather.

f. Move the work around with your free hand to make the cutting easier.

g. Press down harder for wider, deeper cuts.

h. Practice making straight cuts, flowing curves and circles, Fig. 20-16. Do not recut any lines to make them deeper.

Fig. 20-14. Lift transfer film occasionally to see if design is complete before removing the pattern.

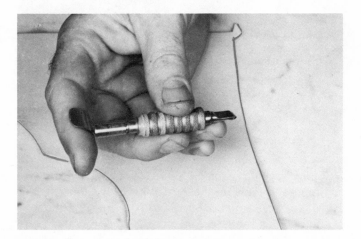

Fig. 20-15. Holding the swivel knife properly. Index finger provides downward pressure.

Fig. 20-13. You can transfer design to leather using plastic transfer film and modeling tool. Another method uses ballpoint stylus and thin tracing paper.

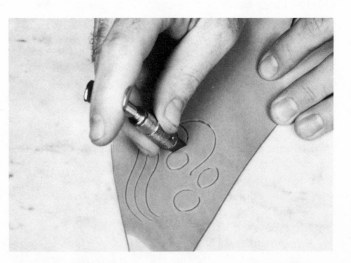

Fig. 20-16. Entering leather at proper blade angle. Free hand moves leather around for easier cutting. Make practice curves before beginning to carve your design. Sharpness of curve is controlled by turning workpiece.

With the damp leather placed on a marble or other hard, smooth surface, follow the design outlines with the swivel knife. Cut about halfway through the leather, Fig. 20-17.

8. The rest of the design is developed using saddle stamps. It is important that stamping be performed on a hard, smooth surface such as marble or glass. Again, it is advisable to practice with each stamp to determine the effect each produces.

USING SADDLE STAMPS

1. Camouflage the design with the camouflage tool.
   a. Hold the shank of the tool between your thumb, index and second finger in a vertical position. Rest your little finger on the surface of the leather to provide support.
   b. Begin at the base of a stem, fern swirl or leaf with the concave edge facing downward. Strike the tool with a mallet.
   c. Move the tool to a new location above the first and strike it again.
   d. Using uniform spacing, proceed toward the top of the stem, leaf or fern swirl. Use lighter blows as you move upward, Fig. 20-18.

2. Shade the design with the pear shader.
   a. Hold the pear shader as you did the camouflage tool, Fig. 20-19.
   b. Begin near the edge of a flower petal or leaf and strike a blow.
   c. Rock the tool along and gradually decrease the pressure on the mallet until you reach the center.
   d. Keep the shaded areas 1/16 to 1/8 in. (1.5 to 3 mm) away from the swivel cuts. Fig. 20-20 shows an area that has been shaded.

Fig. 20-18. Moon shaped impression on design was made with camouflage tool. It adds texture and a flow to design.

Fig. 20-19. Pear shader must be held properly to make an impression on the leather.

Fig. 20-17. Carve design outlines with swivel knife. Be careful not to cut too deeply.

Fig. 20-20. Shading is completed in two areas of design.

3. Bevel the design with the beveler tool.
   a. Hold the beveler in the same way as you did the two previous tools.
   b. Select the elements of your design which you wish to appear to be behind or under an adjacent element. Place the toe (thick portion) of the beveler in the swivel knife cut on the outside edge. Strike with the mallet, Fig. 20-21.
   c. Move the beveler along about a quarter of its width and strike again.
   d. Decrease the striking force as you reach the end of the cut. Be sure always to bevel away from the design elements that you wish to emphasize, Fig. 20-22.
4. Vein the design using the veiner tool.
   a. Hold this tool the same way as the other stamping tools.
   b. Begin near the base of a large leaf and place one side of the veiner next to the center rib of the leaf. The concave side should face downward, Fig. 20-23.
   c. Tip the veiner about 30 deg. and strike it firmly.
   d. Move the stamp along making impressions at regular intervals. Do not stop until you reach the top of the rib.
5. Add the flower centers with the seeder tool.
   a. Hold this tool in the same manner as the others.
   b. Begin on the outside edge of the flower center and strike the tool lightly with the mallet. The leather should be a little drier for this operation.
   c. Move the stamp to a new location and again lightly strike the tool. The seeds should not touch each other.
   d. Space the seeds uniformly in the flower center, Fig. 20-24.

Fig. 20-22. Beveling has been completed around part of design.

Fig. 20-23. Using veiner tool to decorate a leaf.

Fig. 20-21. Beveling of a portion of design has been completed along a swivel knife cut.

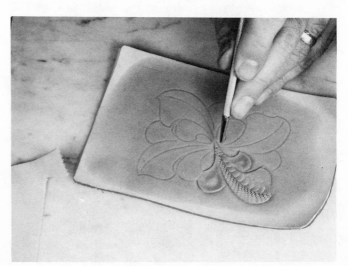

Fig. 20-24. Seeder finishes off decoration in center of design.

6. Further decoration may be added with the stop tool, Fig. 20-25, and the mulefoot stamp. Choose those stamps which produce the desired effect you wish for your design. Fig. 20-26 shows the stop and mulefoot application on the design. The ''V'' shaped depression is the mulefoot.

7. Background the design with the background tool.
   a. Begin next to the design outline with a wedge-shaped or half-round background stamp.
   b. Impressions should barely touch each other as you continue around the design. Be sure to use uniform pressure on the mallet.
   c. Fill in the background area between the design and the border, Fig. 20-27.

8. Make any decorative cuts that you wish with the swivel knife, Fig. 20-28.
   a. Dampen the leather again with a sponge or cloth. Be careful not to use too much water.
   b. Hold the swivel knife like you did to incise the design outline.
   c. Make decorative cuts inside flower petals and stems to add detail, Fig. 20-29. (Fig. 20-30 shows all of the basic steps involved in carving and tooling leather.)

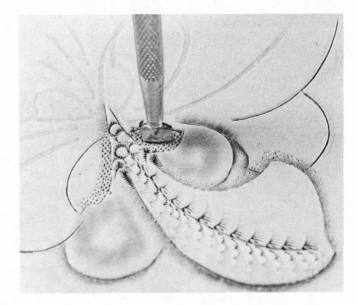

Fig. 20-27. Filling in the background with a background tool. This depresses areas not part of the design.

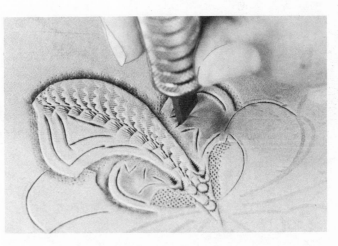

Fig. 20-28. Making decorative cuts with the swivel knife.

Fig. 20-29. Compare completed design with the pattern.

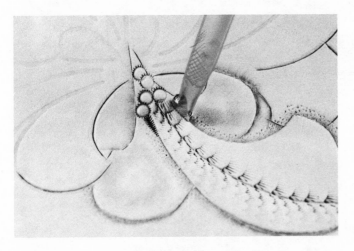

Fig. 20-25. Stop tool is used at end of swivel knife cut to accent line.

Fig. 20-26. Mulefoot stamp is used to accent leaf lines. It makes a V-shaped impression.

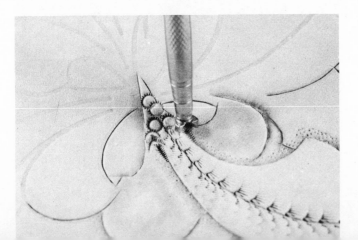

STEP 1. TRANSFER PATTERN   STEP 2. CUT DESIGN   STEP 3. CAMOUFLAGE

STEP 4. PEAR SHADE   STEP 5. BEVEL   STEP 6. VEIN

STEP 7. SEED   STEP 8. BACKGROUND   STEP 9. DECORATIVE CUTS

Fig. 20-30. Closeup photos of carving samples summarize the steps required for carving and tooling leather. Compare your work with these models.   (Tandy Leather Co.)

9. Clean the leather using oxalic acid, Fig. 20-31.
    a. Dissolve 1 tsp. (5 ml) of oxalic acid crystals in 1 pt. (500 ml) of warm water and shake well.
    b. Apply a coat of the acid to the leather using a sponge or small cloth. Use a light scrubbing action to clean stubborn stains.
    c. Clean the sponge and wash the leather surface with clear water to remove the acid from the leather. Note: Be very careful while using this chemical. Follow directions!
    d. Allow leather to dry for about 12 hr. before the next step.
10. Dye the background of the design using a camel hair brush, Fig. 20-32.
    a. Use a commercially prepared leather dye in a color of your choice.

b. Fill the brush and wipe excess dye on the inside edge of the bottle.

c. Begin by placing the point of the brush close to your design and pull it toward you. Follow the outline of the design but be careful not to get dye on the design itself.

d. Dye the background inside the design.

e. Allow the dye to dry before beginning the next step.

11. Apply a coat of leather finisher or leather dressing, Fig. 20-33.

a. Use a small cloth or woolskin to apply the finish. More than one coat may be used, if desired.

b. Let the finish dry thoroughly.

c. Apply a coat of neutral shade paste or shoe wax to the leather. Wait a few minutes, then polish with a soft cloth to develop the shine. This completed, the project is ready for assembly.

ASSEMBLING THE PROJECT

Assembly techniques and materials are important considerations in any leather article. Good quality snaps, key plates, eyelets and locks should be used since leather articles last for years.

SETTING SNAP FASTENERS

Many types and sizes of snap fasteners are available from leather supply dealers. Select one which will function best for the article you have produced.

To set a segma snap:

1. Select the proper setting tools (anvil plate and punches) for the size of snap fastener you plan to use. Find the proper size of punch on the revolving spring punch. If you are not sure of the hole size, punch several size holes in scrap leather first and test.

2. Punch a hole through the leather in the proper location, Fig. 20-34.

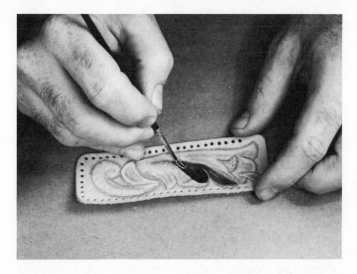

Fig. 20-32. Apply leather dye to a design with a camel hair brush.

Fig. 20-33. Applying a coat of leather dressing to the completed surface. Use a piece of woolskin or small cloth.

Fig. 20-31. Clean leather with oxalic acid solution.

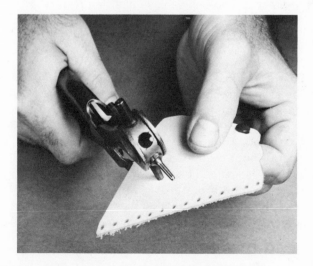

Fig. 20-34. Punching hole for snap with revolving spring punch. Be sure punch is positioned accurately.

3. Assemble the button and socket with the socket on the flesh side of the leather.
4. Use the large punch with the concave surface on top of the snap button to set the button and socket together as in Fig. 20-35. The socket is placed on the anvil plate. Use a mallet to strike the punch.
5. Place the eyelet through its hole from the grain side of the leather and position the assembly on the anvil plate, Fig. 20-36. Locate the stud on the eyelet and, using the correct punch, set the stud.
6. Try the snap to see if it works properly. See Fig. 20-37.

INSTALLING LEATHER LININGS

When all exterior pieces of leather have been carved and stamped and hardware has been installed, cut out and attach the lining. It is generally a good idea to make the lining slightly larger than the exterior piece so that it may be trimmed to fit exactly. Proceed to attach lining as follows:
1. Place the flesh side of the lining and exterior leather pieces face up on the workbench.
2. Apply a thin coat of rubber cement to each piece, Fig. 20-38.
3. When the cement is dry, carefully position the lining over the exterior piece as shown in Fig. 20-39. Avoid wrinkles. The cement will hold the pieces together until they are sewed or laced.
4. Trim away excess lining from the edges of the leather, Fig. 20-40.

LACING

Lacing finishes the edges of handmade leather products. The quality of the lacing job is very important to overall appearance. Follow the instructions. With a little practice you will achieve pleasing results.

Thonging

Before you can begin lacing, you must cut or punch holes around the edge of the project. This is usually done with a thonging chisel but a punch will do the job too.

First, mark a line with the double line marking tool or dividers about 1/8 in. (3 mm) from the edge, Fig. 20-41. This line will be used as a guide for thonging.

Place a smooth piece of wood (end grain) or thick rubber sheet under the leather when thonging. Begin at a corner with a four-prong thonging chisel, Fig. 20-42. Be sure to hold it vertical as you strike it with the mallet. Use a one-prong or three-prong chisel for curved areas. Drive the chisel through the leather the same depth each time to get uniform holes.

Fig. 20-35. Assemble button and socket using a punch and anvil plate. Socket must be on flesh side of leather.

Fig. 20-36. Set stud and eyelet with punch and anvil.

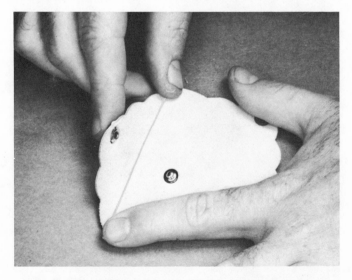

Fig. 20-37. Try out snap to see if it works properly.

Fig. 20-38. Installing linings. Apply rubber cement to each piece and allow to dry before attaching lining.

Fig. 20-39. Positioning lining and project piece for assembly. Lining should be slightly larger than the project. It is trimmed later.

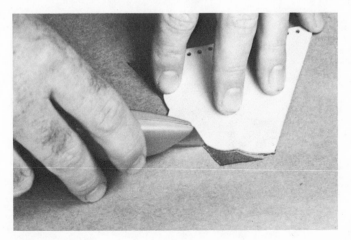

Fig. 20-40. Trim lining to size.

Fig. 20-41. Mark line with dividers to provide guide for thonging.

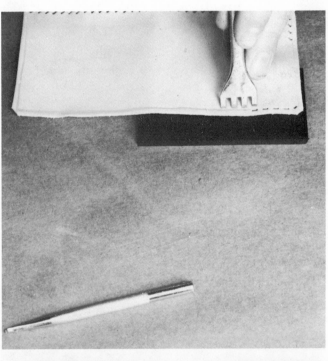

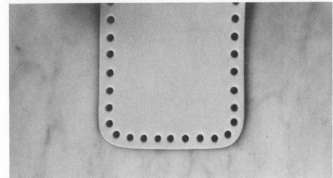

Fig. 20-42. Top. Punching lacing holes with thonging chisel. Hole was punched on corner of the demonstration piece with the one-prong chisel (lower foreground) to make neater lacing job on corner. Place end prong in last hole punched so that all holes will be evenly spaced. Bottom. Lacing holes for this leather project were made with revolving spring punch.

Threading the Needle

Select a two-prong lacing needle for most lacing jobs. Prepare the end of your lace by skiving off one end with a sharp knife, Fig. 20-43. Point the skived end and insert into the open needle as shown in Fig. 20-44. Tap the needle closed with a mallet and be sure that the prongs have pierced the lace.

Load the needle with about 2 yd. of lace each time. If longer pieces are used they will become worn and frayed.

Whip Stitch Lacing

1. Estimate the approximate amount of lace required. Measure the project and then triple the distance.
2. After threading the needle, pierce the opposite end of the lace. with a sharp knife. The cut should be about 1/8 in. long. See Fig. 20-45. You are ready for the first stitch.
3. Pull the two pieces of leather apart slightly and push the needle through the hole in the lining only. Draw the lacing through until about 1/4 in. of the slit end is left hanging out.
4. Moving over to the second hole, push the needle through both pieces of leather and the slit end of lacing as shown in Fig. 20-46.
5. Pull the first stitch tight, Fig. 20-47. Be sure that the lace is not twisted. Continue lacing, tightening each stitch as you proceed.
6. When you have laced around the project to the second hole from the beginning stitch, leave a loose loop. There should be one unlaced hole left between your first and last stitch.
7. Spread the layers of leather and push the needle through the last hole of the top layer. Guide the needle up between the layers of leather and through

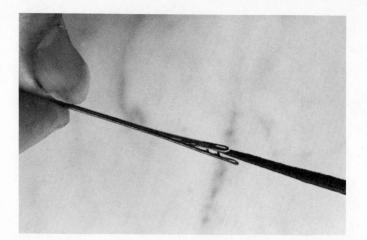

Fig. 20-44. Lacing is inserted over prongs of needle. Tap needle together with light blows of the mallet. Smooth side of lace should face the side of the needle with the longest prong.

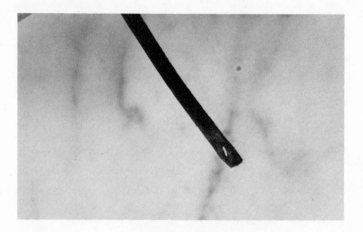

Fig. 20-45. Pierce tail end of lace with sharp knife for distance of 1/8 in. before taking first stitch.

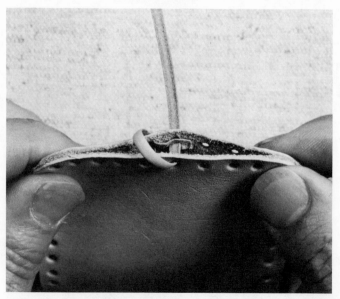

Fig. 20-46. Whip stitch, Steps 1 through 4. Lace is anchored through slit in the loose end.

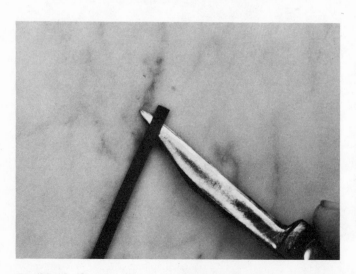

Fig. 20-43. Skiving off the end of lacing thins it to be inserted in the needle.

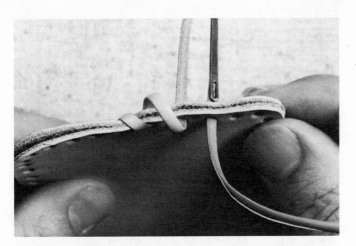

Fig. 20-47. Whip stitch, Steps 5 and 6. Make sure lacing is untwisted and tighten each stitch as you go.

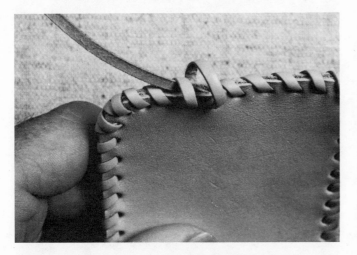

Fig. 20-48. Whip stich, Steps 7 and 8. End of lace has been pushed through last hole in facing leather. It is not passed through last hole of lining but comes out the top after being passed beneath last stitch made.

Fig. 20-49. Whip stitch, Step 9. Lace is ready to be cut off.

the first loose loop as in Fig. 20-48.

8. Tighten the first loose loop over the end of the lace.
9. Pull the lace tight to take the slack out of the last loop. Cut off the end of the lace, Fig. 20-49.

SINGLE LOOP STITCHING

1. Hold the project with the front facing you and begin on the top. Push the needle through from the front. Pull through all but about 3/4 in. (19 mm) of the lacing. Fold this end up and loop the lace around as shown in Fig. 20-50.
2. Lace through the second hole and pull the lacing snug, Fig. 20-51.

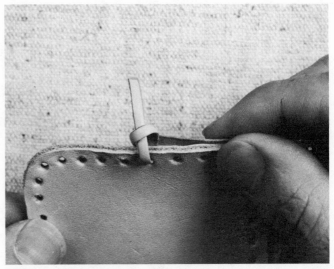

Fig. 20-50. Single loop stitch, Step 1. First loop goes around loose end of lace.

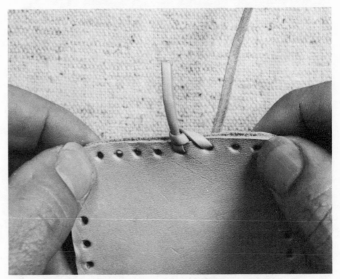

Fig. 20-51. Single loop stitch, Step 2. Do not pull loop too tight.

3. Push the needle under the lace as shown in Fig. 20-52 and pull up snugly.

4. Push the needle through the third hole and form another loop, Fig. 20-53. These first two stitches should not be pulled too tight. They must be adjusted when the lacing is completed.

5. Thread the needle through the last loop made to form the next stitch, Fig. 20-54. Continue threading and looping until you reach a corner.

6. At corners, lace through each hole two or three times to make a neat job of rounding the corner, Fig. 20-55. Continue the previous lacing procedure.

7. When a new piece of lace is needed to complete the project, it may be spliced. Allow 5 or 6 in. (127 or 152 mm) of lace to complete the splice. Start a new lace three holes from the old lace. Separate the leathers slightly and push the newly threaded needle down between the leathers through the hole in the lining. Pull the lace out the back side and leave an inch sticking up, as in Fig. 20-56.

8. Tuck the end of the new lace between the leathers and continue lacing the project with the old one. When you reach the new lace, push the needle through the front hole and up between the leathers, Fig. 20-57.

Fig. 20-54. Single loop stitch, Step 5. Pattern of loops can be seen.

Fig. 20-55. Single loop stitch, Step 6. Two corner holes are laced twice for smooth, rounded appearance.

Fig. 20-52. Single loop stitch, Step 3, is the beginning of second loop. Pull stitch up snugly.

Fig. 20-53. Single loop stitch, Step 4, completes second loop.

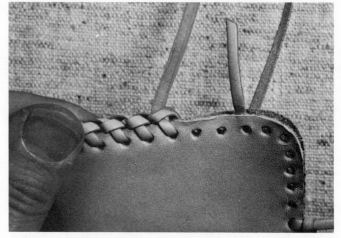

Fig. 20-56. Single loop stitch, Step 7. New lace has been started through hole of lining.

Fig. 20-57. Single loop stitch, Step 8. Last stitch with old lace is brought up between the leathers.

9. Pull the old lace tight and cut off the end of it at an angle. Leave a tail about 1 in. (25 mm) long. See Fig. 20-58.
10. Continue lacing your project with the new lace, Fig. 20-59.
11. Tuck the end of the old lacing between the leathers and lace over it so that it does not show, Fig. 20-60.
12. When you have reached the beginning point, lace through the last hole and under the loop, Fig. 20-61. Insert a stylus under the end of the beginning lace.
13. Pull the lace end out of the loop and leave the loop loose as in Fig. 20-62.
14. Insert the stylus between the leathers and pull the old lace end up through and between the leathers, Fig. 20-63.

Fig. 20-60. Single loop stitch, Step 11. Lace over the old lacing which is tucked between the leathers.

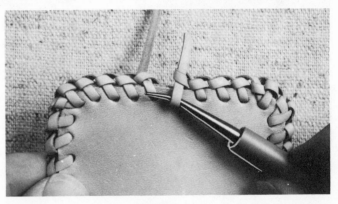

Fig. 20-61. Single loop stitch, Step 12. Use stylus to loosen beginning lace.

Fig. 20-58. Single loop stitch, Step 9. Old lace has been trimmed short. Cut is angled.

Fig. 20-62. Single loop stitch, Step 13. Lace end is pulled out of the loop and loop is left loose.

Fig. 20-63. Single loop stitch, Step 14. End of lace has been pulled out of hole and up between leathers.

Fig. 20-59. Single loop stitch, Step 10. First loop is made with the new lace.

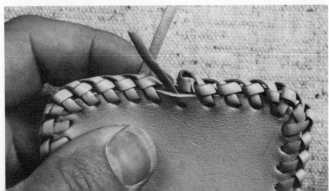

Crafts

15. Push the needle down through the loose loop as shown in Fig. 20-64.
16. Push the needle up through the hole where the old lace end was before and out between the leathers. The needle should be behind the newly formed loop, Fig. 20-65.
17. Tighten the stitches and adjust them to form an even row, Fig. 20-66. Cut off the ends and tuck them between the leathers.

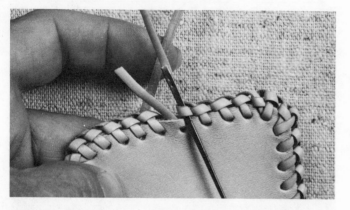

Fig. 20-64. Single loop stitch, Step 15. Bring needle down through empty loop.

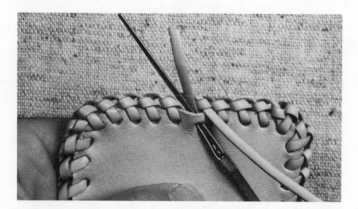

Fig. 20-65. Single loop stitch, Step 16. Final stitch brings needle up through hole and between leathers.

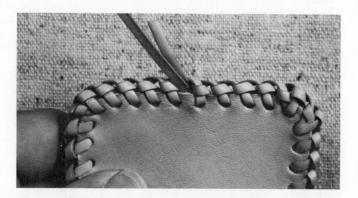

Fig. 20-66. Single loop stitch, Step 17. Lacing is nearly completed. Adjust last stitches for evenness.

SADDLE STITCHING PROCEDURE

Saddle stitching can be used on many craft projects. It is an excellent way to assemble leather parts when lacing is not desired.

1. You will need the following tools for saddle stitching: safety skiver, stitching groover, awl, overstitch tool, 2 needles and some nylon thread. First, skive the edge of the leather to reduce the thickness, Fig. 20-67. Next, gouge a line with the stitching groove about 1/4 in. (6 mm) from the edge of the leather pieces. The groove should be deep enough to contain the thread, Fig. 20-68.
2. Pull the overstitch tool along the groove, Fig. 20-69, to mark the spacing for the stitches.
3. Place the leather on a thick rubber mat and punch stitching holes with the awl, Fig. 20-70. Each hole should be the same diameter.
4. When several holes have been punched, thread a needle on each end of a length of thread. But do not thread it in the usual way. Instead, about 2 in. from the end of the thread, twist it apart slightly and run the needle through the opening with plies evenly divided on either side of the needle, Fig. 20-71. Thread the end into the eye of the needle.
5. Pull the thread up the needle and over the end, Fig. 20-72. Your needle is now threaded so thread will not pull out of the eye. Do the same thing on the other end of the thread.
6. Begin sewing by pushing one needle through the first hole. Pull through about half the length of thread. Now push the needle back through the second hole. Push the other needle through the second hole from the opposite direction. See Fig. 20-73.
7. Pull the thread tight from both sides to complete the first stitch, Fig. 20-74. Continue stitching in this manner until the project is finished.

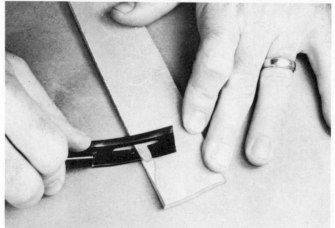

Fig. 20-67. Skive edge of leather with safety skiver to reduce its thickness.

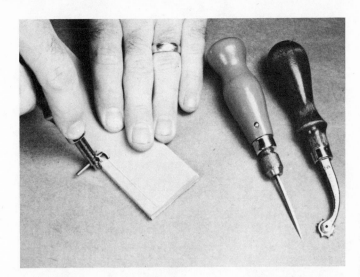

Fig. 20-68. Use stitching groover to gouge a groove for saddle stitching. Awl and overstitch tool are shown at right.

Fig. 20-69. Mark spacing for stitches with overstitch tool.

Fig. 20-70. Punch stitching holes through leather with diamond shaped awl.

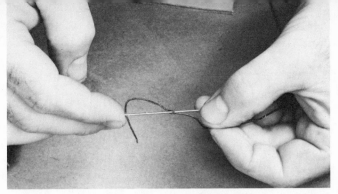

Fig. 20-71. Pass needle through strands of nylon thread. Then pass end through eye of needle.

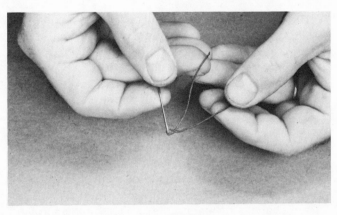

Fig. 20-72. Needle threading is completed. Short end will not slide out of eye.

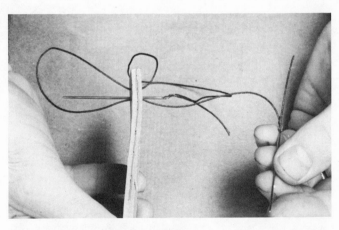

Fig. 20-73. Begin to stitch using two needles from opposite sides.

Fig. 20-74. Pulling the first stitch tight. Wrap thread around hands for better grip.

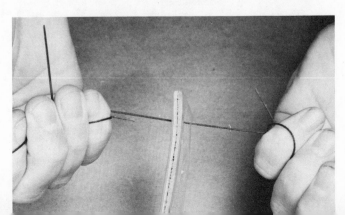

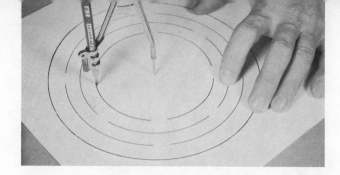

EXPANDED LEATHER

Expanded leather is produced by incising (cutting) flat pieces of leather so that they may be expanded into creative and useful forms as in Fig. 20-75.

You will need a piece of heavy, vegetable tanned leather, a sharp knife, a compass, dividers, awl or modeling tool, a No. 1 and No. 3 round drive punch, a mallet, dyes and finishes.

Fig. 20-76. Make a paper pattern for a hanging planter.

PROCEDURE

1. Draw a full size pattern on paper using a compass, Fig. 20-76. You may want to cut out the paper pattern and expand it to determine whether or not it produces a satisfactory design.
2. Dampen a piece of leather large enough for your project and trace the pattern on the leather with an awl or modeling tool, Fig. 20-77. Be sure to indicate the location of holes.
3. Retrace the lines on the leather using a pair of dividers for greater accuracy, Fig. 20-78.
4. Using a No. 1 drive punch or a revolving punch, make holes at the ends of each line. This reduces the chances of tearing the leather while improving the overall appearance. See Fig. 20-79. Use a No. 3 punch for thong holes if you plan to hang the article using thongs.
5. Cut carefully along each of the lines with a sharp knife as in Fig. 20-80.
6. Apply a finish to the grain side, flesh side and edges. See Fig. 20-81.

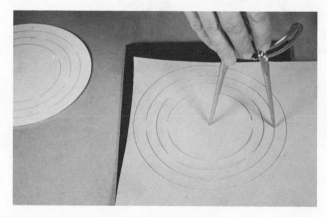

Fig. 20-77. Trace pattern on dampened leather. (Tandy Leather Co.)

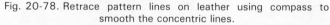

Fig. 20-78. Retrace pattern lines on leather using compass to smooth the concentric lines.

Fig. 20-75. These attractive craft projects were made using expanded leather techniques.   (Tandy Leather Co.)

Fig. 20-79. Punch hole at end of each line to reduce tearing. Use a No. 1 drive punch or a revolving punch.   (Tandy Leather Co.)

7. While it is still damp, expand the leather over a bottle or can to shape it, Fig. 20-82. Allow the article to dry in this position.
8. Attach thongs to your project if you plan to hang it up, Fig. 20-83.

Bands, belts and similar articles may also be made of expanded leather.

LEATHER SCULPTURE

Leather sculpture is the exciting craft of forming shapes out of vegetable tanned cowhide, Fig. 20-84.

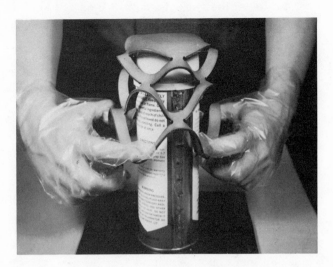

Fig. 20-82. Expand leather over a can. It should remain in this position until dry. (Tandy Leather Co.)

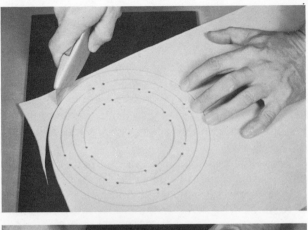

Fig. 20-80. Cut out pattern with a sharp knife. Top. Removing excess leather. Bottom. Cutting concentric lines. (Tandy Leather Co.)

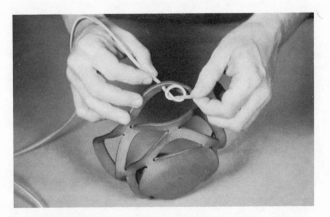

Fig. 20-83. Attach thongs for hanging planter.

Fig. 20-84. Stylized masks were formed from sections of vegetable tanned cowhide.

Fig. 20-81. Apply finish to project.

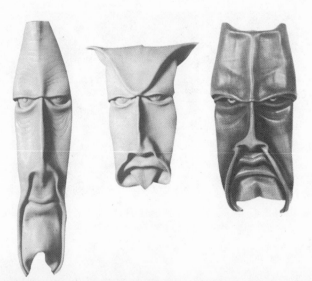

Few tools are needed even if you wish to add fine detail to your creation. Your hands are the primary tools.

1. Think of a basic form which you wish to develop.
2. Pick the size and weight of leather needed to fashion this article. If the project involves deep, sharp folds, then select a light 3-5 oz. (85-142 g) natural leather. Heavier leathers may be used if less contouring and folding is to be done.
3. Dampen the leather as you would for carving and let it dry until most surface moisture has evaporated. Leather that is too wet will not hold its shape. Leather too dry will not bend properly.
4. Fold and shape the leather until you have a sculpture which appeals to you, Fig. 20-85. Generally, it is best to begin at one end and work toward the opposite end. Details may be added with the modeling spoon, Fig. 20-86. Let the leather dry before adding details so that it will retain its shape.
5. Apply a finish if desired. You may also wish to apply spray varnish to the back of the sculpture to make it more durable and rigid.

LEATHER ART

Leather art is the creation of pictures, panels and plaques using leather glued to a backing. The leather used for these works of art may be any type of leather product depending on your design idea. The background material may be masonite, plywood, barn boards or fabric covered backing. The leather designs are attached with transparent white glue. Leather dye, paint, lacquer or spray-on varnish may be used as a finish.

PROCEDURE

1. Cut the backing or panel to proper size and frame if desired.
2. Plan content, size, backing, framing and materials needed for your art piece. Rough out the design on a piece of paper, Fig. 20-87.
3. Cut out the leather parts as shown in Fig. 20-88.
4. Glue the larger pieces into place. Be careful not to get any glue on the faces of the leather pieces, Fig. 20-89.
5. When the glue has dried on the large pieces, glue remaining pieces in place. Features may be modeled and formed into shapes to add realism if the design requires it. Acrylic paint or dye may be used to achieve an interesting effect, Fig. 20-90.
6. Spray with a clear protective finish. Fig. 20-91 shows the completed project.

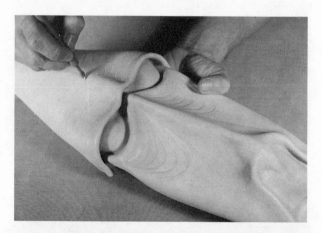

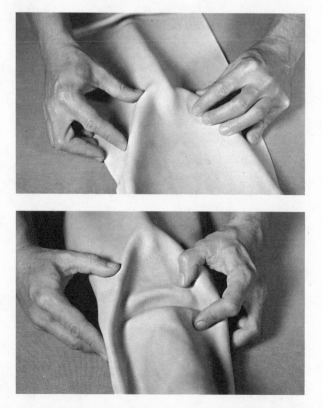

Fig. 20-85. Folding a piece of 4-5 oz. (113-142 g) Live Oak leather to make a mask. Begin at one end and work toward the other end.

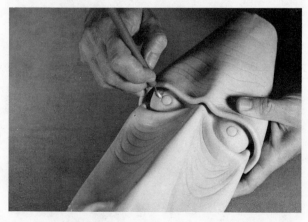

Fig. 20-86. Add details to the mask with a modeling tool.
(Tandy Leather Co.)

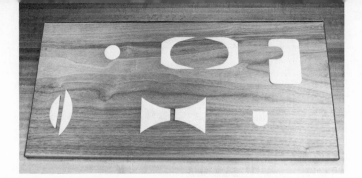

Fig. 20-87. Main elements of the design are cut from paper and roughly positioned on the backing to get an idea how the finished design will look.

Fig. 20-88. Leather parts have been cut out and are ready to be attached to backing.

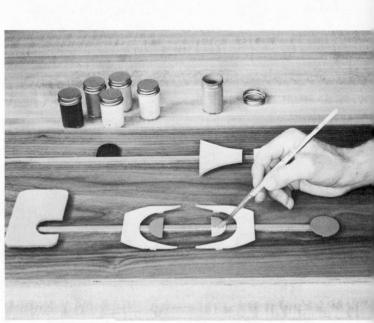

Fig. 20-90. Acrylic paints are used to add color to the design.

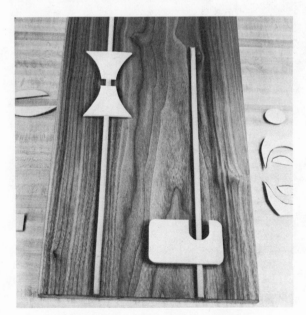

Fig. 20-89. Glue pieces in place.

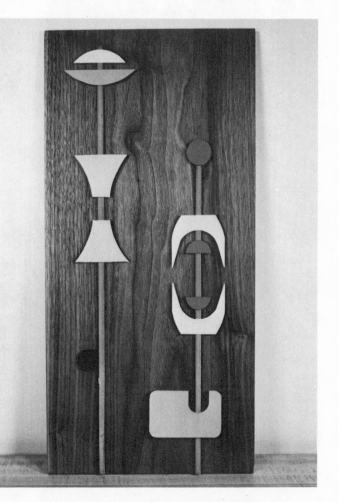

Fig. 20-91. Completed leather art project.

Suggestions for macrame projects. A—Christmas tree ornaments made from beads held together with macrame. B—Macrame pig formed on metal rings. C—Complex hanging planter incorporating all the macrame knots. D—Macrame cat wall hanging. (Peggy Nixon) E—Christmas tree ornaments made from linen cord. F—Wall hanging planter. G—Towel holder with plastic rings and accent beads. H—Lady's purse. I—Macrame border for mirror. J—Decorative necklace using common macrame knots and beads.

Chapter 21
MACRAME

Macrame is the knotting of threads or cords to produce decorative and functional craft items. Though it may look complicated, macrame is quite simple and easy to learn. There are a few basic knots and several variations to be remembered. Once you learn these knots, you can design and fabricate an endless variety of beautiful projects. Among them are jewelry, hanging planters (Fig. 21-1), wall hangings and clothing.

MATERIALS

Macrame materials should be flexible enough to be knotted but not so stretchy that they lose their shape. They may, therefore, include a wide range of cords, as Fig. 21-2 illustrates.

Some cords are not very satisfactory for knotting because they are difficult to handle, because knots tend to slip or because fibers are too fuzzy. Flat leather lacing is hard to control and therefore not a good material for knotting. Nylon cords tend to slip, and knitted worsted yarns are usually too fuzzy and elastic.

Jute is a very popular material for macrame projects. It is economical, available in a wide range of colors and sizes and it knots well. Its main disadvantage is that it will fade when exposed to natural light for long periods of time.

Seine twine (pronounced "sane") is an excellent material and highly recommended. Though stiffer than most twine, it ties well. Other heavier cords, ropes and

Fig. 21-1. This little hanging planter is a good macrame project that is not too hard for a beginner.

Fig. 21-2. These macrame cords are suitable for a wide variety of projects. Left to right: Waxed linen, soutache, heavy rattail, four-ply Thai jute, heavy Thai jute, masons' line, linen, macra-cord, navy cord, waxed nylon, cotton glow cord, macra-line, natural jute and sisal.

twines may also be used successfully.

Linen is a high-quality knotting yarn available in a wide range of colors, weights and textures. It combines well with other materials.

Homespun yarns are more difficult for the beginner to use. They add interest to certain macrame projects, however.

TOOLS

Fig. 21-3 shows the tools and some of the yarns. They are few and simple. A good pair of scissors will be needed for cutting yarns and cords. A measuring device, such as a scale or flexible tape, is a necessity for measuring cord lengths and design features. T pins hold the work in place on a knotting board during construction. The knotting board provides a working surface. It may be purchased or fabricated from a piece of Celotex (fiberboard) or similar material. A covering of grid paper will be useful.

Knotting boards vary in dimensions depending on the size of the project. A good selection of sizes includes 12 x 24 in., 20 x 36 in. and 24 x 48 in. Boards should be lightweight, rigid and soft enough that a pin may be inserted easily.

MACRAME KNOTS AND TERMS

Common macrame knots must be learned before beginning a project. The knots will be explained and illustrated so you may practice them and build confidence. It is helpful to make samples of each knot and its variations as a reference for future work. Use white or natural colored cord for these knots so they will be easier to see.

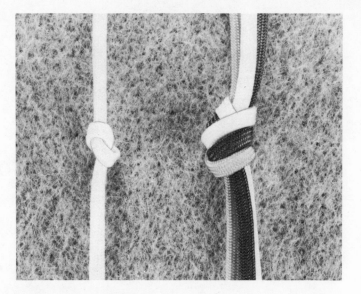

Fig. 21-4. The overhand knot is a basic macrame knot. It may be used to hold several cords together, to create texture, or to end a chain of knots.

Fig. 21-5. Top. Tying a lark's head knot. Bottom. Tying a reversed lark's head knot.

Fig. 21-3. Basic macrame tools—scissors, flexible tape, T pins, knotting board, rings and cords.

OVERHAND KNOT

The overhand knot in Fig. 21-4 may be used to:
1. Hold together a series of cords (called ends).
2. Create texture.
3. End a sinnet. (A sinnet is a chain of similar knots.)

The overhand knot is formed by making a loop and then passing the end through the loop and pulling tight. The procedure is the same when several ends are tied at once.

LARK'S HEAD KNOT

The lark's head knot, or reversed double half hitch, is used to mount ends on a holding cord. To tie it:
1. Find the center of the working cord (this is the cord used to form the knot). Double it to form a loop as in Fig. 21-5. Place the loop over the holding cord.
2. Bend the loop around the holding cord.
3. Put the ends through the loop.
4. Pull the ends tight to complete the knot.

REVERSED LARK'S HEAD KNOT

1. Find the center of a working cord and double it to form a loop as shown in Fig. 21-5. Place it under the holding cord.
2. Bring the loop down in front of the holding cord.
3. Put the ends through the loop.
4. Pull the ends tight to complete the knot.

HALF KNOT

The half knot is basic to macrame. It is tied using three or more cords. The center cord or cords are called filler or core ends. The two outside cords are working or tying cords. To tie the half knot:
1. Place the left working cord (cord 1) over cord 2 and under cord 3 as shown in Fig. 21-6.
2. Place cord 3 under cord 2 and up through the loop formed by cord 1. Pull the outside cords tight completing the knot.

HALF HITCH

The half hitch is another basic macrame knot. It is very practical because it lends itself to a number of variations. Fig. 21-7 shows how to tie it.

DOUBLE HALF HITCH

The double half hitch is made up of two half hitches. The second is tied exactly the same as the first. See Fig. 21-8.

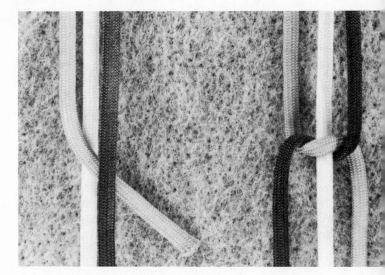

Fig. 21-6. Tying the macrame half knot using three cords.

Fig. 21-7. The half hitch is a simple loop around a second cord.

Fig. 21-8. The double half hitch is made up of two half hitches.

REVERSED DOUBLE HALF HITCH

The reversed double half hitch is also two half hitches. The second half hitch is reversed as shown in Fig. 21-9.

SQUARE KNOT

A square knot is made from two half knots—one right and one left. Four ends are generally used, however more than two core cords may be used. To tie it, refer to Fig. 21-10 and follow these instructions:
1. The two outside or working cords, are 1 and 4. Cords 2 and 3 are the inner cords or core. Place working cord 1 over inner cords 2 and 3 and under working cord 4.
2. Place working cord 4 under the inner cords 2 and 3 and up through the loop formed by cord 1. Pull tight.
3. Place cord 1 over cords 2 and 3 and under cord 4.
4. Place cord 4 under cords 2 and 3 and up through the loop formed by cord 1. Pull tight.

Look closely at the square knot in the illustrations. On one side of the knot the cord appears as a "parenthesis" or curved bar. The rest of the knot appears as a loop through which the other cord passes. It does not matter on which side the bar appears. Fig. 21-11 shows it both ways.

HALF KNOT SPIRAL

Tie a series of half knots all from the same direction, Fig. 21-12. After about five to seven half knots, the work will begin to twist. Without removing the T pins holding the ends, reverse the working cords by turning the knots over in the direction of the twist. Continue making half knots and turning them in the same direction. Do not stop until the desired length is reached. Fig. 21-13 shows an example of a half knot spiral.

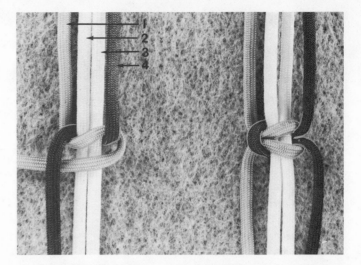

Fig. 21-10. How to tie a square knot. Left. Half the knot has been tied and cord 1 has been brought back over the filler cords to start the second half knot. Right. Cord 4 has been crossed under filler cords and pulled through loop of cord 1. Knot is completed.

Fig. 21-11. Square knot may be tied with bar on left or right as shown here.

Fig. 21-12. This series of half knots is tied from the same direction.

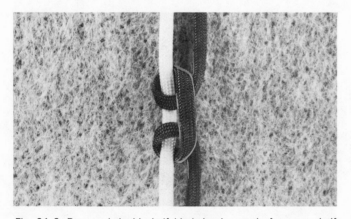

Fig. 21-9. Reversed double half hitch is also made from two half hitches. One hitch is reversed.

SQUARE KNOT SINNET

A square knot sinnet is a series of square knots tied one after the other. Fig. 21-14, as well as Figs. 21-12 and 21-13 are examples.

THE CARRICK BEND

The carrick bend consists of two intertwined loops of cord. It makes an attractive ornament either alone or with other knots. Fig. 21-15 shows how to tie it.
1. Place two cords side by side. The left one is cord 1; the right one is cord 2.
2. Grasp and lift cord 1 at the point where you want the knot to be.
3. Grasp cord 2 by its lower end and start to form a second loop in a clockwise direction.
4. Swing the loop over the top of the lower end of cord 1, then under the upper end of cord 1.
5. Continue over the topside of the loop of cord 1. Go underneath the portion of cord 2 that lies under the loop. Then pull the end of cord 2 back out of the loop.
6. Adjust the knot for best appearance.

Tying the carrick knot becomes easier if you remember to alternately go over or under as you cross each cord.

This knot looks best left loosely tied. It is very decorative when two cords are used on each side. Then, it is known as a double carrick bend.

PICOTS

There are several ways of mounting cords on a holding cord. Two methods, the double half hitch and the reversed double half hitch, have already been discussed. Two other relatively easy methods are the double half hitch with picot and a series of picots as

Fig. 21-13. When several half knots have been made from the same direction, they will begin to twist into a spiral such as this.

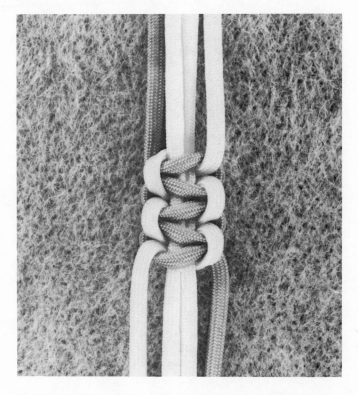

Fig. 21-14. Square knot sinnet is pleasing because of the repetition of the same bars and loops.

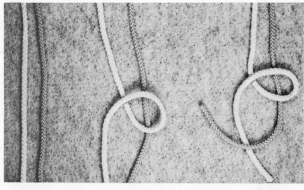

STEP 1 STEP 2 STEP 3

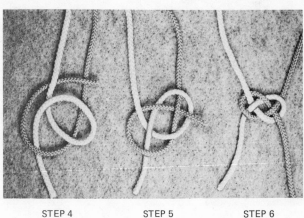

STEP 4 STEP 5 STEP 6

Fig. 21-15. Steps for tying the carrick bend or Josephine knot.

shown in Fig. 21-16 and Fig. 21-17. (A picot is a looped knot which produces a lacy effect.) It may be used with most knots. Fig. 21-18 shows a series of square knot picots.

HORIZONTAL DOUBLE HALF HITCHES

The steps for tying a series of horizontal double half hitches are illustrated in Fig. 21-19 through Fig. 21-23. Follow these instructions:

1. Attach several working cords to a mounting cord using the lark's head knot. Cord 1 on the left side is called the knot bearer. A knot bearer is the unknotted cord over which the working cords are tied. Place cord 1 horizontally across the working cords as in Fig. 21-19 and tie a half hitch on it with cord 2.
2. Complete the double half hitch on cord 1, the knot bearer. See Fig. 21-20.
3. Repeat steps 1 and 2 using cord 3, 4, and so on until all have been used as in Fig. 21-21.
4. Return by tying a second row using the same procedure. See Fig. 21-22 and Fig. 21-23.

VERTICAL DOUBLE HALF HITCHES

Fig. 21-24 through Fig. 21-27 illustrate the steps.

1. Using cord 1, tie a double half hitch on cord 2. Fig. 21-24 illustrates how to begin.
2. Again, using cord 1, tie a double half hitch on cord 3, 4, 5 and so on, until the end is reached, Fig. 21-25.
3. Return by tying a second row using the same procedure. Refer to Fig. 21-26.
4. Begin the third row as you did the first, Fig. 21-27.

Fig. 21-17. Series of picots. As many as desired may be used to form a design.

Fig. 21-18. Square knot picots have been tied along filler cords.

Fig. 21-16. Double half hitch with picot. A picot is a looped knot which produces a lacy effect.

Fig. 21-19. Step 1 in tying a horizontal double half hitch. First half hitch was tied low to allow working room.

Fig. 21-20. Step 2. First horizontal double half hitch is tied.

Fig. 21-24. Step 1. Beginning series of vertical half hitches. Each cord except the first is a knot bearer.

Fig. 21-21. Step 3 in tying a horizontal double half hitch. First row has been completed.

Fig. 21-25. Step 2. Vertical half hitches begin to create a pattern.

Fig. 21-22. Step 4. Beginning second row of horizontal double half hitches. Row is made in opposite direction.

Fig. 21-23. Step 4. Second row of horizontal double half hitches is now completed.

Fig. 21-26. Step 3. Second row of vertical half hitches is started.

Fig. 21-27. Step 4. Begin third row in series of vertical half hitches.

DIAGONAL DOUBLE HALF HITCHES

The following instructions are illustrated in Figs. 21-28 through 21-31.

1. Cord 1 is the knot bearer. Angle it down and to the right across the top of the other working cords. Using cord 2, tie a double half hitch on cord 1 as in Fig. 21-28.
2. Using cord 3, tie another double half hitch on cord 1. Continue this procedure until the end is reached, Fig. 21-29.
3. Cord 2 becomes the knot bearer for the second row. Angle the cord down to the right across the working cords as you did in the first two steps. Using cord 3, tie a double half hitch on the knot bearer (cord 2) as in Fig. 21-30. Complete the row by tying all cords in the same way.
4. Continue the same procedure for the next row, Fig. 21-31, using cord 3 as the knot bearer.

STARTING A PROJECT

If this is your first experience with macrame, you should begin with a simple project such as the hanging planter pictured in Fig. 21-1, or a wall hanging. Plan your project by deciding:

1. Knots to be used.
2. Type, size and color of cord.
3. Kinds of rings, beads and other things.
4. Amount of cord needed.

Collecting the materials in proper sizes and quantities

Fig. 21-30. Step 3. Cord 2 becomes knot bearer for second row of diagonal double half hitches.

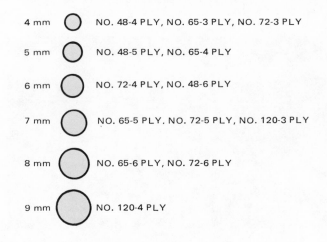

Fig. 21-31. Step 4 in tying a series of diagonal double half hitches. Note that cord 3 has become the knot bearer.

4 mm	○	NO. 48-4 PLY, NO. 65-3 PLY, NO. 72-3 PLY
5 mm	○	NO. 48-5 PLY, NO. 65-4 PLY
6 mm	○	NO. 72-4 PLY, NO. 48-6 PLY
7 mm	○	NO. 65-5 PLY, NO. 72-5 PLY, NO. 120-3 PLY
8 mm	○	NO. 65-6 PLY, NO. 72-6 PLY
9 mm	○	NO. 120-4 PLY

Fig. 21-32. Comparative cord sizes of jute. These are the exact sizes of the cord.

Fig. 21-33. Methods of beginning macrame hangings. First example uses an overhand knot. Second is secured by winding smaller cord around main cords. Third example shows cords tied to metal ring covered with masons' line. Cords in last example are held together with series of square knots and then wrapped (whipped). The wrapping completes the eye.

Fig. 21-28. Step 1. Series of diagonal double half hitches is started almost like horizontal pattern.

Fig. 21-29. Step 2. Row is completed in series of diagonal double half hitches.

may concern the beginner. What size and how much? Fig. 21-32 shows a chart of comparative jute cord sizes.

Calculating the amount of cord required can be a problem. As a rule of thumb, plan for each end to be about four or five times as long as the piece you plan to make. Remember that each end will be doubled for knotting so they should be about eight to ten times as long as the project. When each end is doubled for knotting, it will then become two ends, each about four or five times as long as your project. It is better to waste a little cord than to end up short. After you have completed several articles, you will be able to make a more accurate estimate of the amount of cord needed.

With materials and tools collected and arranged, you are ready to begin. All hangings may be constructed with a loop at the top containing all the cords or attached to a ring, piece of wood or other device, Fig. 21-33. If you plan to make a hanging planter, consider using a welded metal ring because of a hanging planter with pot, plant and soil may weigh 30 or 40 lb.

When working with long ends, butterfly each cord by wrapping the end of the cord around your thumb and little finger in a figure eight pattern, Fig. 21-34. Slide the butterfly off your hand and place a rubber band around the center. The cord is easy to release as needed.

Use any of the knots described to form your design. Remember the design should be functional as well as decorative. For example, Fig. 21-35 shows the procedure for making a double half hitch circle which may be incorporated in your design.

When the project is completed, trim all the cords to the desired length. You may finish off by fraying each cord, tying an overhand knot in the end of each cord or by tying a bead on the end of each cord, Fig. 21-36. Use your imagination!

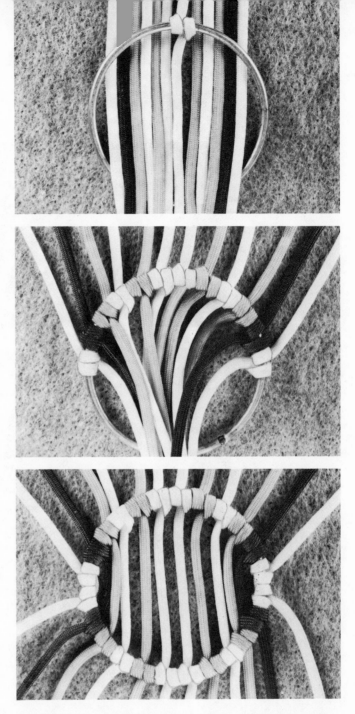

Fig. 21-35. Three steps in making a double half hitch circle. This decorative design may be incorporated in your project.

Fig. 21-34. Butterfly your cords to make them easier to handle.

Fig. 21-36. These are three methods of ending each cord in your macrame project.

185

Suggestions for other marquetry projects. A—Geometric design for jewelry box. B—Maple and walnut veneered checkerboard. C—Finely detailed marquetry using shades of veneer to suggest clouds. D—Wall plaque in mahogany and apple wood. E—Detailed floral marquetry picture. F—Cribbage board of walnut and maple veneer. G—Card table with 64 different woods making up playing surface. Border is walnut.

Chapter 22
MARQUETRY

An ancient craft, marquetry consists of building up an ornamental surface of thin wood veneers to form a pattern or picture, Fig. 22-1. The color and grain of beautiful woods from all over the world are readily available. Glued on flat boards they make delightful designs. Marquetry should not be confused with inlaying. In that craft, the veneer pieces are inserted into recesses cut in a wood panel. In marquetry, the baseboard is covered with veneer, forming designs much like a mosaic. It is easier than inlaying.

Since marquetry is a surface-covering process, it is well suited to craft projects like serving trays, jewelry boxes, chess and checkerboards, pictures or even a table top. Start with a simple pattern or picture—perhaps a geometric design—to develop your skills in cutting and fitting the veneer pieces.

MATERIALS

Two basic materials are required: an assortment of wood veneers and a baseboard of solid wood or plywood. Veneers, generally 1/28 in. (0.9 mm) thick, are available in a wide choice of colors. The range is from light tan to dark brown or purple tints to shades of red. Fig. 22-2 shows several beautiful grain patterns.

Walnut, mahogany, cherry and maple veneers pro-

vide a rich variety of colors for beginning projects. Veneer picture kits are also available at craft and hobby shops. The pieces have already been cut and assembled ready for gluing to the baseboard. While little craft skill is required to assemble the kit materials, they will give a beginner a feel for the process.

Other materials necessary for making your own projects are white glue, contact cement, masking tape, gummed brown paper tape and sandpaper, Fig, 22-3.

Fig. 22-2. Assortment of attractive veneers for marquetry includes both dark and light woods.

Fig. 22-3. Basic materials include gummed brown paper tape, white glue, contact cement, sandpaper, masking tape and paintbrush.

Fig. 22-1. Functional serving tray in marquetry.

TOOLS

Basic hand tools are all that are needed for marquetry, however, they must be used with extreme accuracy. You will need: a good steel rule, small blade knife, mat knife, straightedge, a hand roller, a notched cutting board, veneer saw and a fretsaw. Similar to a coping saw, the fretsaw has a very deep throat and a thin blade. The blade has extremely fine teeth so as not to tear the veneer. Fig. 22-4 shows some of the basic tools.

MAKING A MARQUETRY PROJECT

The critical steps in marquetry are cutting and closely fitting the veneer pieces into the final pattern. The "window method" is one of the best techniques. It can be used for both straight line and irregular shaped designs.

WINDOW METHOD

1. Draw a design full size. Keep lines simple. Each must be cut or sawed from the veneer! Select the colors of veneer for each area and write in the colors on your drawing if the design is complicated. From two to four colors usually look best.
2. Using carbon paper as in Fig. 22-5, trace your design onto a sheet of scrap veneer. This will make an exact pattern for you to follow as you cut out each piece of the design. (It is very difficult to cut out all the pieces for a design from the good veneers and then try to assemble them into the completed design. In this method, you will cut out one piece at a time, shape it, and glue it to the edges of adjoining pieces until the design is complete. This makes the fitting of one piece to another much more accurate.)
3. Starting at a corner, cut out one piece of the design from the scrap veneer, Fig. 22-6. If your design contains all straight lines, use only a sharp knife and straightedge. However, a fretsaw generally works best for most cuts, curves and straight lines. It seldom splits the veneer. When using a knife, make many light cuts with the tip until the veneer is cut through. This will make a better edge and helps prevent splitting of the veneer.
4. Select a piece of veneer of the color chosen for that part of the design. Apply moistened brown tape as in Fig. 22-7. Place the good veneer under the scrap veneer pattern. Use a sharp pencil to trace the pattern onto the brown tape, Fig. 22-8.
5. Cut out the marked veneer with a small blade knife or fretsaw, Fig. 22-9. Carefully follow the pencil line on the brown tape. (Do not cut away the pen-

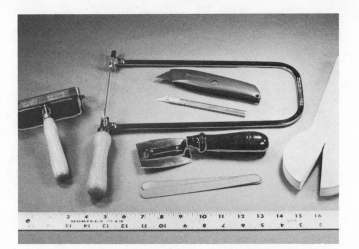

Fig. 22-4. These tools are needed for marquetry: fretsaw with mat knife and X-acto knife inside, hand roller, veneer saw, notched cutting board, emery boards and straightedge.

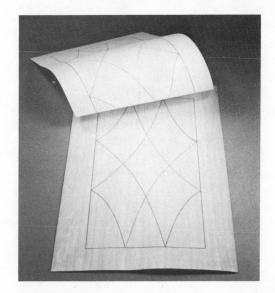

Fig. 22-5. Design is traced on sheet of scrap veneer. The scrap will become an exact pattern as each piece is cut.

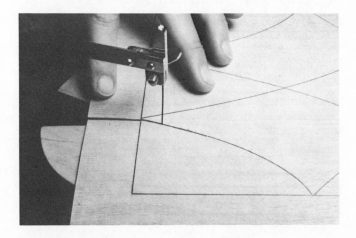

Fig. 22-6. First corner piece of design is cut from scrap veneer. Use fretsaw on notched cutting board. Follow line accurately.

cil line.) Fit the piece back into the opening in the scrap veneer. If it does not fit accurately, lightly sand the edges where it is too big for the opening. See Fig. 22-10. Use masking tape to hold the piece in position in the scrap veneer as shown in Fig. 22-11.

6. In the same way as before, cut out an adjoining piece of the design from the scrap veneer. Trace the shape of this new cutout onto your next color of veneer. Cut this piece out in the same manner. After it has been fitted to the opening, spread a small amount of white glue along the edge that mates with the first piece. See Fig. 22-12. Return

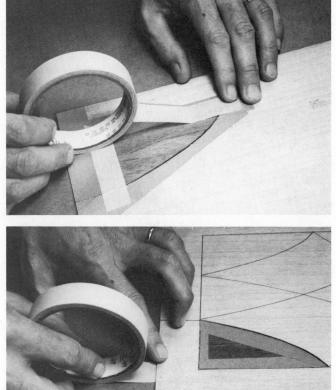

Fig. 22-10. Lightly sand edge of veneer piece with emery board to secure good fit.

Fig. 22-7. Apply gummed tape to veneer piece which will replace first corner piece in scrap veneer.

Fig. 22-8. Trace design through opening (pattern) in scrap veneer onto taped veneer.

Fig. 22-9. Cut out veneer piece along line on brown tape. Use fretsaw or sharp knife.

Fig. 22-11. Masking tape will hold first piece in position in scrap veneer. Top. Apply tape on back side. Bottom. Press tape firmly to edge as shown.

Fig. 22-12. Apply white glue to mating edge of second piece. A narrow piece of veneer makes a good glue spreader.

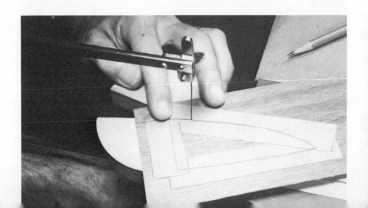

it to the opening so that it becomes glued to the mating edge of the first design piece as shown in Fig. 22-13. Apply masking tape to the joints on the back side to secure the piece in the scrap veneer and to keep glue off of your work area.

7. Continue the cutting and fitting steps with all adjoining pieces. Cut out each shape and glue it back into the scrap veneer. Do one piece at a time until the entire design is completed. If any of the scrap veneer is to be part of the design, glue the surrounding pieces to that section.

8. Remove masking tape from the back as each joint dries. The brown tape, used to trace your pattern, can also be peeled away from the face with a mat knife. Refer, again, to Fig. 22-13. Any paper that sticks is easily removed by sanding, Fig. 22-14, or dampening with a sponge when the design is finished.

Fig. 22-14. Remove remaining brown paper by sanding or rubbing with a dampened sponge.

Fig. 22-15. Press veneer onto plywood with roller after applying contact cement.

Fig. 22-13. Top. Glue and tape second veneer piece in place in the scrap veneer. Glue has been applied only to the mating edges of the first two pieces. Bottom. Carefully peel away brown tape from face with mat knife.

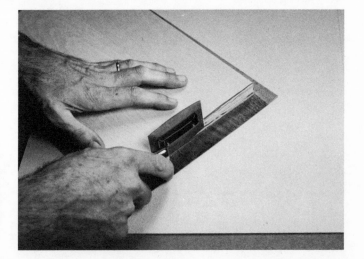

Fig. 22-16. Trim veneer flush with plywood edges. Use a veneer saw to avoid damage to the thin wood.

9. Make a baseboard for your design from a sheet of plywood. For the tray illustrated, cut 3/4 in. plywood the size of your design plus a 1 in. (25 mm) border on all sides. The baseboard should be covered with veneer on the underside and edges. Cut a sheet of veneer slightly larger than the baseboard. Apply two coats on contact cement to the underside of the baseboard and to the veneer. Allow to dry between coats and again after the second coat.

10. Attach the veneer to the back of the baseboard. *If you have never worked with contact cement, be very careful at this point. Once the two cemented surfaces touch, they bond immediately and cannot be shifted.* It is best to lay down overlapping strips of brown wrapping paper on one surface. Position the mating surface over the paper. Then, working from one end to the other, carefully remove one strip at a time bonding as you go. Apply pressure to the surface with a rubber roller as shown in Fig. 22-15. This will assure a tight bond.

11. Trim the veneer flush with the edges as shown in Fig. 22-16. Sand the edges, Fig. 22-17, so the veneer on the edges will conceal the bottom veneer. Cut and glue veneer strips to the edges in the same manner, Fig. 22-18. Trim and sand.

12. If your marquetry design is not square, trim it with a knife and straightedge as in Fig. 22-19. Make an attractive border from a light colored strip of veneer, about 1/8 in. wide. Glue it to a wider band of veneer that compliments the design colors. The border is generally made from the same veneer as that used for the back and edges. Cut the narrow and wide border strips and glue them together as shown in Fig. 22-20. Allow to dry. Border strips should be larger and wider than the baseboard.

13. Tape the border strips to the edges of the design as shown in Fig. 22-21. Cut miters at each corner,

Fig. 22-18. Glue veneer strip to edge of plywood with contact cement. Use care. Contact cement bonds instantly.

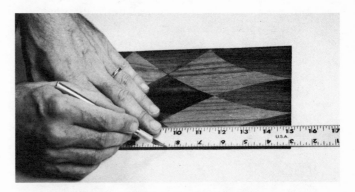

Fig. 22-19. Trim marquetry design square with knife and straightedge.

Fig. 22-20. Glue narrow and wide border strips together with white glue and hold in place with masking tape.

Fig. 22-21. Tape border strips to edges of design. Allow strips to overlap at the ends.

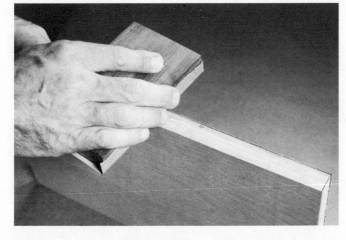

Fig. 22-17. Sand veneer back flush with edge of plywood.

Fig. 22-22, being sure to cut through both border strips to make a tight joint. Remove the masking tape and glue the border edges to the marquetry design.

14. When the edge glueing is dry it is time to attach the design to the base. With the design face down, center the baseboard within the border edges and make pencil marks at each corner. Apply two coats of contact cement to both the baseboard and the back of the design. Allow to dry between coats. When the second coat is dry, place the baseboard on the design in line with the corner pencil marks. Use great care so surfaces do not touch before they are in the right position. Turn the tray over and go over the entire surface with a roller, Fig. 22-23. Trim overhanging border veneer with a veneer saw and sand the edges smooth. Sand the surface smooth with a flat sanding block, Fig. 22-24. Sanding should be done with the grain.

Fig. 22-24. Sand surface smooth with wood block and fine garnet paper. Work with the grain.

Fig. 22-22. Make miter cuts on border veneers. Cut through both borders using knife and straightedge.

Fig. 22-25. Lacquer based sanding sealer provides one of the best finishes used in marquetry.

Fig. 22-23. Roll contact cemented surface veneer with rubber roller to insure good bonding.

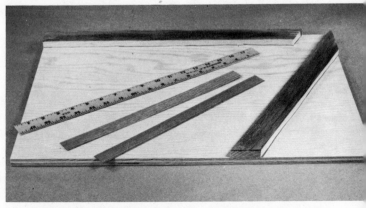

Fig. 22-26. Veneer cutting board is made of 3/4 in. plywood with one wood stop fastened at the bottom and another one at a 60 deg. angle to it along the side.

15. Many finishes are suitable for marquetry work. A penetrating oil finish, lacquer, synthetic varnish or a hard urethane produce beautiful results. Fig. 22-25 shows the application of a good synthetic sanding sealer finish. After two or three coats have been applied and allowed to dry thoroughly, polish with fine steel wool. The tray is then ready for use.

MAKING GEOMETRIC MARQUETRY DESIGNS

A number of projects in marquetry require cutting and fitting of veneer pieces into geometric patterns. Chess or checker boards are typical examples. The following procedure works nicely when using a knife and straightedge to cut straight-sided pieces.

1. A checker board requires eight squares along each side, a total of 64 squares. Half should be made from a dark colored veneer and half from a light color. Walnut and maple provide a good contrast. To cut the individual squares and fit them together accurately would be very difficult. However, the simple cutting board shown in Fig. 22-26 will help you make the cuts neatly and accurately.

2. Select a piece of straight grained veneer and trim one edge with the grain using a small knife and straightedge. Place this edge of veneer against the stop at the bottom edge of the cutting board. Place a metal straightedge, usually 1 1/2 in. wide, against stop on top of the veneer. With a knife, cut the first strip as seen in Fig. 22-27. Make many light cuts with your knife to produce a smooth edge. Remove the first strip and slide the veneer down against the stop and cut each additional strip in the same manner.

3. Apply glue to the edges of each walnut and maple strip. Glue all strips together alternating dark and light strips. Fasten with brown gummed tape as shown in Fig. 22-28. Tape the front side of the veneers since it can easily be sanded off later.

4. Square off one end across the strips, Fig. 22-29. Turn the piece and butt the square end against the bottom stop of the cutting board. Cut strips as shown in Fig. 22-30. The strips now contain dark

Fig. 22-27. Cutting veneer strips with knife. Straightedge and veneer are held against stop at bottom of cutting board.

Fig. 22-28. After edge gluing and butting strips, fasten them with brown gummed tape.

Fig. 22-29. Remove unevenness and square an edge across veneer strips with triangle and knife.

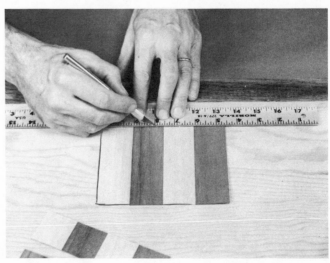

Fig. 22-30. Cut strips across the grain with knife and straightedge to form checker board squares. Tape has been removed for this picture.

and light squares which can be alternately reversed, glued and taped together, as in Fig. 22-31, to form a checker board pattern.

5. Make a border as described earlier. Mount the veneer on the base with contact cement. Fig. 22-32 shows a completed checker board.

6. Other designs can be made from the basic pattern of squares. Use a knife and straightedge and cut across the points of the dark and light squares as shown in Fig. 22-33 to form triangles. After several strips are cut, slide each one along half a square to form a zigzag pattern, Fig. 22-34. Other patterns, formed by sliding or reversing the strips, are shown in Figs. 22-35 and 22-36.

7. Diamond shaped patterns can be made by cutting dark and light strips using the 60 deg. angle edge of the cutting board as a guide, Fig. 22-37. By changing the width of the strips that are cut at an angle, a variety of diamondlike shapes can be produced, Fig. 22-38.

Fig. 22-33. Cutting across the points of dark and light squares with knife and straightedge forms a pattern of light and dark triangles.

Fig. 22-34. Arrange strips to make interesting shapes. Offsetting them half the width diagonally across the squares made this zigzag pattern.

Fig. 22-31. Reversing some strips, alternate dark and light squares to form checker board pattern.

Fig. 22-35. Interesting zigzag pattern of dark pieces is alternated with a chain of light colored squares.

Fig. 22-32. Completed checker board has walnut border and suitable supporting base. (Dave Baird)

Fig. 22-36. Every other strip of veneer can be reversed to form a pattern of triangles.

194

Fig. 22-37. Cutting diamond shaped strips using the 60 deg. angle edge of the cutting board, a knife and straightedge. One edge of veneer must be butted against bottom stop.

Fig. 22-38. An interesting geometric pattern formed by arranging strips to diamondlike shapes.

Alternate metal art projects. A—Aluminum wire sculpture. B—Hang glider of brass with horseshoe nail figure. C—Windmill sculpture from horseshoe nails. D—Horseshoe nail owl on natural wood background. E—Model of antique plane in brass. F—Brass horses on wood. G—Pendant of horseshoe nails. H—Antique car from brass sheet and rod. I—Flower lamp base made from metal. J—Gold cross necklace made from nails.

Chapter 23
METAL ART

Imagine making useful and decorative articles from scraps of sheet metal, nails, bolts, screws, washers and wire. These common items can open up a new exciting world of creativity. You can make Rube Goldberg-like creations, wall plaques, freestanding sculptures, jewelry and countless other useful products. The following sections on nail art, hardware figures and metal sculpture will get you started in the fascinating area of metal art.

NAIL ART

Nail art or nail sculpture, Fig. 23-1, is a unique way to make interesting compositions out of horseshoe nails. Made of soft steel, these nails may be shaped with hand tools and then soldered or glued together to form a finished art piece. Plaques, three-dimensional wall hangings, mobiles, pendants, freestanding sculptures and jewelry are but the beginning of an endless variety of home or personal decorations fashioned from the lowly horseshoe nail.

Fig. 23-1. This delicate necklace is a product of nail art.

TOOLS AND MATERIALS

These tools, shown also in Fig. 23-2, will be useful for most nail art projects:
1. Roundnose pliers—for bending a small radius on the end of smaller nails.
2. Needlenose pliers—for bending larger nails and for making angular bends.
3. Diagonal or side cutting pliers—needed for cutting pieces of wire to length.
4. Soldering gun, iron or small torch capable of producing 600 to 700 °F (316 to 371 °C)—necessary if you plan to solder nails together.
5. Silver solder and flux—preferred for fastening nails together. It is several times stronger than regular solder, will adhere to most metals and stays bright.

Fig. 23-2. Tools and materials needed to make horseshoe nail projects. Articles pictured include steel wool, side-cutting pliers, needlenose pliers, roundnose pliers, files, silver solder and flux, small torch, pipe and dowel pieces, a soldering brick, metal antique finish and a box of horseshoe nails.

6. Small, fine files (flat and round)—useful for removing excess solder and shaping parts.
7. Asbestos sheet or brick—used as a work area when soldering.
8. Steel wool—ideal for cleaning the nails before applying a finish or prior to soldering.
9. Pipe or wooden dowels (in assorted sizes)—for bending nails into larger circles.

In addition to the tools listed, you will need an assortment of horseshoe nails, Fig. 23-3. Although some craft supply stores stock these nails, they are generally hard to find. Harold Mangelsen and Sons, Inc., Omaha, Nebraska, is a large supplier of horseshoe nails and may be a useful source if you have difficulty finding them.

Some type of finish may be desirable. A clear acrylic spray is easy to apply and retains the natural character of the nails. A gold or silver leaf paint is attractive on some articles while a matte black spray is ideal on others. Experiment with the paint on a piece of scrap to be sure that it produces the effect you want.

MAKING NAIL ART OBJECTS

The general procedure for most nail art projects involves planning the project and selecting materials, bending the nails, soldering, applying the finish and displaying the completed work. Some helpful hints follow for each of these procedures. Hopefully, they will assist you in your first project.

Planning

1. Whether you make a project similar to one at the beginning of this chapter or design your own, make a sketch as close to the article's finished size as possible, Fig. 23-4. This will be helpful in making refinements and in visualizing the design.
2. Make a list of tools and materials required. Be sure that you have everything you need before you begin.
3. Select your work area and organize the materials and tools. A brick makes a good soldering surface.

Fig. 23-4. Project idea for three nails—one No. 6 and two No. 2. Each will be bent to the shape shown in the sketch.

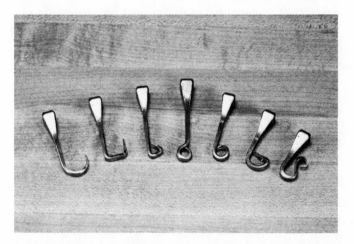

Fig. 23-5. Useful bends for making nail projects. Each is made with one of the pliers. First nail on left has been bent around a dowel rod to form a large radius.

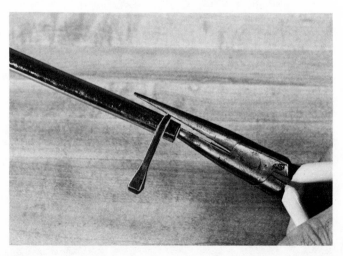

Fig. 23-6. Piece of pipe and large needle-nose pliers are used to bend large radius on nail.

Fig. 23-3. For metal art projects get a supply of horseshoe nails ranging in size from 1 7/8 in. (48 mm) to 3 1/4 in. (82 mm). Notice the variety in head shapes.

Bending Nails

1. Use the type of pliers best suited to produce the desired bend in the nails. Fig. 23-5 shows some of the typical bends.
2. A dowel or pipe may be used to produce larger bends. Fig. 23-6 shows a nail being bent on a small pipe.
3. Different size of dowels or pipes will produce a variety of standard size circles. Experiment before you begin your project.

Soldering

1. Silver-bearing solder and silver solder flux will produce the best results.
2. Be sure that nails are clean and dry before attempting to solder them.
3. Apply a small amount of flux to the surfaces to be soldered, Fig. 23-7.
4. Perform the soldering on a brick, concrete block or asbestos sheet for safety. Remember not to touch the nails. They will be hot after soldering.
5. Heat the nails with a torch to the point where they will melt the solder, Fig. 23-8. Apply a small amount of solder. If you are using a soldering gun or iron, add a small amount of solder to the tip after it is hot, Fig. 23-9, and hold it to the nails until the molten solder flows into the joint. Allow to cool.
6. Do not use any more solder than needed. Extra solder detracts from the appearance and does not add strength.

Applying the finish

1. After the solder has cooled, wash each piece with warm, soapy water. This will remove the flux and add a polish to the solder. An old toothbrush is useful in reaching difficult areas. A cotton swab, saturated with the liquid acid flux, will clean difficult areas. Be sure to wash off all the flux and keep it off your hands.
2. Use a small file to smooth rough spots and remove excess solder, Fig. 23-10. Steel wool may also be used to clean and smooth rough edges.

Fig. 23-7. Apply silver solder flux to the spots where the nails are to be soldered. Use only a drop at each location.

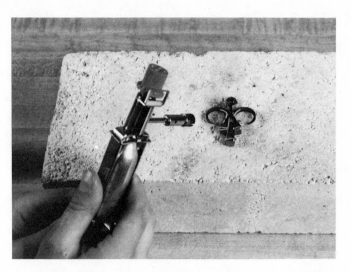

Fig. 23-8. Heat nails with small butane torch. The flux has been applied and a small piece of silver solder is located on each spot to be joined. When nails are hot enough, solder will melt and operation is complete.

Fig. 23-9. Join nails using a soldering gun with silver solder and flux. The gun is not as fast as the torch, but will heat nails to proper temperature.

Fig. 23-10. Touch up rough areas with small file. Nails should be smooth and free from nicks and scratches.

3. Spray the project. Use a clear acrylic spray, silver or gold leaf or other craft paint, Fig. 23-11. A clear, gold, silver or black finish is generally preferred, but the type of project and its use may require another color. Fig. 23-12 shows the completed pendant.

Displaying the project

The way you display your project may be as important as the quality of your work. If you mount it be sure that the base receives the care and planning that you gave the design. Sand rough areas and apply a suitable finish. Consider the possibilities for display: fabric backing, framing, freestanding or hanging.

Many other kinds of nail projects are possible. Study the color illustrations at the beginning of this chapter.

HARDWARE FIGURES

Hardware figures are made from nuts, bolts, washers, pieces of wire and assorted pieces of hardware. Insects, human figures and animals are good subjects for this type of metal art. However, this brief list does not exhaust the possibilities. Look around you for other ideas.

TOOLS AND MATERIALS

Fig. 23-13 shows tools and materials generally required to make hardware figures. You need:
1. Pliers (roundnose, flatnose, diagonal or side-cutting)—for bending wire or strips of metal and cutting wire to length.
2. Tin snips (tinners' hand snips)—for cutting thin, flat metal. (These snips should not be used to cut wire or hardened metal).
3. Soldering gun, soldering iron or small torch—for fastening the various pieces.
4. Silver solder and flux (more desirable than regular 60/40 solder)—for fastening a variety of metals.
5. Hack saw—for cutting pieces too large to snip with diagonal cutters.
6. Vise—for holding parts for cutting and bending.
7. Brick or asbestos sheet—for soldering surface.

An assortment of nuts, bolts, washers and other hardware will be needed to form the parts of your project, Fig. 23-14. Collect as many as you can of various sizes and shapes so that you will have more design possibilities.

The hardware parts may be cemented together using epoxy cement rather than soldering, if desired. Follow the directions on the container.

The usual finish applied to hardware figures is a black spray paint designed for metal application. However, other colors may be brushed or sprayed on. As in other

Fig. 23-11. Several coats of clear acrylic spray should be applied to protect the finish and prevent rusting.

Fig. 23-12. Completed pendant ready to be attached to a chain.

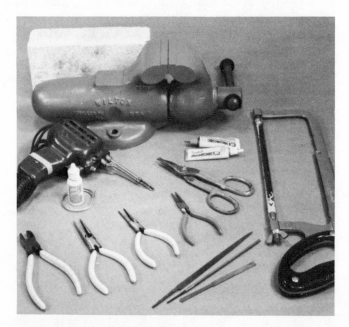
Fig. 23-13. These tools are useful in making hardware figures.

finishing projects, paint a piece of scrap to be sure the paint will produce the right effect. Two light coats are usually better than one heavy coat.

MAKING HARDWARE FIGURES

The basic procedure for making most hardware figures is simple:
1. Plan the project.
2. Select the materials
3. Shape the parts.
4. Fasten parts together.
5. Apply a finish.

PLANNING AND SELECTING

1. Have a design in mind before you begin. Sketch the object or use a picture to help you proportion the parts accurately, Fig. 23-15.
2. Select the hardware that will form each part of the object. Hold these together to determine which arrangement is best, Fig. 23-16.

SHAPING PARTS

1. Some pieces of hardware may need to be cut or shaped. Use the proper tool to perform the operation. Fig. 23-17 shows the wings for an insect design being cut with snips. Fig. 23-18 shows the wings after cutting and shaping.

Fig. 23-15. This picture of a dragon fly is a good subject for a hardware figure project.

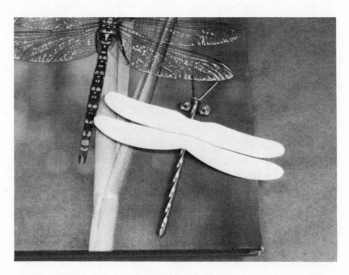

Fig. 23-16. Materials are ''trial'' assembled. The insect will have a nail body, eyes from two small brass nuts with a ''BB'' soldered in the hole, wings of brass foil .005 in. thick and feet of brass wire.

Fig. 23-17. Cut out dragon fly's wings using a pair of tin snips. Try to make smooth cuts and follow your lines.

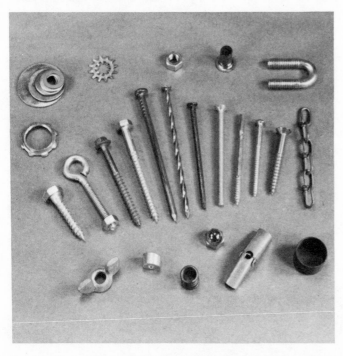

Fig. 23-14. Assortment of nuts, bolts, washers and other hardware may be used to form parts of various projects.

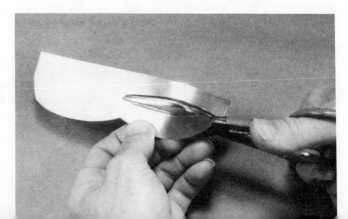

2. If a piece is too small or difficult to hold with your fingers, a vise may be helpful. Remember that sawing produces heat. Allow a part which has just been sawed to cool before handling with unprotected hands.

ASSEMBLING

1. Decide whether you will solder or cement the pieces together. If you have never soldered before, practice on scrap before working on your project. Soldering is faster and the parts can be separated easily if you do not like the effect. Cement should usually dry overnight and it may take several days to attach all the pieces.
2. Work on a brick or asbestos if you solder, Fig. 23-19. Be careful and do not touch the parts until they cool. Fig. 23-20 shows the wings soldered in place. Refer to soldering procedure, this chapter.

APPLYING A FINISH

1. Clean metal parts with soapy water and allow them to dry before applying a finish.
2. Select a paint or clear finish designed for metal and apply it with a brush or spray it on, Fig. 23-21. Try it out first on a piece of scrap.
3. Allow the paint to dry and then display your work.

METAL SCULPTURE

Create a conversation piece or bring back a bit of the past with a metal sculpture crafted from wire and sheet brass. You can choose as your subject one of the early flying machines, automobiles, ships or countless other contraptions in our history. If you are very creative, you can produce your own "machine."

TOOLS AND MATERIALS

The tools required for this type of metal art are few. The following, shown in Fig. 23-22, will be adequate for most projects:
1. Pliers (roundnose, needle-nose, diagonal or side-cutting)—for bending, shaping and cutting small wire.
2. A small pair of tin snips—for cutting thin sheet brass. A pair of heavy scissors may be used for very thin sheet brass.
3. Straightedge and scribe—for drawing out parts on the brass.
4. Soldering iron and rosin core solder—for fastening parts together. A 60/40 rosin core solder is ideal.

One of the few materials needed for metal sculpture is thin sheet brass and some thin steel or brass wire,

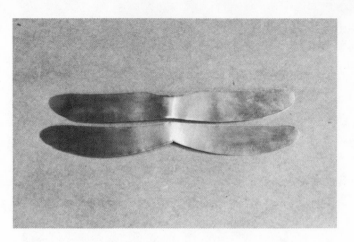

Fig. 23-18. Wings after cutting operation is complete.

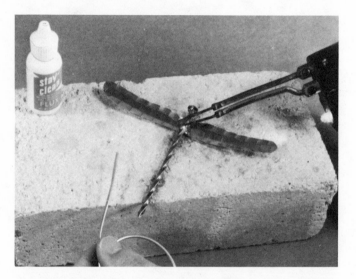

Fig. 23-19. Soldering first pair of wings to nail using soldering gun, silver solder and flux. All parts must be hot enough to melt solder or joint will not hold properly.

Fig. 23-20. Top view of wings soldered in place. Wings are scored with sharp scribe to achieve ribbed effect.

Fig. 23-23. The thickness of brass used will depend on the size and design of the project, but you may want to begin with 0.005 or 0.010 in. sheet first. Experiment with the material before you purchase a large amount. Several wire sizes are available and No. 28 wire would be useful to represent rigging on a ship, old airplane or similar detail. Larger sizes up to brazing rod diameter are useful for structural parts.

Acetone (nonoily fingernail polish remover) may be used to remove rosin from the metal. Use a small brush or cotton wad to soak the surface and brush toward the edge. Ordinary brass polish may be used to remove fingerprints.

A clear spray is needed to protect the shine of the metal. This may be a lacquer type spray or one of the acrylics.

MAKING METAL SCULPTURES

The general procedure for making metal sculptures involves planning the project and selecting materials, cutting the parts, soldering the pieces together and applying the finish. The following hints will help you through your first metal sculpture project.

Planning the project and selecting materials

1. Select a design or make up your own, but have a design in mind before you begin, such as the one in Fig. 23-24. Books on the history of aviation, sailing, or automobiles provide a good source of ideas for metal sculpture projects.

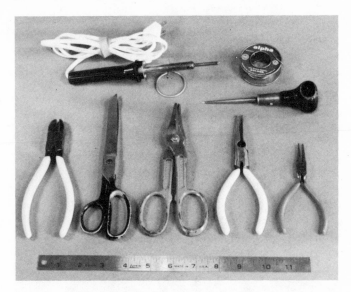

Fig. 23-22. Tools needed for metal sculpture projects: side-cutting pliers, scissors, tin snips, needle-nose pliers, roundnose pliers, measuring device, scribe or awl, soldering iron and rosin core solder.

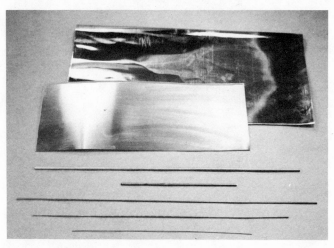

Fig. 23-23. Sheet brass in thickness of 0.005 in. (0.127 mm) and 0.010 in. (0.254 mm) is ideal for most projects. Brass wire and rod from No. 28 to 1/8 in. (3 mm) diameter will meet most project needs.

Fig. 23-21. After eyes and legs are attached with solder, metal is washed in soapy water and dried. Next, finish is applied. Clear acrylic spray is used to protect the finish.

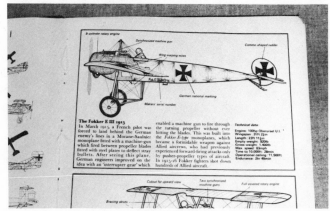

Fig. 23-24. Ideal subject for metal sculpture project is this 1915 Fokker airplane.

2. Plan the size of your project so that you can determine the amount and thickness of brass needed.
3. Make a pattern of the parts from heavy paper, Fig. 23-25, to help in figuring the amount of material needed and in cutting out the parts.

Cutting the parts

1. First, lightly trace the shape of each part on the sheet brass using your pattern. Nearly any sharp object will scribe the metal, Fig. 23-26.
2. Cut out each part very carefully using scissors or snips. Be sure to cut smooth curves and straight lines so that poor work will not spoil your project.

Fig. 23-27. Soldering engine plate to shroud. A small craft soldering iron with 60/40 solder is being used for this operation.

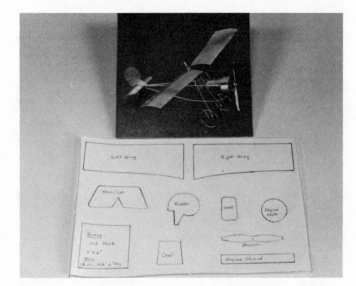

Fig. 23-25. Pattern for each part is drawn on thick paper full size. Photo of the modified design is also shown.

Fig. 23-28. Spray project with clear acrylic spray to protect finish.

Fig. 23-26. Tracing left wing pattern onto a piece of thin sheet brass. Awl or any pointed instrument can be used.

Fig. 23-29. Completed project, a vintage aircraft.

3. Cut wires to length with diagonal or side-cutting pliers. Snips should not be used to cut wire.

Soldering pieces together

1. A light soldering iron (30-40 watts) will be large enough for most small metal sculptures. Use a heavier iron or torch on thick brass.
2. Apply a small amount of rosin core solder to the tip of the iron when it is hot. Hold the molten solder to the pieces to be joined until it flows between them, Fig. 23-27. Remove the iron and hold until the solder cools. Use solder sparingly for neat work. The metal will be hot for a few minutes after you remove the iron.

Applying a finish

1. When all parts have been attached and the object is completed, remove traces of rosin with acetone and fingerprints with brass polish.
2. Spray the project with lacquer or clear acrylic to protect the finish, Fig. 23-28. Display your handiwork when the finish is dry, Fig. 23-29.

Other project suggestions for mosaics. A—Bird picture in mosaic with wood frame. B—Glass bead mosaic coaster. C—Pebble mosaic necklace. (Marge Baird) D—Jewelry box with mosaic tile inlay. E—Small ceramic tile pieces on brass tray. F—Broken glass mosaic design on waste basket. G—Religious figure in mosaic design.

Chapter 24
MOSAICS

An assembly of many pieces of the same or unlike materials which are cemented next to each other to form a pleasing picture or design is called a mosaic. The pieces can be applied to just about any flat or curved surface. Spaces between pieces may be left open or filled with grout.

Mosaics are one of the broadest craft activities known, since most any natural or synthetic materials can be used and arranged in any desired pattern. This gives you the opportunity to design and make mosaic craft projects while giving free reign to your imagination. You have a complete range of texture, color and surface light reflection in the materials you select. Your mosaic may be a simple, patterned design or a complicated picture. Serving trays, trivets, wall plaques, salt and pepper shakers, table tops, jewelry boxes and hot plates are all suitable mosaic projects. Fig. 24-1 shows a trivet project. Instructions will be given on how to make it.

MATERIALS AND TOOLS

Ceramic tile is the most common material used for mosaic projects. They are easy to work with and readily available. However, there are hundreds of other materials from which to select. Glass, metal, plastics, wood, pumpkin seeds, pebbles, beads and buttons are all suitable for mosaics.

Select the basic materials you want to use according to the theme of your design. See Fig. 24-2. Construction of most mosaic projects also requires a tile cement

Fig. 24-1. Ceramic tile hot tray is set off by a walnut frame.

Fig. 24-2. Common materials used for mosaics. Top. Glass and ceramic tile, pebbles, crushed glass, buttons, glass beads and pressed glass shapes. Bottom. Tile mastic, white tile cement, powdered tile grout, silicone grout sealer, white glue, mixing cups and a sponge.

or mastic, white glue, powdered tile grout, a sponge, mixing cups and a suitable grout sealer. These materials are also shown in Fig. 24-2. The object you plan to make becomes the base for the mosaic application. For example, if you are making a hot tray, you will need a board or piece of plywood for the base.

Basic tools include a tile cutter, files, sandpaper, a paintbrush, putty knife, straightedge and tweezers, Fig. 24-3. General woodworking tools will be necessary if you plan to make a mosaic-covered jewelry box or salt and pepper shakers. Unfinished projects are available at craft and hobby stores ready for the application of mosaic designs.

Fig. 24-3. Only a few basic tools are needed for mosaic work.

Fig. 24-4. Apply tile cement to plywood backing with a paintbrush or putty knife.

MAKING A MOSAIC

Whatever your mosaic project may be, you can follow these steps for cutting, applying and finishing the mosaic material.

1. Select or develop the mosaic design you plan to use. Be sure the surface to be tiled is smooth and clean. If you are using tile mounted on a net backing, cut the tile to the size of the base surface. Apply a tile cement, Fig. 24-4, and spread evenly over the whole surface with a paintbrush or putty knife. Place the tile firmly into the cement as shown in Fig. 24-5. Allow to dry overnight. When the cement is dry, spaces between the tile can be filled with grout.

2. A mosaic made from individual pieces of tile is prepared in a similar manner. Cut a piece of 1/4 to 3/4 in. plywood to the desired shape, as for a trivet. Lay out the design by arranging dry tile pieces on the plywood. This will give you an opportunity to

Fig. 24-5. Placing tile with net backing onto cemented plywood base. Backing maintains correct spacing between tiles.

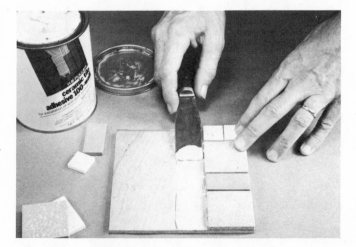

Fig. 24-6. Use putty knife to spread an even coat of mastic on plywood. Apply only enough for one row of tile at a time.

select colors, shapes and correct spacing between tiles. Try to keep the spaces 1/8 in. (3 mm) or less. (If the tile has been glued to a paper backing, simply soak it in water to remove and allow tile to dry.) Apply a small amount of mastic to the plywood surface and begin to fill in the design, Fig. 24-6. Continue to place tile in position, adding just enough mastic as you go along to keep it wet. Press each piece of tile tightly down against the plywood, being sure the mastic squeezes out slightly for a firm base, Fig. 24-7. Align tile flush with plywood edges, as demonstrated in Fig. 24-8. Allow to dry overnight.

3. A special design or picture mosaic is made in the same way except that the pattern is drawn or traced on the base material. Tile must also be cut to the individual shapes of the design. This is done with a tile cutter as shown in Fig. 24-9. Tiles are selected by color and cut to fit each individual area of the design. Cut and cement each piece of tile until the mosaic is complete, Fig. 24-10. Again, try to keep spacing as even as possible between tiles.

Picture mosaics or designs made from other materials such as plastic granules, pebbles, pieces

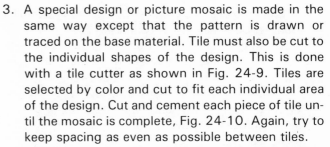

Fig. 24-9. Tile cutter is used to shape tile for part of mosaic design.

Fig. 24-7. Press tile firmly into position in the mastic.

Fig. 24-8. Use wood stick as straightedge to align last row of tile along edge of base.

Fig. 24-10. Random cut tile were used to form this mosaic picture.

of broken glass or beads, are prepared in a similar manner. See Figs. 24-11 and 24-12.

Be sure to use the right adhesive for each material. Tile mastic or cement are not the only adhesives. White glue will work well for many materials. Try a sample and see how well it sticks. White glue is recommended on most materials not being grouted; mastic would detract from the appearance.

4. Spaces between tiles are filled with grout. This is a plasterlike material that also helps to hold the tiles in place. Grout is sold in white and varied colors. Mix with water to a very heavy cream consistency, Fig. 24-13. Pour grout over the tile and use a putty knife to work it into spaces between tiles, Fig.

24-14. You can use your fingers to force the grout into any empty spaces, being sure all air bubbles are removed. Wipe the surface clean with a damp sponge, Fig. 24-15, and cover with a wet towel. Allow to dry overnight. Cement grout need not be covered.

5. After grouting has dried, surface film can be polished away with a paper towel or a lightly dampened sponge. Since grout has somewhat of a porous surface, it can be sealed, Fig. 24-16, to make it more waterproof and easy to keep clean.

6. Cut and attach trim or frame as necessary.

7. Apply finish to projects like jewelry boxes or edges of hot trays. Attach fasteners to wall plaques or mosaic pictures.

Fig. 24-11. Pebble mosaic pendant was made from smooth pebbles taken from a stream.

Fig. 24-13. Mix powdered grout with water to a heavy cream consistency.

Fig. 24-12. Mosaic made from colored glass beads.

Fig. 24-14. Force grout into spaces between tile. Use a putty knife or your fingers.

Fig. 24-15. Clean grouted surface with a damp sponge.

Fig. 24-16. Rub silicone sealer into grouted surface.

Alternate ideas for needlepoint. A—Snoopy and Woodstock in tent stitch. (Jill Minton)   B—Gros point picture in rustic frame. C—Christmas tree ornaments in bargello canvas. D—Bargello pillow cover. E—Advanced needlepoint furniture top of intricate design. F—Decorative wall hanging with beetle design. G—Shopping bag with variety of decorative stitching. H—Owl picture in wood frame. I—Needlepoint picture in fine petit point. (Fran Nelson)

Chapter 25
NEEDLEPOINT

Fig. 25-1. Beginning project, a Bargello needlepoint picture is mounted in custom walnut frame. (Joan Kicklighter)

Are you interested in a craft that is easy to learn, requires few materials, encourages creativity and produces a broad assortment of useful and decorative items? Needlepoint may be just the activity you have been looking for. You can make jewelry, wall hangings, pictures, clothing, accent pillows and dozens of other

articles. This chapter includes instructions for making the needlepoint picture illustrated in Fig. 25-1.

Needlepoint or canvas embroidery is a method of completely covering an open-weave fabric with yarn. There are four basic classifications of needlepoint, based on the fineness of the stitches:

1. Quick point - 3 1/2 to 5 stitches per inch.
2. Gros point - 8 to 15 stitches per inch.
3. Bargello - 14 stitches per inch.
4. Petit point - 16 or more stitches per inch.

Each type lends itself to particular yarns and canvas. As you learn more about needlepoint, these combinations will become clear.

MATERIALS AND TOOLS

Needlepoint is worked with yarn on canvas using tapestry needles which have blunt points and long eyes. Fig. 25-2 shows the tools and materials needed. Needle sizes range from 24 (the finest) to 14 (the thickest) and are chosen to fit the mesh of the canvas. Generally, only Nos. 18, 20 and 22 are required. The

Fig. 25-2. Materials and tools needed for most needlepoint projects. Left. Canvas, needles, yarn, scissors, measuring device, thread, felt tip marker, masking tape and graph paper. Right. Close up of blunt tapestry needles used for needlepoint. Beginner should have several sizes ranging from No. 18 through No. 22.

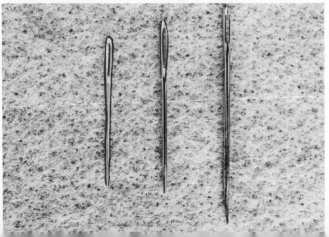

eye of the needle should be slightly wider than the thickness of the yarn. But it must still be narrow enough to slide easily through the canvas openings.

YARN

Yarn for needlepoint must be strong enough to withstand the wear and tear of being pulled through the canvas openings. It must not be elastic, so knitting wool is not acceptable.

Persian wool, a three-ply yarn, works very well. It covers 10 mesh canvas nicely and two plies are suitable for 12 or 14 mesh canvas.

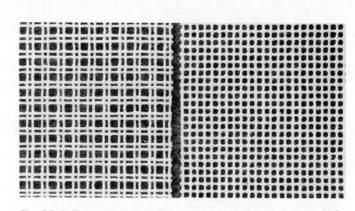

Fig. 25-3. Two basic types of canvas are used for needlepoint. Left. Double thread canvas. Right. Single thread canvas.

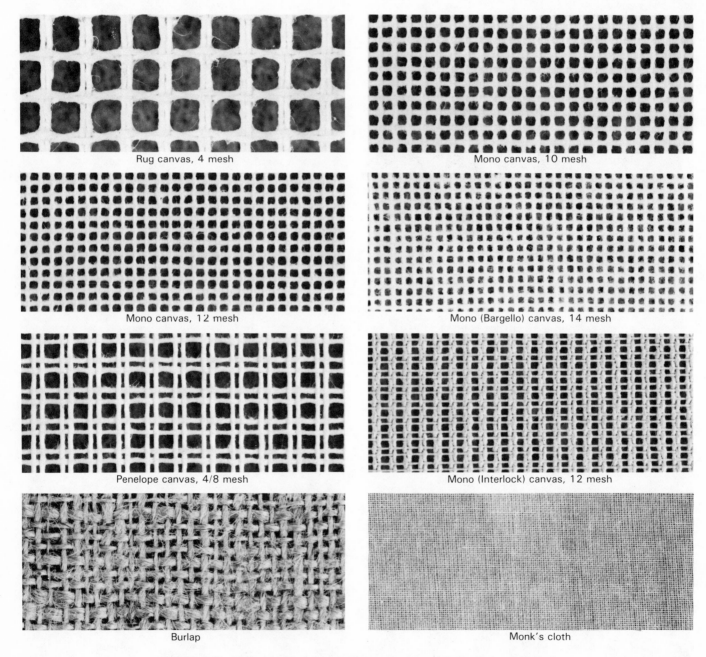

Rug canvas, 4 mesh

Mono canvas, 10 mesh

Mono canvas, 12 mesh

Mono (Bargello) canvas, 14 mesh

Penelope canvas, 4/8 mesh

Mono (Interlock) canvas, 12 mesh

Burlap

Monk's cloth

Fig. 25-4. Typical canvas materials are shown close up so they may be compared.

Tapestry wool is a single-ply yarn. It works well for 10, 12 and 14 mesh canvas.

Crewel wool, a fine embroidery yarn, is acceptable for 16 mesh or finer canvas. Rug wool may also be used for large mesh canvas.

Keep labels from your yarn so that you can match colors and dye lots exactly. A change in dye lot can cause streaking in the background color and ruin the appearance of your project.

CANVAS

Canvas for needlepoint is available in two basic types: single thread and double thread. See Fig. 25-3. There are three classes of single thread canvas which include:

1. Mono which has 10 to 18 holes per inch.
2. Interlock with 5 to 14 holes per inch.
3. Bargello with 14 holes per inch.

Penelope, also called duo, is the only double thread canvas and it has 6 1/2 to 15 holes per inch. Fig. 25-4 compares several types of canvas.

Canvas is made from cotton and, more recently, plastic. Available in widths from 18 to 60 in. (457 to 1524 mm), cotton canvas is either white or tan. Plastic canvas is, of course, nearly colorless. Unless cotton canvas is of good quality, it is likely to fray the yarn.

TOOLS

In addition to yarn, you will need a few small tools:

1. A flexible tape or other measuring device.
2. A pair of shears for cutting the canvas.
3. A small pair of scissors for cutting the yarn.
4. Graph paper for working out the designs.
5. A roll of masking tape for binding cotton canvas edges.
6. Acrylic or thinned oil paints and a small brush for applying your design to the canvas. (Some people use waterproof markers successfully. However, every brand has some colors which will run. They can ruin a needlepoint project during blocking.)

NEEDLEPOINT STITCHES

Many kinds of stitches are used in needlepoint. Whatever name they are called, they are variations of either diagonal, horizontal or vertical stitches. Some of the most popular will be listed. They are also described and illustrated to show how they are made.

TENT STITCHES

The basic needlepoint stitch, illustrated in Fig. 25-5, is called the ''Tent'' stitch. It is the smallest unit in

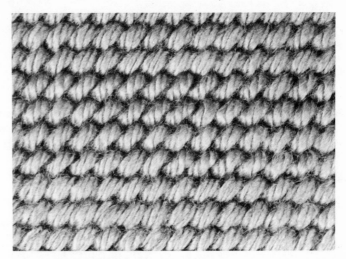

Fig. 25-5. Front side of Tent stitch. This basic needlepoint stitch lays across one intersection of canvas.

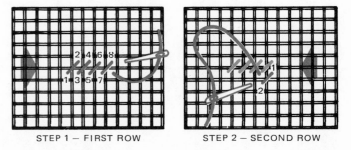

STEP 1 — FIRST ROW   STEP 2 — SECOND ROW

Fig. 25-6. Half Cross (Tent) stitch. Front side of this stitch looks like photo in Fig. 25-5.

needlepoint and is laid across just one intersection of canvas threads. The tent stitch always appears as a flat, even thread, slanting from the lower left to the upper right.

All Tent stitches are identical on the front or right side, but there are actually four variations. The difference between them is seen only on the back side of the canvas. The names of the stitches are:

1. Half Cross stitch. This is a simple, economical stitch used for flat work. It does not provide a heavy cover on the back of the canvas and does not wear well; therefore, it should be used on pictures, wall hangings or pillows where it does not get heavy use. It should only be used on Penelope canvas because the backing is not strong enough to hold the Mono canvas firm. To produce this stitch, the needle goes down through the upper square and up through the lower square. Then the needle moves horizontally and repeats the step in the next square to the left. Fig. 25-6 shows the procedure. At the end of each row, the canvas is turned upside down and the procedure is repeated.

2. Continental stitch. This one is best for working a single row of tent stitches. To make this stitch, move from left to right. Push the needle down

Crafts

through the upper square and up through the lower square two meshes away. To start the second row, turn the work upside down and continue as previously described. Turn the work again as each new row is begun. Fig. 25-7 shows the stitch.

3. Basket Weave stitch. This stitch prevents distortion of the canvas because the direction of work changes after each row, Fig. 25-8. The stitch gets its name from the woven pattern it forms on the

back of the canvas. It looks like old fashioned monk's cloth. On the front, the stitches form a pyramid whose base is at a 45 degree angle to the weave of the canvas. Each successive row dovetails with the previous row.

4. Diagonal stitch. The Diagonal also prevents the canvas from distorting. Fig. 25-9 shows the steps viewed from the back side of the canvas. This stitch forms a diagonal pattern.

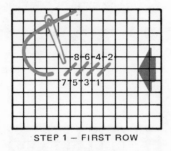
STEP 1 — FIRST ROW

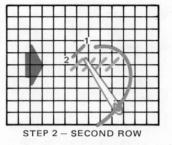
STEP 2 — SECOND ROW

Fig. 25-7. Continental (Tent) stitch. Front looks the same as Fig. 25-5, but stitches are made differently. Compare needle positions with those in Fig. 25-6. Rows are worked in opposite direction of the Half Cross stitch.

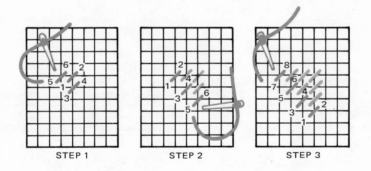

STEP 1   STEP 2   STEP 3

Fig. 25-8. Basket Weave (Tent) stitch. Front is the same as Fig. 25-5 but rows are made in a sloping plane rather than horizontally.

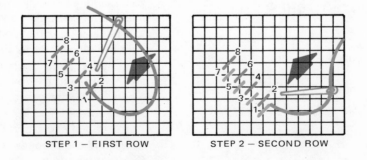

STEP 1 — FIRST ROW   STEP 2 — SECOND ROW

Fig. 25-9. Diagonal (Tent) stitch. Front is the same as Fig. 25-5. While much like the Basket Weave, rows are laid on bottom to top. Work all rows in same direction finishing off at end of each row.

DECORATIVE STITCHES

Unlike Tent stitches, decorative or pattern stitches may cover more than one intersection of canvas threads. They may go in any direction and may share a hole with another stitch. Some of the most popular decorative stitches include: the Cross stitch, the Upright Cross stitch, the Slanting Gobelin, Encroaching Gobelin, Scotch stitch, Scotch stitch variation, Checkerboard stitch, Fern stitch, Florentine stitch, Hungar-

ian stitch, Leaf stitch, Byzantine stitch and the Milanese stitch. These stitches are illustrated in Figs. 25-10 through 25-24. Alongside each procedure is a full color photograph showing how the pattern actually appears on canvas.

As you become more familiar with the stitches try them with different yarns or even with different kinds of canvas. The appearance of some stitches will change dramatically from one yarn to the next. Alternate rows might be worked in different colors.

 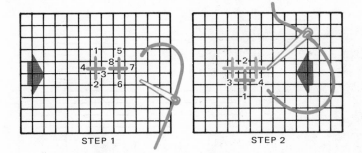

Fig. 25-10. Cross stitch. Begin stitch at the top of the canvas. All rows start and end at left. Numbers show order in which stitches are made. At second row numbering starts over.

 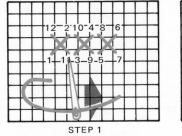 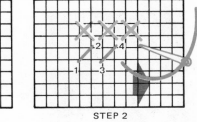

Fig. 25-11. Upright Cross stitch. Start at top of the canvas and work all rows from left to right. At end of each row, turn canvas upside down. Step No. 2 shows first Upright Cross stitch of the second row.

 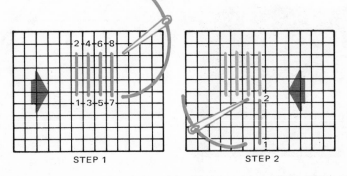

Fig. 25-12. Upright Gobelin stitch. Starting at top of canvas, work first row from left to right. Work second row from right to left. No. 1 and No. 2 of Step 2 show first stitch of second row. This stitch may be worked over two to six threads of canvas.

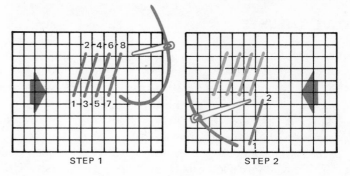

Fig. 25-13. Slanting Gobelin stitch. Start at top of canvas. Work first row from left to right. Work second row from right to left. No. 1 and No. 2 of Step 2 show first stitch of second row. Stitch may be worked over two to six threads.

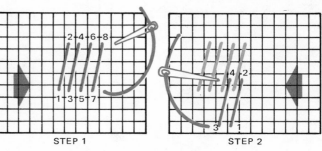

Fig. 25-14. Encroaching Gobelin stitch. Starting at top of canvas, work first row from left to right. Work second row from right to left. No. 1 and No. 2 of Step 2 show first stitch of second row. This stitch may be worked over two to six threads.

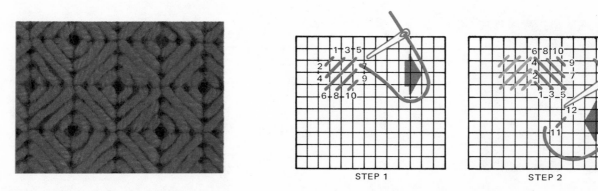

Fig. 25-15. Scotch stitch. Begin at top of canvas and work all rows from left to right. Turn canvas upside down at end of each row. No. 1 and No. 2 of Step 2 show first stitch of next square. No. 1 and No. 2 of Step 3 show first stitch of second row.

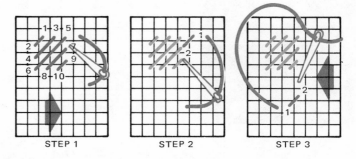

Fig. 25-16. Checkerboard stitch. Start at top of canvas. Work all rows from left to right. At end of each row, turn canvas upside down. No. 11 and No. 12 of Step 2 show position of first stitch of second row.

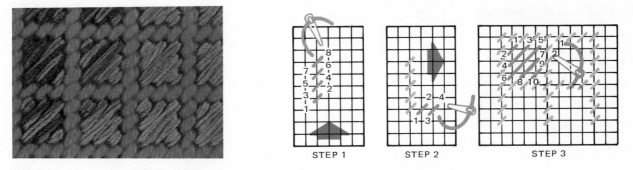

Fig. 25-17. Scotch stitch variation. Start at bottom of canvas. Work outline of squares in Half Cross stitch, Fig. 25-6. First, work all vertical lines and then horizontal lines. Work center of squares last, using Scotch stitch shown in Fig. 25-15.

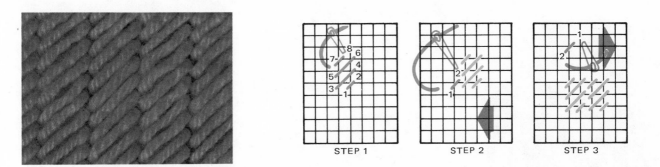

Fig. 25-18. Cashmere stitch. Begin at bottom of canvas. Work all rows from left to right. (A row is made up of two squares; each square has four stitches, a short, two long and one short stitch.) At end of each row, turn canvas upside down. Step 1 shows first square completed. Step 2 shows first stitch of second square. Step 3 shows first stitch (1 and 2) of second row.

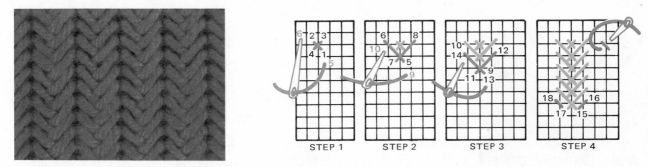

Fig. 25-19. Fern stitch. Work all rows from top to bottom of the canvas. No. 1 through No. 4 show beginning of row. Repeat No. 9 through No. 12 for each stitch. No. 15 through No. 18 of Step 4 show end of row. Step 4 also shows beginning of second row.

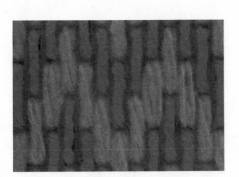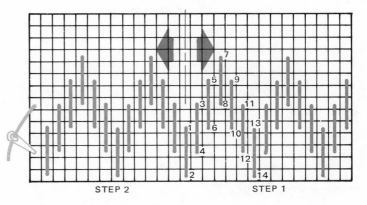

Fig. 25-20. Florentine stitch. Start in center of canvas, Step 1. Work first row from center to sides. Work next rows up toward top of canvas. Turn canvas upside down and work other half, Step 2. Each row may be worked in a different color, if desired.

219

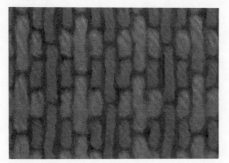
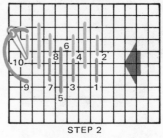
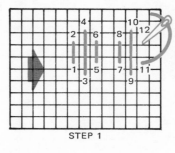

Fig. 25-21. Hungarian stitch. Start at top of canvas. Work first row from left to right (Step 1) and second row from right to left (Step 2). Each row may be worked in different color.

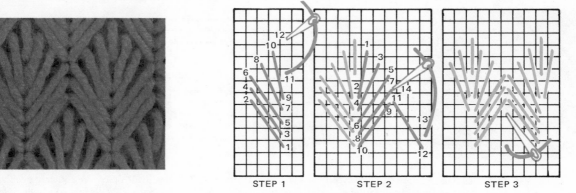

Fig. 25-22. Leaf stitch. Start first row of leaves at top of canvas. Work all rows from left to right. No. 11 and No. 12 of Step 2 show first stitch of the second leaf. Needle in Step 3 is placing top stitch of second row.

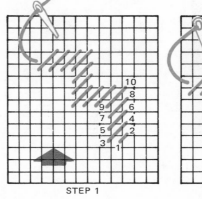
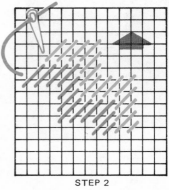

Fig. 25-23. Byzantine stitch. Begin at bottom of the canvas. Step 2 shows second row in progress. When half of work is completed, turn canvas upside down and complete other half. This stitch may be worked in two colors.

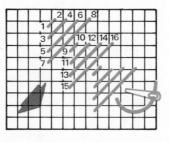

Fig. 25-24. Milanese stitch. Begin at top left side of canvas. At end of each row, turn canvas upside down. No. 1 and No. 2 of Step 2 show first stitch of second row. Complete other half of canvas same way.

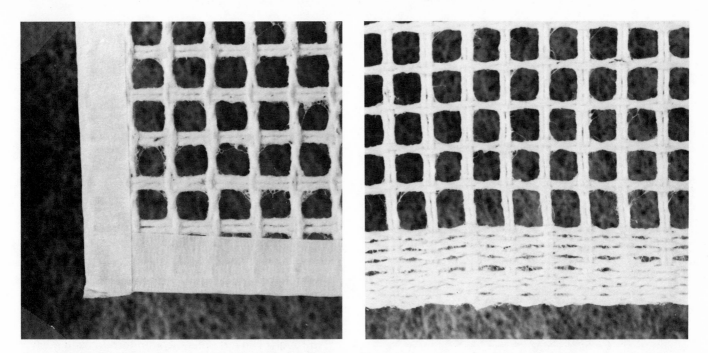

Fig. 25-25. Prepare canvas edging. Left. Bind edge of canvas with masking tape to prevent fraying. Right. This is not required on selvage or woven edges.

MAKING NEEDLEPOINT PROJECTS

Most needlepoint projects involve several common steps. These steps are explained and illustrated to help you produce a satisfactory product on your very first attempt. If you are left-handed, the procedures are reversed. It may help to turn the illustrations upside down.

1. Plan your project carefully and completely. Identify the type and amount of canvas, yarn and other materials that you will need. Check to be sure that you have the proper needles and other tools required for the operations involved. *Note: You may estimate the amount of yarn required by stitching a square inch of canvas and measuring the amount of yarn used. As a rule, a yard of tapestry yarn or of Persian will cover a square inch of tent stitches.*

2. Prepare the canvas. Measure out the amount needed and add 2 in. (51 mm) all around for finishing. Bind the edges with marking tape to prevent fraying, Fig. 25-25.

3. Orient your canvas. Selvages should be the vertical edges. On double canvas, the closely paired threads must run vertically. These directions must be established before placing a design on the canvas or before making any stitches on it.

4. Draw your design on the canvas, Fig. 25-26. You may also wish to indicate the colors. If the canvas is large, form it into a loose roll, leaving a few inches of work space. Pin the remainder in place with safety pins. Unroll the canvas as work progresses.

5. You are ready to begin the stitches. Refer to the stitches presented earlier. Thread the needle with a piece of yarn about 25 in. (635 mm) long. (The yarn will fray if too long a piece is used.) Knot the end. (Note: There are two methods of threading the needle. In the first, loop the yarn around the needle and pull tightly against the needle. Slip the needle out of the loop and bring the eye down on the loop and pull it through. In the second method fold a narrow strip of paper over the end of the yarn and push it through the eye.)

    To start the yarn, put the needle through the canvas from the front, about an inch from where you

Fig. 25-26. Design may be drawn on canvas with acrylic paints or waterproof felt tip markers.

Fig. 25-27. Beginning first stitch on canvas. This one is called the Scotch stitch.

plan to make the first stitch. Catch the yarn on the back with the first few stitches to secure it, Fig. 25-27. Clip the excess yarn after it is secured. Knots are never allowed to remain in a piece of needlepoint.

The basic needle technique is simple to master. Refer once more to the stitching diagrams in Figs. 25-6 through 25-24. The needle comes up through the canvas at odd numbered squares and down through the canvas at even numbered squares. If the canvas is not stretched in a frame, the needle can be pushed down through one square and up through the next in one single motion. In the next motion, the needle and yarn is pulled through both squares at the same time.

However, when the canvas is tightly stretched, it may not be possible to work the needle down and up through the squares in one motion. Then, one hand must work the top while the other hand works the bottom. The right hand starts the needle down through. The left pulls the yarn through and pushes the needle back up again. Fig. 25-28 demonstrates both methods.

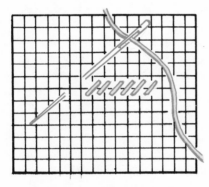
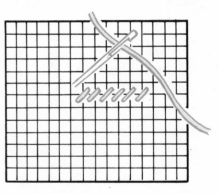

Fig. 25-28. Two methods of making needlepoint stitches. Left. If canvas is not stretched on a frame you can go in and out of canvas with needle in one continuous motion. Right. If canvas is stretched on frame, needle and thread must be pulled through all the way before returning through canvas.

Fig. 25-29. First series of Scotch stitches is completed.

Fig. 25-30. This color photo shows the project well along.

6. Begin stitching your design, Fig. 25-29. Work gently taking care not to pull the thread too taut. If the yarn begins to twist, let the needle hang free. It will unwind. End a length of yarn by threading it through several stitches on the back side of the canvas. Cut off the yarn left over. Fig. 25-30 shows the work well along and in the colors that are being used.

7. When you have completed your needlework, you may notice that the canvas is pulled out of shape. If so, it should be stretched to its proper shape, pinned down about every inch along the border as in Fig. 25-31. Use rustproof pins and dampen the canvas. When it is dry, it should hold its shape. This procedure is called blocking.

8. Complete your project by stitching pieces together, framing or performing other operations required.

Fig. 25-31. Stretching canvas back into shape after stitching is completed. Be sure to use rustproof pins.

Six projects in papier mache'. A—Mask formed on large inflated balloon. B—Primitive mask. C—Turtle on wire form. D—Papier mache' tennis shoe. E—Witch hand puppet. F—The ''Peanuts Gang.'' (Lois Ann Vidolich)

Chapter 26
PAPIER MACHÉ

With a little paste, a coat of paint and a few other common odds and ends, you can transform old newspapers into beautiful and useful objects, Fig. 26-1. Papier maché, which means ''chewed-up paper,'' can be used to make boxes, trays, animals, jewelry, flowers and even furniture.

This craft has remained popular for centuries because the techniques are simple, the materials are readily available and the applications are varied. Papier maché is as flexible as your own imagination. People of all ages enjoy it.

TOOLS AND MATERIALS

Few materials and hardly any tools are required for papier maché. See Fig. 26-2. A file or sandpaper may also be used to smooth and shape your design if desired, but is not necessary.

Fig. 26-1. Papier maché bucket makes a fine flower pot holder. Figures 26-5 through 26-10 show how to make it.

Fig. 26-2. Tools and materials needed for most papier maché projects include paper strips or paper pulp, paste, paintbrushes, gesso (a primer), paint, decorations, sandpaper, and clear acrylic spray.

Either strips of old newspaper or commercial pulp (instant papier mache) can be used as papier mache. Each has its own peculiar characteristics and advantages. Strips of paper work best to quickly build up an area. Pulp takes longer. Delicate shapes with smooth or textured surfaces can be formed using the pulp. It must be purchased at a craft shop and takes longer to dry than strips of paper. Pulp is recommended for small projects because of the cost and high rate of shrinkage of this material. Newspaper is readily available, cheap and useful for a broad range of larger projects.

Wheat paste powder or wallpaper paste is used to hold the paper together. Either may be purchased at a hardware store. The introduction of a small amount of white glue into the paste is recommended to add strength.

Several brushes, in a variety of sizes, will be useful. A small paintbrush can be used to apply and smooth the paste while smaller artists' brushes can be useful in decorating the finished product.

Gesso is generally used to prime the surface for painting after the paste is dry. A composition of plaster of paris and glue, it may be purchased in art supply stores.

Almost any type of paint can be used on a papier mache project. Antique and acrylic finishes are especially suitable for some objects. An acrylic spray coat, varnish or lacquer may be used to make the papier mache more water-resistant and durable. The type of object and intended use will largely determine the type of paint to use.

A variety of decorations should be collected to add a finishing touch to your project. Such items as colored tissue paper, construction paper, fancy wrapping paper, string, yarn, beads, shells, ribbon and fabric scraps are very useful for papier mache objects. Bottles, wire, balloons and styrofoam, Fig. 26-3, may also be used to form the basic shape.

Fig. 26-3. These materials may be used to form basic shapes of a papier mache' projects.

Fig. 26-4. Project has been selected and materials gathered. Supporting shape will be an empty cardboard bucket such as those sold at paint stores. Design approach here is to make it look like a woven basket.

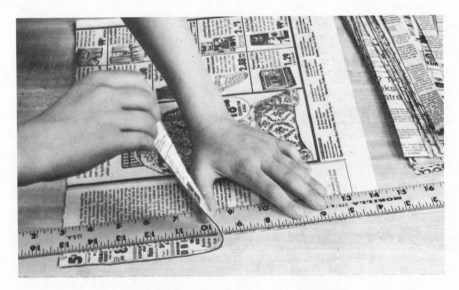

Fig. 26-5. Tear newspaper into narrow strips.

MAKING PROJECTS OUT OF PAPER STRIPS

The procedure discussed here will help you get started in this interesting craft. More complex projects will understandably require additional steps.

1. Plan your project. Decide what to make and how to support the papier mache' while it is wet, Fig. 26-4. Bottles, cans, wadded-up paper, clay, light bulbs, wire mesh and styrofoam may be used to form the basic shape and provide support. Supporting shapes may even remain partially visible becoming an element in the finished design.

2. Select or build the support structure for your project.

3. Tear or cut newsprint into strips about 3/4 in. (19 mm) wide and 10 or 12 in. (254 or 305 mm) long, Fig. 26-5. Torn edges will blend together better than cut edges. If the paper seems hard to tear, maybe you are tearing across the grain. Turn it 90 deg. and try again.

4. Mix paste in a large container following directions. Add a small amount of white glue to the mixture. Immerse several strips in the paste for a few minutes, Fig. 26-6. Each strip should be thoroughly soaked and coated with the paste.

5. Take one strip at a time from the paste and remove excess paste with your fingers or a brush, Fig. 26-7. Your fingers will probably work best.

6. Apply the strip to your support structure, Fig. 26-8. Smooth it in place or form the shape you want. Remove air bubbles and excess paste.

7. Cover the structure with layers of strips until you have formed the desired shape, Fig. 26-9.

Fig. 26-7. Remove excess paste with fingers or brush.

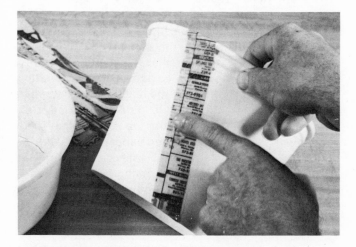

Fig. 26-8. Apply first strip to backing. Press strip down until it is smooth. Remove all air bubbles.

Fig. 26-6. Allow paper to soak for several minutes in paste. Be sure each strip is completely covered with paste.

Fig. 26-9. Several layers of strips have been attached to bucket to produce three-dimensional effect.

8. When the object is completed, let it dry thoroughly. Drying may take overnight or several days, depending on the thickness of the material and the drying conditions. Some shrinkage will occur. If you are not satisfied with the result after it shrinks, wet the object and apply more paper and paste. Continue this procedure until you are happy with the shape. After the project has dried, you can sand or file it if you want a smoother surface.

9. Prime the surface with gesso, for painting. Use a paintbrush to spread the gesso, Fig. 26-10. When it is dry, paint it to suit your taste.

10. Apply the finishing touches needed to add character and detail to your creation. Spray with clear acrylic to protect the finish. Display your project, Fig. 26-11.

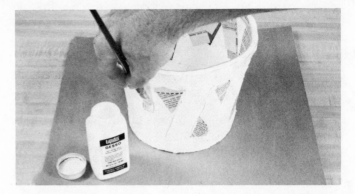

Fig. 26-10. Priming the surface of the project with gesso for painting. Gesso acts as a filler and sealer.

MAKING PROJECTS OF PAPER PULP

Paper pulp also needs some kind of support until it is dry. It can be used over the same type of support materials as paper strips. However, when a large wire mesh is used, it should be covered with paper strips first. Pulp would fall through the holes. Other materials such as balloons and bottles should also be covered with strips first to form a base for the paper pulp.

Follow these steps when using paper pulp:

1. Plan your project and collect the required materials, Fig. 26-12. If the project requires a foundation of paper strips, put those on first using wallpaper paste. See Fig. 26-13.

Fig. 26-11. After painting, completed project will be attractive and quite durable.

Fig. 26-12. Materials required for making a puppet from paper strips and paper pulp. In addition to these materials, gesso, paint and trim will be needed.

228

2. Mix the paper pulp with water until the particles are moistened as shown in Fig. 26-14. Do not saturate to the point where they become soggy; it will take too long to dry. Mildew is likely to develop and could ruin your project. If mildew does develop, spray it with a disinfectant. Form the parts which do not require a foundation. See Fig. 26-15.

3. Apply the pulp to your form with a spatula, palette knife or use your fingers, Figs. 26-16 and 26-17.

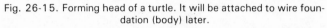

Fig. 26-15. Forming head of a turtle. It will be attached to wire foundation (body) later.

Fig. 26-13. Balloon covered with paper strips is foundation for a puppet head. Eyes, nose and mouth will be fashioned from instant papier mache'.

Fig. 26-16. Attach turtle's head to wire shape.

Fig. 26-14. Mixing paper pulp. Add only enough water to dry flakes to make them stick together in uniform mass.

Fig. 26-17. Applying paper pulp to wire mesh. This mesh has 1/4 in. (6 mm) squares — fine enough so that paper strips are not required.

Fig. 26-18. Smooth shape with palette knife.

Fig. 26-21. Acrylic paints are being used to finish project.

Fig. 26-19. Set completed papier mache' turtle where it can dry.

Fig. 26-22. Completed turtle is painted in vivid colors.

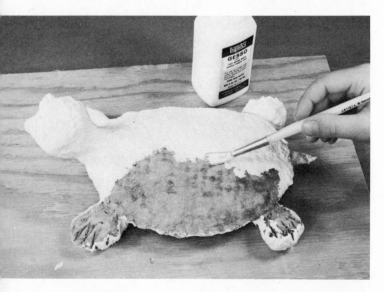

Fig. 26-20. After the paper pulp has dried for a few days, apply primer to all surfaces.

Fig. 26-23. Instant papier mache' eyes, nose and mouth have been added to the puppet's head. Hair and teeth were attached last. Face is being painted with acrylic paint.

Develop the shape and allow pulp to dry, Figs. 26-18 and 26-19. Shrinkage will be great using this material and you may have to refine your design with several applications. Let each coat dry before adding another.

4. When the project is thoroughly dry, prime it with gesso before painting as shown in Fig. 26-20.

5. Select paints and apply finish using brushes in appropriate sizes, Figs. 26-21. Careful brushwork will produce a beautiful finish, Fig. 26-22.

6. Add facial details to puppet head, Fig. 26-23, and apply finish. Fig. 26-24 shows completed puppet.

Fig. 26-24. Puppet witch is trimmed in a hat made from cardboard and a cape of burlap.

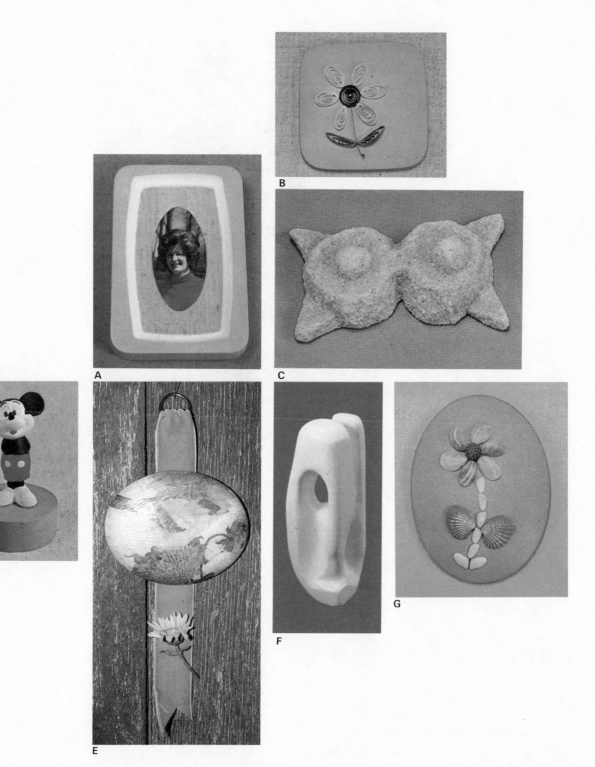

Plaster casting projects. A—Plaster frame with photo mounted on fabric backing. B—Plaster of paris plaque with quilled flower. C—Abstract plaster casting with a sand finish. D—Mouse figurine. E—Decoupage plaque attached to ribbon. F—Plaster form cast to rough dimensions and scupltured. G—Plaster plaque decorated with acrylic paint and a shell flower.

Chapter 27
PLASTER CASTING

As a craft material, plaster of paris is easy to work and fun to use. You can cast plaques, figurines and make impressions for a very small investment in materials and time. People of all ages enjoy the creative expression that this craft provides. See Fig. 27-1.

MATERIALS AND TOOLS

A key material for this craft, the plaster, may be purchased as "casting plaster," "art plaster" or "plaster of paris." The plaster should be fresh and dry. It has a short shelf life and should be stored where it is dry. Since it cannot be reused, mix only the amount you intend to use.

You will also need a mixing bowl, measuring cup, spatula for mixing and a little white glue. The mixing bowl should be large enough to hold all that you will need for a given project. Of course, you will need water. Fig. 27-2 shows the materials and tools you should have on hand.

If you plan to make a plaque, you will need a mold and a piece of rustproof wire for hanging the plaque. A wide assortment of plastic molds are available at craft and hobby shops. See Fig. 27-3.

Fig. 27-2. Materials and tools required for casting plaster of paris. From top clockwise. Plaster, mixing bowl and spatula, rubber latex, measuring cup, artists' brush and wire, molds, figurine and white glue. A small quantity of water is also needed.

Fig. 27-3. Assortment of plastic molds are made for casting plaster of paris.

Fig. 27-1. One of the projects you will learn to make in this chapter is this plaster of paris impression.

Molds for casting figurines may be made by painting several coats of white liquid latex over the pattern. Latex may be purchased at craft and hobby shops. If the container does not have a brush attached to the lid, then you will need a small brush.

Plaster may be poured in a pie pan or almost any container for making impressions. Select a shape and size suitable for your project.

MAKING PLASTER OF PARIS PLAQUES

Plain and detailed plaques are easy to cast using plaster of paris. The following procedure is recommended:

1. Select the mold and support it around the edges with sand, pieces of Styrofoam or blocks of wood, if required. Fill the mold with water to determine the amount of plaster required. Pour the water into your measuring cup so you will know how much you need. (You will need about 1 1/2 parts plaster to 1 part water.)

2. Pour the water into a mixing bowl. Measure out the plaster of paris and slowly "sprinkle" it on top of the water, Fig. 27-4. Let the mixture stand for about a minute and then begin to stir using your spatula, Fig. 27-5. Add a few drops of white glue to make a smoother casting. After the plaster has been mixed thoroughly, let it stand for a minute before pouring it into the mold. (Never beat or whip the mixture; this will cause air bubbles.)

3. While waiting for the plaster prepare the mold. Wash it out with a little liquid detergent in a cup of water. It should be left wet, but with no water standing in it. You may need to pin the mold in place on its support.

4. Pour the mixture into the mold moving the bowl back and forth until the mold is filled, Fig. 27-6.

Fig. 27-5. Stir plaster until it is smooth and thoroughly mixed.

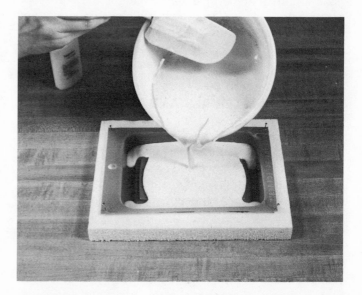

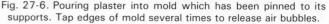

Fig. 27-6. Pouring plaster into mold which has been pinned to its supports. Tap edges of mold several times to release air bubbles.

Fig. 27-4. Mix measured amounts of plaster and water. Measure precise amounts before mixing. Note how mold is supported by Styrofoam.

Fig. 27-7. Hanger wire is embedded at top of plaque just before plaster sets up.

5. When the plaster has set a few minutes, embed the support hanger as shown in Fig. 27-7. Move the hanger back and forth several times to settle it in place.

6. Allow the plaster to dry for an hour or more; then gently force it out of the mold with your fingers. See Fig. 27-8. Let the plaque dry completely. This will take a day or more depending on the humidity. Fig. 27-9 shows completed castings of different shapes and sizes.

7. Apply a finish to the plaque. You can use antiquing, spray paints, acrylics, wood grain finishes or decoupage, Fig. 27-10. The completed plaque is a suitable frame for a photograph, piece of art or whatever you wish to display.

MAKING PLASTER OF PARIS FIGURINES

Figurines are small art objects which may be easily cast in a latex mold. Latex is a flexible, stretchy substance purchased in liquid form. It is used to make a one-piece mold. To make a latex mold and cast figurines, follow these steps:

1. Select a figurine that you would like to reproduce. Remove dust, oil or other foreign material from the model. If it is made from copper, brass or synthetic oil-based clay, apply a coat of clear arcylic lacquer. This will seal the surface and act as a release agent. Place the model on a base and brush on one coat of latex covering about an inch of the base, Fig. 27-11. Be sure to completely cover the object and try to avoid bubbles. The latex painted on the base will form a casting lip.

2. Allowing 30 minutes or more drying time between coats add more coats. (White latex will turn a beige color when ready.) Continue applying coats until the mold is between 1/16 and 1/8 in. (about 2 or 3 mm) thick. Larger objects should have a thicker mold and may require 10 or 12 coats. Let the mold dry for 48 hours after the last coat.

3. Carefully remove the mold from the model, Fig. 27-12. (Note: If your model is rather large, form

Fig. 27-9. These plaster of paris plaques are ready for decoration.

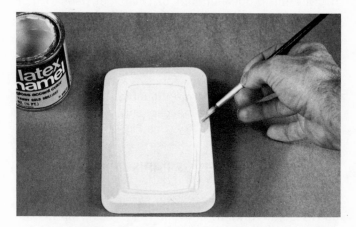

Fig. 27-10. This frame plaque is being painted with a coat of latex enamel paint.

Fig. 27-11. Figurine receives several coats of liquid latex to form mold for casting.

Fig. 27-12. Remove latex mold from the model. The latex will stretch and return to its original shape.

Fig. 27-8. Releasing the casting from the plastic mold. Be careful not to chip the edges.

two plaster halves around the outside of the mold before you remove it from the model. Latex will stretch and may become distorted from the weight of large amounts of plaster.)

4. Pour soapy release agent or soapy water into the latex mold. Slosh the solution around, Fig. 27-13, and pour out the excess. Support the mold in loose sand, Fig. 27-14, or the plaster coating if you have made one.

5. Mix the proper amount of plaster of paris (1 1/2 parts plaster to 1 part water) and pour it into the mold. See Fig. 27-15. Work the plaster in the mold with a thin piece of wood to be sure all crevices are filled and bubbles come to the top.

6. Allow the plaster to dry for several hours. Then very carefully remove it from the mold.

7. Shape the base as needed and apply the finish when the casting is dry. See Fig. 27-16.

MAKING PLASTER OF PARIS IMPRESSIONS

Impressions of objects such as leaves, hands, feet and decorative knots may be made using plaster of paris. The procedure follows:

1. Select a container for the plaster. An aluminum pie pan as shown in Fig. 27-17 will do. Also select an object for the impression.

2. Measure the amount of water needed to fill the container and pour it into the mixing bowl. Measure the proper amount of plaster and mix thoroughly. Pour the mixture into the container, Fig. 27-18.

3. Let the mixture set for a few minutes after tapping the container several times to remove bubbles. Press the object into the plaster to form the impression, Fig. 27-19. Do not push the object too deeply into the plaster. When the mixture begins to harden around the object, it may be removed.

4. Let the plaster cure for 24 hours and then remove it from the container. Apply the desired finish when the plaster is dry, Fig. 27-20.

Fig. 27-14. Mold has been placed in sand for support and is ready to be filled with plaster.

Fig. 27-15. Pouring properly mixed plaster into the mold. Tap mold or use a wire to release bubbles. Add more plaster if needed.

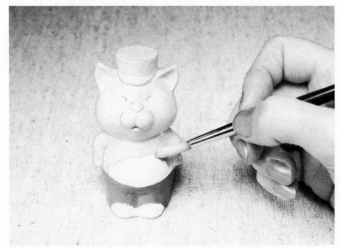

Fig. 27-16. Apply a finish of acrylic paint to the figurine.

Fig. 27-13. Fill mold with soapy solution to act as release agent before filling with plaster. Pour out all the soapy solution.

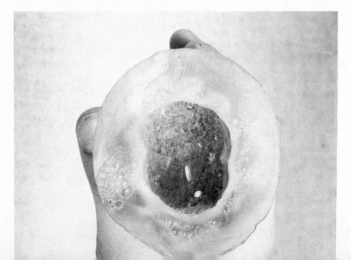

Fig. 27-17. This small pan is an excellent container for holding a plaster impression.

Fig. 27-19. The object has been placed on the plaster and has settled into place. The rope this knot was made from was colored so it would photograph better.

Fig. 27-18. Pouring the proper amount of plaster into the container. See section on casting plaques for mixing instruction. Carrick bend knot, shown at right, is the subject of this impression.

Fig. 27-20. Object has been removed from plaster and plaster has been taken from its mold. (Impression was painted with model lacquer to improve visibility.)

Plastics project suggestions — a dozen or more. A—Kitchen recipe holder. B—Five-sided picture/photograph holder. C—Functional and decorative napkin holder. D—Freestanding picture frame of smoked sheet plastic. E—Clear acrylic display boxes. F—Recipe box with slip-on lid. G—Smoke gray acrylic letter holder. H—Small card holder. I—Opaque white holder for calculator. J—Recipe box with hinged lid. (Dave Baird) K—Desk organizer. L—Sheet-and-tube pen and pencil holder. M—Marble game made of clear sheet acrylic. (Ann Arbor Plastics, Inc.)

Chapter 28
PLASTICS CRAFTS

By simply cutting, forming and shaping plastic sheet, rod or tube, you can fashion many interesting and functional craft items. The material, often called "Plexiglas" or "Lucite," is an acrylic plastic with many unusual characteristics.

Acrylic is highly transparent, can be heated and formed at very low temperatures, is quite hard and cements very easily to form strong joints. With these properties, it is ideal for craft projects. What to make? Try picture frames, desk trays, napkin holders, lamps, coasters, templates, clocks and a variety of jewelry. More than likely, you can add others to the list.

MATERIAL

Acrylic plastics are available in many sizes, shapes and colors. However, most acrylic used for craft projects is clear or colored flat sheet. Most sheet plastic is masked (paper covered) to protect the glossy surface during construction. A variety of colored and textured sheets, resembling the brilliance of stained glass, is also available for special projects. If you need round or square rod and tubing, these come in standard sizes. They can be purchased in almost any length. Stock acrylic materials are shown in Fig. 28-1.

You should also have on hand an acrylic solvent cement, a solvent cement applicator, clear, thickened cement, plastic cleaner, mask remover, masking tape, some wood for making jigs or forms for bending, and acrylic paint. See Fig. 28-2.

TOOLS

Most standard woodworking and metalworking tools also work well for cutting and shaping acrylic materials. You will probably need a cutting tool, coping saw, hacksaw, sandpaper, emery boards, an assortment of

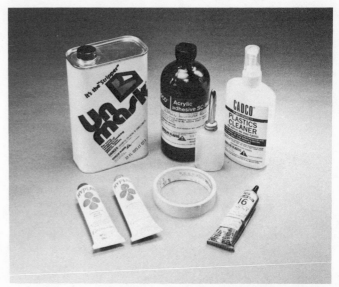

Fig. 28-2. Materials most frequently required when working with acrylic plastics are a liquid paper mask remover, solvent cement, plastics cleaner, acrylic paints, masking tape and a tube of clear, thickened cement.

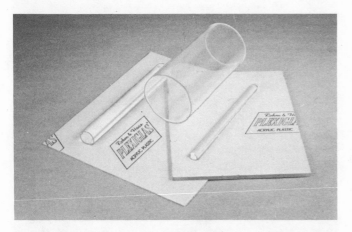

Fig. 28-1. Acrylic sheet, rod and tube can be purchased in a variety of stock sizes.

files, a straightedge, toothpaste and buffing compound. See Fig. 28-3.

A hand drill or portable power drill and a saber saw can be used to complete most operations. A jig saw cuts acrylic sheet quite well. However, it is probably best not to use other machines, such as a table saw or bandsaw, unless they have special blades for cutting plastics. A strip heater, Fig. 28-4, and an oven should supply enough heat for bending and forming.

CUTTING AND SHAPING PLASTICS

The following steps for cutting, shaping and forming, are typical.
1. When cutting acrylic sheet to size for your project, hold a straightedge firmly in position and scribe a line with a cutting tool across the sheet as in Fig. 28-5. Place the scribed line at the edge of the bench. Hold it firmly with one hand and snap off the extending piece by applying pressure with the other hand as shown in Fig. 28-6. Smaller pieces can be snapped in a woodworking vise. Do not remove the masking paper.

   Scribing and snapping the plastic sheet is used only for straight cuts. Curves should be cut with a saw. Short straight cuts can be made with a hacksaw.
2. Extremely large curves can be cut using the saber saw or jig saw. However, most craft work is small enough so that the coping saw works very well. Trace your pattern on the masked plastic and make your cut just outside of the pencil line, Fig. 28-7. Use a fine-tooth blade.

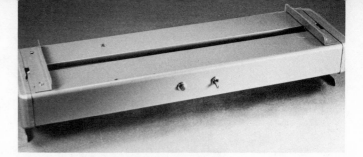

Fig. 28-4. A standard plastic strip heater is used for bending plastic.

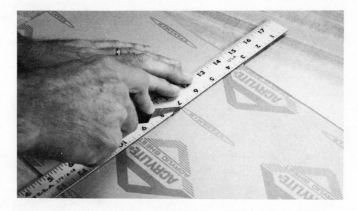

Fig. 28-5. Scribing line with plastic cutting tool and straightedge. This is done in preparation for "snapping" plastic.

Fig. 28-6. Snapping plastic sheet at edge of bench. If scribing was done properly, break will be clean and straight.

Fig. 28-7. Cut curved line with coping saw.

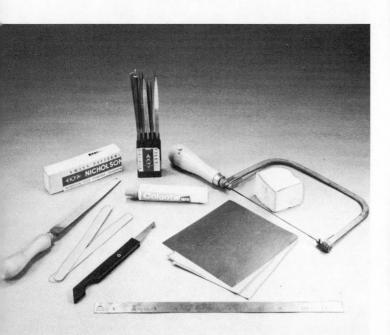

Fig. 28-3. These basic tools are used in plastics work.

3. To cut internal shapes, first drill a hole inside the pattern design. Use a drill press, hand drill or portable power drill, Fig. 28-8.

Insert one end of the coping saw blade through the hole. Reattach the blade to its handle and tighten. Cut out the internal pattern shape, Fig. 28-9, and remove the blade in the same manner.

4. The saw marks or unevenness from snapping the edges of acrylic sheet can be removed by filing, sanding and polishing. Start by draw filing the edge as shown in Fig. 28-10. Leave the masking paper on the plastic. When the filing is complete, wrap a fine grit sandpaper around a wood block and sand the edge as in Fig. 28-11. Work down to a very fine grit of "wet or dry" paper to give the edge a high polish. For a higher gloss, rub the edge with a damp cloth to which a small amount of toothpaste has been applied, Fig. 28-12. A buffing compound on a

Fig. 28-10. Draw filing on edge of plastic sheet. Work carefully to keep surface flat.

Fig. 28-8. Drill hole inside design shape with hand drill.

Fig. 28-11. Smooth edge with fine sandpaper and wood block.

Fig. 28-9. Cut out internal shape with coping saw.

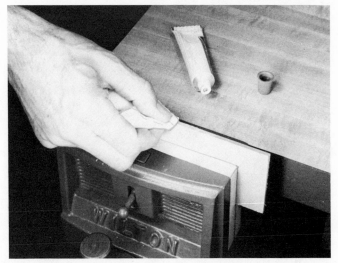

Fig. 28-12. Polish edge with toothpaste and soft damp cloth.

cloth wheel may also be used as shown in Fig. 28-13. Curved edges can also be sanded and polished in this manner.

5. Saw marks left after making internal cuts are generally more difficult to remove. Small files, fingernail emery boards or sandpaper wrapped around a pencil or flat stick should be used. See Fig. 28-14. Polish with toothpaste if desired.

6. Bond acrylic materials with a solvent cement or thickened cement. The solvent cement is a clear liquid and is best applied with a solvent cement applicator. Always remove the masking paper before cementing. See Fig. 28-15.

Since the cement dissolves the plastic surfaces and dries to make a bond, care must be taken not to let any cement touch the polished surfaces. They can easily be spoiled by the cement's chemical action.

Prepare the edges by filing flat and smooth. Do not polish. Assemble the joint. Use masking tape, rubber bands or a wood fixture to hold the pieces in place. Apply the cement with an applicator as shown in Fig. 28-16. Capillary action draws the cement into the joint where the edges are touching. The best joint is produced where complete contact is made between edges. A light pressure will give a strong bond in a few moments. Fig. 28-17 shows the cemented joint.

Joining sheet surfaces to obtain thicker material for a project is done in much the same manner. Wet the surfaces with solvent cement, slide them together and clamp until dry. The handle for a letter opener is made in this way.

Fig. 28-14. Smooth internal edge with emery board.

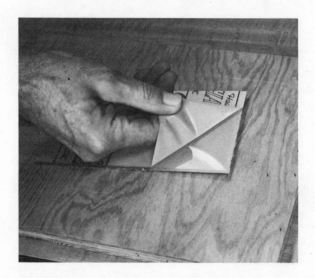

Fig. 28-15. Peel masking paper from plastic sheet before assembly.

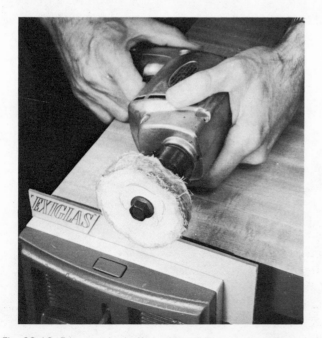

Fig. 28-13. Edge can be buffed with polishing compound on cloth wheel which is attached to a power drill.

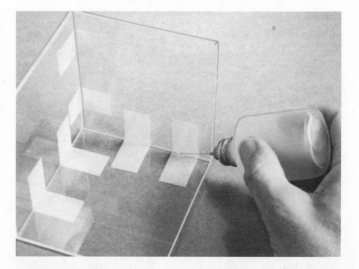

Fig. 28-16. Apply solvent cement to joint with applicator. Tape holds joints in correct position until cement sets.

7. Simple bends can be made by heating acrylic sheet over a strip heater until soft, Fig. 28-18. Bend to desired angle and hold until cool. To obtain exact angles, bend the heated sheet and tape it to a wood jig until cool as in Fig. 28-19. Make the bend in the direction away from the heated surface. A variety of shapes can be obtained in this manner as shown by the illustrated projects. Always remove the masking paper before heating and bending.

8. Projects requiring that sheet acrylic be twisted or formed into compound curves can be softened by heating in an oven. Set the oven at 300 °F (140 °C) and place a smooth cookie tin or sheet of aluminum on the oven rack. Remove the masking paper from the plastic and place the sheet on the cookie tin. Allow the sheet to heat for about five minutes. Wear soft gloves to remove the hot sheet from the oven and quickly form the plastic around your fixture to shape it. See Fig. 28-20.

Use felt on fixtures to protect the plastic. Wood grain may leave marks on the hot plastic sheet. A variety of jigs and fixtures can be made out of pieces of softwood and dowel rods to form acrylic sheet to your design pattern. Use your imagination in designing such jigs. The following projects show how most of the preceding operations are applied.

MAKING PLASTIC PROJECTS

You may want to try several basic projects in acrylics to get started in plastic crafts. See Fig. 28-21. Plastic templates can offer a variety of design possibilities.

Fig. 28-18. Heat plastic sheet over strip heater with masking paper removed to soften it for bending.

Fig. 28-19. Bent plastic sheet is taped to wood jig for cooling.

Fig. 28-17. Cemented joint with masking tape removed. Never apply cement over tape.

Fig. 28-20. Form hot sheet around wood fixture covered with felt.

Darts for sewing patterns, personal insignias and mechanical drawing templates are just a few of the things you can make.

1. Lay out your design on a piece of paper or a file card. Cut the required size from acrylic sheet 1/16 in. thick. Trace your design on the masked plastic as shown in Fig. 28-22.

2. Drill a small hole in each section of the design to insert the coping saw blade for cutting, Fig. 28-23. Carefully cut out the design following your pencil lines.

3. Use small files and emery boards to dress (smooth) the inside of the design. When filing is complete, trace the template on a piece of paper to see if the edges match your pattern. Dress any edges that are irregular and trace again.

4. File and polish the outside edges of the sheet to eliminate roughness. When this has been done the template is ready to be used, Fig. 28-24.

Fig. 28-22. Trace design on masking paper using carbon paper.

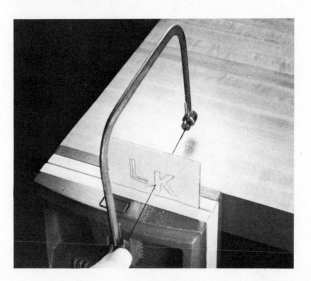

Fig. 28-23. Insert coping saw blade through hole in plastic and cut out design.

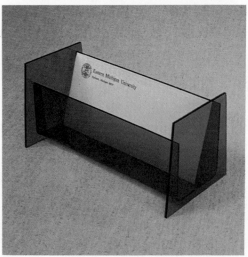

Fig. 28-21. Plastic projects are easy to cut and shape from sheet acrylic. Top. Bracelet. Bottom. Letter holder.

Fig. 28-24. File edge of design with a flat jewelers' file to remove roughness and irregularities.

PICTURE HOLDER

Interesting picture holders can be made from clear acrylic sheet. This type of project requires little more than heating and bending.

1. Determine the size of holder needed for the picture. You will need a piece of 1/8 in. acrylic sheet about three times the length of your picture. Example: if the picture is 5 x 7 in. (127 x 178 mm), cut a sheet 8 x 15 in. (203 x 381 mm). This holder is made to enclose a horizontal picture of these dimensions.
2. File and polish the edges. Remove masking paper from both sides.
3. Place the sheet on the strip heater 3 in. (76 mm) from one end to make the bend for the base, Fig. 28-25. Be sure to make your bend away from the heated surface and hold in place until cool. This takes only a few minutes.
4. Make next bend 6 in. (152 mm) from the opposite end or midway between the ends of the flat face. Place on strip heater with base down and heat until pliable. Make the bend and clamp as shown in Fig. 28-26. This forms the lip for holding the photograph. Allow to cool, remove clamps and polish with plastics cleaner. The finished picture holder is shown in Fig. 28-27.

PLASTIC BRACELET

A plastic bracelet makes a good beginning project that involves heating in an oven and bending around a solid form. Any variety of richly colored acrylic sheet can be used.

1. Prepare a design for the bracelet and cut it out of stiff paper. Trace the design on a 1/8 in. masked acrylic sheet, Fig. 28-28.

Fig. 28-26. After heating, bend hot plastic quickly. Hold the bend in place with spring clamps. Felt strips protect surface.

Fig. 28-27. Picture is held by fold at top.

Fig. 28-25. Heating plastic to make bend for base of picture holder. Place plastic squarely on the heater.

Fig. 28-28. Trace bracelet design on masked acrylic sheet.

2. Cut out the bracelet blank with a jigsaw or coping saw, Fig. 28-29. Carefully saw just outside your pencil line.

3. File and polish the edges to the degree of gloss you desire. Remove the masking paper and lay the plastic on a sheet of aluminum or a cookie tin. Place in an oven at 300 °F (149 °C) and heat until pliable, about five minutes.

4. Remove the hot blank from the oven with soft gloves. Quickly wrap around bracelet form and hold until cool, Fig. 28-30. Refer to the chapter on laminating for making a wood bracelet form. Fig. 28-21 and Fig. 28-31 show the completed bracelet.

LETTER HOLDER

A letter holder involves cutting, cementing and bending. It also lends itself well to the use of colored acrylic sheet.

1. Plan your design using a curved body and flat ends. Trace the pattern for the ends. Make the body 10 in. (254 mm) long and wide enough—about 9 in. (228 mm) to form the U-shaped section. See Fig. 28-32. Use a 1/8 in. sheet.

2. Cut out, file and polish all edges and remove masking paper. Place the ends aside until later. They are ready for assembly.

3. Form the body using the strip heater. Make right angle bends 3 in. (76 mm) from each end.

4. Use a solvent cement to bond ends of holder to body as shown in Fig. 28-33 and allow to dry. Fig. 28-21 and Fig. 28-34 show the letter holder ready to use.

Fig. 28-30. Hold hot sheet plastic around fixture until cool.

Fig. 28-31. Bracelet is polished and ready to wear.

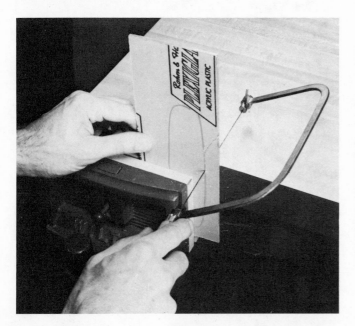

Fig. 28-29. Cut out bracelet blank with coping saw.

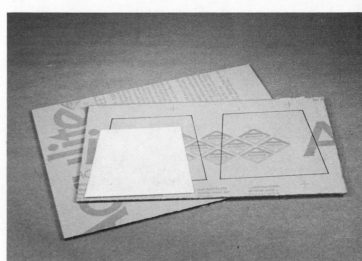

Fig. 28-32. Shape has been traced for ends and sheet cut for body of letter holder.

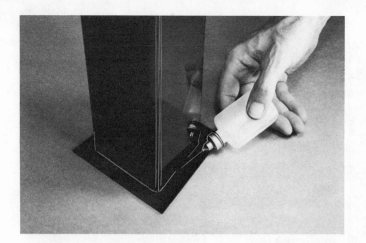

Fig. 28-33. Cement end to body with solvent cement in applicator.

Fig. 28-34. Letter holder was made from smoke gray acrylic sheet.

Suggestions for additional pottery projects. A—Small pinch pot ash tray. B—Slab vase and matching pinch pot. C—Thrown vase with multicolor glaze. D—Square pinch pot candle holder. E—Slab salt and pepper shakers. F—Coffee cup with red overglaze. G—Thrown bowl with simple decoration. H—Brightly colored bud vase. I—Wheel thrown jar with flattened sides. J—Sugar and creamer set with large pitcher. K—Coffee mug from slab clay. L—Slab decorated pendant. M—Slab dresser tray, free-form design. (Linda Baird Kerr) N—Slab planter. O—Wheel thrown base for hurricane lamp. P—Wheel thrown flower pot. Q—Leaf decoration on small slab necklace.

Chapter 29
POTTERY

Projects made from fire-hardened clay are generally called pottery. Working with clay to produce a variety of functional and decorative pottery can be exciting.

Soft clay can be formed by hand or with simple tools into almost any shape. No drawings or exacting equipment are needed. Once shaped to your satisfaction, a pottery piece should be allowed to dry thoroughly before it is glazed and fired. However, some pieces can be made without glazing and firing.

You may want to try some simple projects first. Then, when you have the feel of forming and working the clay, try your hand at some advanced designs. Candle holders, hot trays, mugs, sugar bowls and cream pitchers, jars and vases are not difficult to make after you have experience. The potter's wheel can be used to form cylinders for bowls and vases.

MATERIALS

A good clay, of course, is the basic material for all pottery work. It can be purchased either dry or dampened. Dampened clay will probably give you more reliable workability and more satisfactory results. It comes ready to use. Usually, the package contains instructions for firing color and temperatures.

You will also need a selection of glazes in different colors. Glaze is both a decoration and a waterproofing material. It is usually applied in a liquid form and, when fired, covers the surface with a thin layer of glass. Prepared glazes, available at craft and ceramic stores, are best.

TOOLS

Tools used for shaping and decorating pottery projects are inexpensive. You will need a good ruler, a rolling pin, some burlap, a knife, sponges, cutting wire, small paintbrushes and modeling tools. See Fig. 29-1. A taut wire stretched across the edge of your workbench is convenient for cutting lumps of clay. A potter's wheel is necessary for thrown pieces and a kiln is required for firing.

Fig. 29-1. Tools used in pottery. You will recognize most of them. The pieces in the center of the picture are wood modeling tools. A hand wire cutter is shown at bottom left.

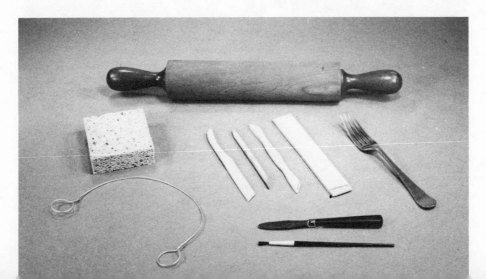

WEDGING THE CLAY

Clay as received from the supplier, needs to be squeezed and pressed to remove trapped air and to form a smooth, even texture. This process is called "wedging."

Wedge the clay by pressing it with the palms of your hands as in Fig. 29-2. Fold it over itself again and again while continuing to press it flat. Wedging should be continued until the clay is very plastic and smooth.

To test the clay, form it into a lump and slice it on a taut wire. Examine the cut surface for presence of air bubbles. Slap the pieces together on the workbench and continue wedging and slicing until all air bubbles are removed, Fig. 29-3.

Fig. 29-4. Decorated pinch pot with green glaze is an easy first project in pottery.

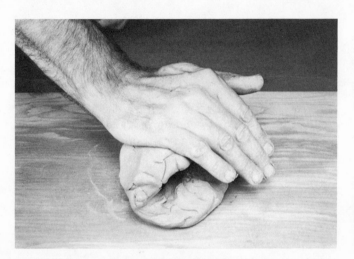

Fig. 29-2. Wedging clay with palms of hands. This is a process of folding and flattening to remove air bubbles.

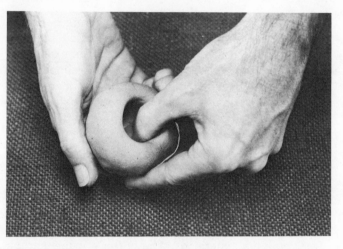

Fig. 29-5. Depress clay with thumb to form inside of pinch pot.

Fig. 29-3. Slicing lump of clay on a taut wire. This step will reveal presence of air bubbles.

MAKING A PINCH POT

A pinch pot, Fig. 29-4, is a simple pottery project. It is an easy way to get used to the feel of forming clay and does not require any tools except for decorating. Follow these steps:

1. Shape a lump of clay (about the size of a small apple) into a ball by squeezing and rolling it around in your hands.
2. Begin forming an opening in the ball by pressing the thumb of one hand into the clay while rotating the ball with the other, Fig. 29-5. Enlarge the opening in the pot by slowing rotating the ball of clay while squeezing between your thumb and fingers as shown in Fig. 29-6.
3. Slowly form the pot to the final size by pressing the sides (walls) to an even thickness. A small pinch pot can be completed at this stage into an oval or circular form.
4. By continued working of the clay with thumb and fingers, the pot can easily be formed into a small vase with a narrowed top. To narrow the top, lap the walls over each other as in Fig. 29-7 and continue pinching and lapping until the neck is the right size. Bend the top of the wall over slightly to form the lip. Smooth all surfaces with your fingers or a sponge before decorating. Texture with modeling tools or stamps for surface decoration, Fig. 29-8.

MAKING SLAB POTTERY

The slab process of forming clay is basic for making many pieces of contemporary pottery, Fig. 29-9. A ball of clay is flattened with a rolling pin to the right thickness and trimmed.

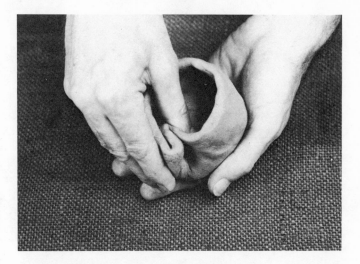

Fig. 29-7. Lap walls over each other to narrow neck.

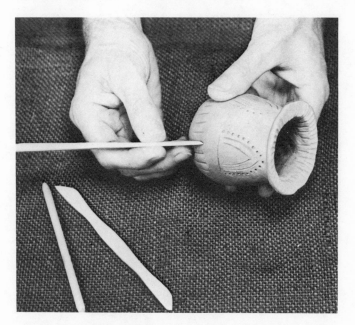

Fig. 29-8. Using modeling tool to decorate surface.

Fig. 29-6. Enlarge bowl of pinch pot by squeezing with thumb and fingers as clay is rotated in the hands.

Fig. 29-9. Slab pottery made from potter's red modeling clay. It was fired with a clear glaze.

Fig. 29-10. Form slab of clay with rolling pin.

Fig. 29-11. Apply slip to scratched edges with a brush.

Fig. 29-12. Join first two edges with modeling tool.

To make a slab project such as a jar, tray or flower box, follow these steps:

1. Place a piece of plastic sheet on the workbench to protect it from moisture. A damp piece of burlap provides a good surface for rolling out clay.
2. Select two strips of wood 3/8 to 1/2 in. thick. Lay them parallel on the burlap the width of your slab.
3. Place a ball of wedged clay between the wood strips and form it to an even thickness with a rolling pin as shown in Fig. 29-10. The burlap gives one side an even texture and keeps the clay from sticking to the plastic sheet.
4. Cut the slab into four pieces with a knife. These will become the sides of a rectangular jar. Allow the clay to dry enough (usually a few hours) to become stiff. This is necessary to prevent sagging during assembly. However, it should still be soft enough to pinch when making joints. Try this for all slab work.

Fig. 29-13. Trim excess clay of base along sides of jar with a knife.

5. Scratch all edges to be joined with the points of a fork. Apply slip (watery clay) to the scratched edges, Fig. 29-11.
6. Join the first two sides by pressing grooves into the joint on the inside. Use a modeling tool as in Fig. 29-12.
7. Join remaining sides in the same manner to form the rectangular jar.
8. Stand the jar on another slab of clay to form the base. Trim the base even with the sides of the jar, Fig. 29-13.
9. Use a modeling tool to join the base on the inside in the same way the sides were joined.
10. Decorate the outside corners by pinching with your fingers. See Fig. 29-14. This is not only decorative but it also helps to make the joints much stronger.
11. Add handles on either side by cutting two strips of clay. Press one end onto side near top of jar and join the other end to the lower side as shown in Fig. 29-15. Allow a loop large enough to grasp comfortably.
12. Allow the jar to dry. Glaze and fire it or leave it unfired. (Pottery left unfired should be allowed to dry completely. Since the clay is porous, it should not be allowed to come in contact with water when in use. Unfired pottery is also brittle; handle it with care.)

You may want to experiment with texturing slab surfaces for decorating pottery pieces. Figs. 29-16 and 29-17 illustrate a few of the many techniques you can use in decorating.

Fig. 29-15. After scratching surfaces well, join handles to jar with slip. Press them on with finger while supporting wall on inside.

Fig. 29-16. Surface decorations were made with modeling stick, head of bolt and bottle cap.

Fig. 29-17. Decorations can be made with table fork, fingernail, toothbrush or other tool.

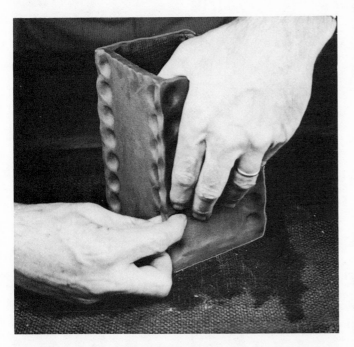

Fig. 29-14. Pinching outside corners with fingers. Besides providing decoration this step squeezes corners more tightly together.

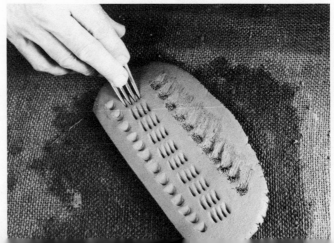

MAKING COIL POTTERY

Coils of clay, formed by hand, can produce a number of different pieces of pottery. See Fig. 29-18. To form coils:

1. Prepare clay in the manner described for slab projects. Be sure the clay has been completely wedged.
2. Start rolling a ball of clay on a damp board with both hands. Move your hands along the clay strip until a smooth, even coil is formed. Try to keep the diameter of the coil in proportion to the project you plan to make. Prepare a dozen or more coils about 16 in. long for a small pitcher. Cover the coils with a damp cloth until you are ready to use them.
3. Cut a circle from a thin slab of clay. Begin forming the pitcher by wrapping a coil around the slab base, Fig. 29-19. Continue laying up coils of clay. Use a modeling tool to join the coils to the base and to each other from inside the bowl. This will seal the clay together but will not show on the outside.
4. Continue to add coils, sealing both the ends and edges as you go along, Fig. 29-20. Try not to flatten the coils as you build up the walls, Fig. 29-21. The last few coils should be expanded outward to form the spout, Fig. 29-22. Add the handle by pressing single or braided coils into the top and side surface, Fig. 29-23. Allow to dry completely.
5. Glaze and fire. These steps are described later in the chapter.

MAKING POTTERY ON THE WHEEL

It takes time and practice to become skilled in using the potter's wheel. However, a few basic instructions should help you get started. Follow these steps for throwing a clay project:

1. Wedge the clay as for any other project, form it into a ball and place it on the wheel plate. Start the

Fig. 29-19. Wrap first coil around slab base.

Fig. 29-20. Add coils, sealing both ends and edges on the inside.

Fig. 29-21. Use a knife to smooth outside joint. This helps to keep coils rounded.

Fig. 29-18. Coil pitcher with green over brown glaze.

wheel turning and force the clay to the exact center of the wheel. Keep your hands moistened with water and steadily press the clay into a solid cylinder as shown in Fig. 29-24.

2. When the ball of clay has been perfectly centered, use your thumbs to force a hole in the top while your fingers keep the outside turning true, Fig. 29-25. Slowly open up the center while pulling the clay up to form a cylinder as shown in Fig. 29-26.

3. Now draw the cylinder up with both hands to thin the walls and form your desired shape. Cut off the

Fig. 29-24. Form clay into solid cylinder.

Fig. 29-22. Form spout from expanded coils. Shape carefully with the hands.

Fig. 29-25. Using thumbs to open hole in top of clay.

Fig. 29-23. Triple coil handle is pressed in place.

Fig. 29-26. Slowly pull up sides of cylinder.

uneven top with a knife or handle-mounted pin, Fig. 29-27. Smooth the inner and outer walls of the cylinder with moistened fingers to obtain the texture you desire. Trim the excess clay away from the base with a flat wood stick while the wheel is turning, Fig. 29-28.

4. Stop the wheel and unfasten the cylinder from the base plate by pulling a wire through the clay at the base plate surface. Gently slide the cylinder from the base plate onto a board and allow it to dry completely. Your thrown clay project is now ready for glazing and firing.

GLAZING AND FIRING POTTERY

To apply glaze to your project and fire it in the kiln:

1. Most pieces of pottery are fired twice. The first or "bisque" firing hardens the clay so that it is not brittle. It also makes the pottery much easier to handle while applying the glaze. Place your pottery piece in the kiln, Fig. 29-29, and slowly raise the temperature.

2. Small tapered cones made of ceramic materials are used to determine the correct firing temperature, Fig. 29-30. The cones are placed in the kiln so that they can be seen through the peep hole. They will melt and sag as higher temperatures are reached. Three cones are generally used following a melt temperature numbering system. Bisque firing is usually done using a cone 6 to a cone 8. The higher the cone number the sooner it will bend.

3. As cone 8 bends and cone 7 begins to sag, turn off the kiln and allow your pottery piece to cool slowly. Most clay and glazes indicate cone temperatures for firing.

4. Allow the piece to cool overnight and then remove it from the kiln.

5. Select the color or colors of glaze to be used. Glazes can also be applied by pouring or spraying. However, brushing works very well, makes application easy and requires less equipment. Brush three coats of prepared liquid glaze over the pottery piece. The glaze is thick, so brush it on heavily being careful to overlap previous applications, Fig. 29-31. When dry, add decorative colors with a small brush as desired.

6. Choose the correct firing cones for the glaze used and place them in the kiln so they can be seen through the peep hole. Place your glazed pottery pieces on a rack in the kiln and turn on the heat. Carefully watch the cones. When the second cone

Fig. 29-28. Trim excess clay away from base with flat modeling tool.

Fig. 29-27. Trim top level. Use small pin tool.

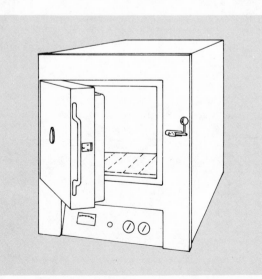

Fig. 29-29. Small kiln is used for firing and glazing pottery.

begins to sag, turn off the heat and allow to cool overnight. Good glazing and firing of pottery takes experience. Experiment with different temperatures until you consistently obtain good results.

Fig. 29-30. Cone in center has begun to sag while cone on right has melted, indicating firing temperature has been reached.

Fig. 29-31. Brush glaze on coil pitcher in preparation for firing.

Quilling craft suggestions. A—Flower design on black background and framed in gold. B—Small wooden box with quilled design on lid. C—Sewing box with quilling design under glass. D—Variety of quilled designs using both coils and scrolls.

258

Chapter 30
QUILLING

Butterflies, birds, flowers and Christmas trees all have something in common. They are good subjects for ''paper filigree'' or ''quilling.'' Quilling is the art of rolling and bending narrow strips of paper into coils which are then assembled into familiar shapes.

If you enjoy meticulous and creative work, then quilling is a natural for you. You can make beautiful pictures, Fig. 30-1, decorate common household items or form three-dimensional objects. All you need is a few materials, a little patience and some creative effort.

MATERIALS AND TOOLS

The basic material for quilling is paper in narrow strips about 1/8 in. wide and 20 in. long (3 by 508 mm). See Fig. 30-2. The paper should be heavy enough

Fig. 30-1. Quilling produces exquisite designs such as this butterfly.

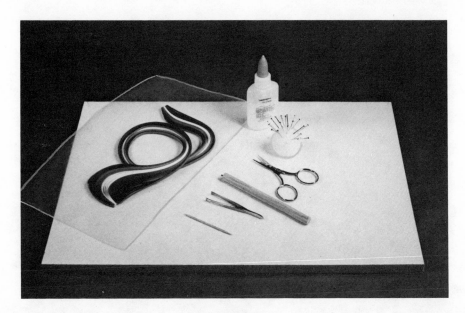

Fig. 30-2. Materials needed for quilling include quilling paper, glue, toothpick, tweezers, quilling tool, manicure scissors, pins, waxed paper and a piece of fiberboard.

to retain its shape, but light enough to roll smoothly. Precut quilling paper, in a variety of colors, is sold at craft and hobby shops.

If you prepare your own, cut the strips with the grain of the paper so that the rolls will be smooth. When you are not sure which way the grain in your paper is running, tear a piece of it. Paper tears straighter with the grain. Paper strips can be as narrow as 1/16 in. (1.5 mm) or as wide as 1 in. (25 mm). However, 1/8 in. (3 mm) is the most popular size.

Also needed is a quilling tool, a toothpick or a corsage pin for rolling the paper. The quilling tool has a hollow metal cylinder at one end. The cylinder has a small slit cut along one side which holds the end of the paper strip. Fig. 30-3 shows a quilling tool. Any small cylindrical object may be substituted if you do not have a quilling tool.

Other tools and materials needed include: white glue for joining the coils, manicure scissors, tweezers, straight pins, waxed paper and fiberboard or cardboard backing for assembly.

Fig. 30-3. A quilling tool is a hollow metal tube with a slit on one side. This is attached to a large wooden handle.

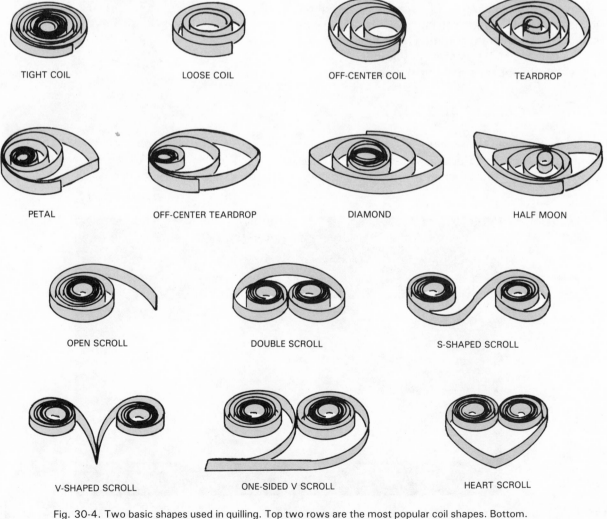

TIGHT COIL   LOOSE COIL   OFF-CENTER COIL   TEARDROP

PETAL   OFF-CENTER TEARDROP   DIAMOND   HALF MOON

OPEN SCROLL   DOUBLE SCROLL   S-SHAPED SCROLL

V-SHAPED SCROLL   ONE-SIDED V SCROLL   HEART SCROLL

Fig. 30-4. Two basic shapes used in quilling. Top two rows are the most popular coil shapes. Bottom. Typical scroll shapes.

BASIC SHAPES

Coils and scrolls are the two basic classifications of shapes used in quilling. There are several variations of each type.

COILS

Coils are formed by rolling quilling paper around a quilling tool or toothpick. Tight coils are glued without allowing the strip to unwind. Loose coils are allowed to unwind until the desired size is reached. Off-center coils are made from loose coils with the center moved to one side. The loops are glued together where they touch. Teardrop coils are loose coils which have been pinched on one side to form a pointed shape. Off-center teardrops are made in the same way as an off-center coil except that one side is pinched to form a pointed end. Other shapes such as petals, hearts, diamonds and half moons are also possible. All are made from loose coils that are fastened together with glue where the loops touch.

SCROLLS

Scrolls are similar to loose coils. The sole difference is an outside end which is free to connect to other shapes or form part of a larger design. The same techniques are used to form scrolls that were used for coils. Fig. 30-4 shows several coil and scroll shapes.

QUILLING A DESIGN

Before you begin a specific design, try some of the coils and scrolls illustrated. Once you master the technique, concentrate on a specific article. Following these steps will help you carry your project through in an orderly fashion.

1. Organize your materials and select a design. Draw the design full size on a piece of paper. Place the paper on your work board and cover it with waxed paper. The lines will be visible through the waxed paper and the glue will not stick to it. Fig. 30-5 shows the layout.

2. Begin your first coil by attaching the end of a paper strip to the hollow tube in the quilling tool, Fig. 30-6. If you do not have a quilling tool, use a toothpick. Dampen the end of the paper slightly if it is difficult to start on the toothpick. Experiment with different lengths of paper until the proper size coil or scroll is produced. Maintain an even pressure as you roll. Select colors which compliment each other.

3. Where required, glue coils or scrolls as soon as you remove them from the tool, Fig. 30-7. Pin each coil

Fig. 30-5. Pattern for a butterfly is placed under a piece of waxed paper on a piece of fiberboard.

Fig. 30-6. Starting a coil using the quilling tool. The end of the paper strip is slipped into the slit.

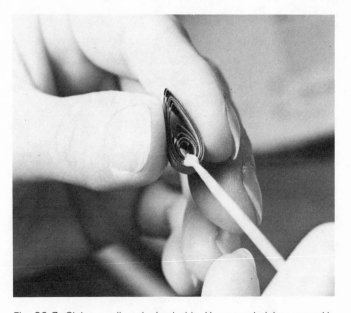

Fig. 30-7. Gluing a coil on the back side. Use a toothpick to spread it between loops.

down and apply a small drop of glue, Fig. 30-8. Use a toothpick to work the glue between the layers of paper. Glue closed coils to the right size before pinching them.

4. Glue each coil where it touches another one, Fig. 30-9. If the design is to be attached to a surface such as a plaque or fabric backing, you can form the design on that surface if you wish.

5. Continue forming coils and scrolls until your design is complete. See Figs. 30-10, 30-11 and 30-12. Rhinestones or shells may be used for eyes or for other decoration. Now that you know the procedure, concentrate on design and form some interesting shapes.

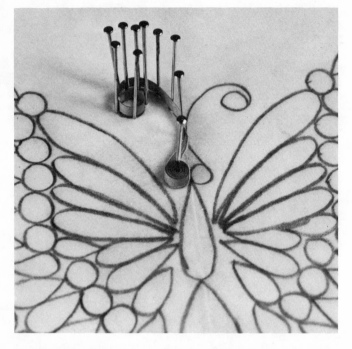

Fig. 30-8. First piece of the design is shaped and pinned in place over pattern.

Fig. 30-10. Body of butterfly is complete and has been pinned down to dry.

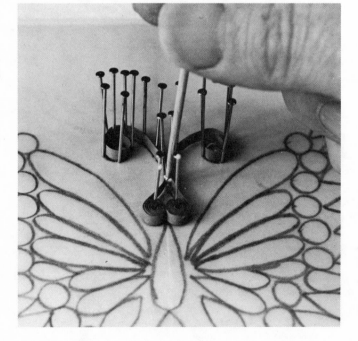

Fig. 30-9. Each coil is glued where it touches another coil. Work glue between coils with a toothpick.

Fig. 30-11. Different size coils are made and matched before they are glued in place.

Fig. 30-12. Completed butterfly still on waxed paper. It will be removed and cemented to a plaque.

Ideas for rugmaking. A—Hooked rug on heavy fabric backing. (Linda Baird Kerr)   B—High quality woven rug in butterfly design. C—Rug woven from fabric scraps. D—Unique advanced work in beautiful design. E—Woven rug with open spaces to accent design. F—Beautiful wall hanging in intricate design.

Chapter 31
RUGMAKING

Rugmaking is fun and anyone can do it. Handmade rugs can be knotted, hooked, woven or braided. All of these methods require very little in the way of tools or equipment.

KNOTTED RUGS

Several types of knotted rugs can be made by hand. The most popular include Rya, Latch-Needle and Tufted.

RYA RUGS

Rya (pronounced ree'-ah) rugs are simple and easy to make using a Swedish knot called the Ghiordes (Yor'-deez) knot and rya wool yarn. A rya rug, Fig. 31-1, has a shaggy cut pile which lends itself well to contemporary themes. Create any size you desire. Simply sew sections together. This method of rugmaking is as appropriate for beginners as it is for persons experienced in the craft.

Materials

The foundation for the rya rug is a double-mesh canvas usually about half cotton and half hemp, Fig. 31-2. A special rya backing is also used. It has narrow openwork rows spaced at 1/2 in. (13 mm) intervals. The canvas should be about 1 in. (25 mm) larger than the finished product.

Yarns may be made of wool or synthetic materials. Rya is a two-ply wool yarn produced in a wide variety of weights and colors.

Colors may be combined to produce an endless variety of patterns. Yarns of different colors may also be used in a single needle to give a variegated (many colored) effect.

Fig. 31-1. This hooked rug is made on canvas using a latch needle.

Fig. 31-2. Double-mesh canvas having about four squares per inch is commonly used for rya rugmaking.

You will need several large, blunt canvas or tapestry needles. Size No. 13 either curved or straight will do. Use a ruler or gage stick to measure to height of the pile as you make the rug. You will also need a grease pencil to draw your design on the canvas. See Fig. 31-3.

MAKING A RYA RUG

1. Plan the size and design. Sketch it on a piece of paper, Fig. 31-4, and then transfer the design to your canvas with the grease pencil. You may indicate colors with felt-tip markers if you wish.

2. Calculate the amount of yarn needed. Figure double the length of the pile and add 1/2 in. (This will be the amount of yarn needed for one knot.) Multiply this by the number of knots in one row (3 1/2 per inch for Rya backing) and by the number of strands threaded in the needle. Usually three or four strands are used together. When you know the amount of yarn required for one row of knots, multiply by the number of rows of knots (about one every 1/2 in.). The resulting figure is the total number of inches of yarn needed. Divide by 36 to convert the amount to yards.

   For comparison, consider that a 37 by 52 in. rug with 2 in. pile requires about 1677 yd. of yarn (125.5 yd. per sq. ft.).

   If you are working in SI metric, consider the problem in this way: How much yarn is needed for a rug 94 cm by 132 cm if each strand of a knot is 6 cm long and four strands are being used in each knot. There are 0.7 knots per centimetre.

Fig. 31-3. Rya rugmaking also requires two-ply wool yarn, a blunt tapestry needle, grease pencil and a gage stick for measuring the height of the pile.

Fig. 31-4. Rug design is first drawn on a piece of paper for easy reference and for calculating materials needed.

Knots per row	= 0.7 x 94	= 134
No. of rows	= 0.7 x 132	= 188
Total knots	= 134 x 188	= 25 192
Amt. of yarn	= 25 192 x (4 x 6)	= 604 608 cm
		= 6 046 m
Yarn per cm²	= 6 046 m x 12 408 = 0.48 m (or 48.7 cm)	

3. If the canvas does not already have a woven border, stitch a narrow hem around the edge to prevent the canvas from fraying.
4. Cut skeins of yarn into length of 36 in. (914 mm). Thread several canvas needles with three or four strands of yarn as shown in Fig. 31-5.
5. Begin your work at the lower left-hand corner of the canvas. Put the threaded needle down through the canvas alongside the first pair of threads, Fig. 31-6. Bring it back up through the opening to the left of the two threads. (Imported rya rug backing has three threads instead of two.)
6. Pull the yarn through to the left, leaving 2 in. hanging down.

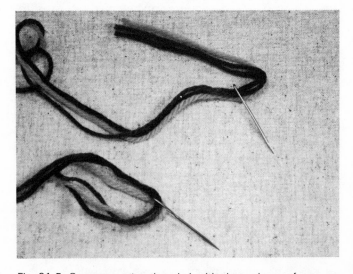

Fig. 31-5. Canvas needles threaded with three pieces of yarn are ready to be used.

7. Bring the needle back to the right and take the next stitch under the next two right-hand strands. Bring the needle up through the hole where you began, Fig. 31-7. Pull the yarn through until it is tight, Fig. 31-8 and Fig. 31-9. The result of steps 5, 6 and 7 is to make a loop around two sets of vertical strands.

8. Place the gage stick (this measures the length of the loop) over the right-hand thread and wrap the yarn over the top forming a loop, Fig. 31-10. This forms the Ghiordes knot. Do not pull it too tight. You must be able to remove your gage later.

9. Push the needle through the next square (hole) to the right of the last occupied square. This is the beginning of the next loop. Bring the needle up through the left-hand square already occupied by the first loop. Finish the second loop in the same way as the first.

Fig. 31-8. Pull yarn through to form knot.

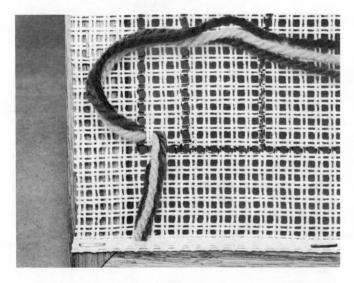

Fig. 31-6. Start first knot in lower left-hand corner of canvas.

Fig. 31-9. Knot is completed.

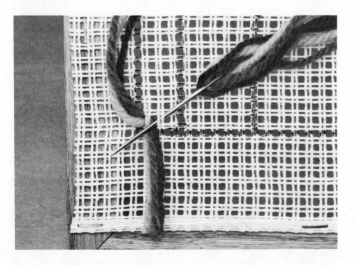

Fig. 31-7. Second half of knot is formed by entering the square just to the right of previous stitch.

Fig. 31-10. Lay gage over first knot and loop yarn over it before entering next square of the canvas to begin next knot. Different width gages may be used to produce piles of different length.

10. Continue making loops across the canvas from left to right, moving the gage along as you work if it is not long enough to reach across the rug. Change colors as required by your design. Proceed as you did in making the first knot.

11. When you have completed a row, cut the yarn along the edge of the gage or slip it out and cut the loops, Fig. 31-11. Fig. 31-12 shows the first row after it has been cut.

12. Begin the second row at the lower left-hand side just above the first row. Skip one horizontal row of squares and proceed across, tying knots as demonstrated in Fig. 31-13. You are on your way!

LATCH-NEEDLE RUGS

Latch-needle rugs are similar in appearance to rya rugs, but the knot is made with the latch needle or latch hook shown in Fig. 31-14. Precut yarn pieces are used. The latch at the top of the needle opens and closes permitting the needle to be loaded and drawn through the canvas holes.

Materials

The fabric backing for latch-hooked rugs must have a coarse, open mesh. Rug canvas having a double horizontal and vertical thread (mono or penelope canvas) is generally used. A coarse mesh, 3 1/2 or 4 squares to an inch, is suitable. See Fig. 31-15.

Yarn pieces for latch-hooked rugs may be wool, orlon or rayon and cotton blended rug yarn. You may purchase precut pieces 2 5/8 in. (66 mm) and longer, Fig. 31-16. Or, if you prefer, cut your own.

Purchase a latch needle with a straight or curved shank. Select a size appropriate for the canvas you plan to use.

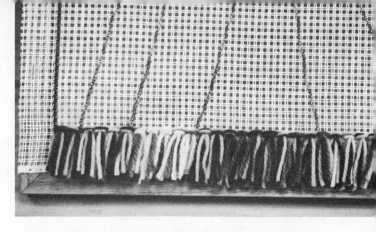

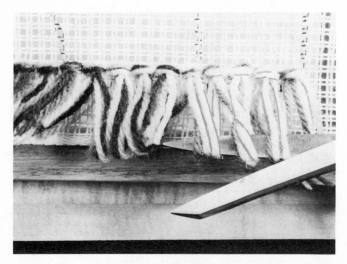

Fig. 31-11. Cut loops after first row is completed.

Fig. 31-12. First row has been completed and loops are cut.

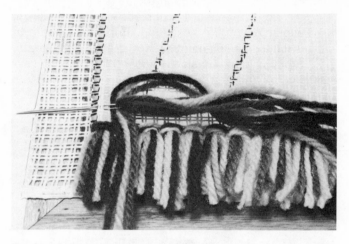

Fig. 31-13. Begin second row of knots. Skip a square between rows.

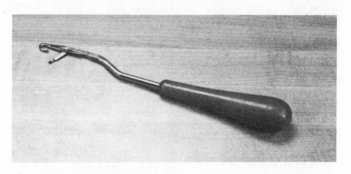

Fig. 31-14. Common latch needle used in making latch-needle rugs. Some needles have the straight shank but this one is curved.

Fig. 31-15. Double horizontal and vertical thread canvas is commonly used for latch-needle rugs. This canvas has 3 1/2 or 4 squares to the inch and is called a mono or penelope canvas.

MAKING A LATCH-NEEDLE RUG

1. Sketch the size and design of your rug on paper.
2. Transfer the design to the front side of the canvas. You will be working from the topside. Indicate colors with water colors or felt-tip markers if you wish, Fig. 31-17.

3. Tape the edges of the canvas with masking tape and attach it to a frame.
4. Calculate the number of yarn pieces that you will need of each color by counting the canvas squares in each color. Each square requires one piece of yarn.
5. Begin working in the lower left-hand corner of the rug. Using the latch needle requires four motions. First, open the latch by pressing it back against the shank. Insert the hook down through a square of the canvas and up through the square above it. See Fig. 31-18.
6. Lay the piece of cut yarn under the shank of the needle and pull the two ends of the yarn together over the top, Fig. 31-19.

Fig. 31-16. Precut yarn pieces are used for latch-needle rugmaking. They may be purchased precut or you can cut your own. Standard length is about 2 5/8 in.

Fig. 31-18. First step in attaching a piece of yarn with the latch needle. First, open the latch, then insert hook down through the first square and up through the square above it. Begin in the lower left corner.

Fig. 31-17. Design has been transferred to canvas using felt-tip markers and water colors to indicate proper colors.

Fig. 31-19. Lay a piece of yarn flat under shank of needle and grasp the two ends of the yarn together over the top as shown in photograph. The looped yarn can also be slipped onto needle before it is inserted in canvas, if preferred.

Fig. 31-20. Bring yarn ends around to left side in back of latch and under hook.

Fig. 31-23. First row is completed and second has begun.

Fig. 31-21. Close latch and slide hook through canvas and the loop of yarn. Pull yarn ends completely through the loop.

Fig. 31-24. Full color shot of rug about half completed. Design is clearly visible even through the long pile.

Fig. 31-22. First knot is completed.

Fig. 31-25. Photograph of backside of rug shows stitches very clearly.

7. While holding the yarn ends, bring them around to the left side in back of the latch, and forward under the hook, Fig. 31-20.

8. Close the latch with your left hand and guide the hook as you pull the handle back toward you with your right hand. The hook will slide through the canvas square and then through the loop of yarn, Fig. 31-21. The knot is tied to the canvas as shown in Fig. 31-22.

9. Tie the next piece of yarn in the square to the right of the first one. When the first row is finished, move to the row above and again work from the left to the right, Fig. 31-23. Continue until you have the knotting completed. Fig. 31-24 shows the rug in full color about half finished. The backside of the rug is shown in Fig. 31-25.

10. Finish off the edges. Fold back the canvas and stitch it down to the backside, Fig. 31-26. Then sew rug binding to the edge with heavy thread. The rug binding should be about 1 in. wide. See Fig. 31-27 and Fig. 31-28.

TUFTED RUGS

Tufted rugs are very easy to make and are excellent projects for the beginner. Tufts of yarn are tied to a foundation or backing. Your design can be simple or intricately detailed. Look about you for ideas.

Materials

The backing is usually made from burlap, monk's cloth or any heavy, firm material. Tufts may be made from yarn or cotton thread. A canvas needle anchors the tufts to the backing. A crayon, pencil or other marking device will be needed to mark and identify each tuft. A piece of cardboard for making the tufts and a pair of scissors complete the list of materials needed. See Fig. 31-29.

Fig. 31-27. Rug binding is stitched to outside edge of rug.

Fig. 31-28. Binding is stitched on inside edge and mitered at corners.

Fig. 31-26. Canvas edges have been folded down and stitched to the back of rug to secure them.

Fig. 31-29. Materials needed for tufted rugs include burlap or other heavy cloth, yarn, canvas needle, marking device, a piece of cardboard for making tufts and scissors.

MAKING A TUFTED RUG

1. Plan your design and mark pairs of dots 1/2 in. (13 mm) apart on the backing material, Fig. 31-30. Use colored crayons. The dots may be lined up in rows or staggered.
2. Make tufts. Wrap yarn around a 1-1 1/2 in. (25-38 mm) piece of cardboard or board 15 to 20 times, depending on the weight and texture of the yarn, Fig. 31-31.
3. Slip the wrapped yarn off the board. Using a 6 in. (13 mm) piece of yarn, tie the end of the tuft to hold it together as in Fig. 31-32. The tails of the piece of yarn will be used to fasten the tuft to the backing.
4. Thread one tail onto a canvas needle and push it through one of the dots on the backing. Now push it back through at the location of the other dot. Duplicate this procedure with the other tail going in the opposite direction. See Fig. 31-33.
5. Tie tails together in a firm knot like the one shown in Fig. 31-34.

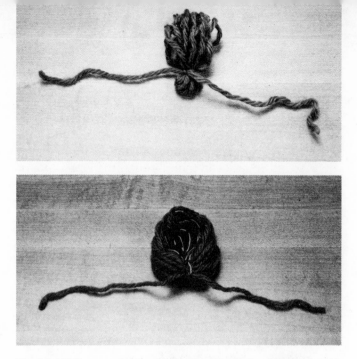

Fig. 31-32. Two methods of tying the end of a tuft to hold it together. Top. Yarn is wrapped around bunched end. Bottom. Yarn is tied through the loop.

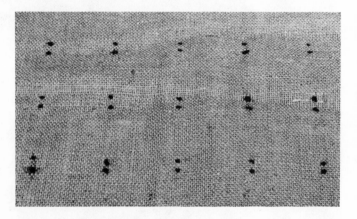

Fig. 31-30. Pairs of dots are spaced about 1/2 in. (13 mm) apart to locate position of tufts.

Fig. 31-33. Each end of tie yarn has been threaded on a canvas needle and pushed through the fabric on one dot and up through at the other dot.

Fig. 31-34. Tie tails into tight knot on front side of fabric.

Fig. 31-31. Wrap yarn around piece of cardboard to form tuft.

6. When all the tufts have been attached, clip the loops to form the pile, Fig. 31-35. Clip tails (left from tying) to length of pile.
7. Finish edges with facing material. Fig. 31-36 shows the completed pile.

HOOKED (PUNCH NEEDLE) RUGS

Hooked rugs are made by forcing loops of yarn or cloth strips through a burlap or canvas backing to form a pile surface. The materials are usually very coarse.

Traditionally, hooked rugs were made with a Susan Bates steel needle. But, today, the shuttle needle, Columbia Minerva hook and walking hook are preferred. These newer mechanical devices are faster and ensure greater accuracy since they regulate the stitches and pile height.

Materials

Most hooking methods require a frame either purchased or built from 1 by 2 in. boards, Fig. 31-37. The foundation or backing should be a good grade of burlap or a two-ply monk's cloth large enough to allow for a 3 in. (76 mm) hem on all sides.

You will also need a needle or hook. Fig. 31-38 shows materials and tools. Any of the hooks on the market will do the job. Select either a hand needle, shuttle hook, punch needle, Columbia Minerva hook or speed hook. Practice with the hook on scrap material until you feel confident with it.

MAKING A HOOKED RUG

1. Plan the rug design and outline it on the foundation material.
2. Attach the foundation to the frame with thumbtacks, staples or lace it. Note: The speed hook,

Fig. 31-36. Pile of tufted rug should look like this.

Fig. 31-37. Hooked rug frame is made from a 1 by 2 in. board. It is used for making punch needle rug.

Fig. 31-35. Insert shears carefully through each tuft and cut the loops to form the pile.

Fig. 31-38. Materials for hooking a punch needle rug. They include a punch needle (two sizes are shown), yarn, fabric, rugmaking frame and Saf-T-back liquid.

shuttle hook, Columbia Minerva hook and punch needle are used on the back of the foundation causing loops to form on the right side. The hand needle is used from the front.

3. Using the needle or hook, outline your design with stitches and then fill in between the outlines, Figs. 31-39 and 31-40. Fig. 31-41 shows the topside of the completed section after it has been clipped.

4. When the rug is hooked, fold the hem flat against the back and sew it in place. The corners will lay flat if you miter them.

5. Paint the backside with a nonslip material, Fig. 31-42. This will seal the rug and help prevent skidding. One quart will cover about 12 sq. ft.

WOVEN RUGS

Woven rugs are made by stringing thread, cord, twine or narrow strips of cloth across a series of evenly spaced vertical cords. The vertical cords or threads, called the "warp," are strung on a sturdy wooden frame known as a loom. The material being threaded crosswise is called the "weft" or filler threads.

THE UPRIGHT LOOM

There are several types of looms you can purchase or build, but the upright loom is simple to make and entirely adequate for the job.

The loom should be large enough to make your entire rug. For the first try, make a smaller rug, not over 2 by 4 ft. (51 by 102 mm).

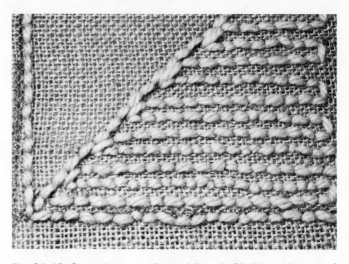

Fig. 31-40. Space between diagonal lines is filled in with rows of evenly spaced stitches.

Fig. 31-41. A completed section after the loops were clipped. Fibers fill up space between rows.

Fig. 31-39. Outlining design with punch needle. Loops should be the same height and distance apart.

Fig. 31-42. Paint back of a hooked rug with a nonskid material.

Building the Loom

Use 1 by 3 in. (25 by 76 mm) oak or other hardwood for the frame. You will need two pieces 60 in. (1524 mm) long for the sides and two pieces 36 in. (914 mm) long for the ends. This frame is large enough for a 2 by 4 ft. rug.

Make lap joints at the corners as shown in Fig. 31-43. Bolt the pieces together with 1/2 in. bolts. Simpler but not as sturdy is a butt joint, Fig. 31-44. Be sure your frame is square.

Now scribe a line on the face of each end 3/4 in. from the inside edge. Use this line as a guide for the nails which will support the warp threads. Use finishing nails 1 1/2 to 2 in. long. Drill holes along the lines slightly smaller than the diameter of the nail 1/2 in. apart. Do not drive the nails all the way through. See Fig. 31-45.

OTHER TOOLS AND MATERIALS

In addition to the loom, you will need:
1. Heavy cord, warping twine or strips of cloth selvage edge.
2. A shuttle to carry the weft back and forth, over and under the warp threads.
3. A warp stick which spreads the warp threads apart so the shuttle may be passed through.
4. Yarn or strips of cloth for filler or weft. (If strips of cloth are used, they should be 1 1/2 in. (38 mm) wide with the edges turned so that they will not ravel.)

Fig. 31-45 shows the materials needed for making woven rugs.

Fig. 31-44. A butt joint should be predrilled and nailed. While not as strong as a lap joint, it is easier to make if you have few woodworking tools.

Fig. 31-45. To make a woven rug you will need a loom, heavy cord for warp strings, shuttle to carry the filler through the warp, warp stick and strips of cloth or yarn.

Fig. 31-43. A lap joint is strong and excellent for the corners of a rug loom. A bolt and wing nut are ideal for quick disassembly and storage of the loom.

MAKING A WOVEN RUG

1. Tie the warp with a slip knot to the first nail at the upper left-hand side. Keeping the cord tight, go around behind the first nail at the lower left-hand corner and the one next to it. Now return to the top and go around behind the next two nails, Fig. 31-46. Continue until the loom has been warped. Tie the warp to the last nail.

2. Thread the shuttle.

3. Insert the warp or shed sticks. "Weave" them through the warp, alternating over and under each successive string. Be sure to start the second stick the opposite of the first so that it goes under the warp strings that the first stick goes over. See the method in Fig. 31-47.

4. Turn the first stick on edge to open a path for the shuttle carrying the weft. Start to weave at the lower right-hand corner about 6 in. (152 mm) above the nails, Fig. 31-48.

5. When the left side of the loom is reached pull the weft tight (not too tight) and remove the stick. Now, turn the other one on edge. This will open the way for the weft to weave to the right. If you are using cloth, fold the edges of the cloth as you weave and keep the weft pushed tightly together, Fig. 31-49.

This method is known as "plain" or "tabby" weaving. You can vary the colors or textures as you

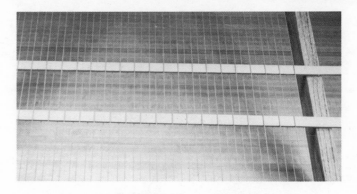

Fig. 31-47. Warp or shed sticks are inserted flat.

Fig. 31-48. Passing shuttle through warp threads the first time. Warp stick is turned on edge to open path for shuttle.

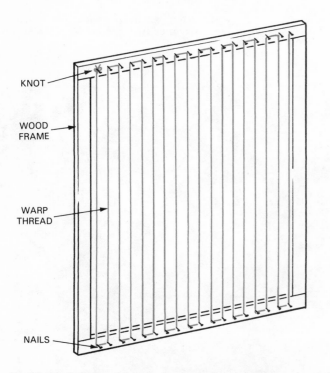

KNOT

WOOD FRAME

WARP THREAD

NAILS

Fig. 31-46. Stringing the loom. Begin at upper left-hand corner and work across to other end. Go around the first two nails and then back to the top again. Continue in this manner until loom is warped. Tie warp thread to last nail.

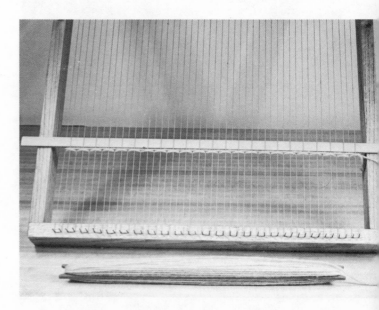

Fig. 31-49. Keep weft (filler yarns) pushed tightly together so that a smooth texture is formed.

weave to develop a design or a random pattern. See Fig. 31-50.

6. As the shuttle empties, add more material. Sew additional strips together with a machine or by hand. Continue the process until the rug reaches the right size.

7. When the weaving is finished, remove the rug from the loom by cutting the pair of threads over the center nails on one end. Tie these two threads together tightly against the weft of the rug, Fig. 31-51. Tie every other pair of threads on each end as you work from the middle toward the edges. Tie the remaining threads, finishing up with the corner threads. Do not cut off the extra thread. It may be used to form a fringe at the ends of the rug.

BRAIDED RUGS

Braided rugs are made from woolen strips of cloth. If you can make a braid, you can make a rug. Use new material, if you wish, but scrap pieces from old clothes work just as well. In fact, many rugmakers prefer used materials.

MATERIALS AND TOOLS

You will need a supply of woolen cloth. A heavy, soft, firm material such as a camel's hair coat produces even braids and is easy for the beginner to work. An army blanket is also very acceptable.

Flannel is generally too thin and will require a wider strip. Very likely it will form extra folds as you braid.

You will need a large darning needle, thimble, safety pins, a large tapestry needle, sewing twine for lacing the braids together, rubber bands, flexible tape and scissors, Fig. 31-52.

Fig. 31-50. Second color is added to rug as weaving progresses.

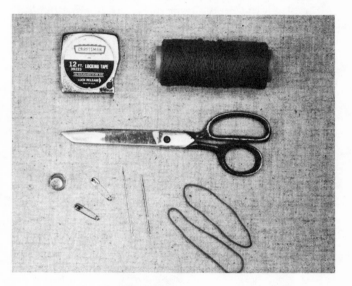

Fig. 31-52. Materials and tools for braided rugs.

Fig. 31-51. Warp threads are tied in pairs when weaving is completed. Begin in middle on one end and tie every other pair. Do the same on the other end and then tie remaining pairs. Ends of strings may be left untrimmed to form a fringe.

MAKING A BRAIDED RUG

1. Prepare the cloth by taking apart clothing at the seams. Wash the pieces. If you have purchased new cloth, washing is not necessary. Determine the width of strips by rolling a piece of material to form a strand of the braid. Widths will range from 1 to 3 in. (25 to 76 mm) depending on the thickness of the material and size of braid desired. Make a sample strand before you cut all your strips, Fig. 31-53. Tearing is preferred; it is faster and more accurate than cutting.

2. Join strips together by placing one on top of the other right side up at right angles, Fig. 31-54. Stitch the pieces diagonally and trim off the corners.

3. To begin braiding, attach three strips together with a safety pin. Follow these steps:
   a. Take the brown over the white toward the left.
   b. Take the plaid over the brown toward the right.
   c. Take the white over the plaid toward the left, Fig. 31-55.
   d. Take the brown over the white toward the right.
   e. Take the plaid over the brown toward the left.
   f. Take the white over the plaid toward the right, Fig. 31-56.
   g. Take the brown over the white toward the left, and so on.

   Practice this procedure until you can produce a round, smooth braid. There should be no creases or folds on the top or underside of the braid.

4. Braid a length of strands and begin forming the rug by holding the braid in position with safety pins. Form a spiral and stitch the braids together, catching the touching sides of braid alternately.

Fig. 31-54. Two strips are joined at right angles and sewed across the corner.

Fig. 31-55. Beginning to braid three strands of cloth together. Be sure to keep the folded edges rolled to the center of each strand.

Fig. 31-56. Braid is underway. By now you should know the procedure for braiding.

Fig. 31-57. Beginning a rug with completed braid. Stitch braids together with a darning needle and hide the threads. Keep rug flat as you work.

Fig. 31-53. A braiding strand with edges rolled in. This piece of material is 2 in. (51 mm) wide.

Hide the thread between the strands as shown in Fig. 31-57.

5. When the rug reaches the proper size, begin to taper the cloth strips to end the rug. Roll into small tubes as you did while braiding and blindstitch using sewing thread and needle. Braid these strips to their end and lace to your rug. Sew one of the strips under another one and wrap the two remaining strips around each other and sew together. Fold the tapered end down and stitch it securely to the adjacent braid, Fig. 31-58. The rug is finished.

Fig. 31-58. Rug should be finished off by tapering braid and sewing it securely in place to the braid beside it.

Punch needle rug with symmetrical design. Refer to page 273.

The beautiful woven rug was made on a rug loom. See page 276.

Suggestions in sand art. A—Simple sand pattern in straight jar. B—Sculpture in curved vase. C—Flower sand sculpture combined with floral arrangement. D—Clown policeman painted in sand. E—Geometric sculpture done in cut bottle. F—Use of color shading in sand painting. G—Sand painting design done on mahogany plywood. H—Sand sculpture scene in sheet acrylic container.

Chapter 32
SAND ART

Sand art, as a craft medium, has become increasingly popular. Materials are inexpensive, techniques are easily learned, self expression is unlimited and it is unique!

The two major types of sand forms are generally known as sand painting and sand sculpturing. Some of the most interesting projects are decorative paintings, sculptures in glass containers, vases, terrariums, planters, jewelry and serving trays. Sand art also can go hand in hand with bottle cutting, since a variety of interesting glass containers may be cut rather than purchased.

MATERIALS AND TOOLS

A good selection of clear glass or plastic containers is basic for sand art projects. See Fig. 32-1. Colored sand, plywood for picture backings, carbon paper and white glue, Fig. 32-2, are also needed.

Fig. 32-1. Containers of many different shapes are used for sand art projects.

Fig. 32-2. Colored sand, white glue, carbon paper and plywood are the other materials needed for sand art.

Colored sand is available under several brand names which will vary in color, intensity, grain size and cost. Some are nontoxic and colorfast. Select good quality sand for lasting beauty. Use colors that compliment your design and are in line with the decorating mood you have set.

Sand art requires only a few simple tools. A wide paintbrush is handy for spreading the initial adhesive. A few small paintbrushes are useful for painting the design. A spoon is pressed into service as a modeling tool. Most of these tools may be found around the home and should be bent or shaped to sculpture your particular design. A selection of tools for sand art is shown in Fig. 32-3.

SAND PAINTING

Fig. 32-4 is a sample of sand painting. The first step is to prepare a design. It should be made full size. Use a pencil on medium weight paper. Include all the details. Every sand painting is made the same way. Use the following procedure:

1. Select a piece of thin plywood for your design. Place it on a paper-covered work area.
2. Prepare the adhesive, mixing one part water with three parts white glue. Stir well.
3. Using a wide brush, spread an even coat of adhesive over the entire plywood surface, Fig. 32-5. Quickly pour the desired color of background sand on the wood, Fig. 32-6. Spread it over the whole surface.
4. Allow the glue to "set;" then tilt the plywood on edge and tap lightly on the back so that all loose sand falls onto the paper, Fig. 32-7.
5. Always save unused sand. Pick up the paper and pour the excess sand back into the container. See Fig. 32-8.
6. Apply a second coat of sand in the same manner when the first background coat is completely dry.
7. Trace your design on the sand background with a pencil and carbon paper, Fig. 32-9. These lines will be hidden by the sand coating as the picture progresses.
8. Use a small brush to paint the outlines of the design with glue as in Fig. 32-10. Apply sand as you did in making the background. When the glue has set, tilt the background board again to remove excess sand. See Fig. 32-11.
9. In any sand painting, apply all of one color at a time before starting with another color. In this way, you can keep excess sand of different colors from becoming mixed together. Allow each color to dry completely before continuing with the next step of the process.
10. When the outlines are complete, paint glue along the edges of the outlines, then fill in the entire

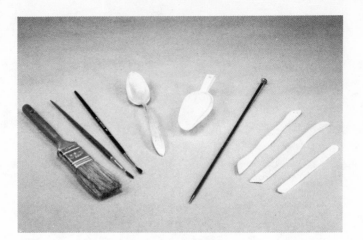

Fig. 32-3. Tools for sand art include both wide and small paintbrushes, a spoon, measuring scoop, knitting needle and wood modeling tools.

Fig. 32-4. Sand painting of ladybug was done in four colors of sand.

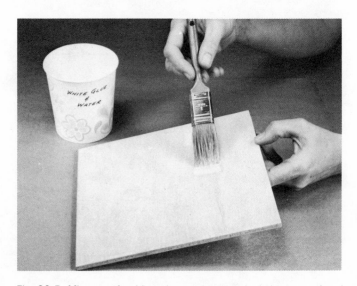

Fig. 32-5. Mixture of white glue and water is being spread on plywood board.

Fig. 32-6. Pour background sand on wet adhesive base.

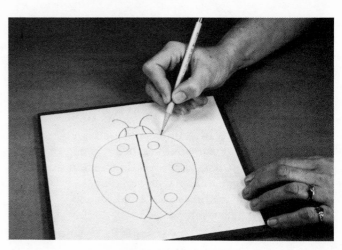

Fig. 32-9. Tracing design on background. Lay carbon paper over background and transfer outline onto background sand.

Fig. 32-7. Tilt board so loose sand will fall away leaving an even coat on the surface.

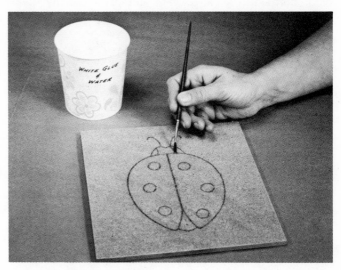

Fig. 32-10. Paint outline of design with glue.

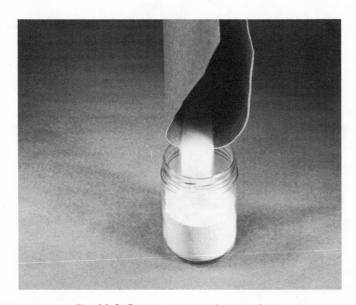

Fig. 32-8. Return excess sand to container.

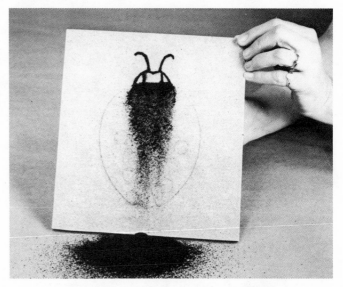

Fig. 32-11. Remove excess black sand by tapping back of board.

area, Fig. 32-12. Apply the desired color of sand. Use this procedure for all areas of your picture. Be sure not to let the glue dry before covering it with sand. For large areas, spread glue and sand in small sections. Do not attempt to do the entire area at one time.

11. For best results, apply two coats of sand to all lines and areas of your design, just as you did the background. Place your brushes in a cup of water when not in use. This will keep them soft and clean for the next application of glue.

12. If you want to frame your sand painting, refer to Chapter 16 on Framing.

SAND SCULPTURING

Using sand to form a three-dimensional design in a clear container is called sand sculpturing. Any clear glass or plastic container may be used, but it is wise to plan your sculpture idea first and then find a container that will work with your design. The magnitude of the project is up to you. You may want to make a simple, decorative table sculpture or a complicated hanging planter with sand and flowers.

For any such project, you will need an interesting glass container. Fig. 32-13 shows a number of inexpensive ones that are suitable for many different types of sculpturing. A visit to glass shops, craft stores, chemistry labs or department stores will give you an opportunity to select the size and shape you desire. Many nonreturnable bottles, such as salad oil jars and jelly glasses, are also satisfactory. You can also make flatsided plastic containers by cementing together thin acrylic sheets to form cubes or rectangular boxes.

Fig. 32-12. Paint solid areas with glue mixture.

Fig. 32-14. Smooth and level sand with small paintbrush.

Fig. 32-13. Glass containers are available in great variety for different types of sand sculpturing.

MAKING A SAND SCULPTURE

The following procedure is basic to all types of sand sculpturing. Variations for special projects are covered at the end of the chapter.

1. Spread layers of newspaper over the work area and place your container on the paper.
2. Gather the colors of sand required for your design, a spoon, pointed tools and a small paintbrush.
3. Start a simple, layered design by pouring one color of sand into the container. Level and smooth the surface with a paintbrush, Fig. 32-14. Brush down sand sticking to the sides before pouring the next layer.
4. Pour each color of sand to the same depth and level. Smooth with a brush in the same manner as the first. The layered design should then look like the one shown in Fig. 32-15.
5. Contoured layers are formed by shaping the top edges of each layer with a spoon or paint brush as shown in Fig. 32-16. The center of the sand need not be contoured.

6. You can produce many abstract patterns by making points in each layer or a number of layers of sand. After two or more layers have been poured, use a pointed tool to form the V shapes. Push the tool gently into the sand while holding it against the container wall. Slowly draw the tool toward the center of the container. Sand from the upper layers will flow in to form the shapes shown in Fig. 32-17. A variety of designs can be made in this manner using flat or pointed tools.

7. Designs and pictures can be sand sculptured with a spoon and a wood stylus. For mountains, lakes, clouds or faces, copy a picture or sketch the shape you desire. A lake scene and a boat will be formed in the following procedure.
   a. Pour the basic sand color into the container and begin shaping the waves with the spoon.
   b. Use the stylus to shape the boat bottom as in Fig. 32-18.

Fig. 32-15. Six layers of colored sand are leveled and smoothed.

Fig. 32-17. Forming pointed shapes in sand layers with a long knitting needle. Press needle into sand along edge of glass to depth desired. Then move needle toward center.

Fig. 32-16. Each layer of sand is first leveled and then contoured by pressing spoon down against inside of glass and drawing sand toward center of container.

Fig. 32-18. Draw blue sand away from side of glass with wood stylus to form hollow for boat hull. Hollow is then filled with red sand.

c. Add the necessary colors of sand to form the sail as shown in Fig. 32-19.

d. After building up the picture evenly in small sections all around the container, use the knitting needle to form the mast as in Fig. 32-20.

e. Keep the center of the container filled with sand to prevent the walls from eroding. Use waste sand or other materials, Fig. 32-21. They will not show when the project is completed.

8. Always pour the sand with a spoon from behind the desired shape on the container wall.

9. When the design is sculptured, fill the container with sand to desired height.

10. Seal the surface of the sand to keep the sculpture from shifting. Two methods work very well.

a. With a spoon, add a small amount of lacquer to the total surface.

b. Mix some sand with white glue and carefully pour a thin layer over the surface, Fig. 32-22.

HELPFUL HINTS

1. An error can be corrected by drawing the sand away from the glass into the center of the container.

2. To make floral pieces, place a block of Styrofoam (rigid expanded polystyrene plastic) in the center of the container and sculpture the sand design around the foam in the basic manner. Completely cover the block and then gently force the floral stems into the foam. A container with a glass lid may also be used for floral pieces.

3. Sand sculpture vases can be made by placing a test tube inside your container. Start your design with sand to a depth that will bring the test tube flush

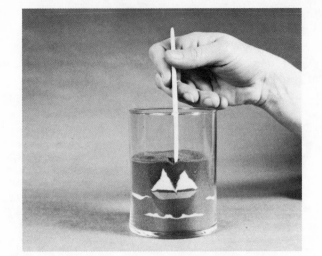

Fig. 32-20. Knitting needle is used to form mast. Point tool into white sail sand and withdraw it toward center of container.

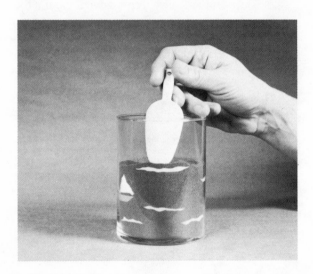

Fig. 32-21. Fill center of sculpture with waste sand.

Fig. 32-19. Gently pour white sand down container wall with spoon to build up mound for the sail.

Fig. 32-22. Pour mixture of sand and glue over horizon to seal sculpture and keep sand from shifting.

with the top of the container. Finish sculpturing around the tube and seal the sand at the top. Use the vase for live flowers, filling the test tube with water.

4. Be sure that both the sand and container you use are completely dry so the sand will flow easily and not stick to the glass.

5. Large containers require a great deal of sand, however, beach sand or waste sand can be used to fill the center since it will not be seen.

6. To make flower planters and terrariums, use the same basic method. Be sure to leave enough room to spoon in about 2 in. of potting soil. Plants or cactus should then be arranged in an interesting setting. Wood chips and stones often add a different dimension to sculptured planters.

Screen printing craft ideas. A—T-shirts screen printed with names. B—Photographic film stencil on wood plaque. C—Christmas card made using paper stencil method. D—Multicolor print for framing. (Norm Delventhal) E—Greeting card reproduced from a photographic film stencil. F—Wood plaque with screen print. (Sarah Lawrence) G—Three color fabric print using photographic film stencil. (John Rocus) H—Fabric print from lacquer film stencil. (Connie Grove) I—Place mat in two colors printed from photographic film stencil. J—Print on mirror prepared from photographic film stencil. (Gerald Smith) K—Design printed on brass foil and etched.

Chapter 33
SCREEN PRINTING

Screen printing or "serigraphy" is based on the principle of the stencil and is one of the most popular of the graphic arts. The process is simple. Once learned, it is an excellent method of printing your own greeting cards, display signs, fabrics, pictures and countless other items. See Fig. 33-1.

MATERIALS AND TOOLS

Relatively few materials and tools are needed for screen printing, Fig. 33-2. A check list would include:
1. Screen material.
2. Frame.
3. Base.
4. Squeegee.
5. Inks, paints, thinners and fillers.
6. Masking or paper tape.
7. Lacquer film stencil material.
8. Paper toweling.

SCREEN

Most important is the screen itself. Any of several types of fabrics may be used: organdy, silk, copper mesh or monofilament nylon. Organdy, though far cheaper, is not nearly as good a screen fabric as silk. It sags and the prints are not as sharp and clear. A good silk fabric may be used over and over dozens of times and will remain tight.

A fabric with a medium fine mesh (No. 12) is recommended for most projects. If you have a fine copper screen, it may be used with reasonable results. Still, it is not as good as silk for craft projects. Monofilament

Fig. 33-1. This banner was screen printed using a paper stencil.

Fig. 33-2. Most of the tools and supplies needed for paper stencil and film stencil screen printing are shown here.

nylon is a very durable fabric that prints nearly as well as silk and is cheaper. Again, a No. 12 mesh, double-weight fabric is the best for screen work. This fabric is available from some graphic arts suppliers.

FRAME

The screen fabric is attached to a frame, usually rectangular and usually made from wood. Corners may be reinforced with metal angle plates. Small frames may be constructed from 1 by 2 in. (25 by 55 mm) pine.

The inside dimensions of the frame should be about 3 in. (7.5 cm) wider and 8 in. (20 cm) longer than the print size. It is important that the frame be sturdy and straight. The screen fabric may be stapled to the underside of the frame or attached with a woven strip forced into a groove in the frame. See Fig. 33-3.

The frame is generally hinged to a plywood base several inches larger than the frame. For sizes up to 18 by 24 in. (46 by 61 cm), the base may be 1/2 in. thick but it should be 3/4 in. (2 cm) for larger frames. A table top could be used for very large projects.

The frame is attached to the base with hinges having removable pins, Fig. 33-4. These are known as slide-pin hinges and are necessary so that the frame may be easily removed for cleaning and repair.

SQUEEGEE

A squeegee is used to draw the ink back and forth across the screen to print the image. It consists of a thick rubber blade fastened to a wooden handle. It should be an inch or two shorter than the inside width of the frame.

INKS AND PAINTS

Ink or paint for silk-screen printing may be opaque or transparent printers ink, poster ink, lacquer-based ink, oil paint or tempera paint. Matte poster-color ink is generally recommended for printing on paper.

In addition to the ink, you should have:
1. Some transparency base which makes the ink less opaque.
2. Some extender base which will make the ink last longer.

Mix the extender with the ink using one part base to two parts ink. The mixture should have the consistency of thick cream.

SOLVENTS AND FILLERS

The proper solvent or thinner for the ink and filler you are using is important. (The filler is used to block openings in the screen where you do not wish ink to pass.)

Oil-based inks or paints can be removed from the screen with paint thinner. Lacquer-base printing medium is removed with lacquer thinner.

Water-soluble fillers should be used with oil or lacquer-base inks. If you use water-base inks, such as tempera that clean up with water, use a lacquer-base filler. Many printing inks and solvents are flammable. Be careful. Use them in a well-ventilated room.

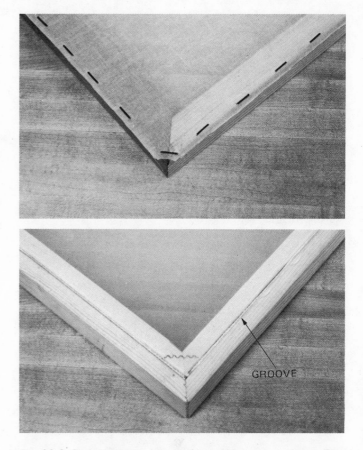

Fig. 33-3. There are two methods of attaching screen to frame. Top. Organdy screen material is stapled to underside of frame. Bottom. Silk screen material can also be attached to frame using woven fabric strip forced into groove cut into wood. This frame is top quality.

Fig. 33-4. Silk screen frame should be attached to base with removable pin hinges or some device which is easily disengaged.

MAKING A SCREEN PRINT

Stencils for screen printing are of several types:
1. Paper stencils.
2. Block-out stencils
3. Tusche stencils.
4. Film stencils.
5. Photographic stencils.

Preparation of three of these stencils will be explained. However, a few details should be clarified before you attempt to produce a stencil.

1. The design on the stencil is right reading (faces the same direction as the printed image). If you have done linoleum block printing, you know that the image on the block is reversed.
2. You will need a stencil for each color you plan to print.
3. Either make a frame for each color or print the required quantity of one color. Then strip the stencil from the screen and attach the second one.
4. Registration (exact positioning) of each color is very important for good results. Registration pins or tabs should be used to position the paper exactly. See Fig. 33-5. You can make these from heavy paper or buy commerically made ones. Hold them in place with masking tape.

PAPER STENCIL METHOD

The paper stencil is simply a piece of paper with the design cut into it. The openings in the paper will form the image when the squeegee is pulled across the screen. The paper stencil is pasted or taped to the screen. This method lends itself to thick applications of paint and large-area work of simple design. Follow these steps:

1. Plan your design and make a full size drawing on a piece of cardboard or heavy paper. Indicate colors if more than one color is to be used.
2. Center the drawing under the screen and tape it to the plywood base with masking tape.
3. Attach registration tabs to the base along the sides of the master drawing. Remove the frame from the base and set it aside, Fig. 33-6.
4. Select a piece of heavy, transparent bond paper as large as the opening in the frame. If you do not have a piece that large, paint in a border of filler (block out) or use brown paper tape to seal the edges and form an inkwell. Be sure there are no pinholes.
5. Cover the master drawing with the transparent bond paper and tape it down.
6. Trace the first design you want printed on the paper. Remove the paper and cut out the design with an X-acto knife or other sharp instrument, Fig. 33-7. This is the stencil.

Fig. 33-5. Commercial and homemade registration pins and tabs are shown on the base. Paper tabs work just as well and will not damage the screen as these metal pins might. Place tape over metal pins if you use them.

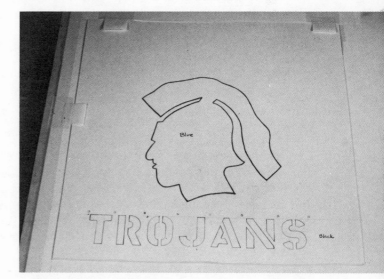

Fig. 33-6. Master drawing is in place on the base and registration tabs are properly located. This is a two-color design.

Fig. 33-7. Cut out the first color design with an X-acto knife. The master drawing is under a piece of heavy transparent bond paper.

7. Place the stencil over the master drawing again in proper position, Fig. 33-8. Place a piece of masking tape, folded so that it is sticky on both sides, on each corner of the stencil.

8. Reattach the frame to the base and carefully lower it over the stencil. The tape should adhere to the screen.

9. Raise the screen, Fig. 33-9. Remove the master drawing from the base.

10. Lower the frame and make an inkwell inside the frame using paper tape, Fig. 33-10.

11. Mix the ink or paint to the consistency you want. Raise the screen slightly and block it up so it will stay in this position.

12. Pour the ink along the inside hinge edge of the screen and lightly squeegee the ink over the screen, Fig. 33-11. This action, called ''flooding the screen,'' will attach the stencil to the screen.

13. Begin to print. Put a blank piece of paper between the registration tabs and lower the screen. (Remove the blocking used in the previous step.) Hold the squeegee at a slight angle (about 60 deg.) and make a single pass over the screen as shown in Fig. 33-12.

14. Raise the frame and carefully remove your print, Fig. 33-13.

15. Repeat this procedure for every print: put a clean piece of paper between the tabs, lower the screen, make a pass with the squeegee, raise the screen and remove the print. If you are printing only one color, this completes the process. Allow the prints to dry.

16. Put several newspapers under the frame and clean the screen. First remove the used stencil and tape. Then, use solvent to remove ink and filler, Fig. 33-14. Dry the screen with paper toweling.

17. If you plan to print a second color, begin the process all over again after the first color is dry. Return to Step No. 2. Fig. 33-15 shows the setup for the second color. Fig. 33-16 shows the second color printed on the design. You can print as many colors as you wish on a single sheet by repeating the procedure.

FILM STENCIL METHOD

The film stencil produces precise detail with sharp, fine lines. It is made from a double-layer film which is usually the lacquer soluble type.

The design is cut through the top layer of the film with a sharp knife. Then the film is fastened to the screen. The bottom layer is peeled off to expose the design.

The following steps will show you how to make a screen print using a film stencil.

1. Draw your design full size on a piece of illustration

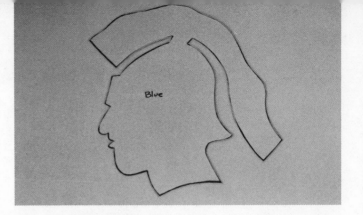

Fig. 33-8. Stencil has been cut out and is placed over master drawing for proper alignment. It is ready to be attached to underside of screen with four pieces of tape. Fold tape so it is sticky on both sides and put a piece on each corner.

Fig. 33-9. Stencil has been attached to underside of the screen. Frame is raised to a vertical position. Master drawing has been removed from the base. If available, doublefaced tape can be used to attach stencil to screen.

Fig. 33-10. Brown paper tape has been used here to form inkwell inside frame. Tape overlaps stencil several inches on each side to prevent ink from seeping through to printing surface.

Fig. 33-11. Flooding the screen. Frame is raised slightly before this first pass is made.

Fig. 33-12. Making first print. Make a pass with the squeegee. At end of pass, lift squeegee with excess ink and return it to hinge side of screen.

Fig. 33-13. First print was made on piece of scrap paper to examine reproduction quality.

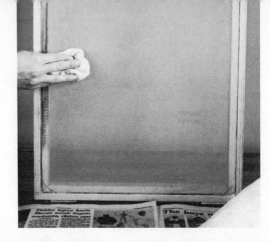

Fig. 33-14. Clean screen after printing first color. Use proper solvent and lightly rub screen with rags or paper towels until clean and dry.

Fig. 33-15. Stencil has been cut and attached to screen for producing second color.

Fig. 33-16. Printing is completed in two colors.

board or heavy paper. Cut the paper to size or indicate the size with a pencil line. Place it on the plywood base under the frame. Tape it in place with masking tape. Attach registration tabs to the base. Remove the frame, Fig. 33-17.

2. Cut a piece of film at least 2 in. (51 mm) larger than the area to be reproduced. Place the film over the design and tape it down. The smooth or lacquer side should face up.

3. Cut the design through the top layer only. Use a film stencil knife or X-acto knife, Fig. 33-18. *Be careful, use very light pressure. Hold the knife the way you would hold a pencil. Make long, smooth cuts.* Straight lines may be cut with a metal straightedge as a guide. Templates may be used for circles or other common shapes.

4. Strip the lacquer film from the areas to be printed. You can easily lift a corner of the film with the knife point. Examine your work for accuracy and completeness, Fig. 33-19.

5. Reattach the frame to the base and remove all but four small pieces of tape holding the stencil to the master design. Lower the screen over the stencil. Now you are ready to fasten (adhere) the film to the screen.

6. Make two pads by folding soft cloths three or four times. Wet one with adhering thinner and rub lightly once or twice in a small spot on the screen. Rub the area immediately with the second cloth, lightly at first and then heavier. Note the change in appearance of the film when it is adhered.

7. Remove the original copy and place several layers of newsprint under the stencil.

8. Continue the process described in Step 6 until the stencil is adhered to the screen, Fig. 33-20. The film must be held tightly against the screen during this process.

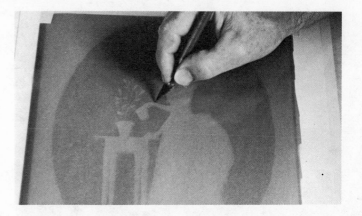

Fig. 33-18. With lacquer stencil in place, design shows through. Cut stencil with an X-acto knife. Use light pressure and be careful not to cut through backing.

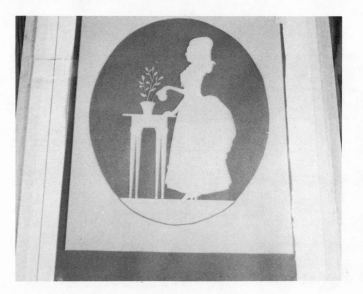

Fig. 33-19. Stencil after stripping. Lacquer film has been removed from area to be printed.

Fig. 33-17. Master drawing, produced on heavy paper, is placed on base and located in the registration tabs.

Fig. 33-20. Adhere stencil by wetting small area with one cloth pad and immediately rubbing the spot with a second dry cloth. The film changes color slightly when it is fastened properly.

9. When the film is adhered to the screen, lift the frame carefully. Allow the stencil to dry for five or ten minutes.

10. Strip the backing from the stencil as shown in Fig. 33-21. The design should be open now for ink to pass through.

11. Stop (block) out the surrounding area with paper tape or filler. You are ready to apply the ink and print.

12. Mix the ink to proper consistency and pour it into the frame which is slightly raised. Flood the screen with the squeegee and place the printing paper between the registration tabs.

13. Make a pass with the squeegee and raise the frame to examine the first print, Fig. 33-22. Make the rest of the prints.

14. When you are finished, remove the frame from the base and dissolve the stencil with lacquer thinner. Use a stack of newspapers and a cloth. Dry the screen. If you plan to print a second color, repeat the procedure.

PHOTOGRAPHIC STENCIL METHOD

The photographic film stencil method of making screen prints is the most precise of the three techniques. But you do not need to understand photography nor do you need special or costly equipment. The materials needed are shown in Fig. 33-23.

The drawing of the design (the positive) should be made on transparent tracing paper with black ink, crayons or dark pencil. Do not use felt tip markers.

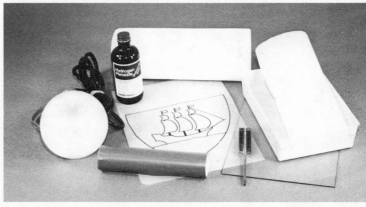

Fig. 33-23. Materials needed to make a photographic film stencil print include transfer stencil, a drawing of the design on transparent paper, hydrogen peroxide, a light source, piece of glass as large as the drawing, tray for developer (not aluminum), thermometer, paper toweling and organdy screen.

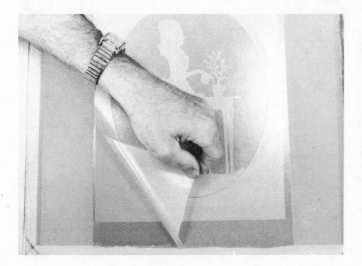

Fig. 33-21. When the stencil has dried for 5 or 10 minutes, backing may be peeled off to expose printing area.

Fig. 33-22. Examine quality of first print.

Thermal transparencies or photographic transparencies also work very well. In any case, the image must be opaque.

Film used for making a photographic stencil is a presensitized screen process film. "Ulano Blue Poly" and "Ulano Hi Fi Green" are two popular films. Both will give good results and are developed with hydrogen peroxide and water.

The light source for exposing film may be as simple as using the sun. However, it is better to use a sun lamp or flood light if you do not have access to a carbon arc and vacuum frame. Experiment with the time required to expose the film using your chosen light source. A reasonable exposure is from 5 to 10 minutes.

Follow these steps:

1. Produce a drawing (positive) on transparent tracing paper with opaque ink, Fig. 33-24, or obtain a thermal or photographic transparency of your design. The lines must be opaque where you want the image to print. The light must shine through the positive. Be sure to use transparent paper, glass or acetate sheet. The design might even be cut from black construction paper. You will need a positive for each color you wish to print.

2. Experiment with a small piece of film to determine the length of exposure needed with your light source. You can do this by taking different exposures on a strip of film. Expose the first segment one minute, the next two minutes and so on until the longest exposure is 10 minutes. See Steps 3 and 4 and Fig. 33-25. Use a section of your positive over the strip so that the exposure time will be accurate.

3. Using the information learned from the test strip, expose the film for the proper exposure time. Arrange the film with the emulsion side down and the positive on top of it face down. Hold both flat with a piece of glass. Turn on the light source, Fig. 33-26. (The emulsion side can be easily identified by touching a damp finger to the surface of the film. The emulsion side feels sticky.)

4. When the exposure is complete, place the film in a tray of developer made up of one part peroxide and two parts water. The temperature of this solution should be under 80 °F (27 °C). Agitate the film for 1 1/2 minutes and take it out of the developing solution.

5. Place the developed film on a piece of glass, emulsion side up. Rinse it with water between 90 and 100 °F (32 and 38 °C). Spray the water gently over the film at an angle. When the design is washed out, rinse the film briefly in cold water, Fig. 33-27.

6. Transfer the film to your work area and place it on several paper towels, emulsion side up. Lay the screen over the film in the desired position and

Fig. 33-24. Design is drawn on transparent tracing paper using black ink. Lines must be opaque so no light shines through them.

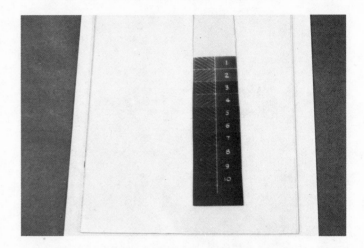

Fig. 33-25. Trial exposures are made to determine the best exposure time. Be sure to have a line image on your positive test sheet so you can examine the quality.

Fig. 33-26. Exposing film for photographic film stencil. Glass sheet is used to hold them flat during exposure.

296

press down. Blot the screen to adhere the film to it. See Fig. 33-28. When the excess water has been removed and the color no longer comes off on the paper towel, stop blotting. Fig. 33-29 shows the underside of the screen with film adhered.

7. Prop the screen up so air can circulate around both sides to dry the film. Drying time will be approximately 30 minutes depending on the humidity. When the screen is dry, peel the back off the film, Fig. 33-30.

8. After the backing has been removed, block out the remaining nonprinting area with brown paper tape, pieces of cardboard or liquid masking to plug the screen. See Fig. 33-10. Be sure to tape the edges carefully to prevent ink from running out there, Fig. 33-31.

9. Refer to Figs. 33-11 through 33-14 for printing and cleanup procedure.

10. When the printing is completed and you wish to remove the film from the screen, use hot water and bleach. Rub lightly.

Fig. 33-29. Underside of screen with film adhered.

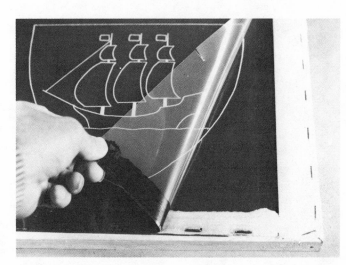

Fig. 33-30. Peel backing off film after it has dried for 30 minutes or more. It will usually change color slightly when dry. If the film looks stringy or pulls away from screen when you are peeling off the back, stop and wait for it to dry longer.

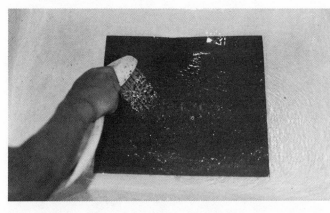

Fig. 33-27. Rinsing film in a sink. Image is beginning to appear.

Fig. 33-28. Blot screen to adhere film to it. Continue this until excess water is absorbed and no color comes off on paper towel.

Fig. 33-31. Tape around edges of screen to contain the ink.

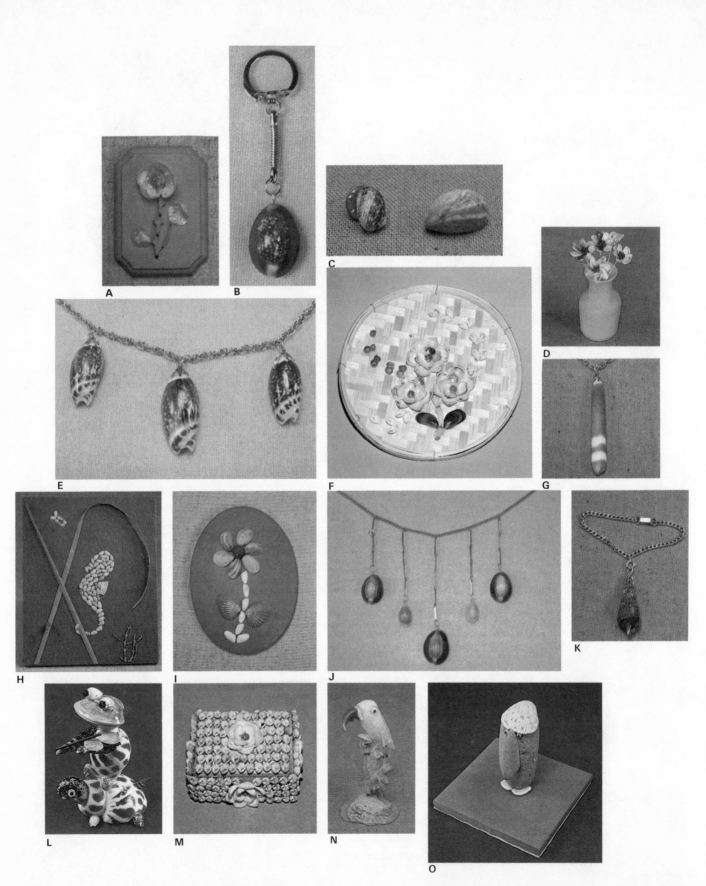

Exciting ways to craft with shells. A—Shell flower on painted wood plaque. B—Key fob features large cowrie shell. C—Tie tacs. D—Small vase holds flowers made from coquina shells. E—Necklace of matched olive shells. F—Floral pattern of shells is attached to woven background. G—Necklace fashioned from stone sea urchin. H—Shell picture mounted on fabric backing. I—Shell picture glued to painted plaster of paris plaque. J—Necklace of cowrie shells. K—Bracelet made from single auger shell. L—Frog and turtle figurines. M—Shell jewelry box. N—Parrot figurine perched on piece of coral. O—Shell figurine on terra cotta tile base.

Chapter 34
SHELLCRAFT

Over the centuries, seashells have been used as personal decoration, cooking utensils and money. Colorful and exotic shells have also played a role in art and religious ceremonies. Shells may be crafted into jewelry, pictures, figurines and flowers.

MATERIALS AND TOOLS

Shells are the external skeletons of animals called mollusks and are available in a variety of sizes, shapes and colors, Fig. 34-1. The smallest shells are microscopic; the largest weight over 600 lb. (272 kg). They may be collected on beaches, retrieved under water or purchased in craft and hobby shops. One advantage to buying shells from a supplier is that they are already cleaned and often are polished. Preparing shells which have the animal still living inside can be a tedious and disagreeable task.

Some of the most useful tools for shellcraft projects are shown in Fig. 34-2.

Pliers and wire cutters are useful for attaching chains and jump rings when making jewelry. Tweezers are helpful in handling small shells and hardware. Necklaces and bracelets, which are strung like beads, require a needle and thread for stringing. The file removes sharp edges on shells and hardware. The electric drill may be used to make holes through shells for stringing or other attachments. A few other materials such as cement, jewelry findings, backings and background objects may be required for some shellcraft projects.

MAKING SHELL JEWELRY

Shell jewelry is one of the most popular types of shellcraft. The variety is almost endless and may range

Fig. 34-1. This collection of shells includes cowries, turban shells, scallops, lucine clam, olive shells, top shells, coquina, snails, coral, conch shells, pectens, abalone, stone sea urchin, cat's paw and auger shells.

Fig. 34-2. Tools and materials for shellcraft include: shells, round-nose pliers, wire-cutting pliers, needle-nose pliers, tweezers, large sewing needle, bead twine, file, electric drill, cement, jewelry findings and blocks of styrofoam.

from very simple to complex. If this is your first experience with shell jewelry, begin with an easy article and work up to the more difficult.

SIMPLE SHELL JEWELRY

A necklace similar to the ones pictured in Fig. 34-3 is easy to make. Simply cement a bell cap, Fig. 34-4, to your favorite shell and attach it to a string, wire or chain. Use epoxy cement or clear craft cement to attach the bell cap. Allow cement to dry for the specified time before handling.

Another method of attaching the shell: drill a small hole through it, Fig. 34-5, and clamp a ring or hook through the hole. Be careful not to break the shell or drill into your finger. Clamp the shell lightly or embed it in a piece of styrofoam before drilling.

A single shell may be worn around the waist or wrist in the same fashion as the necklace. Use your imagination.

For a slightly more involved type of necklace, belt or bracelet string several shells on a string, wire or chain.

Again, the shells may be attached with bell caps, hooks or drilled holes. Fig. 34-6 shows several shells on a string forming a necklace.

Try to plan your shell article to make use of natural variations in the shells themselves, Fig. 34-7. For example, you may use larger shells in the middle as in

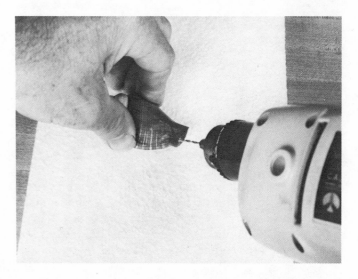

Fig. 34-5. Drilling a hole through a large shell. The shell is placed on a piece of styrofoam to help hold it steady while drilling.

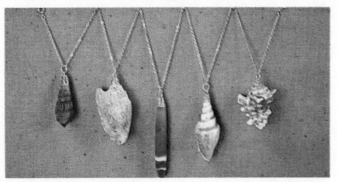

Fig. 34-3. Simple shell necklaces are easy to make.

Fig. 34-6. This necklace was made by stringing shells one after the other. Holes were drilled through each shell.

Fig. 34-4. Bell caps used for attaching shells to a chain or other piece of jewelry.

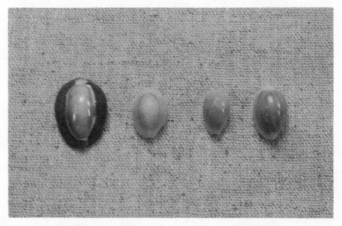

Fig. 34-7. Cowries make beautiful jewelry and are readily available at shell shops.

Fig. 34-8, or much smaller shells between large ones.

Shells may also be combined with beads in the same design. Choose materials which compliment each other.

Shells may be sprayed with clear acrylic. This will add gloss and reduce wear.

Other types of jewelry—tie tacks, cuff links, pins and earrings—may be produced by attaching shells to the appropriate jewelry findings, Fig. 34-9. You can select from a wide variety of findings at craft and hobby shops.

MORE COMPLEX JEWELRY

Shell jewelry may be made more complex by adding other shells and using combinations of jewelry findings. Fig. 34-10 shows a necklace in which several shells are attached to a decorative chain with findings. To make a similar piece of jewelry:

1. Select the shells and chain and choose the appropriate findings, Fig. 34-11.
2. Cement a bell cap to each shell, Fig. 34-12.

Fig. 34-8. The three shells in each photo will form a nice pattern in a piece of jewelry.

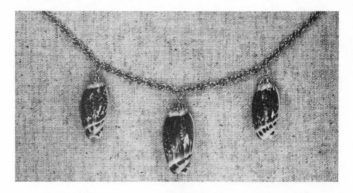

Fig. 34-10. Necklace with three matched shells is an attractive piece of shell jewelry.

Fig. 34-11. These materials are all that is needed for three-shell necklace.

Fig. 34-9. This assortment of findings shows variety of materials available for making shell jewelry.

Fig. 34-12. Cementing bell caps to shells. Press them into styrofoam block to dry.

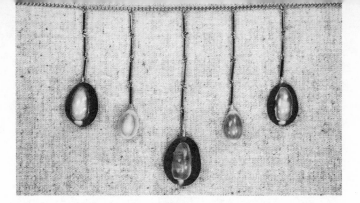

Fig. 34-15. Different lengths of decorative chain add to beauty of this cowrie necklace.

3. When the cement has dried, attach three jump rings to the chain, one for each shell, Fig. 34-13. Be sure the spacing is exact for a balanced effect. First, attach the middle ring at the exact center of the chain; then the other two on either side.

4. Attach a jump ring and hook or other fastener to the ends of the chain, Fig. 34-14. Check for proper length before completing this operation.

Pieces of chain may be added to the main chain so that the shells will hang at different lengths, Fig. 34-15. The bracelet shown in Fig. 34-16 would make a nice companion for this necklace. Interesting, complex jewelry pieces may also be made by stringing shells in various patterns and shapes.

MAKING SHELL FLOWERS

Beautiful artificial flowers may be made with shells. The shape and color of the shells lend themselves to flower designs. Two favorites are coquinas and cockleshells, Fig. 34-17. They are used to form the petals. If you have never made shell flowers before, follow these steps:

1. Lay out the tools and materials needed, Fig. 34-18. These will include: about seven shells of the same size for each flower, cloth covered florist wire large enough for a stem, cement, tweezers, needle-nose pliers, side-cutting pliers, a small bottle with clear plastic wrap stretched over the top and some small seeds or pine cones for the flower centers.

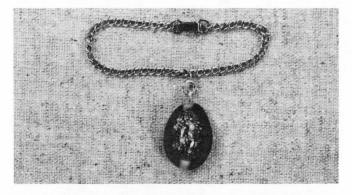

Fig. 34-16. A cowrie bracelet is easy to make and will complement other jewelry made from these beautiful shells.

Fig. 34-17. The little shells on the right are coquinas or butterfly shells. The larger ones are cockleshells. Both are favored for shell flowers.

Fig. 34-18. These are the tools and materials you will need for making shell flowers.

Fig. 34-13. Attach jump rings to chain with needle-nose pliers.

Fig. 34-14. Attach fastener to end of necklace chain.

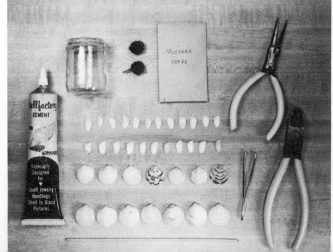

2. Form a slight depression in the plastic stretched over the small bottle. Select shells for petals which have the hinges on the same side. Begin to nestle the shells into a flower shape, one at a time, with a drop of glue between each shell, Fig. 34-19. Overlap the edge of each shell the way many real blooms are formed.

3. With all the petals in place, spread a drop of glue in the center and sprinkle a few small seeds on the glue for the flower center. See Fig. 34-20. Let the glue dry for at least an hour before removing the flower from the bottle.

4. Cut a length of florist wire for the stem. Form a loop on one end and bend it at a right angle to the stem. Glue it to the backside of the flower as in Fig. 34-21. When the glue is completely dry, the flower is ready to display. A coat of clear acrylic spray may be applied to the flower if you wish. Fig. 34-22 shows a beautiful shell flower made with cockleshells.

Make several shell flowers and form a bouquet in a small container. Floral clay or styrofoam may be used to hold the stems.

MAKING SHELL PICTURES

If you have a bag of assorted shells, you may have enough to make a picture. If you do not already have the shells, they can be purchased from shell dealers or craft shops.

Birds, flowers, fish and other easily recognized shapes make good subjects for shell pictures. There are many techniques for making pictures; however, the following instructions may help you get started.

1. Plan your picture and collect the materials. A wide assortment of shells is generally needed. Other

Fig. 34-20. Mustard seeds have been sprinkled on drop of cement to form flower center.

Fig. 34-21. Glue the wire stem to backside of flower. Hold stem while glue sets.

Fig. 34-19. Flower petals (coquina shells) are held in place with a drop of glue between each shell.

Fig. 34-22. Completed cockleshell flower. Pine cone forms its center.

materials such as feathers, a piece of driftwood or bits of polished stone may also be used. Select some kind of backing. Heavy illustration board, plywood or canvas board is excellent. Of course, you will need glue. The background can be painted, left natural or covered with fabric, depending on the subject and your preference. Fig. 34-23 shows some of the materials commonly used for shell pictures.

2. Prepare your backing and decide on the subject, Fig. 34-24. Make a full size sketch and select the materials.

3. Pick out the shells to be used for various parts of the picture and cover one section at a time. Apply glue to the backing or to the shells. Begin to put the shells in place, Fig. 34-25.

4. Continue covering your design with shells until you have the picture completed. Add any finishing touches with other materials that you wish. See Fig. 34-26.

5. When the glue is dry, spray the picture with clear acrylic and frame it if you desire.

MAKING SHELL FIGURINES

Shell figurines are miniature sculptures. Possibilities are almost unlimited. To get started:

1. Select a large shell, piece of coral, or other material to use as a base.

2. Arrange several shells to see if they produce the desired sculpture. Fig. 34-27 shows the materials

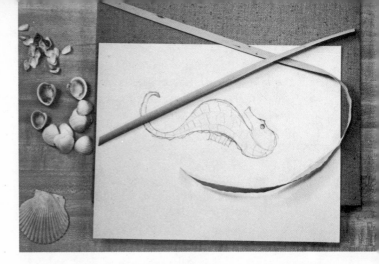

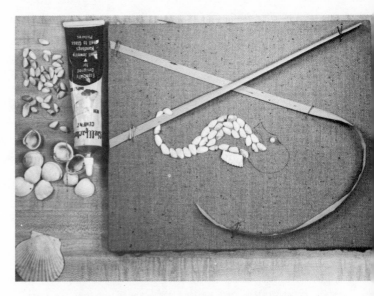

Fig. 34-24. Beginnings of shell picture. Seahorse will be fashioned from coquina shells.

Fig. 34-25. Shell picture underway with some of the shells in place. Design has been traced on backing to insure accuracy.

Fig. 34-23. The "raw" materials of a shell picture. Backing is a piece of 1/2 in. plywood which has been covered with fabric.

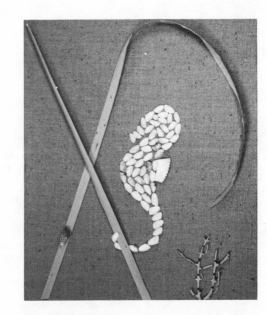

Fig. 34-26. Completed shell picture is ready for display.

used for a simple figurine. Arranged in this fashion, you can see what the finished piece is going to look like when completed.

3. Using white glue or any fast-drying cement, begin to assemble the major parts of the figurine. See Fig. 34-28. Allow the glue to dry before adding other parts. (A glue gun works well for assembling figurines because the glue dries very quickly.)

4. Assemble other parts and attach them to the main body of the figurine, Fig. 34-29.

5. Add details such as eyes, mouth or background materials to your figurine to increase realism, Fig. 34-30. A felt-tip pen works well for eyes, mouth and similar small detail.

6. Spray the finished product with clear acrylic to protect it.

Fig. 34-27. These random materials will become a parrot sitting on a branch.

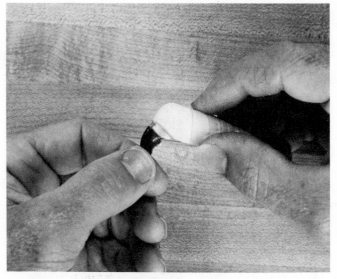

Fig. 34-29. Beak (crab claw) is glued to the body (auger shell) of bird.

Fig. 34-28. Attaching coral branch to oyster shell base. Hold parts in place until they are dry enough to stand alone.

Fig. 34-30. Completed figurine has cat's paw shell for feet and a bead eye.

Ideas for framing silhouettes. A—Silhouette cemented over beautiful photographic background. B—Freehand silhouette attached to plaster plaque. C—Trio of contact print silhouettes made with photographic enlarger. D—Children's silhouettes mounted in matching circular frames. E—Silhouette of old man copied from wood carving. F—Angel fish silhouette matted for display.

Chapter 35
SILHOUETTES

Silhouettes are generally thought of only as profiles cut from black paper, Fig. 35-1. However, any shadowlike representation made by filling the outline of an object with a solid color is a silhouette.

The silhouette has remained popular because of its ability to communicate instantly. Portrait silhouettes, Fig. 35-2, first became popular in mid 1700 and continue today as a popular art and craft form. Silhouettes may be used as wall decorations, signs or elements of other art forms. But most important, making silhouettes is fun. Anyone can do it.

TOOLS AND MATERIALS

Few tools and materials are needed to produce a silhouette. A small pair of sharp scissors or an X-acto knife and paper will do for most projects, Fig. 35-3.

The cutting instrument must be sharp to produce crisp lines, an important characteristic of this craft. A good pair of manicure scissors is ideal for small details.

Fig. 35-2. A truly effective silhouette must capture the outstanding characteristics of the subject.

Fig. 35-3. Tools and material required to make silhouettes.

Fig. 35-1. This silhouette captures the important features of the subject as well as a photo and presents it in a dramatic way.

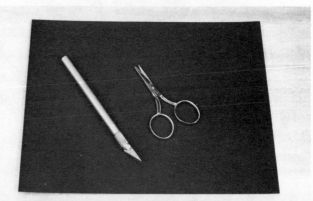

Fig. 35-4. Top. This silhouette is the reverse of Fig. 35-1. It can be cut from white paper and mounted on black background or the remains of a black silhouette may be mounted on white paper to form the image. This particular example is made from the trimmings from Fig. 35-1. Bottom. This silhouette was cut from white paper and mounted on a black background.

Traditionally, silhouette paper has been thin black paper especially designed for the purpose. However, any paper or thin material may be used. Instead of cutting silhouettes from black paper, plain white paper may be used and placed on a black background. See Fig. 35-4.

MAKING A SILHOUETTE

There are several methods of making silhouettes:
1. Cutting a shape from memory.
2. Casting a shadow on paper then tracing it out.
3. Using a photographic process to produce an object outline.

The first two techniques do not require specialized equipment and may be used by anyone. The third technique requires a camera and an enlarger in addition to the materials already named.

CUTTING A SHAPE FROM MEMORY

This method is so simple that instructions are hardly needed. However, these steps may be helpful on your first attempt.
1. Collect the materials and tools that you will need—scissors and paper.
2. Decide on a shape or find a picture in a book that you wish to duplicate. Simple shapes of natural objects are very effective. Fig. 35-5 shows a few.
3. Cut out the shape and examine it for proportion and scale, Fig. 35-6. Make any adjustments that you think necessary.
4. Mount the silhouette on a piece of illustration board or other backing, Fig. 35-7. Use a drop of glue to hold it in place and frame it behind glass. The glass will hold the paper flat.

Fig. 35-5. Step 2. These common shapes are instantly recognized and make good silhouette subjects.

PROJECTING A SILHOUETTE

You will need a light source for this method. A candle, flashlight or the sun will project an image onto your paper. Follow these steps:

1. Select a piece of paper large enough for the silhouette.
2. Attach the paper to a wall, floor or other flat surface so that you can trace around the shadow.
3. Position your subject and light source to produce the desired image. Try to eliminate all distortion, Fig. 35-8.
4. Attach silhouette paper to the backing paper, look at the faint image. Trace around the shadow with a sharp, soft pencil, Fig. 35-9.
5. Cut out the design with scissors or an X-acto knife.
6. Mount the silhouette, Fig. 35-10, as previously described.

Fig. 35-8. A setup for projecting a silhouette. Subject is placed in front of a piece of illustration board where a light shines on it casting a shadow. (Light has been shaded for photographic purposes.)

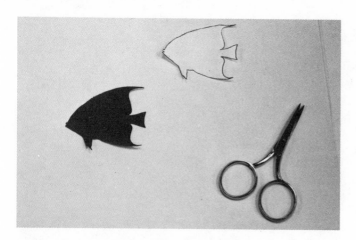

Fig. 35-6. Step 3. Original drawing was used as a pattern and silhouette was cut from black paper. It should be compared to the original drawing for accuracy.

Fig. 35-9. Trace around the shadow with pencil.

Fig. 35-10. Completed silhouette mounted on a piece of illustration board. Subject is placed beside the finished product for comparison.

Fig. 35-7. Step 4. Silhouette has been mounted on piece of illustration board and placed under glass to hold paper flat.

PHOTOGRAPHIC SILHOUETTES

Complex shapes may be accurately reproduced in silhouette using the photographic method.

1. Select the subject for your silhouette and position it in front of a brightly lighted surface such as a white wall. The subject should be very dimly lit to produce as great a contrast as possible, Fig. 35-11.
2. Position the camera, loaded with black and white film, in front of the subject. Aim at the white background. Set the exposure for the lighted surface and take the picture. The subject should be greatly underexposed and therefore appear as a clear area on the negative when it is developed. The background will appear very dark.
3. Put the developed negative in an enlarger and project the image on a piece of black silhouette paper, Fig. 35-12. You can make the finished silhouette any size desired by changing the magnification on the enlarger. Fig. 35-13 shows a close-up of the image. Use maximum light to produce a clear image. Trace the outline with a sharp pencil.
4. Cut out the outline and mount it using the procedure previously described, Fig. 35-14.

Fig. 35-11. Subject is placed in front of brightly lighted white wall. Exposure is set for background rather than the subject. This will produce a silhouette such as this one.

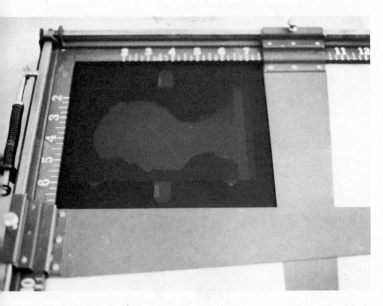

Fig. 35-12. This projected image is made by an enlarger on black silhouette paper. Image may be traced and cut out to form finished product. The size of the image can be adjusted with the enlarger.

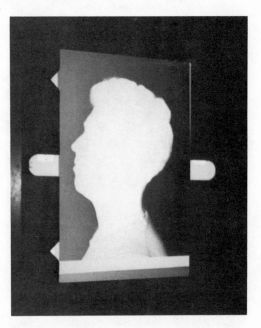

Fig. 35-13. Close-up of image shows clarity of subject lines.

Fig. 35-14. Completed silhouette is mounted on white paper and placed under glass.

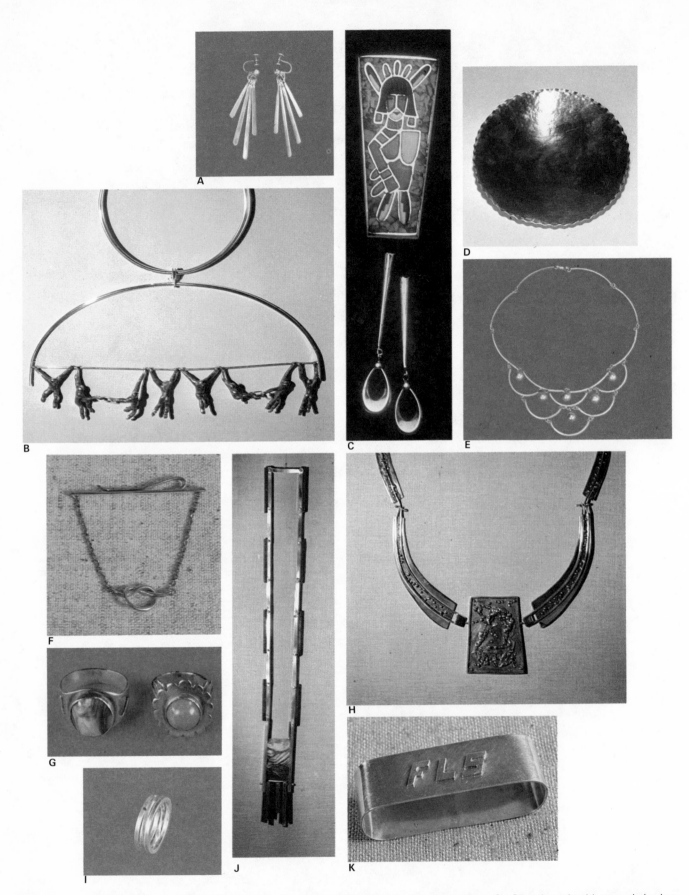

Samples of silversmithing you can do. A—Silver earrings formed from flat sheet. B—Choker necklace. C—Silver brooch with enameled colors. D—Small pin tray hammered from sheet pewter. E—Necklace of silver wire and balls. F—Tie clasp of brass rod and chain. G—Stones in silver rings. H—Pewter necklace. I—Sterling silver ring. J—Pewter pendant and necklace chain. K—Napkin ring of silver with silver initials. (Fran Nelson)

Chapter 36
SILVERSMITHING

Cutting, shaping and fastening silver and other valuable metals is generally known as silversmithing. The metals used each have their own unique properties of color, texture and hardness. Besides silver there are pewter, copper, brass and aluminum to choose from. The silversmith, indeed, has a wealth of materials from which to create functional and beautiful objects.

Some of the most interesting craft projects are ladles, candle snuffers, cheese spreaders, napkin holders, bowls and trays, candlesticks, bracelets and many other variations of jewelry. Many simple projects can be completed in one evening while advanced work may take a number of days. See Fig. 36-1.

MATERIALS

Select the metals carefully. Silver is expensive, yet it is well worth the cost for many small projects. The best silver is sterling. It contains about 92 percent silver and 8 percent copper. The copper gives it added strength.

Silver, as well as the other metals used in silversmithing, is available in many sheet thicknesses and a variety of small square and round rods. These are the forms you will most often need.

Pewter is an alloy of tin mixed with other metals to give it better working properties and a rich, satin lustre. Copper and brass provide interesting color and strength to projects. However, they tarnish easily so they are generally protected with a clear finish.

Aluminum is available in many degrees of hardness. It forms and shapes quite readily, takes a variety of finishing textures, and, being least expensive, is ideal for many large projects. Materials you will likely need are shown in Fig. 36-2. With the exception of the pickling solution, these are purchased ready to use. Preparation of the acid for pickling is explained later.

Fig. 36-2. Silversmithing materials. Top. Supplies you will need include sheets of pewter, brass, copper, aluminum and silver along with round brass rod and square silver rod. Bottom. Other products the silversmith may need: silver polish, acid pickling solution, rubber cement, silver solder flux, paraffin, silver solder and fine steel wool. Not shown but necessary is an assortment of fine sandpaper.

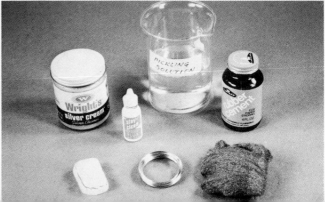

Fig. 36-1. Attractive, useful utensils are well within the skill range of the beginner in silversmithing.

TOOLS

Some of the major silversmithing tools are shown in Fig. 36-3. Nearly all tools needed are found in general craft shops.

A small sandbag is useful for shaping curved bowls and spoons. Other tools used for specific projects are common to most shops.

SILVERSMITHING FLAT SHEET

Some of the most interesting silversmithing is done with a small sheet of metal and a few tools. Basic skills can be developed through flat-work projects. This will prepare you for more advanced work. Follow these instructions for making a cheese spreader:

1. Select or design a pattern for the project you want to make.
2. Draw the outline on a sheet of heavy white paper.
3. Cut out the pattern with scissors and glue it onto a sheet of 14 or 16 ga. sterling silver, Fig. 36-4. The paper pattern can be removed later.
4. Use a jewelers' saw or coping saw with a very fine tooth blade to cut out the metal shape, Fig. 36-5. Carefully follow your pattern as you cut. If the saw tends to stick, rub some paraffin on the blade as shown in Fig. 36-6.
5. When the shape has been cut out, file the edges until completely smooth, Fig. 36-7. Filing also takes out any unevenness due to cutting and prepares the edges for final finishing. Use a fine-cut file and clean it frequently with a file brush.
6. Peel off the paper pattern and lightly round the edges of the project with a fine jewelers' file or sandpaper wrapped around a small wood stick. An emery board often works well for this.

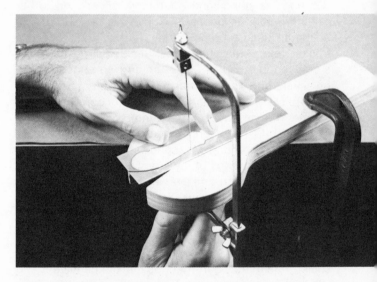

Fig. 36-4. Glue paper pattern onto silver sheet with rubber cement.

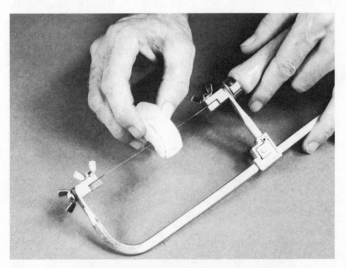

Fig. 36-5. Cut out silver with jewelers' saw on notched board.

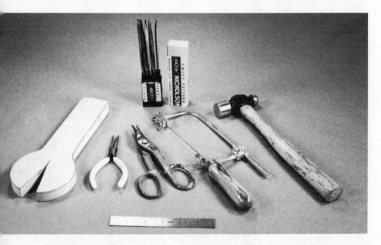

Fig. 36-3. These basic tools are generally required for silversmithing. Top. A set of fine jeweler's files. Left to right. Notched cutting board, needle-nose pliers, tin snips, jewelers' saw, ball peen hammer. Bottom. Steel rule.

Fig. 36-6. Rubbing paraffin on jewelers' saw blade will keep it from binding during sawing operations.

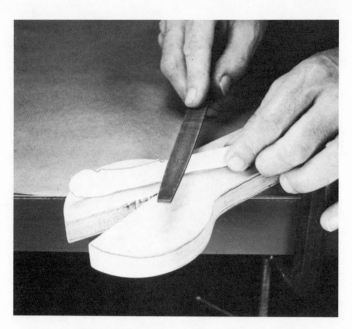

Fig. 36-7. File edges of cheese spreader smooth.

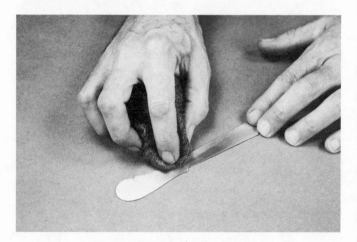

Fig. 36-8. Finishing the spreader with fine steel wool. This operation gives the silver a soft lustre.

Fig. 36-9. Polishing cheese spreader with silver polish will give it a bright finish.

7. Finish the edges and faces of the silver with very fine "wet or dry" abrasive paper or very fine steel wool, Fig. 36-8. Both give a nice lustre to the silver. A bright polish can be obtained by buffing with a soft cloth and commercial silver polish, Fig. 36-9.

SILVERSMITHING A CONTOURED PROJECT

Forming, shaping and stretching of metal requires additional skill. Bowls, spoons and ladles are fashioned in this manner. Any of the metals mentioned can be used as a less expensive substitute for silver. Follow these steps to make a contoured project:

1. Prepare a drawing of the project.
2. Cut a pattern from thin cardboard, such as a file card, of the top view, Fig. 36-10. If your project is a round bowl, lay out the pattern with a compass.
3. Select the metal sheet. In this case, a blank of aluminum is used. See Fig. 36-11.

Fig. 36-10. Pattern of top view of ladle is cut out of cardboard.

Fig. 36-11. Aluminum starting blank at left will be enlarged by hammering until it is slightly larger than the pattern at right.

4. Hammer the large end of the blank on an anvil to a disc size just a little larger than the pattern disc, Fig. 36-12. Work from the outer edges in. The flat end of a ball peen hammer is satisfactory.

5. The hammering will harden the metal. If it becomes too stiff it may crack. Anneal (soften) the metal as shown in Fig. 36-13 by heating the area to a dull red color. Quickly dip it into a bucket of water. You may have to anneal the metal a number of times.

6. Form the neck and handle of the ladle in the same manner. Hammer the surface and edges until the metal blank is slightly larger than the pattern. Overlap hammer marks so that the surface is fairly smooth.

7. Sand both sides with a fine abrasive and finish with fine steel wool. (It is easier to sand and smooth the blank before it is hammered to the final shape.)

Fig. 36-14. Pattern has been traced on aluminum with felt tip pen.

Fig. 36-12. Spreading disc end of aluminum with flat end of ball peen hammer. Use even, overlapping blows.

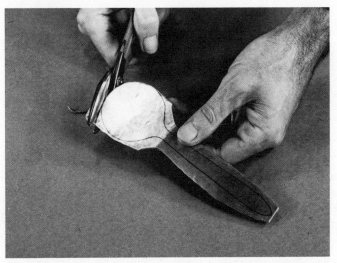

Fig. 36-15. Cut out shape of ladle with tin snips.

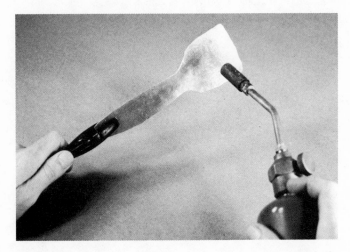

Fig. 36-13. Heating spoon end of ladle with propane torch will relieve tensions which could cause cracks.

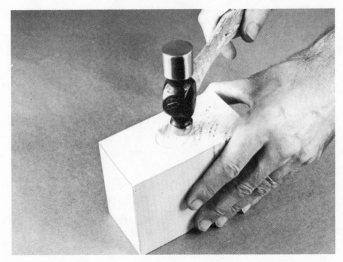

Fig. 36-16. Form a circular depression in hardwood block. It will be used to shape spoon of ladle.

8. Lay the ladle pattern on the formed aluminum and trace the outline with a fine felt tip pen as shown in Fig. 36-14.

9. Cut out with tin snips, Fig. 36-15. File edges to their final, flat shape.

10. Prepare a hardwood block, Fig. 36-16, for forming the spoon contour. With a ball peen hammer, make depression in the end grain to the diameter and depth of the spoon part of the ladle.

11. Place the spoon part of the ladle in the center of the hollow. Gently strike the metal with a polished, rounded end of the ball peen hammer. Continue tapping the metal until it takes the hollow shape you want. See Fig. 36-17. Anneal the metal whenever it becomes too hard. Rotate the ladle as you hammer to form as smooth a contour as possible. File rough edges.

12. Since aluminum is fairly soft, the handle can be easily bent to the proper curve by hand as shown in Fig. 36-18.

13. Give the ladle a final polishing with moistened, fine, wet or dry, abrasive, waterproof paper.

14. Scrub with fine steel wool which has been rubbed with wet soap, Fig. 36-19.

SILVERSMITHING A RING

Rings make interesting beginning projects in silversmithing involving silver soldering along with forming processes. Basic rings can be made from different shapes of silver. A variety of silver mountings may be attached with solder.

The procedure used can be adapted to many other forms and shapes of ring design. In this design, three rings are fastened together.

1. Determine the length of silver rod needed for one ring. If a ring gage is not available, measure around your finger with a narrow strip of paper and mark the overlap on the strip. For example: ring size 6 needs 2 1/4 in. (57 mm) of material, while ring size 7 1/4 requires 2 3/8 in. (60 mm).

2. Cut two pieces of 1/16 in. square rod, Fig. 36-20,

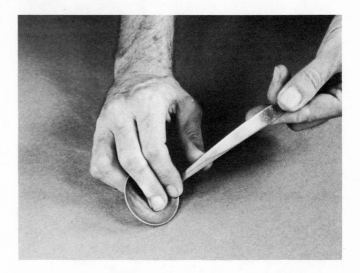

Fig. 36-18. Bend handle to shape by hand.

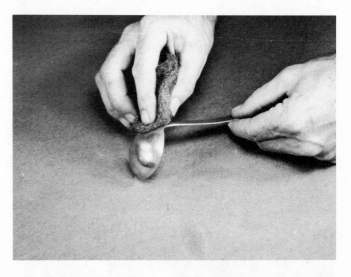

Fig. 36-19. Final polishing is done with steel wool and wet soap.

Fig. 36-17. Hammering spoon end of ladle into wood block depression.

Fig. 36-20. Cutting square rod with jeweler's saw in small vise. Paper protects silver from vise jaws.

slightly longer than the exact length needed for a ring. A jewelers' saw works best but wire cutters can also be used. File the ends to bring them to exact length, Fig. 36-21.

3. The third piece should be cut about 1/2 in. (13 mm) longer. This allows for shortening that occurs while it is being twisted. Twist this piece by clamping one end in a vise while gripping the other end with pliers. Pull on the wire as you twist to keep it straight, Fig. 36-22. Cut the ends to the correct length and file smooth and square.

4. Bend each piece around a tapered mandrel, Fig. 36-23. A round metal bar can also be used if it is the correct size. Make the bend so that the ends are in good contact for soldering. See Fig. 36-24. Use a wood or rubber mallet to gently tap the ends together.

5. When the joint is fitted, stand the ring on edge, joint up, on a clean asbestos block. Brace it with smaller pieces of asbestos.

6. Apply liquid silver soldering flux to the joint as shown in Fig. 36-25. Cut a very small piece of silver solder and place it over the joint.

Fig. 36-23. Bend silver rod around tapered mandrel.

Fig. 36-24. Form ring with rubber mallet so ends make good contact.

Fig. 36-21. File ends flat and square.

Fig. 36-22. Twist silver rod to make a fairly tight spiral.

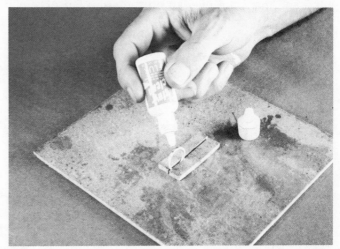

Fig. 36-25. Apply liquid silver solder flux to joint in preparation for silver soldering.

7. Heat the side of the joint with a propane torch until the silver becomes red hot and the solder flows through the joint, Fig. 36-26.

8. Allow to cool below red hot, grip with tweezers and drop the ring into a pickling solution, Fig. 36-27. This solution, one part sulfuric acid and ten parts cold water is prepared ahead of time.
   Always add the acid slowly to the water. Never add water to acid since a small explosion can result causing serious burns.
   Pickling is a method of quickly cleaning metals. It removes oxides (fire scale) and used flux.

9. Remove the ring from the pickling solution with silver wire or a wood stick and rinse in water to remove traces of the acid. Do not use metal tools. The acid may attack the surfaces. Be careful: acid spilled on your hands can cause serious burns. Wash immediately with plenty of cold water.

10. Smooth the joints of the rings with jewelers' files, Fig. 36-28. Solder the three rings together. Follow Steps 5-7. Clean rings again in the pickling solution. Shine with silver polish. Completed ring is shown in Fig. 36-29.

You may not want to solder the rings together so that you can wear them separately or as a set, Fig. 36-30.

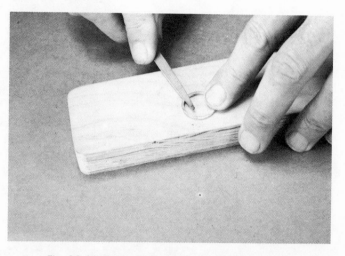

Fig. 36-28. Smooth joint of ring with jewelers' file.

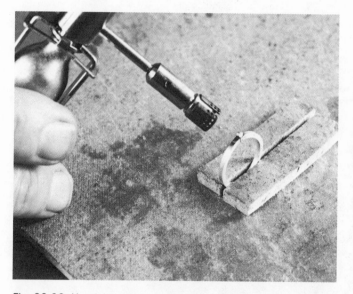

Fig. 36-26. Heat side of joint with small butane torch until solder melts.

Fig. 36-29. Ring is polished and ready to wear.

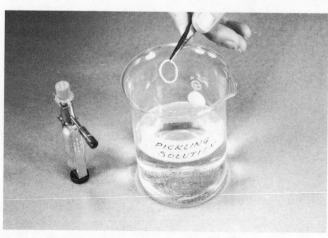

Fig. 36-27. Drop ring into pickling solution with tweezers.

Fig. 36-30. Same three rings are left unfastened to be worn separately or as a set.

Nine idea starters in stained glass. A—Leaded window pane. B—Copper foil technique for flower window hanging. (Nancy Kermode) C—Seasonal pressed glass with lead and wire. D—Pressed glass with lead came. E—Lead and wire with cut glass. F—Leaded window hanging with wire attachments. G—Stained glass mobile. H—Stained glass jewelry box with lead came. I—Stained glass window using copper foil technique.

Chapter 37
STAINED GLASS

Although the art of working with stained glass has been practiced for thousands of years, modern stained glass craftwork has become very popular as a hobby. In the past, the use of stained glass has primarily been confined to windows for churches, public buildings and homes. Today, however, the basic craft form is directed toward smaller projects which would include such items as window hangings, jewelry, decorative pictures, door panels, lampshades, mirror and picture frames, mosaics and glass sculpture.

The most exciting aspect of stained glass is the beauty of light streaming through the many colors and textures of the glass itself. There are so many ways you can combine shapes and colors of glass in your projects that you will find working with stained glass a fascinating craft. See Fig. 37-1.

GLASS

The term "stained glass" actually refers to glass that is colored while it is being made. It does not mean that stain is applied in any manner. Two types of glass are used in stained glass craftwork: hand-blown and machine-made.

Hand-blown glass is produced by blowing a large, hollow tube which is split while still hot and flattened on a stone surface. This glass contains beautiful surface textures and colors but is quite expensive.

Machine-made glass is rolled into sheets or pressed into molds. Molding produces a variety of shapes that may be used in projects without further cutting. Most craft projects are made from machine-made glass. There is a wide selection of colors and textures. Fig. 37-2 shows samples of stained glass purchased for project work. Select the glass after you have decided upon a project design and colors. It is expensive, so plan to purchase only the amount you will need. Most stained glass is about 1/8 in. thick.

Fig. 37-1. Working in stained glass is not as hard as it may seem if you follow steps carefully. Top. Leaded glass panel. Bottom. Copper foil glass star.

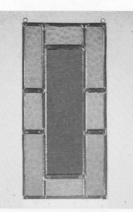

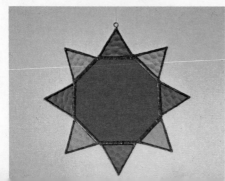

Fig. 37-2. Assortment of textured stained glass and pressed glass shapes. These are available at craft shops.

OTHER MATERIALS

You will need lead came (strips of lead material) to hold pieces of colored glass together, Fig. 37-3. Copper foil, Fig. 37-4, is used for the same purpose in a different joining technique. You should also have some tracing paper, lightweight cardboard, masking tape, plaster of paris, glazing putty and patina, Fig. 37-5. Use a large piece of insulation board to protect the work table and provide a good cutting surface.

The most necessary tools required for stained glass work are shown in Fig. 37-6. You will also need a soldering iron with supplies, (also shown in Fig. 37-6), a framing square or heavy straightedge and a good steel rule for measuring.

With these materials and tools you can use the following procedures to make a variety of stained glass projects. Since most stained glass work requires glass cutting, you would do well to practice on less expensive window glass until you have developed the necessary skill to make accurate cuts.

CUTTING GLASS

Glass is actually not cut, but scored (scratched) with a glass cutter, Fig. 37-7, and then snapped along the scored line. Of most importance in glass cutting is scoring the line. If the line is scored correctly the glass will snap sharp and clean. Try the following technique.

1. Place a piece of glass on the padded work table covered with insulation board or many layers of newspaper. Clean the glass thoroughly. A soft cloth dampened in turpentine does a good cleaning job and also lubricates the surface.

2. Keep the glass cutter in a small jar with just enough turpentine to cover the cutting wheel. This will lubricate the wheel so it can make a good scored line on every cut.

3. Lay a straightedge across the glass and score a line with the glass cutter. Hold the cutter vertically against the straightedge. Start at the far edge of the glass and draw the cutter toward you with an even pressure, Fig. 37-8.

4. As you score a number of lines, you should become familiar with the feel and sound of the scratch. It should feel like a steady, continuous cut and have a light scratching sound. *The scored line must be continuous or the glass will not snap evenly.* If you hold the glass up to a light, you can tell if there are any spaces where the glass did not score.

5. *Never try to run the cutter over a scored line a second time. It will make the score worse and dull the cutter. Make a continuous score, do not start and stop.*

6. Snap large pieces of glass by placing the scored

Fig. 37-3. Top. Coils of lead came in 6 ft. (1829 mm) lengths. Center. Sections of U-lead with a single channel, H-lead with round flange and double channel; H-lead with flat flange and double channel. Bottom. Section of flat-flange H-lead is shown with related terms.

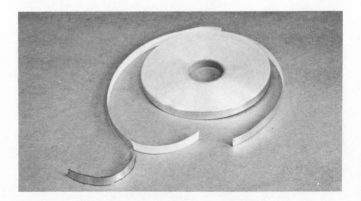

Fig. 37-4. Copper foil with adhesive backing is made up in rolls.

Fig. 37-5. Important materials for stained glass work are glazing putty, plaster of paris, patina solution and masking tape.

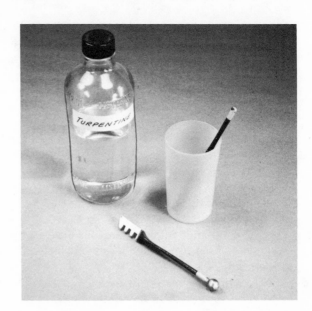

Fig. 37-7. Glass cutter with ball end for tapping and plastic container with small amount of turpentine to lubricate cutter wheel.

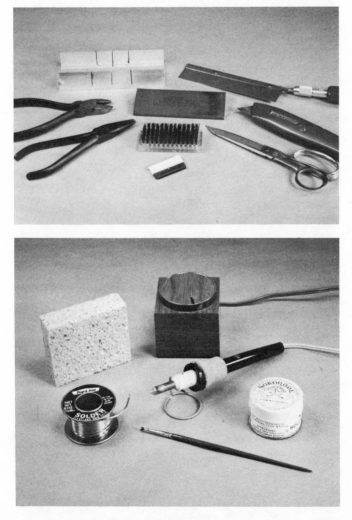

Fig. 37-6. Basic tools. Top. Razor saw and aluminum miter box, wire cutters, pliers, whetstone, mat knife, scissors, stiff brush and double edge razor blades. Bottom. Small soldering iron (with rheostat to control heat below melting point of lead), paste flux, flux brush, solid core solder and sponge.

Fig. 37-8. Top. Scoring line on stained glass with cutter in vertical position against straightedge. Bottom. Similar method is used for scoring picture glass for framing.

line just over the edge of the workbench. Hold glass flat against the bench top with one hand and snap the glass using a slight downward pressure with the other. Glass may also be snapped by gripping the glass with fingers of each hand close to the line. Apply pressure from below and pull slightly away from the line. If the scored line is good, the glass will snap with a very slight pressure, Fig. 37-9. It is a good idea to wear safety glasses since small particles of glass may chip off and fly into your face.

7. Small pieces of glass are often difficult to snap by hand. Use pliers as shown in Fig. 37-10. Glass may also be tapped from the back side of the scored line to make it snap. Use the ball end of the glass cutter, Fig. 37-11.

8. Curved cuts are generally made by following a cardboard pattern with the glass cutter as shown in Fig. 37-12. Snap the glass by hand or by

Fig. 37-10. Snapping a small piece of glass on scored line using pliers. Glass will break cleanly.

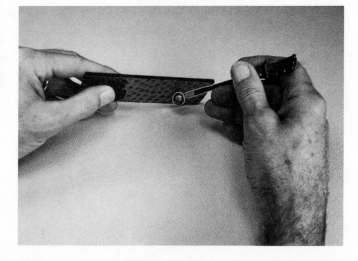

Fig. 37-11. Glass can also be snapped by tapping with ball of cutter behind scored line.

Fig. 37-9. Top. Snap glass on scored line by pressing thumbs and fingers together and applying a slight upward and outward pressure. Bottom. Glass snaps easily on a good scored line.

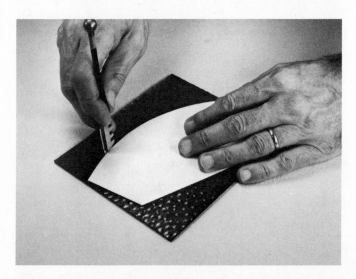

Fig. 37-12. Score a curved line by following cardboard pattern with glass cutter.

tapping from below. Circles are cut in the same manner except that additional scored lines must be made tangent to the circle, Fig. 37-13. Snap these pieces off by hand or tap from below.

9. If a scored line does not break sharp, use wire cutters to remove any irregularities or excess material as shown in Fig. 37-14.

10. Remove sharp edges by rubbing gently with a whetstone, Fig. 37-15.

STAINED GLASS WITH LEAD CAME

A leaded glass project is an assembly of glass shapes held together with lead came. Flat pieces of glass are fitted into the H-shaped came and joints are soldered wherever two pieces of came meet. U-shaped came is generally used on the outside edges of panels. A simple window hanging is a good beginning project.

Use the following procedure.

1. Make a full size sketch of your design on drawing paper.

2. Prepare two copies of the design on heavy paper. One will be cut into individual patterns to serve as guides for cutting the glass pieces. The other will be used as a guide for assembling the glass and lead came parts.

   a. Attach tracing paper over your drawing and trace along the center of each part of the design. This will actually be the centerline of the lead came.

   b. Transfer this design to two sheets of heavy paper using carbons.

   c. Number each piece for size and color reference and then cut out patterns, Fig. 37-16, from one sheet. The glass patterns must be cut about 1/16 in (1.5 mm) smaller than the original size. This will allow for the thickness of lead came that fits between each piece of glass.

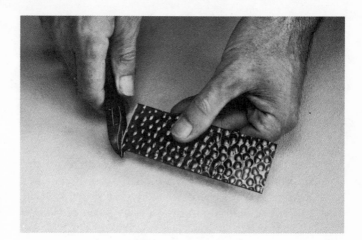

Fig. 37-14. Wire cutters do best job of grozing (nipping away small pieces of glass).

Fig. 37-15. Remove sharp edges on glass with whetstone.

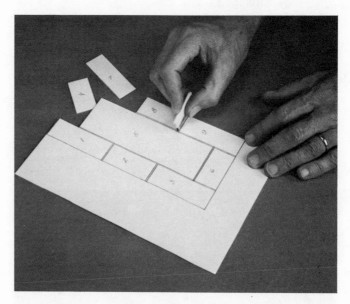

Fig. 37-16. Cut out patterns for window panel with two single edge razor blades taped together. A piece of cardboard is placed between the blades to hold them about 1/16 in. apart. Pattern shears are available but expensive.

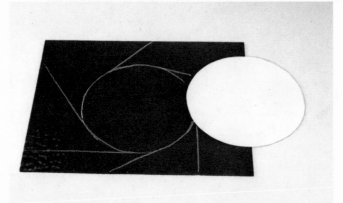

Fig. 37-13. Scored circle on glass has scored tangent lines (lines touching the scored circle) to snap sections of glass away.

3. Attach the other copy of the design to a 1/2 or 3/4 in. plywood base with masking tape. This will become your working surface. Nail small wood strips, called lath strips, along the bottom and left side of the design, Fig. 37-17.

4. Place each pattern piece on desired color of glass and score around the pattern with a glass cutter. Snap short, straight cuts with your fingers or pliers.

5. Lay each piece in its proper position on the assembly design, Fig. 37-18, to see if the total pattern is correct. You should have about 1/16 in. (1.5 mm) opening between each piece of glass in the pattern.

6. Lead came is very soft and flexible and requires stretching to make it rigid. Place one end of the lead came in a vise and pull on the other end with pliers until rigid, Fig. 37-19.

7. Cut two pieces of U-lead came slightly longer than the sides of your design. Use a razor saw or knife as in Fig. 37-20. Place these strips along the bottom and left side of the assembly pattern to form square corner. Carefully press first piece of glass into each slot of the came forming the corner, Fig. 37-21. Cut a piece of H-lead came 1/16 in. shorter than the width of the exposed glass, Fig. 37-22.

8. Continue to cut lead strips and fit glass pieces as shown in Fig. 37-23. Fig. 37-24 pictures the final assembly. Always try to keep the design shapes directly over the correct shapes on the assembly pattern. Cut off ends of first two border strips of lead to correct length. Fasten lath strips at top and right side to hold assembly tight for soldering as shown in Fig. 37-25.

9. Prepare lead joint for soldering. Be sure joints are a tight fit and lie flat.

   a. Clean each joint with fine steel wool and apply a very small amount of flux, Fig. 37-26. This is necessary because the solder will flow where the flux has been applied and makes it stick to the lead.

Fig. 37-17. Nail lath strips at bottom and left side of design at right angles to each other.

Fig. 37-18. Check assembly by placing each piece of cut glass on the pattern.

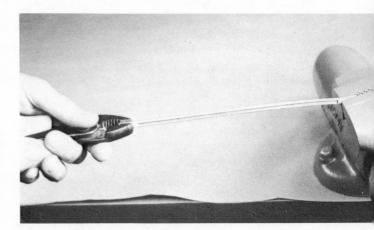

Fig. 37-19. Stretching lead came makes it rigid. Small pieces of wood in lead channel keep ends from being crushed.

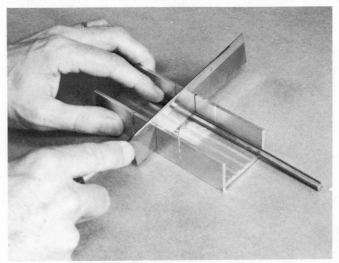

Fig. 37-20. Cut U-lead with razor saw and miter box. A knife can be used but it may crush the soft lead.

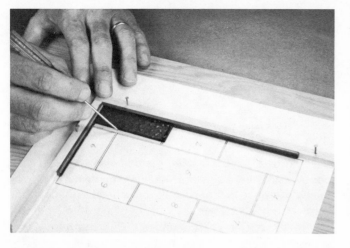

Fig. 37-21. Fit first piece of glass into corner of U-lead with small screw driver.

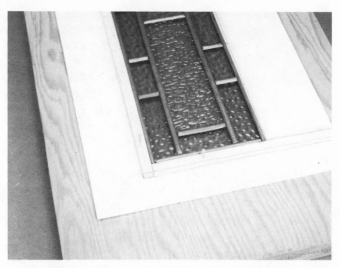

Fig. 37-24. Final assembly of glass and lead came is ready for the soldering operation.

Fig. 37-22. Short piece of H-came has been fitted to top of first glass piece. It is cut 1/16 in. shorter than glass width, leaving room for overlap of next lead strip.

Fig. 37-25. Nail lath strips at top and right side to hold assembly securely for soldering.

Fig. 37-23. Carefully fit one glass piece at a time adding lead as you go to build up the panel.

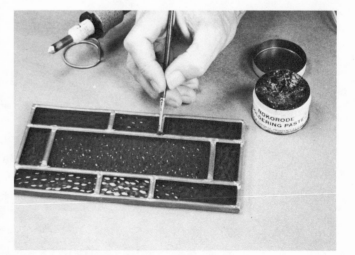

Fig. 37-26. Apply paste flux to joints with brush.

b. Be sure your soldering iron is tinned if it has a copper tip. To tin the tip, file smooth, heat the iron and dip in paste flux. Melt a small piece of solid wire solder on the tip. Wipe off excess on a damp cellulose sponge, Fig. 37-27.

10. Add solid wire solder to the joint and heat with tip until it begins to melt, Fig. 37-28. Withdraw the iron straight up and see if a small layer has covered the joint surface. (Note: As soon as the solder melts remove the soldering iron, since further heating may easily melt the lead came.)

11. Completely solder all the joints on one side and wipe off excess flux with a rag. Turn the project over and solder all joints in the same manner.

12. If you plan to hang the panel, solder a copper loop at the two top corners.

13. If any of the glass pieces appear to be loose, carefully press down the edges of the came with a small dowel rod.

14. Clean both sides of the panel by scrubbing it with a small brush and sawdust or plaster of paris, Fig. 37-29. Dust and polish with window cleaner. The panel is now ready for hanging, Fig. 37-30.

15. The lead can be given an antique look by applying patina solution with a rag.

16. A panel or window can be weather proofed by forcing putty between the lead came and glass pieces with your fingers. Remove excess putty and wipe clean.

STAINED GLASS WITH COPPER FOIL

The procedure for making stained glass projects with copper foil is very similar to the lead came method. The main difference is that copper foil is used in place of the came and glass pieces are cut the exact size since the foil takes up very little space. This method works especially well with small pieces of glass since the foil is very pliable and is easier to apply to curved surfaces.

1. Lay out the design, trace and cut glass patterns from heavy paper.

2. Mount the assembly pattern on a plywood board and follow the same procedure as described for lead came work.

Fig. 37-27. After tinning tip of soldering iron with solder wipe it bright on damp sponge.

Fig. 37-29. Scrub panel with paster of paris to remove any hardened flux left on surface after soldering.

Fig. 37-28. Solder is melted onto lead joints.

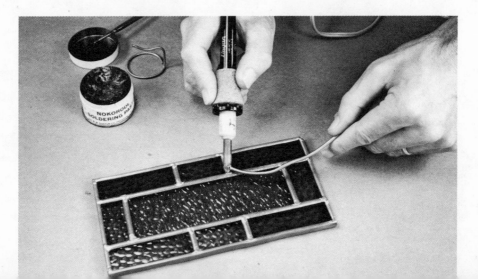

3. Cut glass and fit each piece on the assembly pattern as in Fig. 37-31. If gaps occur, recut the glass.

4. Use copper foil tape in place of lead came to join the pieces of glass. Center a strip of foil on the edge of a cut glass piece and wrap around glass, Fig. 37-32. Then bend over the extra foil to form a U channel around the edge of the glass. Press the foil tightly and smoothly around the glass with a wood stirring stick. See Fig. 37-33.

5. Apply foil to the remaining pieces of glass and lay them back on the assembly pattern.

6. Paint liquid soldering flux with a small brush on all exposed foil surfaces. Tack assembly together with the soldering iron and solder at each corner and then flow solder over all copper foil surfaces, Fig. 37-34. Turn the panel over and repeat the soldering on the other side. Tin the foil edges with solder until all copper is covered.

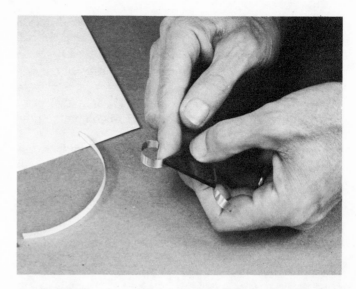

Fig. 37-32. Wrapping copper foil around glass piece. Adhesive backing is toward glass.

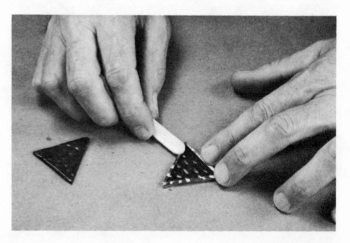

Fig. 37-33. Press foil tight around sides of glass with wooden stick.

Fig. 37-30. Stained glass window panel is completed.

Fig. 37-31. Fitting pieces of cut glass on the assembly pattern. They should be same size as pattern.

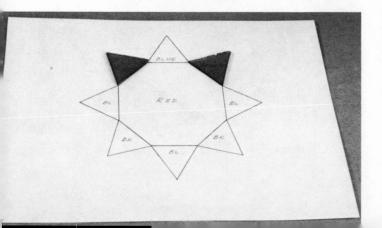

Fig. 37-34. Flowing solder over copper joint surfaces. Solder can be built up to look like lead.

7. Clean the panel as in lead came work. Projects of this type can be strengthened by soldering a strip of copper wire around the entire edge.

8. If you are making a window panel, attach rings for hanging.

9. Apply patina solution, Fig. 37-35, if a dull gray antique appearance is desired. The completed star is shown in Fig. 37-36.

Other small stained glass projects can be made by using preshaped pressed glass pieces. No glass cutting is required. Just form lead came around the desired glass shapes and solder them together to obtain your design. You may get some project ideas from page 320.

RESTORATIONS

Restoring old stained glass windows has become a popular craft activity. Often they are used as interior panels or to replace clear glass windows. Most repair work requires taking worn or broken window sections apart, Fig. 37-37, and replacing missing glass with new pieces, Fig. 37-38.

Fine examples of the stained glass art are to be found in churches, Fig. 37-39. Also, see Fig. 37-40.

Fig. 37-37. Removing piece of glass from window after melting soldered joint.

Fig. 37-35. Apply patina solution to solder to achieve a dull antique appearance.

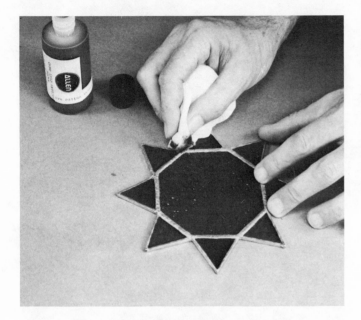

Fig. 37-36. Stained glass star is ready for hanging in a window.

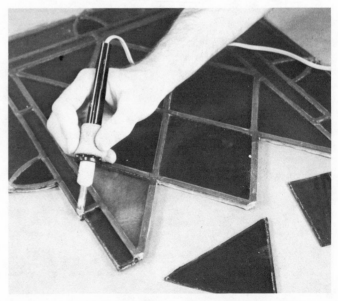

Fig. 37-38. Soldering leaded joint during a restoration of old stained glass window.

Fig. 37-39. Many fine examples of stain glass work are found in churches. Much can be learned from studying them.

Fig. 37-40. Decorative stained glass window uses lead came.

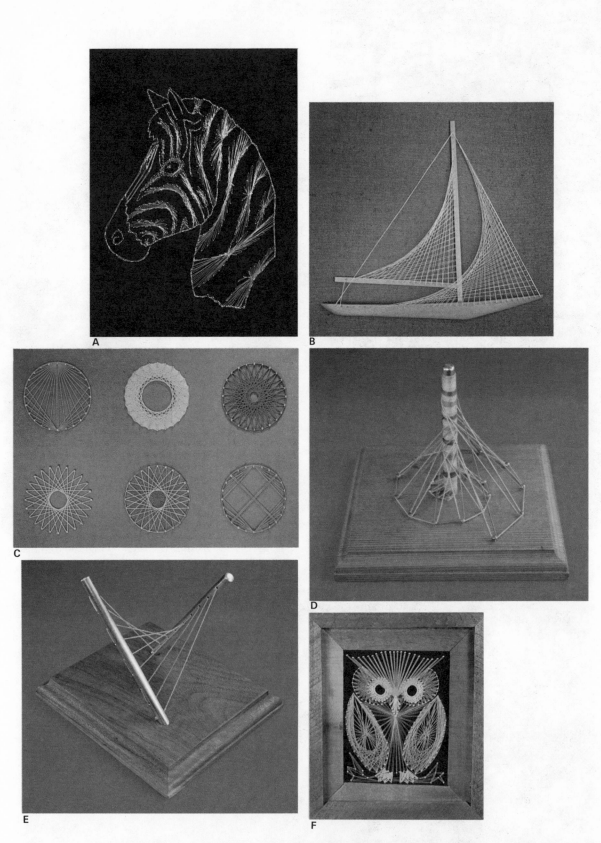

Six alternate suggestions in string art. A—Silver wire zebra strung on black velvet backing. B—Sailing ship with sails of aluminum wire. C—Variations of a basic circle form an attractive plaque. D—Three-dimensional convolute design. E—Warped surface string design is made from thread, aluminum rods and walnut wood. F—Rustic owl framed in rough sawn cedar.

Chapter 38
STRING ART

String art is the creation of decorative designs using string, wire or yarn stretched over nails, dowels or through holes in a backing. There are many types of string art and endless applications. Designs may be two-or three-dimensional. They may be combined with other media to form some part of a work of art. String art is fun and relaxing for people of all ages, Fig. 38-1.

MATERIALS

The materials needed to create string art projects are varied but simple, Fig. 38-2. Some type of stringing material is a basic requirement. Almost any kind of yarn, string, fishing line, masons' cord, wire, leather lacing or plastic fibers is suitable. Choose stringing materials which compliment the basic design. Experiment with different kinds to determine which you like best.

Fig. 38-1. Constructing this hollow circle geometric design can be fun for people of all ages.

Fig. 38-2. Tools and materials needed to make most string art projects include stringing materials, dowels or plywood backing, nails, white glue, measuring device, scissors, coping saw, needle-nose pliers, compass, protractor, pencil, staple gun, awl, brushes, hammer and sandpaper.

All string art designs must be attached to a framework or backing. Nails and brads are appropriate for many designs. Length and type of nail will depend on the number of strings it must support and the thickness of the backing. Be sure to choose a kind which will not rust and ruin your creation. Brass and aluminum nails about 1 in. long are good choices.

Plywood is the backing material preferred by most string art enthusiasts. It can be cut to any shape or size, is easily obtained and may be finished in many ways.

For very small string art pieces, 1/4 in. plywood may be used. For larger projects select thicknesses of 1/2 or 3/4 in. Thicker backing holds nails better and does not warp as readily. Backing may also be covered with fabric or other materials.

Some string art creations are attached to dowel rods instead of a backing. Dowel material may be purchased at hardware stores and lumber suppliers in a wide assortment of sizes (diameters). Most are in 3 ft. (91 cm) lengths. Choose a size which will withstand the tension of stringing.

Some projects will require glue and/or paint. White

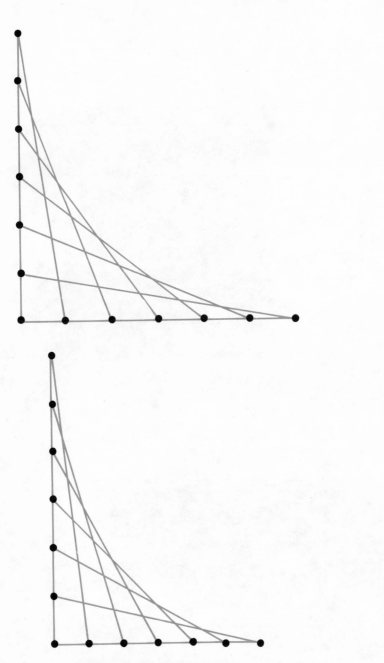

Fig. 38-3. Top. A right angle with equal legs forms part of a circle when string is stretched between nails along the legs. Each leg has the same number of nails equally spaced. Bottom. This right angle has one side shorter than the other. The overlapping of straight lines forms a curve. Both sides contain the same number of nails.

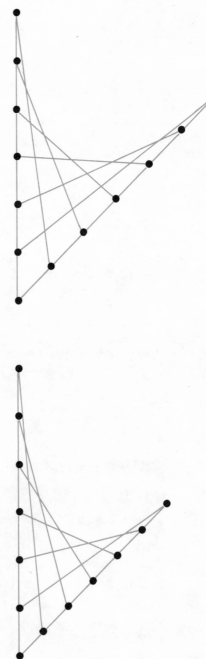

Fig. 38-4. Acute angles (having less than 90 deg.) with equal and unequal sides. Neither of the arcs formed has a center point.

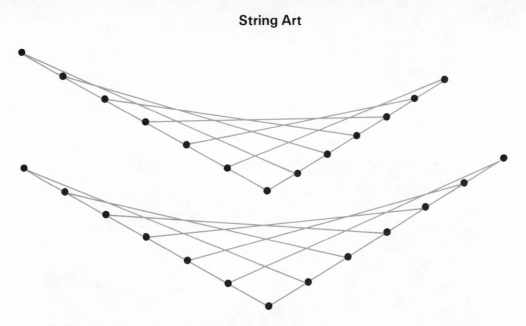

Fig. 38-5. On obtuse angles (more than 90 deg.) intersecting lines form long sweeping curves.

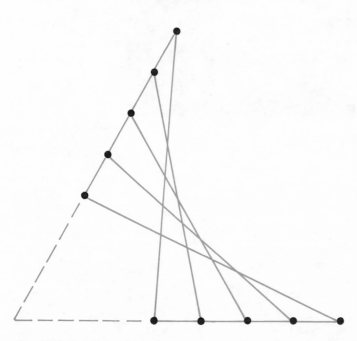

Fig. 38-6. Two lines which do not come together to form an angle create an interesting design.

glue is the choice of most hobbyists because it is economical, strong and easy to use. Flat or gloss enamel are the usual paint choices.

TOOLS

Among the tools you will need for string art projects are a hammer, measuring device, scissors, some type of saw, pliers and wire cutters (if you string with wire). Other accessories which may be required are sandpaper, brushes, pencils, compass, protractor, staple gun and hand drill. Select the tools that you will need after you have planned your project.

TWO-DIMENSIONAL DESIGNS

String art designs are produced mainly from straight lines. They often appear as curves in the finished product. Simple geometric shapes form the basis of these designs and once you understand the principle involved, you can create your own unique shapes. Some of the basic forms are illustrated to help you get started.

CURVE IN A RIGHT ANGLE

A right angle measures 90 degrees of a circle. It may or may not have sides of equal length. See Fig. 38-3. (Note: The nails are all spaced exactly the same distance apart in this design.)

The string is tied to the first nail (tying on) and to the last nail (tying off). Use a secure knot and a spot of clear glue. Trim off the end close to the knot for neater appearance.

Fig. 38-3 also shows a right angle design with different length sides. It is important, however, that both sides contain the same number of accurately spaced nails. Of course, the spacing of the nails in the shorter leg will be closer.

CURVES IN ACUTE AND OBTUSE ANGLES

An acute angle contains less than 90 deg. while an obtuse angle has more than 90. Fig. 38-4 shows two acute angles. One has sides equal and the other has unequal sides. Fig. 38-5 shows obtuse angles with equal and unequal sides.

Some lines would form angles, but are not extended until they meet. These lines form open-ended curves as shown in Fig. 38-6.

CIRCULAR DESIGNS

To create any circular design, divide the circle into a number of equal parts. A large circle should be divided into 72 parts of 5 deg. each. This will produce a finely detailed design. Small circles may have fewer divisions. Use a protractor to mark off the circle, Fig. 38-7.

Once the placement of the nails has been determined and they have been inserted, you can create different designs by varying the stringing order. Fig. 38-8 shows

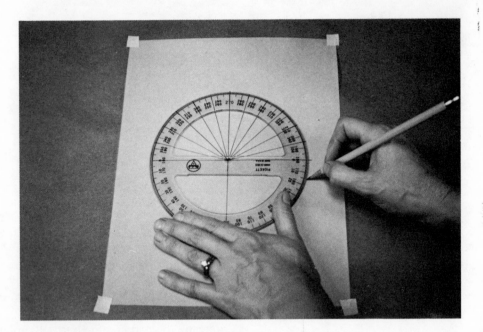

Fig. 38-7. Protractor may be used to divide circle into desired number of parts. A circle has 360 deg.

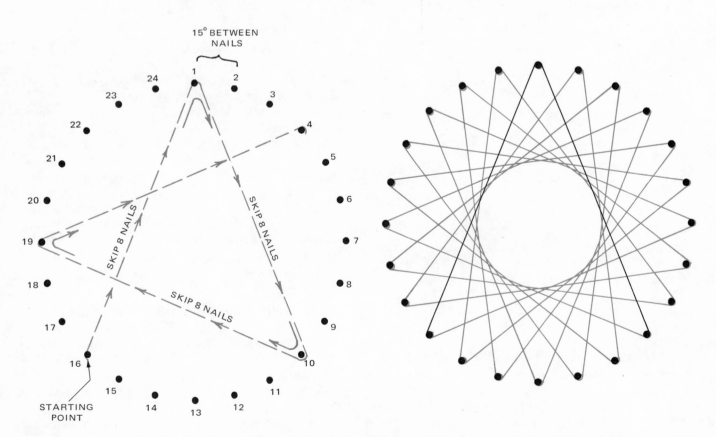

Fig. 38-8. Open circle stringing design. Left. Basic stringing pattern. Right. Pattern is completed when string has looped all nails once and starting point is reached.

String Art

the technique for an open circle.

Using the protractor as shown in Fig. 38-7, place a pencil mark every 15 degrees of the circle. Marks must be evenly spaced around the circle or the design will be crooked. Drive in a nail at every pencil mark.

Stringing can start on any nail. The design is created by pulling the string across the circle and catching a nail opposite. Be sure always to skip eight nails between loops.

Continue looping the string around every ninth nail until the starting point is reached. Figs. 38-9 through 38-11 show other possible designs.

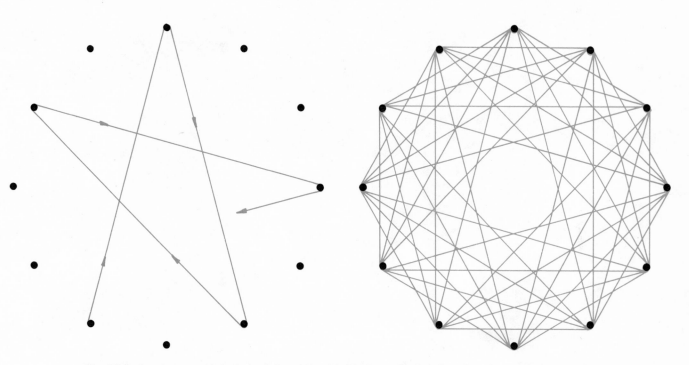

Fig. 38-9. Another open circle design is formed by skipping four nails each time; then three, two and one nail.

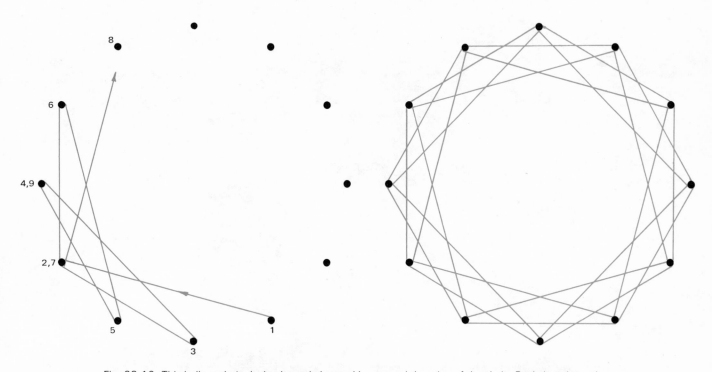

Fig. 38-10. This hollow circle design is made by working around the edge of the circle. Begin by tying string to any one of the nails. Skip two nails and wrap counterclockwise around nail. Go back to nail next to starting point. Repeat sequence until starting point is reached. Smaller center may be formed by skipping three or four nails instead of two.

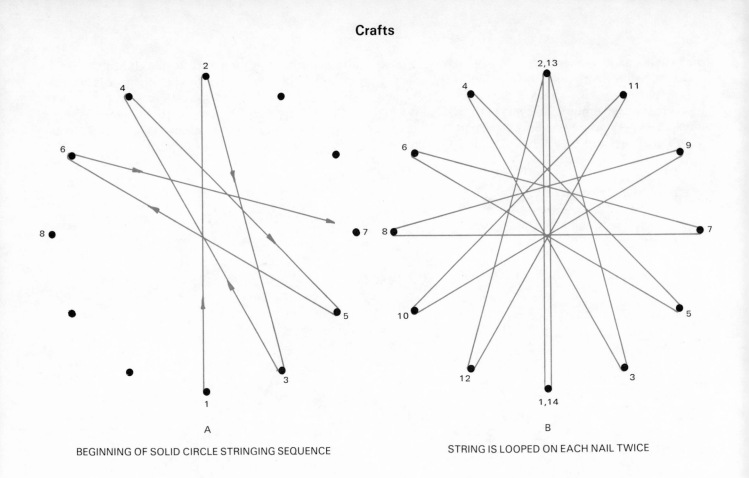

A

BEGINNING OF SOLID CIRCLE STRINGING SEQUENCE

B

STRING IS LOOPED ON EACH NAIL TWICE

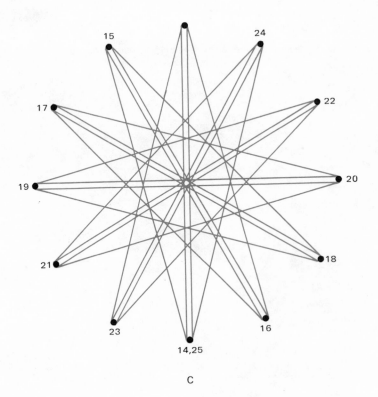

C

Fig. 38-11. Solid circle design may be made by stringing directly across circle and back to nail immediately to right of previously strung nail. Continue this operation until the design is symmetrical and ends at starting point. A—Sequence for first eight nails. B—Starting back to starting point. C—Completed design.

FREE FORMS

Free forms are easy to create with string art. Two different techniques are widely used. The first uses holes drilled through the backing rather than nails for attaching the strings. The string is threaded back and forth through the holes. A spider's web would be easy to create using this technique.

The second technique uses filler to complete a design. Odd-shaped areas do not lend themselves to an ordered stringing procedure. Therefore, filler string is woven back and forth to cover the space enclosed by the nails. Fig. 38-12 shows the use of filler on an irregular shape. The irregular shape is made by stretching the stringing material from one nail to the next in a process called outlining.

EDGING

Edging is used to close in and give shape to a circle or curved form. The result is a border similar to a woven edge and provides a finished appearance to the basic form.

Two basic types of edging are shown in Fig. 38-13. Inside edging is generally used in a circular design while outside edging may be used on a circle, an irregular or a straight edge.

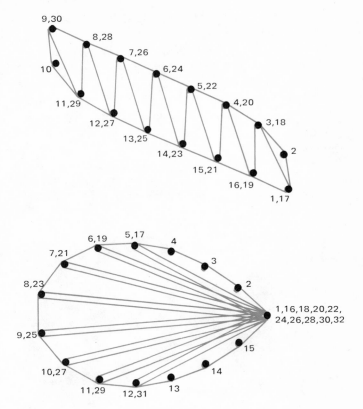

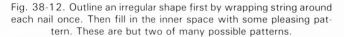

Fig. 38-12. Outline an irregular shape first by wrapping string around each nail once. Then fill in the inner space with some pleasing pattern. These are but two of many possible patterns.

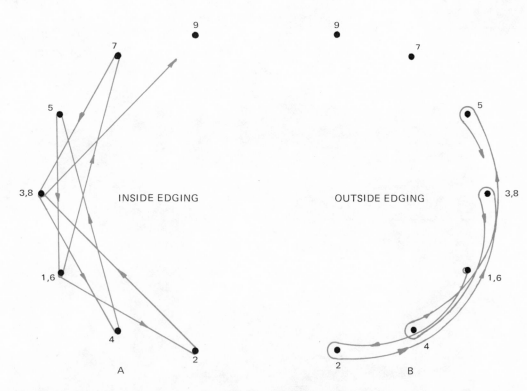

Fig. 38-13. Special stringing sequence is needed for developing edges. A—Make inside edging by skipping one nail to right of starting point and proceeding to nail on immediate left of starting point. Repeat pattern until design is complete. B—Outside edging is similar to inside edging but string is always on outside of nails. Select point to begin, pass string on the outside of next nail on left and then move right past two nails and begin the sequence again. Repeat until design is completed.

STRING ART ON BACKING

The backing is a very important part of the total product. It provides support for the design elements and forms the background against which the design is viewed. Choose a piece of material of an appropriate size. It should be at least 4 in. (10 cm) larger, each dimension, than the design. This will provide a 2 in. border.

To produce string art on the backing:

1. If you plan to stain or paint plywood, be sure to sand it first with fine sandpaper.

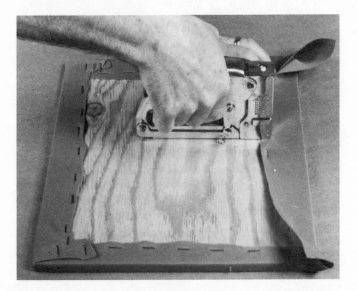

Fig. 38-14. Covering a backing with fabric. Staple gun is fast and holds cloth securely.

2. Dust off the surface and apply the finish. It is frequently a good idea to try the finish on a scrap piece to view the final effect before going ahead. Allow the finish to dry for the time recommended.

3. If fabric covered backing is to be used, attach it with a staple gun as shown in Fig. 38-14. Lay the fabric face down on a flat clean surface. Place the backing material (plywood) on top of the fabric, face down. Fold the fabric over the backing and staple it securely. Do not pull the fabric too tight. It may stretch out of shape.

4. With backing prepared, transfer the design to it. Place a full-size paper pattern on the backing in its proper position. Tape it down or hold it securely by some means. It is very important that the pattern does not move. If the backing is easy to nail into, drive nails or brads through the pattern into the backing. Be sure the nails are positioned accurately and all are the same height, Fig. 38-15.

If nailing is difficult, drill holes in the backing slightly smaller than the nails. When all the holes have been drilled, remove the pattern and insert the nails.

5. String the design, Fig. 38-16. Tie the end of the string to the nail at the starting point. Trim off excess string, but be certain that you have a secure knot. The string applied first will be at the back of the design. If you plan to use more than one color, plan the sequence so the right colors are in the foreground.

When the design is completed, tie the string off securely. Sometimes, a drop of glue will help secure the knot.

Fig. 38-15. Nailing brads through paper pattern into backing material. Small block of wood is used as height gage to check each nail.

STRING ART ON DOWELS

One type of string art is called an Ojo de Dios (pronounced o'-ho day dee'-ohs). It is Spanish for "Eye of God" and is an ancient good luck sign. The Ojo is made by weaving various colored yarns on dowels or sticks to create interesting and beautiful shapes and designs.

The simplest Ojos are made from two crossed dowels, some yarn and a little glue. To make one:

1. Notch the center of each dowel so the two pieces fit snugly together and are no thicker than one dowel. Apply white glue to the joint and clamp until dry, Fig. 38-17.
2. Select the yarn. Put a line of glue along the back of the joined dowels before wrapping the yarn. The glue, when dry, will hold the yarn in place. While holding the yarn underneath at the intersection bring it diagonally across the front. Then go beneath the dowels and back across the top on the opposite diagonal, Figs. 38-18 and 38-19.

Fig. 38-16. This string art is the design shown in Fig. 38-8. Center circle is created by straight sections of string!

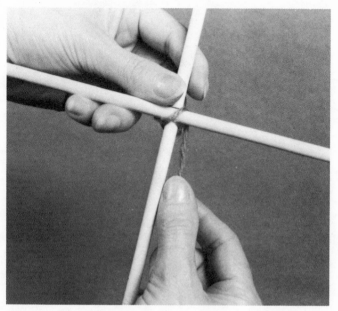

Fig. 38-18. First step in wrapping yarn on dowels to make an Ojo. Hold yarn behind one dowel and bring it diagonally across front of intersection of two dowels.

Fig. 38-17. Notched and glued dowels are clamped together. They will form base of an Ojo de Dios - a good luck symbol.

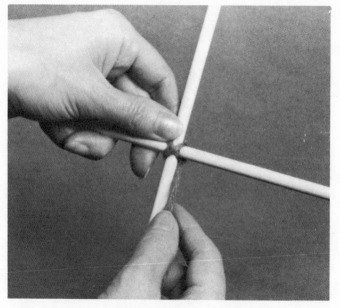

Fig. 38-19. First sequence is completed by bringing yarn back over dowels on opposite diagonal. This method is called "flat wrap."

3. Begin to wrap the yarn around the dowels using a flat wrap on each dowel, Fig. 38-20. This is the simplest wrap and is generally used to form the center or "eye" of the design. It is made by bringing the yarn over and around each dowel in turn. Fig. 38-21 shows the back side of the design. When you have completed one yarn color, make a half hitch and put a few drops of glue on the back side of the dowel to hold it.

4. Start a new piece of yarn on the next arm. Put a drop of glue on this knot too, and continue wrapping, Fig. 38-22. After you have used two or three colors of yarn, you may wish to try a "recessed wrap." The reverse of the flat wrap, it is made by winding the yarn under and around each dowel. See example in Fig. 38-23.

5. Most Ojos have an arrowhead formation on each dowel. "Arrowing" is formed by wrapping two opposite dowels on the back side. Wrap the yarn under and around the dowel twice. Then go back to

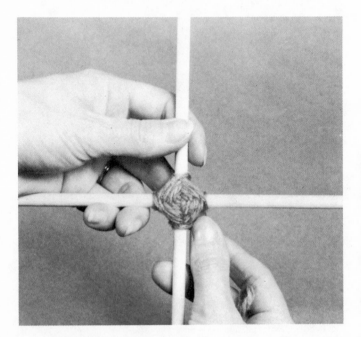

Fig. 38-20. Proceeding with the flat wrap to form the "eye" of the design. Loop yarn around each dowel.

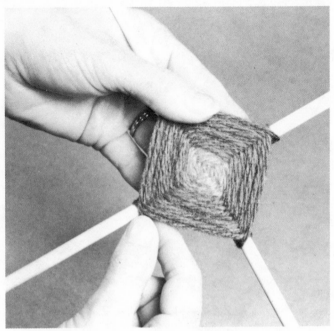

Fig. 38-22. Second color of yarn has been completed.

Fig. 38-21. Backview of flat wrap design. See how yarn encircles each dowel.

Fig. 38-23. Begin "recessed wrap" by reversing flat wrap.

the dowel where you started and wrap the yarn under and around that dowel twice. Fig. 38-24 shows the method. When arrowheads are completed on two arms, tie off the yarn and repeat the procedure on the other two arms. See Fig. 38-25.

6. Finish each dowel end by wrapping with yarn until it is covered as in Fig. 38-26. Secure the yarn with a knot.

7. Feathers, pompons or other decorative items may be added to the dowel ends. See Fig. 38-27 and Fig. 38-28. The Ojo de Dios, Fig. 38-29, is ready for display.

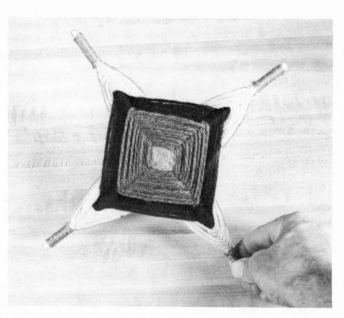

Fig. 38-26. Wrap each dowel end with yarn to completely cover it.

Fig. 38-24. This type of wrap is called "arrowing." It is formed on two opposite dowels on the back side. Wrap yarn under and around dowel twice and then go to other end and repeat.

Fig. 38-27. Steps in making a pompon for the arms of the Ojo. Wind several loops of yarn around two fingers until it forms a sizable hank as shown at left. Cut the hank at opposite ends to get a bundle of short yarns. Tie bundle in its center with another short piece of yarn.

Fig. 38-25. Arrowing is completed on all arms of the Ojo.

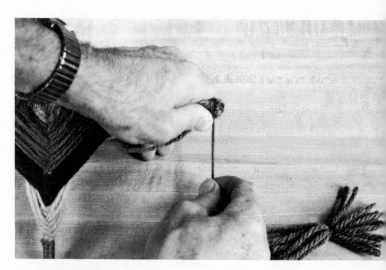

Fig. 38-28. Form yarn pompon around dowel end and tie it tightly with a piece of yarn. Do this on each dowel.

A third dimension may be added to an Ojo by adding other arms to the design. A three-dimensional Ojo makes an interesting mobile.

THREE-DIMENSIONAL STRING ART

Three-dimensional string art is merely an extension of the two-dimensional designs presented earlier. You may decide to try a single-curved surface such as a cylinder, cone or convolute, Fig. 38-30. Or, a more complex warped surface such as the shapes in Fig. 38-31. A more difficult shape to represent is the double-curved surface. Examples of double-curved surfaces include the shapes in Fig. 38-32.

These shapes may be strung inside clear sheet acrylic boxes or on metal rods supported on an attractive base. See Fig. 38-33.

Fig. 38-29. Completed Ojo is ready for display.

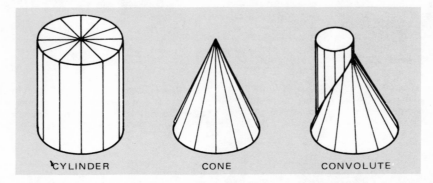

Fig. 38-30. Three dimensional string art designs patterned after these single-curved surfaces can be very exciting.

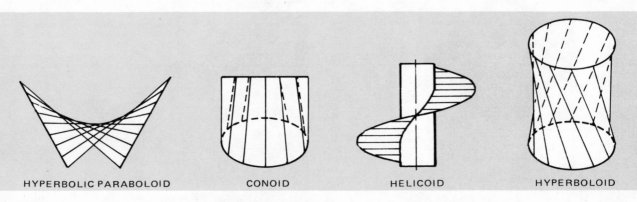

Fig. 38-31. Warped surfaces are more complex than single-curved surfaces, but add interest.

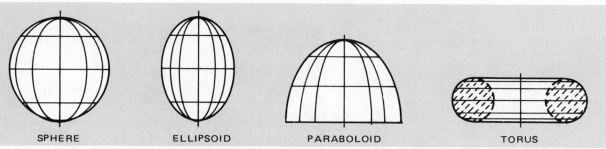

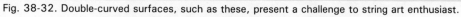

Fig. 38-32. Double-curved surfaces, such as these, present a challenge to string art enthusiast.

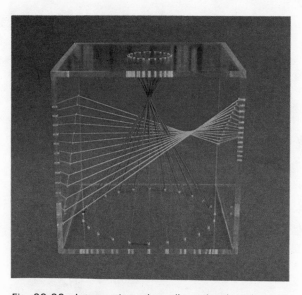

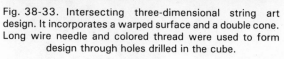

Fig. 38-33. Intersecting three-dimensional string art design. It incorporates a warped surface and a double cone. Long wire needle and colored thread were used to form design through holes drilled in the cube.

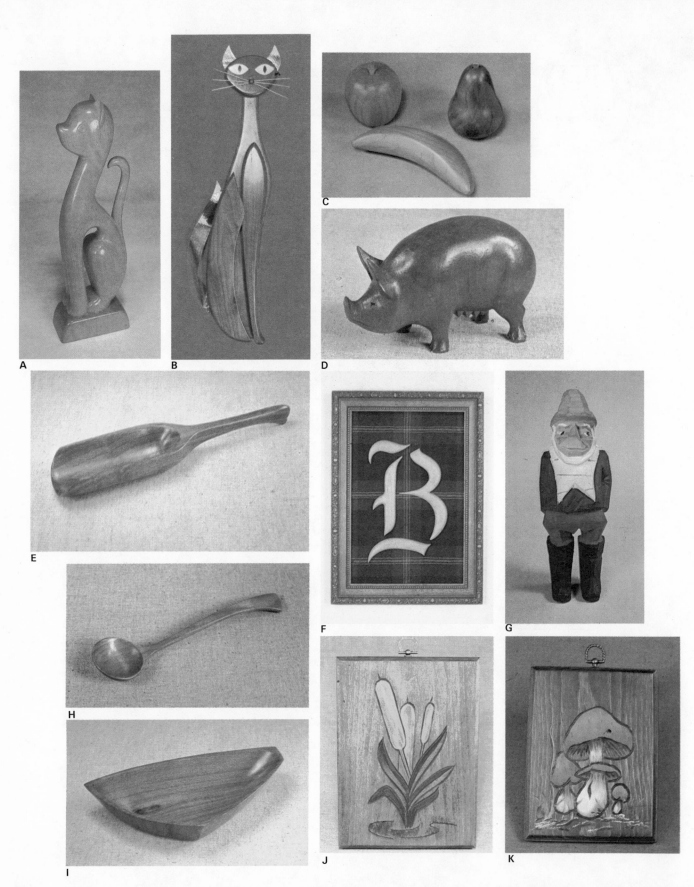

Alternatives for woodcarving. A—Excellent craftwork in wood. (Eldon Rebhorn). B—Stylized figure carved in individual pieces and then assembled. C—Different woods carved into fruit. D—Full carving in mahogany. E—Sugar scoop. F—Silhouette carving mounted on plaid backing. G—Painted statue made by whittling. H—Carved walnut spoon. I—Walnut dish finished in lacquer. J—Surface carving stained and painted. K—Painted surface carving over stain.

Chapter 39
WOODCARVING

Carving wood is one of the oldest and most interesting craft activities. Every piece of wood has a character unique in grain, color, texture, shape and beauty. It is very exciting to select a piece of wood and begin planning a useful and beautiful object. With experience, you will be able to visualize the shape of the object you want as you view a block of wood. You will then decide the best methods for removing the excess material. There is no limit to the number and style of functional and beautiful products that can be carved from wood. Fig. 39-1 is a beautiful, functional example of the carving craft.

MATERIALS

Many woods are suitable for carving. But, in every case, the wood must carve easily while offering the object function and beauty. Some woods, like hickory,

are very hard and make carving difficult. Others, such as cedar, are so soft that they splinter and become fuzzy. Hardwoods, such as walnut, cherry, butternut, teak and mahogany, are highly desirable. The beauty of these woods, adds to the value of the carved project. For projects that are to be stained, painted or given a clear finish, pine, basswood and poplar are satisfactory.

TOOLS

A number of tools are required for different types of carving, Fig. 39-2. A set of wood carver's tools are used for many carvings as are gouges, chisels and scrapers. Wood may be shaped also with carving knives, files and rasps.

A coping saw is used a great deal for roughing out shapes before carving begins. A notched cutting board

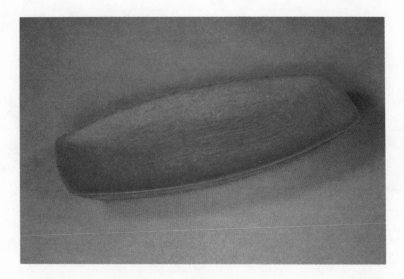

Fig. 39-1. Carved teak dish has beauty which only fine wood could impart.

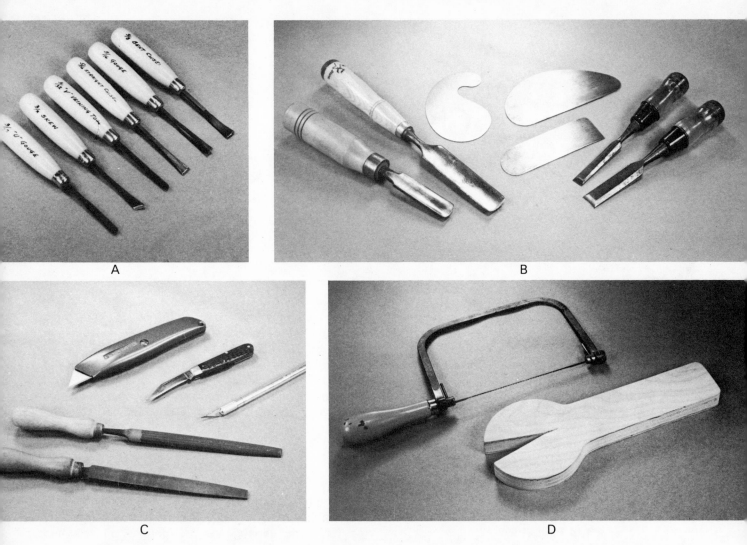

A B C D

Fig. 39-2. These hand tools should be in the well stocked woodcarving tool box. A—Wood carvers' tools include a U-shaped gouge, skew (slanted) chisel, V-shaped veining tool, straight chisel, shallow gouge and a bent shank gouge. B—Carving gouges, curved hand scrapers and wood chisels are also useful to the carver. C—Mat knife, pocket knife, small blade knife, wood rasp and file. D—Coping saw is always used with notched cutting board.

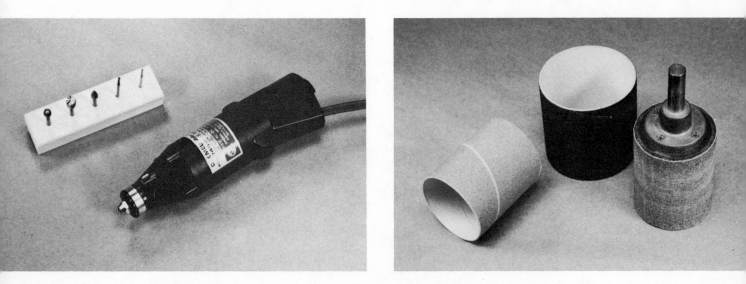

Fig. 39-3. Small portable power drill is useful for woodcarving. Left. Drill and assorted burrs. Right. Sanding drum with coarse to fine rolls.

is a useful companion to the coping saw. Some detailed carving work can be done with a hand-held power tool, Fig. 39-3, left, but it is best used for removing large amounts of wood quickly.

Other valuable power tools are the jig saw, bandsaw, disc sander and drum sander. See Fig. 39-3, right.

All cutting tools used for wood carving must be kept extremely sharp so the cuts are clean and smooth. Dull tools tend to tear the wood leaving marks that are difficult to remove. Even worse, they cause more accidents than sharp tools. Keep a whetstone at hand to restore a keen cutting edge whenever necessary, Fig. 39-4.

MAKING A HOLLOW CARVING

For the beginner, a hollow carving like a bowl or dish is a good project. Design a pleasing shape for the top and side views by making a number of sketches. A simple free-form design, like the one shown in Fig. 39-5, is easier to carve and will help you develop skill.

Trace the design onto a thin, stiff piece of cardboard. Cut out the pattern forming a smooth curve or line as the design requires.

TRANSFER OF PATTERN AND CARVING

Select a piece of wood large enough to overlap the pattern by 1/2 in. (12 mm) on all sides and thick enough to provide at least 1/4 in. (6 mm) of stock for the wall thickness at the bottom. Then proceed as follows:

1. Place your pattern on the stock so that its length is parallel to the grain of the wood. Hold the pattern firmly on the wood and trace a dark line around the edge with a pencil, Fig. 39-6.
2. In order to determine the wall thickness of a dish or bowl for carving purposes, sketch a pencil line about 1/4 in. (6 mm) inside the pattern line as shown in Fig. 39-7.

Fig. 39-4. Honing an outside bevel gouge with a whetstone. Use the stone frequently to keep fine edge on tools.

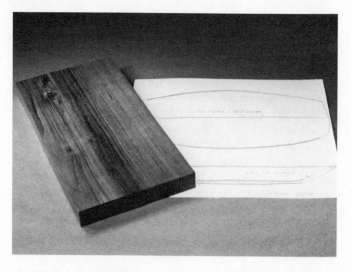

Fig. 39-5. Completed design with piece of teakwood in mind. Drawing shows all three dimensions.

Fig. 39-6. Trace around pattern on wood. Use pencil.

Fig. 39-7. Sketch line inside pattern line for carving.

3. Fasten the piece of wood in a vise or clamp to a bench top and begin removing stock as in Fig. 39-8. Use an outside bevel gouge and mallet. To remove the material, work from the outside edges toward the center at even depths. Continue this process until you have reached the desired contour and depth. Check the depth of a hollow carving as shown in Fig. 39-9. Be sure to complete all hollow carving and shaping before removing any outside material. In this way, you will always have a solid block to clamp to the bench. When rough gouging has been completed, use the gouge without the mallet to remove ridges and uneven areas. This is called finish gouging.

4. After finish gouging, even out and smooth the hollowed surfaces by scraping. Hold the curved scraper firmly and pull or push it with the grain of the hollow surface. See Fig. 39-10. Continue scraping away wood until the surface feels smooth to the touch and all gouge marks have been removed.

5. Sand the hollow surface with garnet or aluminum oxide paper. Start with a 120 grit (medium) and work down to a 220 grit (fine). Continue sanding until all scratch marks are removed. Always sand with the grain of the wood.

6. Sculpture (round over) the inside edges using a chisel, Fig. 39-11. Then sand to remove the sharp edges and give your project a graceful and finished appearance.

SHAPING THE OUTSIDE

1. A band saw is generally used to rough out the outside shape of the project, Fig. 39-12. However, a coping saw may be used for thinner carvings or carvings with sharp curves (such as a dish with an extended handle).

   When using the band saw, tilt the table to the correct angle to provide for the desired wall thickness. In most cases, the wall thickness will vary from 1/8 to 3/8 in. (3 to 9 mm) depending on the size and shape of your carving. Always use your pattern line as a guide.

2. Shape and smooth the outside of the carving with a spokeshave, file or disc sander, Fig. 39-13. Follow the side view of your drawing to obtain the desired shape and keep the wall thickness even around the hollow section. Carvings with graceful, thin lines are much more beautiful than those with heavy edges and thick bottoms.

3. Sand the outside of your carving in preparation for finishing, Fig. 39-14. A sanding block with a felt or rubber pad works well for heavy sanding of the outside shape. Apply the finish, Fig. 39-15. (Finishes are discussed at the end of the chapter.)

Fig. 39-8. Shape inside of dish with outside bevel gouge and mallet.

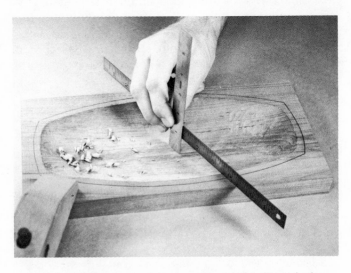

Fig. 39-9. Check depth of carving with straightedge and rule.

Fig. 39-10. Scrape inside of dish with curved scraper to remove ridges.

Fig. 39-11. Round off top edges with wood chisel.

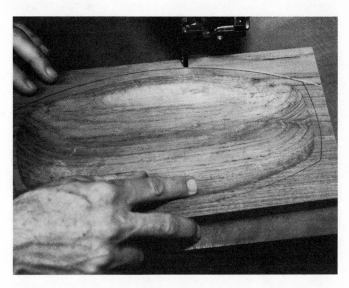

Fig. 39-12. Cutting outside of dish with band saw table tilted. This could be done with a coping saw but it is hard work!

Fig. 39-13. Shaping outside of carving with spokeshave. File or disc sander also works well.

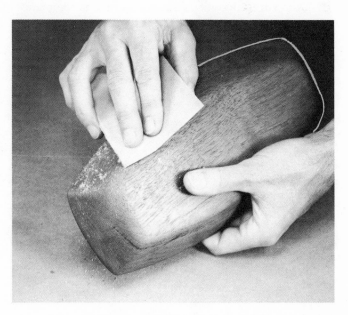

Fig. 39-14. Sand outside of carving with the grain.

Fig. 39-15. Apply penetrating oil finish with rag.

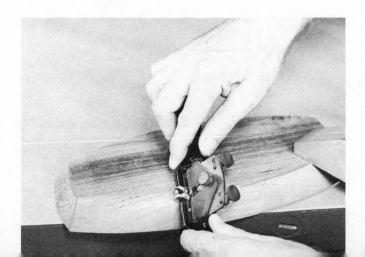

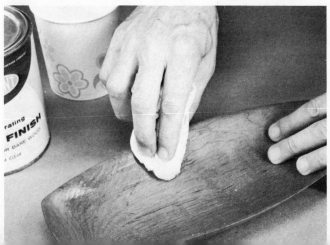

Crafts

IRREGULAR CARVINGS

Some hollowed out carvings do not have one flat, straight surface. Many salad servers, spoons, forks, ladles and scoops are of this type. Such carvings require a slightly different procedure than is used for a bowl or dish having a flat base. Patterns for an irregular shape are prepared as for a regular shape. There must be a top view and a side view. Shaping follows these steps:

1. Trace the side view pattern onto the block of wood. See Fig. 39-16. Carefully cut out this shape on the band saw.
2. Trace the top view onto the new curved surface, Fig. 39-17.
3. Lay out the shape for the hollowed section on the top view.
4. Carve out this section as shown in Fig. 39-18 and sand.
5. Carefully band saw the top view following the traced line, Fig. 39-19.
6. Complete the outside surfaces in the same manner as carving a dish. Sculpture the edges, sand smooth and apply the finish, Fig. 39-20.

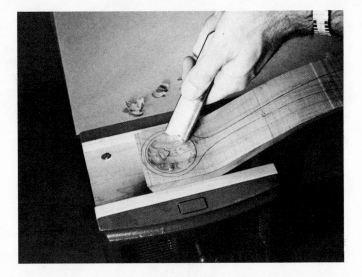

Fig. 39-18. Carve hollow section of spoon with gouge.

Fig. 39-16. Trace pattern of side view on block of wood.

Fig. 39-19. Cut out top view of carved spoon.

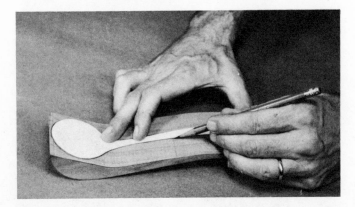

Fig. 39-17. Trace pattern of top view on new curved wood surface.

Fig. 39-20. By any standards, finished spoon is beautiful.

SILHOUETTE CARVINGS

Both silhouette and wall carvings have flat backs and sculptured fronts. In this respect they are similar. A silhouette is made by carving individual pieces of wood and placing them together in a way that plays up the main parts of a figure. The parts left out will be filled in by the imagination of the viewer.

The parts are usually made from a dark wood, walnut for example, and are mounted on a light-colored background. Contrasting woods and fabrics are both used for the background material. Most silhouette carvings are framed and used as wall hangings.

Design your silhouette carvings so that the viewer will be attracted by the unusual arrangement of the parts. Fish, birds, animals and sailing ships may provide ideas for a silhouette carving.

WALL CARVINGS

Wall carvings are similar to silhouettes except that they are made from one piece of wood. In most cases, wall carvings are decorative designs meant to add spots of beauty in the home. Abstract shapes, flowers and silhouettes all provide ideas for a beginning wall carving project.

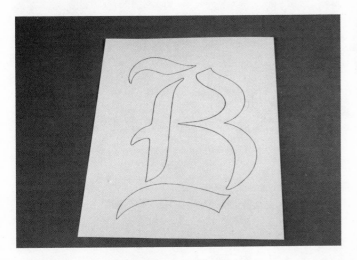

Fig. 39-21. Full size drawing was made of individual parts for initial letter "B".

Fig. 39-22. Patterns are traced onto 1/2 in. cherry.

HOW TO MAKE THEM

Since silhouettes and wall carvings are similar, the same procedure is used for both.

1. Select a design and make a full size drawing on cardboard. See Fig. 39-21. Cut out the pieces with scissors and trace them on flat pieces of wood, Fig. 39-22. Smooth, free-form lines provide an attractive outline shape for this type of carving.

2. Using a band saw, jig saw or coping saw, cut out the shapes. Stay on the outside of your pencil line, Fig. 39-23.

3. If there are internal cuts, bore holes in the open areas on a drill press or with a hand drill as shown in Fig. 39-24.

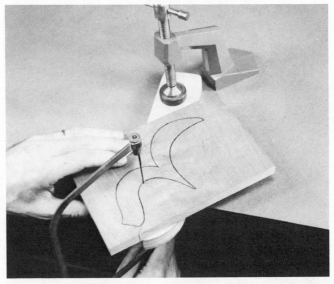

Fig. 39-23. Cut out wood shape with a coping saw, band saw or jig saw. Stay just outside pencil line.

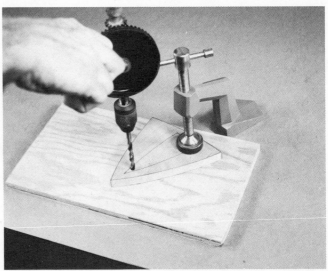

Fig. 39-24. Drill hole in open area to insert coping saw blade.

4. Use the jig saw or coping saw to cut out the internal openings, Fig. 39-25. The blade must be removed, slipped through the bored hole and replaced in the handle.

5. Carve and sculpture the edges as you would a dish in hollow carving. Use a spokeshave, rasps and assorted files to form the contours you want, Fig. 39-26. Shapes with much detail are easily formed using a hand-held power tool and an assortment of burrs, Fig. 39-27. Carving tools may also be used. Edges of inside cuts may be shaped with the aid of a round file.

6. After final shaping, sand smooth, working from a coarse to a fine grit sandpaper, Fig. 39-28. Always sand with the grain. Apply appropriate finish.

7. Silhouettes may be glued to a backing and framed as you desire, Fig. 39-29.

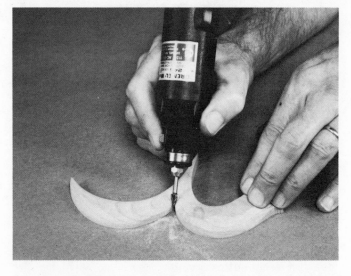

Fig. 39-27. Shaping curved groove with burr in hand-held power tool. Power tools remove wood faster than hand tools.

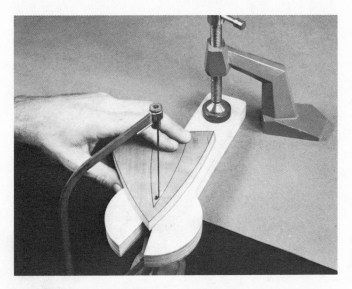

Fig. 39-25. Cut out internal opening with coping saw.

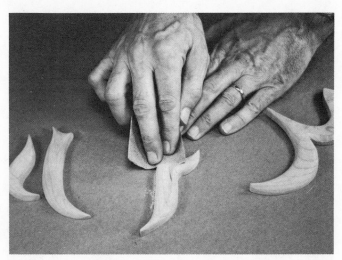

Fig. 39-28. Sand with grain to smooth curved surface.

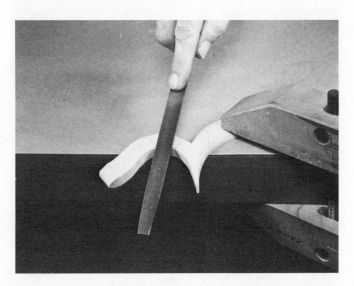

Fig. 39-26. Inside curves may be shaped with wood rasp.

Fig. 39-29. Silhouette carving has been mounted on fabric backing and framed.

8. Attach a wallhanger to the backs of wall carvings so they will hang straight. Metal and fabric hangers are available for this purpose.

SURFACE CARVING

Most surface carving is used for decorative purposes. One of the oldest and simplest forms of carving, it is used to produce the designs on trays, wall plaques, family crests, jewelry boxes or a name plate. Many terms are used to describe the various types of surface carvings. *Incised line, chip* and *relief* are three of them. Combinations of these are used to produce many carving designs.

Incised line carving is one of the easiest. It consists primarily of cutting grooves into the wood surface tracing the outline of the pattern. A V or U-shaped gouge is used. Small pieces of wood are removed as carving progresses.

Chip carving refers to the process of cutting triangular or wedge-shaped chips or slivers from the wood surface. Carving chisels, utility knives and standard pocket knives are generally used to produce this design

Relief carving is nothing more than incised line carving with some of the background cut away to make certain areas appear to be raised. Both knives and carving tools are used.

The following procedure can be used for each of these surface carving techniques.

1. Sketch your design on a piece of white paper and select the wood appropriate for the carving. See the design shown in Fig. 39-30.
2. Transfer the design to the wood.

3. Clamp wood to the bench and use a V-shaped gouge to incise the outline shapes of the cattails, Fig. 39-31. Make these cuts by using a number of passes rather than one long, deep groove. Remove only a small amount of wood at a time to control the depth and width of the cut. Cut carefully across or with the grain to avoid tearing the fibers. Make diagonal cuts the way the grain lays whenever possible. Cutting against diagonal grain may deflect the gouge from the pattern line.
4. Chip carve the three top leaves. Sketch a line through the center of each leaf and use a knife to cut this line to desired depth rising to the surface at each end of the leaf, Fig. 39-32. Slant your knife

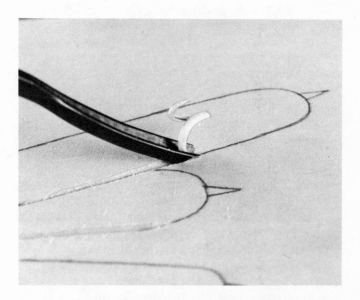

Fig. 39-31. Making an incised line cut with a V-gouge. Work with grain wherever possible.

Fig. 39-30. A simple design such as this is best for a first project in surface carving.

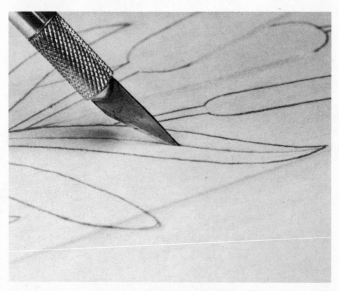

Fig. 39-32. Use knife, held vertically, to make first cut through center of leaf.

and make a slicing cut along the length of the leaf toward the bottom of the first chip cut. See Fig. 39-33. Cut slowly and remove pieces as you go along. Continue the slicing cuts until a V-shaped leaf is formed.

5. Use two forms of relief carving to give the feeling of depth around the leaves and pool of water.

   a. Make an incised line or stop cut (where relief cuts end) around the leaves, Fig. 39-34.

   b. A shallow relief cut is then made by slanting your knife and slicing away wood up to the incised line cut, Fig. 39-35.

   c. Try to work across the grain toward the stop cut. Do not slice deeper than the bottom of the stop cut or splitting may spoil your work. Depth is obtained around the pool of water by making incised line cuts as shown in Fig. 39-36.

   d. A shallow gouge can be used to give a deeper relief around the incised line cuts, Fig. 39-37.

6. Whether to sand a surface carving is a matter of personal taste. Many woodcarvers prefer to leave tool and knife marks. Others like to remove all carving traces. If you do sand, use the edge of a piece of sandpaper or an emery board, Fig. 39-38, to smooth carving details. Carefully smooth backgrounds with a fine grit sandpaper. Be careful not to spoil your carving by rounding over details that should be sharp and clear.

7. Surface carvings will accept many attractive finishes. They can be stained, painted or left natural with only a clear, protective finish. Fig. 39-39 shows one method of finishing. Other finishes are discussed at the end of the chapter. The completed surface carving is shown in Fig. 39-40.

Fig. 39-34. Making an incised line cut around leaf. This will prevent ragged edge being formed from relief cuts.

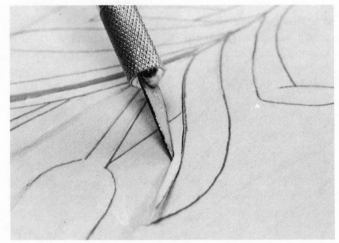

Fig. 39-35. Make shallow relief cuts with knife slanted toward incised line.

Fig. 39-33. Making slanted cut along edge of leaf toward bottom of first chip cut. Make additional cuts up to edge of leaf. Repeat on opposite side.

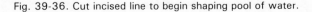

Fig. 39-36. Cut incised line to begin shaping pool of water.

WHITTLING AND FULL CARVING

A full carving is usually the most difficult. This is undoubtedly due to the fact that you must learn to visualize the form in three dimensions. There is a tendency to carve the object with relatively flat sides like rounding the corners off of a cube. This is often due to fear of carving too deep. Full carving, often called "carving in-the-round", requires that you "see" the form in your mind from all directions. To attain this, it is often wise to make up a model of the figure from modeling clay. This material is soft and moldable. It is easy to build up sections and cut away others to gain a feeling for the shape of the carving. It should give you a great deal of confidence when you begin shaping a block of wood.

WHITTLING

Whittling is a good way to get acquainted with full carving a simple figure. Whittling is actually a simple

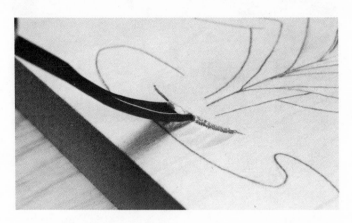

Fig. 39-37. Shallow gouge is used to give deep relief to incised lines.

Fig. 39-38. Sanding detail of carving with emery board. Some carvers prefer to leave carving marks in finished work.

Fig. 39-40. Surface carving has been stained and finished.

Fig. 39-39. Applying walnut stain to the carving with a cloth. Stain strikes in deeper over depressed areas.

form of full carving and requires only a few tools: a good sharp pocket knife or hobby knife, a coping saw and a carving skew.

Try the following procedure for whittling a three dimensional object.

1. Select or design the outline of the figure. Prepare a drawing of the front and side views, or the views that show the most detail. See Fig. 39-41.

2. Prepare a piece of wood, (poplar, white pine or basswood are easy to carve). Lay out the pattern on all four surfaces, Fig. 39-42. Thin sections should run with the grain as much as possible so they will not break so easily.

3. Use a band saw, jig saw or coping saw to cut the outline shape for the jump ring as shown in Fig. 39-43. Cut just outside your pattern line. If part of your pattern has been removed by the first cutting, retrace or sketch that section and cut in the same manner.

4. With a sharp knife, begin shaping the four bars of the cage as in Fig. 39-44. Carefully remove just enough wood so that the cylinder remains as large as possible. Continue making V-shaped cuts along the sides until the knife will pass through at each corner as shown in Fig. 39-45.

5. Round the cage bars with a knife, Fig. 39-46.

6. Round the cylinder with long thin shaving cuts, Fig. 39-47.

7. Now, cut the cylinder free, top and bottom, with a knife. Carve the top of the cage flat and smooth.

8. Carefully hold the cylinder in one hand and begin carving the ball or cylinder as shown in Fig. 39-48. Carve the opening in the bottom of the cage in the same manner as the sides.

9. Using the point of the knife, carve the hole for the jump ring, Fig. 39-49. Round the outside edges of the ring. Check the carving to be sure all parts are equally shaped and edges rounded.

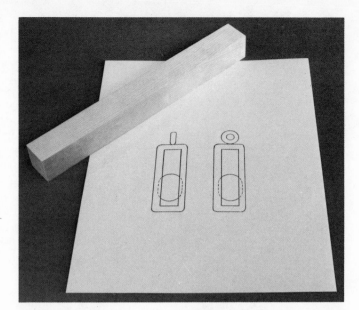

Fig. 39-41. Drawing shows front and side views for whittling a ball-in-cage.

Fig. 39-42. Lay out pattern on wood block with pencil and rule.

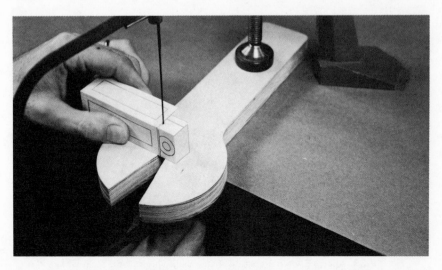

Fig. 39-43. Use coping saw to cut away excess wood around jump ring.

Fig. 39-44. Beginning to shape bars of cage with knife. Continue to deepen stop cut and make wedge-shaped cuts to remove wood.

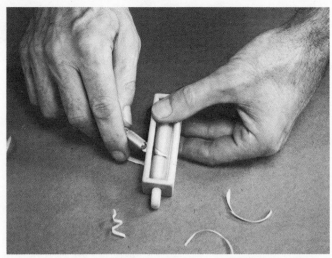

Fig. 39-47. Long thin shavings round out the cylinder.

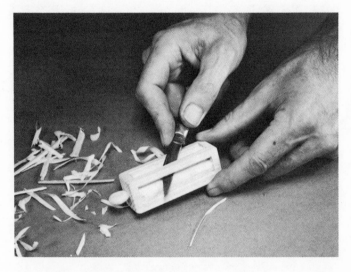

Fig. 39-45. Opening has been made between bar and cylinder.

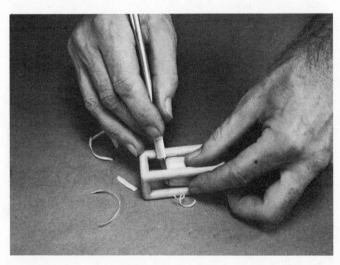

Fig. 39-48. Shave end of cylinder with light knife cuts while holding it tightly.

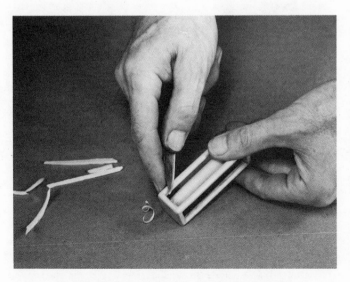

Fig. 39-46. Round bar of cage with shaving cut.

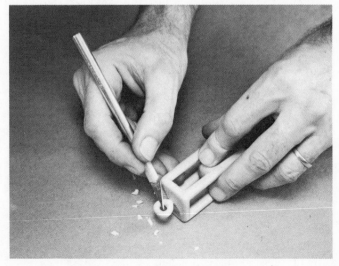

Fig. 39-49. Round jump ring with knife point.

10. Sand all surfaces using strips of sandpaper, Fig. 39-50, or an emery board. Apply a clear finish and polish smooth with fine steel wool. Thread a soft leather thong through the jump ring to complete the ball-in-cage necklace. See Fig. 39-51.

CARVING

Full carving differs from whittling in the type of tools used. While whittling primarily depends upon the skillful use of a knife, full carving usually involves the use of many carving tools and sanding devices. In a full carving project, which may range from a small table figure to a life-sized object, carving generally becomes more detailed.

Two major areas should be carefully studied before you begin a full carving. First, the problem of holding the block of wood becomes more difficult. Some solutions are the following:

1. Leave extra stock at the base of the object so that it can be clamped in a vise. This wood can be cut off later.
2. A variety of wood clamps can be used as shown in Fig. 39-52.
3. Screw a piece of wood to the bottom which may be clamped to a bench or held in a vise.
4. Use a sandbag which will conform to the shape of the figure and hold it in place.

Secondly, most detail carving is done on curved surfaces. Grain direction then becomes more of a problem. Carefully watch the grain direction as you carve so as not to accidentally chip out areas that are part of the figure.

Use the same procedure as in whittling. A good beginning technique is to copy a figure you like which is made out of some other material. It is easier to visualize the shaping of the figure as carving progresses. Use carving tools and make the same types of cuts you would in wall carvings. Most full carvings should be sanded smooth. This removes tool marks, gives the figure a realistic appearance and exposes the grain patterns of the wood. See Fig. 39-53.

FINISHING TECHNIQUES

Since wood is so beautiful as a natural material, many woodcarvers feel that a carving should remain just as it is when the tool makes its last stroke. This would be quite desirable. However, there are many reasons why carvings should have a finish. Most woods, being porous, collect dust and dirt that is difficult to remove. Carvings should also be protected from damage by nicks and scratches, cracks from changes in humidity and ordinary wear. There is also the problem of protecting carved objects (such as salad bowls and serving trays) that come in contact with

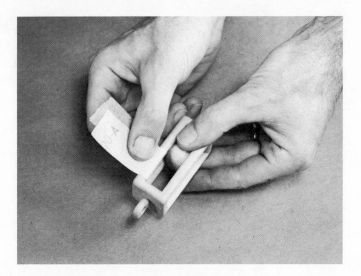

Fig. 39-50. Smooth edges with sandpaper strip.

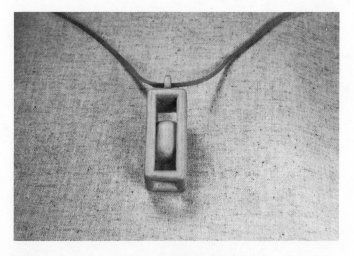

Fig. 39-51. Completed ball-in-cage with leather thong. Clear finish has been applied.

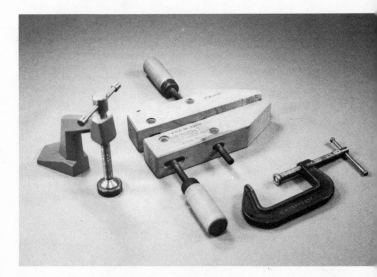

Fig. 39-52. A hold-down clamp, handscrew or C clamp can be used to hold full carving project.

food. Finally, finishes generally enhance the beauty of wood by bringing out the color and emphasizing the grain pattern.

WAX

Waxing brings out the grain pattern, produces a soft semigloss and makes a very attractive surface. It is not waterproof or scratch resistant. Therefore, it should only be used for decorative carvings. Use a good paste wax or pure beeswax dissolved into a paste by addition of turpentine. Apply two or three generous coats by rubbing heavily into the wood surface. Allow to dry between coats and buff with a lint-free rag.

PENETRATING FINISHES

Penetrating finishes produce one of the most natural looking surfaces possible. Especially with beautiful woods like walnut or teak, the color becomes very rich.

Linseed oil and tung oil should be applied heavily, allowed to soak in and the surface wiped clean. You can apply as many coats as you wish to achieve the best color and durability.

Penetrating resin finishes are probably the easiest and most protective finishes you can apply. They contain oils to penetrate the wood and plastic resins which harden the surface as they dry. Apply resin with a rag and keep surfaces wet for 15 minutes. Wipe off excess with a clean rag and allow to cure for at least 24 hours. Two more coats should be applied in the same manner. After final drying, rub with fine steel wool and buff with a soft cloth.

SURFACE FINISHES

Surface finishes are built-up finishes. Application usually starts with a sealer followed by a number of top coats that cover the wood surface. The sealer does not allow the top coats to penetrate further, so the build-up begins. Most surface finishes are a type of lacquer or synthetic varnish. Since there are so many on the market, carefully follow the manufacturer's directions for application. In general, lacquers provide a hard surface, dry rapidly and come in a semigloss which is ideal for some carvings. Use a soft, natural bristle brush and apply a coat of sanding sealer. Rub smooth with fine steel wool. Apply two coats of clear lacquer. When dry, rub with steel wool and buff with a soft cloth.

Varnishes are applied in much the same manner. However, most varnishes give a high gloss surface which is not as attractive on wood carvings. Varnishes also dry very slowly and are apt to pick up a good deal of dust on the surface. Lacquers and varnishes are also available in spray cans.

Fig. 39-53. Full carvings show beautiful grain and finish.

STAIN

Staining is often used to darken light colored woods and to even out the color of darker woods. It is a method of giving the wood a tint or shade without concealing the grain pattern. Water, spirit and oil stains all work satisfactorily.

Apply the stain according to the manufacturer's directions. Always test the stain you select on a scrap piece of wood of the same type as your carving. Apply stains with a soft brush. After they have dried, finish them with wax, oil, lacquer or varnish.

PAINT

Painting is sometimes used to finish softwoods, such as basswood or pine, which may not have an attractive color or grain pattern. A realistic look can be achieved by painting some carvings like birds or leaves, but think before you paint. Beautiful carvings usually look better with a more natural finish.

Flat or gloss enamel may be used. A lacquer sealer or coat of shellac makes a good base so that the paint does not soak in and painting detail is easier. Paints may also be used on some carvings to produce a textured effect. Paint the entire carving. After the paint has dried slightly, wipe it off with a soft cloth. The paint that has penetrated the pores or soft grain will often give an interesting, highlighted effect. When dry, finish with a coat of wax.

Other woodcraft projects. A—Decorative bookends. B—Wall plaque for storing keys. (Mark Lindsay) C—Woodcraft picture made from pieces of cove molding. D—Decorative woodcraft puzzle. E—Simple wooden ware for kitchen use. F—Picture puzzle from two sheets of plywood. G—Playing card holder from glued blocks cut on bandsaw. H—Small easel for holding pictures and plaques. I—Desk caddy for file folders. J—Salt and pepper shakers with filler hole drilled in bottoms. K—Jewelry box with teak stain.

Chapter 40
WOODCRAFT

For those who just like to make something out of wood, woodcraft projects are a very popular activity. In general, these activities allow a great deal of personal expression and the end products are useful. Projects may be simple or hard to make, depending on your personal preference, Fig. 40-1.

Most of the enjoyment comes from the freedom to design and make a project you like. You do it your own way. Specific drawings and dimensions are seldom required and you are completely free to use the materials and tools you need in a manner you feel will produce the best results.

The range of woodcraft projects is broad. Some interesting items include salt and pepper shakers, a wood handbag, cutting boards, a jewelry box, game boards, toys or a tool box.

MATERIALS

Any number of different types of wood are available for woodcraft projects. Most lumberyards stock softwoods such as white pine, redwood and fir. They also carry many of the good hardwoods—maple, oak and even walnut—for small special projects. Plywood and chipboard should not be overlooked, since they work quite well for many projects. Different types of glue, sandpaper, fasteners and finishes are about all the other materials needed.

TOOLS

Since the processes involved in making woodcraft projects are simple shaping, fastening and finishing, general woodshop hand tools are all that are required. Tools used in a home workshop are satisfactory. Different methods of sawing, drilling and planing are the most commonly used processes.

A miter box is often used for making accurate cuts with a saw. Clamps are sometimes necessary for

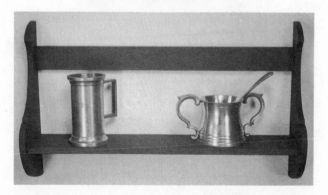

Fig. 40-1. Functional woodcraft projects add beauty and interest to home or office.

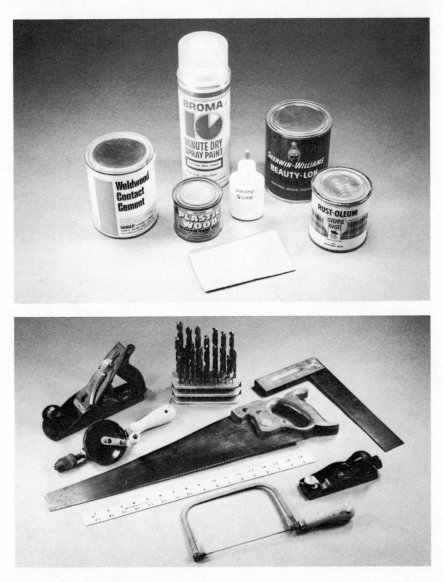

Fig. 40-2. Top. Materials common to woodcraft are contact cement, clear plastic spray, varnish, paint, plastic wood, white glue and sandpaper. Bottom. Some of the most-used tools for woodcraft are a jack plane, set of twist drills, try square, hand drill, handsaw, block plane, ruler and coping saw.

Fig. 40-3. Bookend pattern is placed on wood and traced.

Fig. 40-4. Use small handsaw to cut tapered side of bookend.

holding wood pieces and gluing assemblies. Power tools can also be used if they are available. Materials and tools are shown in Fig. 40-2.

MAKING A FLAT WOOD PROJECT

Many valuable but simple projects are made from one flat piece of wood or plywood. Try the following procedure for layout and construction of a bookend.

1. Make a number of sketches and select the one you like best. You may see a picture of a project in a magazine or book that you like. Make a sketch from the picture.
2. Lay out your design on a piece of thin, stiff cardboard. Cut it out with scissors.
3. Select a piece of wood and trace the pattern on it, Fig. 40-3. Always use a pencil. Ink from a ball point pen is difficult to sand away. Also, be sure the grain of the wood runs along the length of the design shape.
4. Use a handsaw to cut the ends and tapered sides, Fig. 40-4. Make cuts just outside the pencil lines so that you can see the lines when smoothing the edges. A power saw can be used, but these cuts are short and easy to make with a handsaw.
5. Smooth the edges with a block plane, Fig. 40-5, being sure to keep the edges flat and straight with the pencil lines. Remove all saw marks with the plane.
6. Using a steel rule as a guide, lay out the pencil lines for the beveled (slanted) edges, Fig. 40-6. Hold the wood in a vise or clamp it to the bench and plane the three beveled edges, Fig. 40-7. Smooth these bevels as accurately as you can to the pencil lines. Sand all surfaces in preparation for painting, staining or a clear finish.

Fig. 40-5. Use sharp block plane to smooth edges.

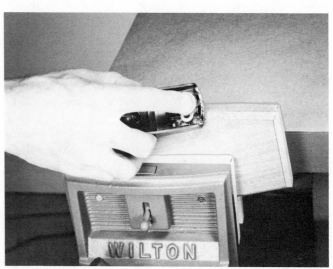

Fig. 40-7. Beveled edge is shaped with a block plane.

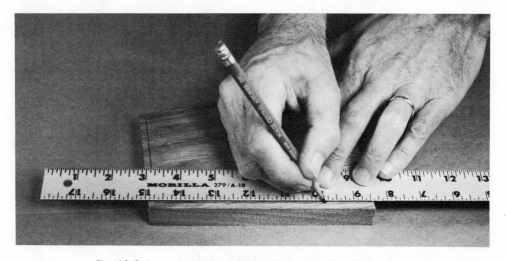

Fig. 40-6. Lay out guidelines for beveled edge with pencil and rule.

7. Select a thin sheet of metal or plastic for the base. Hard, thin aluminum sheet is easy to cut and drill. Cut a piece of an appropriate size with a pair of tinners' snips or a hacksaw, Fig. 40-8. File the edges smooth. Drill two holes at one edge for attaching to the bottom of the wood. Fasten with small wood screws as shown in Fig. 40-9.

8. Apply the finish as described in Chapter 39. Felt can be fastened to the metal base with white glue to protect table or bookshelf surfaces. Fig. 40-10 shows the completed bookend.

MAKING A WOOD BLOCK PROJECT

Projects like salt and pepper shakers, candlesticks or a pen and pencil holder usually require a thick block of wood. If the wood available is not thick enough for the project you plan to make, several pieces can be glued together. Use white glue and clamps or a heavy weight to join such pieces.

Since the basic operations are similar for these items, the following procedure for making a pen and pencil holder should serve as a guide.

1. Cut a block of wood to length with a handsaw or band saw, if available. Plane all sides smooth with a block plane or jack plane, Fig. 40-11. Use a sharp block plane or coarse sandpaper to smooth the end grain on the top and bottom.

2. Lay out the spacing for the holes in the top. Decide upon the size of holes you will need to hold different pens, pencils or felt tip markers you may be using. The depth of the holes will depend on their length so that they stand at a fairly even height. About half the length of a ball point pen makes a good depth. Mark spots for holes with a center punch or ice pick, Fig. 40-12.

3. Drill holes. Use a hand drill, portable power drill or drill press. Select the twist drill size required. A common wood pencil fits a 5/16 in. (8 mm) dia. hole nicely. Drill the holes slowly to allow chips to escape without overheating. To keep the drilled holes straight, use a try square as a guide as shown in Fig. 40-13.

4. Sand surfaces smooth and carefully round over the edges of the drilled holes as shown in Fig. 40-14.

5. Apply paint or other finish and attach decoration such as an initial, interesting coin or a decal. See Fig. 40-15. Decorative items are easily attached with contact cement.

MAKING A WOOD PROJECT

Some woodcraft projects require the assembly or fabrication of a number of pieces of wood. In most cases, gluing, nailing or using wood screws will do the job. The following procedure is typical of cutting, shap-

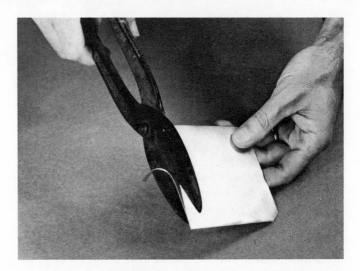

Fig. 40-8. Cut thin sheet of aluminum with tinners' snips.

Fig. 40-9. Fasten metal base to bottom of wood with small flat head wood screws.

Fig. 40-10. Bookend was given clear plastic spray finish.

Fig. 40-11. Smooth sides of wood block with jack plane.

Fig. 40-12. Make layout for holes and mark centers with ice pick.

Fig. 40-13. Drilling holes with portable power drill. Use try square as guide for making holes straight.

Fig. 40-14. Round edges of drilled holes with fine sandpaper wrapped around finger.

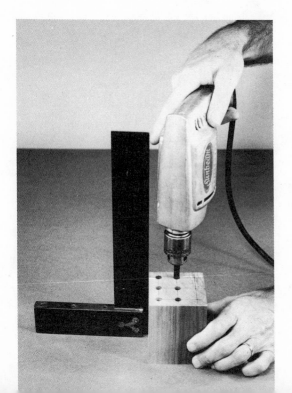

Fig. 40-15. Finished pencil holder has been decorated with interesting coin.

ing and fabricating almost any style of wall shelf. Plywood works well for projects of this type.

1. Prepare a design for the ends, shelf and supporting strip. Make a cardboard pattern for the ends. Trace the pattern onto 3/8 in. (9 mm) plywood as shown in Fig. 40-16.

2. Carefully cut the curved shapes of the ends with a coping saw, Fig. 40-17. Be sure to stay just outside pencil lines to retain the shape when sanding.

3. Sand the faces and edges smooth with sandpaper and a block of wood. Inside curves are easily smoothed by wrapping sandpaper around a short piece of broom handle or a dowel rod, Fig. 40-18. Lightly round over all edges so they will not be sharp to the touch.

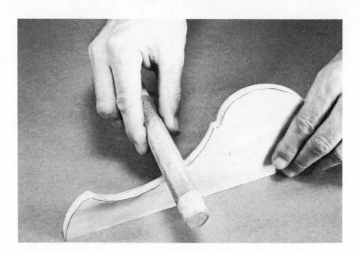

Fig. 40-18. Sand inside curves with sandpaper wrapped around dowel rod.

Fig. 40-16. Tracing pattern of shelf end on 3/8 in. plywood. Try to use up scraps.

Fig. 40-19. Square off end of shelf with pencil and try square.

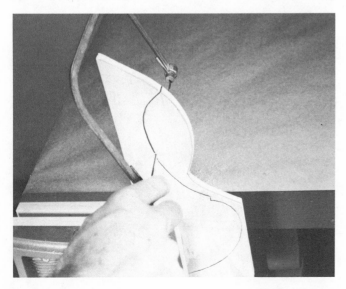

Fig. 40-17. Cut out shelf end with coping saw.

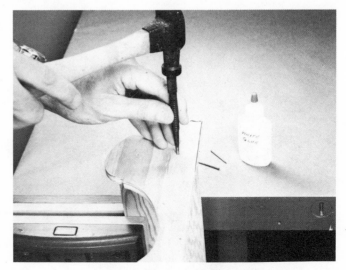

Fig. 40-20. Set nail heads below surface with nail set.

4. Cut the shelf and supporting strip to width with a handsaw. The shelf can be made any length that fits your needs. Square off the ends of the supporting strip and shelf to the same length, Fig. 40-19. Be sure to cut off the pieces accurately with a saw since they must form a neat, square joint with the ends.

5. Use white glue and small finishing nails to assemble the ends, shelf and supporting strip. A hole drilled smaller than the size of the nail helps keep the plywood from splitting. Set the nail heads below the surface with a nail set as in Fig. 40-20. Fill the holes with plastic wood or water putty. When the plastic wood is dry, sand smooth and the shelf is ready for finishing, Fig. 40-21. Paint or apply the finish you want. Metal picture hangers can be fastened to the top of each end piece to secure the shelf to a wall.

Fig. 40-21. Plywood wall shelf is ready for finishing.

GLOSSARY

BASKETRY

BASE: Bottom of a basket whether woven or made of one solid piece of wood or plywood.

FOOTING: Row of interlocking reeds woven under the solid base of a basket.

HONG KONG GRASS: Coarse grass which may be twisted into thin ropes for basket weaving.

PAIRING: Weaving with two reeds at same time.

PIECING WEAVERS: Method of starting new weaver when old weaver runs out.

PLAIN WEAVING: Also called simple weaving. Passing single weaver over one stake and under the next in alternating pattern.

PINE STRAW: Needles of the longleaf pine or southern pine which reach a length of 18 in.

RAFFIA: Dried leaves of palm frond found mainly in Madagascar.

REED: Woody, flexible, stemlike material used widely for basketry. Often obtained from core of the rattan or cone palm and cut round by special coring machines.

STAKES: Also called spokes. Upright reeds around which weaving is done.

STROKE: One complete movement of weaving reed.

UPSETTING: Fixing stakes firmly in place with three-ply coil weave.

WALING: Strip of braided weavers whose purpose is to provide accent to weaving pattern or to strengthen basket work.

WEAVERS: Reed, cane or straw used to weave sides or base of a basket.

WILLOW: Thin branches of willow tree. Slightly heavier and harder to weave than reed.

WOOD-BASE BASKET: Basket whose base is made of solid piece of wood or plywood.

WOVEN-BASE BASKET: Basket with base made of reed woven in flat shape.

BATIK

BATIK: Method of printing on cloth using a series of wax deposits which are added one by one between a series of dyeing operations.

BRUSH BATIK: Batik method in which brushes are used to apply hot wax to large areas of cloth before dyeing.

STAMP BATIK: Method of batik in which wax is applied to cloth with special shapes. These shapes are dipped into hot wax and pressed onto dry cloth.

TJANTING BATIK: Batik method characterized by fine detail. Usually, a tjanting tool is used to apply the hot wax.

TJANTING TOOL: Metal container with long thin spout used for applying thin line of melted wax on cloth during batik operations.

BEADWORK

BEADING: Art of creating craft items by stringing beads in various designs and patterns.

BEAD LOOM: Wooden or plastic frame on which thread or cord can be strung for beadwork.

BUGLE BEADS: About the same diameter as seed beads but longer.

E BEADS: Similar in shape but three times larger than seed beads.

ROCAILLES: Similar to seed beads except for their square holes; often substituted for seed beads.

SEED BEADS: Smallest beads used in beadwork. Usually round and hollow they can be made from plastic, metal or glass.

SOUTACHE: Braided material with a herringbone pattern used for stringing beads.

TWILL BEADING: Also called "peyote" beading. Method of beading which produces a solid texture; often done around a core of rope to develop a spiral pattern.

BLOCK PRINTING

BLOCK PRINTING: Method of reproducing several copies of a design or symbol using raised designs fashioned in durable, hardened materials. Surface design is inked and pressed onto surface to be printed. Similar to relief printing.

BRAYER: Rubber faced roller with handle designed to spread ink on relief printing surfaces.

LINOLEUM BLOCK: Linoleum surfaced block used for block printing. Image to be printed is carved on surface of linoleum.

MASKING: Technique for printing using thin pieces of paper placed over areas receiving ink.

OFFSETTING: In block printing a method of printing in which a brayer is used to ''pick up'' the image from a relief surface transferring it to the substrate (printing medium).

RELIEF PRINTING: Printing done from a raised surface.

RUBBING: Method of relief printing in which any textured surface can be the ''printing block.''

CALLIGRAPHY

CALLIGRAPHY: Art of decorative handwriting or penmanship.

CHANCERY CURSIVE: Style of calligraphy with a contemporary look. Suited for greeting cards, announcements, invitations and less formal lettering.

GOUACHE: Pronounced ''Gwash,'' a pigment used in opaque watercolors; also, the method by which these watercolors are used.

HOLDER: Handle for holding nib of writing pen.

ILLUMINATE: To decorate manuscript with gold or silver or brilliant colors or with elaborate designs (scrolls) and miniature pictures.

NIB: Metal tip of lettering pen which holds ink supply; point of lettering pen which touches writing surface.

OLD ENGLISH TEXT: Calligraphic style of writing or hand lettering noted for its elegance.

CANDLEMAKING

CANDELILLA WAX: Brittle wax with high melting point often used in candlemaking.

CARNAUBA WAX: A hard, brittle wax taken from the leaves of the carnauba palm. Noted for its high melting point, it can be substituted for stearine in candlemaking.

HAND DIPPING: Technique used in candlemaking when molds are not used. Bare wicking material is dipped into container of hot wax repeatedly by hand with intermittent periods of cooling.

PAPER CORE WICKING: Stiff wicking made of twisted paper. Considerably stiffer than regular wicking, it is more easily inserted into a candle after the candle has been molded.

STEARINE: White powdery material added to wax during candlemaking. Its purpose is to make the candle harder so it will not sag in hot weather. Also, the candle will be more opaque.

CASTING PLASTICS

BREAKAWAY MOLD: Mold which is removed from completed casting by destroying it.

CATALYST: A substance which causes a chemical reaction to take place when mixed into the substance to be changed. In plastics, it causes liquid resin to harden.

EMBEDMENT: Plastic casting process in which articles are placed in an open mold while polyester resin is poured around them. The clear resin solidifies around the article making a permanent display of the object.

GEL: To thicken (as plastic hardener reacts to plastic resin).

HARDENER: Chemical which, when added to polyester resins, causes them to harden. A catalyst.

MOLD RELEASE AGENT: A powder or liquid which will keep cured plastic from adhering to sides of mold.

POLYESTER RESINS: Thermosetting plastic materials usually purchased as a liquid and used for casting projects in plastic.

COLLAGES

ASSEMBLAGES: Three-dimensional collages made from objects such as stones, scraps of wood, parts of a clock or any material which has bulk.

COLLAGE: An arrangement of pictures, illustrations or any other objects placed artistically on a background. Taken from a French word meaning ''pasting.''

OVERLAY TECHNIQUE: Collage method in which smaller illustrations are pasted over a background illustration.

UNDERLAY TECHNIQUE: Method of adding a small illustration within a larger one by slitting the larger illustration and slipping a portion of the smaller one through the slit from underneath.

DECOUPAGE

CRAFT KNIFE: Knife with thin, light blade which is kept very sharp. Cutting edge usually does not run along its length but slopes across the end of the blade. Handle is usually heavy. Blades may be detachable.

DECOUPAGE: Application of illustrative material to any surface using several coats of a clear finish such as varnish, lacquer or a plastic finish. Illustrations might include old greeting cards, pieces of wallpaper or specially prepared commercial prints. Usually applied to furniture or plaques.

GESSO: Plaster of paris, whiting or gypsum mixed with

glue or size. Used as a primer to prepare a surface for painting or gilding.

LACQUER: A fast drying varnish which forms a film and cures because of evaporation of the solvents. Contains nitro cellulose along with various gum resins and solvents.

ENAMELING METAL

CLOISONNE: Enameling technique which utilizes copper wire to form or enclose areas for different colors.

ENAMEL COATINGS: Finely powdered glass to which are added metal oxides and chemicals to get properties such as color and elasticity. Coatings may be transparent or opaque.

ENAMEL EASE: Solution which acts as a flux when applied to a metal surface in preparation for enameling. It causes the enamel to stick to the metal surface in an even coating.

ENAMELING: Application of a coating to a surface by heating to a high temperature a covering of finely powdered glass.

JEWELERS' SAW: Very small, fine-tooth metal cutting saw. Blade is replaceable.

KILN: Special oven capable of attaining a high temperature. Used in craftwork for metal enameling, firing of pottery and other purposes requiring high heat within an enclosed space.

PICKLING: Preparation of copper surfaces for enameling by dipping in a solution of one part nitric acid and six parts water.

SGRAFFITO: Enameling technique. Second color of enamel powder is dusted over base coat. Blunt or sharp tool is used to scratch a design through the dusted coat. The second coat is then fired.

STENCILING: Enameling technique involving masking off parts of the base coat and applying contrasting colors of enamel to the exposed sections.

SWIRLING: Decorative technique used in enameling. Several coats of different color enamel powder are dusted on the surface. When the powder has melted it is stirred with a swirling tool.

FLOWERCRAFT

FLORIST TAPE: A plastic adhesive tape made green in color to blend with plant colors. Used by florists and hobbyists to attach flowers to wire stems and/or fastening devices.

FLORIST WIRE: Wire used by florists to extend and stiffen the flower stem.

GLYCERINE (OR GLYCEROL): Sweet, syrupy liquid used as a solvent or plasticizer.

LIQUID PLASTIC FILM: A plastic resin which has high surface tension causing it to bridge wide gaps while

stretched in a thin flim. Used in making artificial flowers.

SILICA GEL: A form of silicon dioxide which looks like coarse white sand. Grains possess many fine pores and are used as an absorbent (to collect things such as moisture).

FOIL TOOLING

FOIL: Very thin metal sheet used especially in craftwork where three-dimensional shapes are easily produced by tooling. Copper, brass and aluminum are the preferred metals.

LIVER OF SULPHUR: A chemical solution used to artificially tarnish metal such as copper; consists of sulfurated potash.

MODELING TOOL: In foil tooling an instrument with a smooth spoon end used to raise the design.

SMOOTHING TOOL: Hand tool used to flatten background in foil tooling.

STIPPLING: Making sharp indentations in a surface with a sharp point to provide texture.

TRACING TOOL: Round-pointed instrument used in tooling foil to trace the pattern and outline the design.

LAPIDARY

BAROQUE: One of the basic forms of gems. Baroque gems are formed by tumbling irregular and unusual shapes of stones.

CABOCHON: Gem shape in which the gem is cut to a geometric shape and then ground to a dome on upper surface.

CERIUM OXIDE: Polishing agent used to give gemstones their final finish.

DOP STICK: Stick to which stone is attached while it is shaped into a cabochon.

FACET: One of basic forms of gemstones. The stone is cut to many faces and the facets meet at a point. Facet cutting is usually done on transparent stones.

LAPIDARY: Art or craft of cutting and polishing stones.

LEVIGATED ALUMINA: Fine polishing agent used to give gemstones their final finish.

PRECIOUS STONES: True gems such as diamonds, emeralds, rubies and sapphires.

SEMIPRECIOUS STONES: Less valuable stones such as agate, jasper, selenite, gypsum, quartz and amethyst.

TIN OXIDE: Polishing agent used to polish gemstones.

TUMBLING: Polishing gemstones by placing them in a tumbling container along with coarse abrasive grit and water.

LEATHERCRAFT

CHROME TANNED LEATHER: Leather which has been chemically treated with chromic salts to produce a tough, firm, water-resistant material.

DOUBLE LINE MARKING TOOL: Leatherworking tool used to mark lines as guides for lacing.

EDGE BEVELER: Similar to leather gouge in design. Intended to cut away and round edges of leather before using an edge creaser.

EDGE CREASER: Rounds edges of leather and places a small groove near the edge.

EYELET SETTER: Sets eyelets in leather. Consists of a solid metal cylinder with a pointed end. This tapered end is placed in the eyelet and struck lightly with a small mallet. This flares the eyelet.

FID: Similar in appearance to a pick, this tool is designed to open lacing slits.

GARMENT COWHIDE: A thinner, more flexible leather used for belts, shoes and bags.

GOUGE: Cutting tool designed to cut shallow grooves in leather so it will fold smoothly. End of tool is concave and cut back in a shallow V. Cutting edge is on the V which is pushed along the leather.

LACING NEEDLE: Needle with eyelet large enough to accept leather thonging used for lacing.

MODELING TOOLS: Small tools for tracing and pressing designs in leather.

REVOLVING SPRING PUNCH: Makes holes through leather. Similar in appearance to a pliers. One jaw holds six cylinders which can be turned to select size of cylinder. Other jaw holds an anvil which supports leather as cylinder cuts out the hole.

SADDLE STAMPS: Tools designed to produce decorative imprints on leather being tooled. Includes: background tools, bevelers, camouflage, pear shader, veiners, stops, seeder and mulefoot.

SIMULATED LEATHERS: Hides from domestic animals treated to look like skins of wild animals such as alligator, shark and turtle.

SKIFE: Knife designed to thin and taper edges of leather which are going to be joined. Also used for skiving. Consists of a handle and a holder which accepts certain types of razor blades. Blade is held so cutting edge is over a slot in the center of the holder.

SKIVING KNIFE: Special knife designed to cut and thin edges of leather. Blade is short and tapers sharply to a rounded point. Works well on any thickness of leather but must be kept sharp.

SNAP BUTTON SET: Tools for setting snaps in leather consisting of base or anvil and cylindrical punch. Cylindrical punch is struck with a small mallet. Punch cuts holes in the leather and sets the snap.

SPACING WHEEL: Tool for marking equally distant spaces on leather as a guide for punching holes.

SUEDE: Leather whose surface has been buffed or sanded to produce a velvety nap. Usually made from lambskin.

SWIVEL CARVING KNIFE: Designed for cutting partway through leather being tooled. Blade turns 360 degrees on handle. It is used for outlining patterns on leather.

THONGING: Cutting holes or slits in leather edge in preparation for lacing.

THONGING CHISEL: Punches slits through leather in preparation for lacing. May have one or several prongs.

TOP GRAIN LEATHER: Some leather is split. The upper half or top layer is referred to as top grain. The flesh layer is almost always sueded.

TRACER MODELING TOOL: Device for tracing designs on leather and for depressing the leather.

MACRAME

BUTTERFLY: Wrapping cord or line between thumb and forefinger in a figure eight pattern. Used in macrame to shorten up long pieces of cord. Rubber band slipped over cord keeps it rolled up.

HOLDING CORD: In macrame, a cord which is the beginning point for other cords going in different directions than the holding cord. Other cords are knotted onto a holding cord.

LARK'S HEAD KNOT: Reversed double half hitch used in macrame to mount ends of cords to a holding cord.

MACRAME: Art of knotting threads or cords to produce decorative and functional craft products.

SINNET: In macrame, a chain of similar knots tied for decorative purpose.

SQUARE KNOT SINNET: Series of square knots tied one after the other.

WORKING CORD: Cord used to form the knot in macrame.

MOSAICS

GROUT: A material much like plaster which helps hold tile in place and seals areas between tile pieces.

MASTIC: An adhesive material used to attach tile to backing materials. Also often used as a sealer.

MOSAICS: Assembly of many pieces of the same or different materials side-by-side in such a way that it forms a design.

TILE: Pieces of fired clay, stone or cement frequently used in mosaic crafts.

NEEDLEPOINT

BARGELLO: Needlepoint which has 14 stitches to the inch.

BLOCKING: Method of straightening needlepoint work by pulling it straight and pinning it down to a rigid surface. It is dampened and left to dry.

CANVAS: Backing material used for needlepoint.

Usually woven material with large mesh to accept the needlepoint yarns. There are many mesh sizes, for example: Mono (10 to 18 holes per inch), Interlock (5 to 14 holes per inch), Penelope (double threaded and 6 1/2 to 15 holes per inch). Canvas is made from cotton or plastic in either white or tan.

CREWEL WOOL: A fine embroidery yarn popular for needlepoint.

GROS POINT: Needlepoint which has 8 to 15 stitches per inch.

NEEDLEPOINT: A craft or method of covering an open-weave fabric completely with yarn.

PETIT POINT: Needlepoint which has 16 or more stitches to the inch.

QUICK POINT: Needlepoint which has 3 1/2 to 5 stitches per inch.

TAPESTRY NEEDLE: Large needle with blunt point and large eye. Suitable for use with needlepoint.

TENT STITCHES: Basic needlepoint stitch. Smallest unit in needlepoint, it is laid across just one intersection of canvas threads. Stitch always appears as a flat, even thread slanting from the lower left to the upper right.

POTTERY

BISQUE FIRING: First firing of clay to harden it so that it is not so brittle.

CONES: In pottery, ceramic material placed in a kiln to indicate temperature.

FIRE: To heat green (unfired) clay in an oven or kiln at high temperature to increase durability and strength of the clay.

GLAZE: A liquid mostly made up of oxides which is applied to the surface of ceramic wares to form a moistureproof and often decorative, lustrous coating.

KILN: Oven for firing clay products. Heated electrically, these ovens are capable of extremely high temperatures.

PINCH POT: Pottery product formed by hand. Clay is first shaped into a ball; then the ball is hollowed out with the thumb and fingers until it takes the shape of a small pot.

POTTERY: Craft consisting of shaping articles of clay; usually accompanied by firing and glazing to make clay more durable and attractive.

SLAB POTTERY: Pottery fashioned by first forming the clay into slabs. The slabs are cut and bent into various flat-sided shapes and containers.

SLIP: A watery clay solution used in pottery.

WEDGING: A preparation process involving squeezing and pressing pottery clay to remove trapped air.

RUGMAKING

LATCH NEEDLE or LATCH HOOK: Needle used in rugmaking which has hook at one end that can be opened or closed at will by changing the position of a hinged section.

LATCH NEEDLE RUG: Rug made using a latch hook; yarns are looped and tied around a stiff, woven base.

RYA RUG: A rug made of wool yarn and having a shaggy cut pile which lends itself well to contemporary themes.

RYA YARN: Yarn made in two plies in a wide variety of weights and colors. Colors are often combined to produce an endless variety of patterns.

SCREEN PRINTING

BASE: In screen printing, a flat surface, usually made of plywood, to which the printing frame is attached by hinges. It also supports the substrate during the printing operations.

FRAME: In screen printing, the rectangular support made of wood across which the screen is stretched.

PHOTOGRAPHIC STENCIL: A screen printing stencil prepared from light-sensitive materials. The image is exposed on the stencil material and the stencil is developed with hydrogen peroxide and water. This treatment dissolves the stencil material over the image area so the ink can pass through.

REGISTRATION TABS: Stops or guides attached to the base of the screen frame in screen printing. Their purpose is to position the paper accurately during printing.

SCREEN: In screen printing, a fabric with a coarse weave. Its purpose is to support the stencil and allow ink to move through portions of the stencil onto the paper. Screen may be made of nylon, organdy, copper or silk.

SCREEN PRINTING: Printing done with a stencil. Stencil is affixed to a screen stretched across a wood frame. Ink is squeegeed across the screen and goes through holes in the stencil to form an image on paper or other substrate (surface).

SQUEEGEE: A thick rubber blade attached to a wooden handle. It is used to draw the ink back and forth across the screen where small amounts are forced down through the screen to produce an image below on the substrate.

STENCIL: In screen printing, a sheet of material through which ink cannot pass except where portions have been etched or cut away. The image to be printed is placed on this material before it is affixed to the printing screen.

SHELLCRAFT

ABALONE SHELL: Covering of a rock-clinging gastropod. The shell is somewhat like that of a clam and is lined inside with mother of pearl. One edge has a row of small holes.

AUGER SHELL: Elongated spiral shell which comes

from the gastropod mollusk of the family Terebridae.

PECTENS: A bivalve mollusk of which the best known is the sea scallop. The shell is used in jewelry making.

CONCH SHELLS: Skeletal deposits (protective coverings) of mollusks. The shells are large and spiraled, large at one end and tapering toward the other end.

COQUINA SHELLS: Shell of a small marine clam.

CORAL: Skeletal deposit produced especially by certain marine anthozoan polyps (sea-dwelling creatures). The red and salmon pink coral, from which jewelry is made, comes from the Mediterranean Sea and off the coasts of Japan.

COWRIE SHELLS: The glossy and brightly colored shell of numerous univalve marine gastropods. The shells are relatively small and somewhat oval shaped. The shell opening is long and narrow protected with curved lips.

MARINE SHELLS: The protective coverings of various mollusks. They are composed of substances secreted by the glands of the mollusks and consist mostly of carbonate of lime.

SILVERSMITHING

ANNEALING: Softening of metal by heating it to a dull red color then quickly cooling it.

BALL PEEN HAMMER: Hammer with a smooth ball-shaped head used for shaping metals.

FLUX: A substance applied to metals being joined by soldering to free them from oxides and make joining them easier.

MANDREL: Tapered cylindrical bar used to hold objects with a hole in them while they are being shaped or machined. A ring, for example, is shaped around a mandrel.

OXIDES: Mixtures of an element with oxygen. This is a process which takes place naturally on the surfaces of metals exposed to air. These mixtures must be removed for good bonding of metals.

PEEN: To shape by striking with a ball peen hammer.

PEWTER: An alloy (mixture) of tin and lead formerly used as kitchen utensils. Now used in silversmithing to create craft items both useful and decorative.

PICKLING: Acid treatment given to silver and other metals to quickly clean them. Pickling solution is one part sulfuric acid and ten parts cold water.

PLANISH: To toughen and smooth metal, such as silver, by hammering.

SILVERSMITHING: Craft of working silver into useful and decorative products. Term also applied to working of less expensive metals such as aluminum, pewter, copper, etc.

STERLING SILVER: An alloy of 92 percent silver and 8 percent copper. The addition of copper gives the silver added strength.

STAINED GLASS

GLASS CUTTER: Device, often hand held, for cutting glass in straight or curved patterns. Consists of a small metal wheel whose outer perimeter is ridged to produce a thin scratch or score when drawn across the surface of the glass. The wheel is set in a small handle and revolves on a spindle.

HAND BLOWN GLASS: Glass produced by blowing a large hollow tube which is split while still hot and flattened on a stone surface. Such glass contains beautiful surface textures.

LEAD CAME: Strips of lead used as border and to fasten stained glass pieces together. Came is usually shaped in an "H" cross-sectional pattern or a "U" shaped cross-sectional pattern.

PATINA: A surface appearance of something grown beautiful with age; often treasured as a result and sometimes produced artificially with acids. For example, weathered copper or bronze takes on a green color. Lead dulls to a soft gray.

STAINED GLASS: A craft, thousands of years old, in which sections of colored glass are artfully combined into beautiful windows formerly used in churches, museums, public buildings and homes. Now, the basic craft form is directed to include such items as window hangings, jewelry, lampshades, door panels, mosaics and glass sculpture. The stained glass craft involves cutting glass and using lead to fit it into a decorative form.

STRING ART

EDGING: In string art, an arrangement of the string to form a decorative border.

FREE-FORM STRING ART: String art designs which are not geometric or formally balanced.

OJO DE DIOS: A traditional string art design made by weaving various designs on dowels or sticks. The name means "Eye of God" and the design is an ancient Spanish good luck charm.

STRING ART: Creation of decorative designs using string, wire or yarn stretched over nails, dowels or holes in the background. Designs may be two or three dimensional.

THREE-DIMENSIONAL STRING ART: String art in which the stringing materials not only run parallel but at an angle to the background. In some cases the string may wrap around and be strung on both sides of the base. Spheres, ellipsoids, paraboloids and toruses are examples of geometric, three-dimensional designs.

TWO-DIMENSIONAL STRING ART: String art which has all stringing material running parallel to the background.

VARIOUS WOODCRAFTS

CAUL: Shape around which wood laminations are formed.

CHIPBOARD: A material made up of wood chips glued together to form sheets.

COPING SAW: Light saw with thin, flexible blade mounted on a U-shaped frame. Intended for cutting tight curves in thin wood stock.

FRAMING: Technique of producing picture frames. May include, mitering of corners, cutting rabbets, gluing, nailing, feathering, etc.

FULL CARVING: A carving in which all surfaces of the wood are shaped. Sometimes called "carving in the round."

FRET SAW: Narrow bladed, fine-toothed saw held under tension in a frame. Used for cutting curved outlines.

MARQUETRY: Craft of building up an ornamental surface of thin wood veneer pieces to form a pattern or picture. Suited to covering surfaces of serving trays, jewelry boxes, chess and checkerboards, pictures and small table tops.

MITER CLAMP. In picture framing, a device for holding wood framing pieces at mitered angle while joint is fastened with glue or nails.

PENETRATING FINISHES: Finishing materials which soak into the surface of the wood. Tung oil and linseed oil are examples.

PLASTIC WOOD: A wood filler made from plastic. It is applied in a putty state and allowed to harden. Its main purpose is to fill gouges and defects in wood prior to finishing of the wood surface.

RABBET SIZE: In picture framing, dimension of the rabbeted edge of picture molding. Dimension is determined by dimensions of matted picture.

SILHOUETTE CARVING: A carving made by shaping only main parts of the design from wood. They are placed in such a way that the imagination is made to fill in the missing parts of the design.

SPOKESHAVE: A drawknife with end handles turned at right angles to the plane of the cutting edge. Used to plane convex or concave surfaces.

STOCK PICTURE FRAME MOLDING: Picture framing wood on which all shaping operations have been performed with exception of cutting and mitering.

SURFACES FINISHES: Wood finishes which sit on and seal the surface of the wood. Lacquers and varnishes are in this classification.

VENEER: In wood, a thin sheet usually with a beautiful grain pattern.

WHITTLING: A simple form of full carving. Main difference is in the tools. Whittling can be done with only a pocket knife or a hobby knife. A coping saw and a carving saw may also be pressed into use.

WINDOW METHOD: In marquetry, method of shaping veneer pieces. Pattern of each piece is made by cutting out each piece from scrap stock. "Hole" is used as pattern for good veneer.

WOOD CARVER'S TOOLS: Specially shaped cutting tools used for carving of wood.

MISCELLANEOUS CRAFTS

ACETONE: A solvent. One of its uses is to remove rosin from metal.

FIGURINE: Small carved or molded statue; sometimes called a statuette.

HOT-WIRE CUTTER: An electrical device consisting of a nichrome wire stretched across a frame. A heating element heats up the wire so it will cut foamed plastic materials without requiring a sharp cutting edge.

LAPPING PLATE: Flat surface such as thin sheet of steel or old cookie tin used to hold abrasives for smoothing cut surfaces of bottles.

MASKING PAPER: In plastic work, the protective paper placed over the surface of sheet plastic.

PALETTE KNIFE: Knife with flexible steel blade and no cutting edge. Used to mix colors, apply thick paint, papier mache or other soft materials used in arts and crafts.

PHOTOGRAPHIC SILHOUETTE: A silhouette made by photographing a subject which is lighted from the side opposite the camera. Side facing the camera is in deep shadow and appears gray or black in the printed picture.

PLAQUE: In craftwork, an ornamental base often serving as support and background for craft or art designed as a wall decoration.

PLASTER OF PARIS: White powder made from gypsum. Used chiefly for casts and molds or in craftwork to cast figurines, etc.

QUILLING: Art of rolling and bending narrow strips of paper into artistic shapes.

QUILLING TOOL: Small round tool which has one hollow end (forming a cylinder). Paper is attached to cylinder end via a small slot and wrapped into a "quill."

SILHOUETTES: Shadowlike representations of people and objects. In craftwork, the shape is often cut out of black paper which is then placed on a white background for contrast.

SOLVENT CEMENT: Special adhesive to join sheet plastic. It works by dissolving a small amount of the plastic on each of the surfaces being joined. When the material rehardens, the surfaces are permanently joined.

SCORING: In bottle cutting, scratching a fine, clean line into surface of bottle to provide a break line.

STRIP HEATER: Heater designed to heat plastic along a straight line for purpose of softening sheet plastic so it can be bent or shaped.

INDEX

Index

Index

Index

ACKNOWLEDGMENTS

We wish to express our appreciation to those individuals and companies who contributed projects, ideas and illustrations for the preparation of this book.

Special credit is given the authors' wives, Joan Kicklighter and Marge Baird, for their untiring assistance in the selection and preparation of materials and projects.